S.O. GAMMAGE.
40 SQUADRON.
1944 - 1945

M Lihou' Dur g the Halir Nigri
W. bomber oper 1944-45

Chns Wad '40 Sq.' (Bomber Command
Profile N° 12)

# SWEEPING THE SKIES

# Sweeping the Skies

*A History of 40 Squadron Royal Flying Corps
and Royal Air Force, 1916–56*

DAVID GUNBY

The Pentland Press
Edinburgh – Cambridge – Durham – USA

First published in 1995 by
The Pentland Press Ltd
1 Hutton Close
South Church
Bishop Auckland
Durham

ISBN 1-85821-190-5

Typeset by Carnegie Publishing, 18 Maynard St, Preston
Printed and bound by Antony Rowe Ltd, Chippenham

This book is dedicated to all those who gave their lives while serving with 40 Squadron, Royal Flying Corps and Royal Air Force, and in particular to the crew of Wellington X, MF 458, A-Able, who were shot down at Dobrohost, Slovakia, on the night of 4/5 October 1944.

Pilot Officer Arthur Leslie Mayers
Flight Sergeant Vallance McCall
Warrant Officer Charles Herbert Gunby
Sergeant Harry Walker Hesketh
Sergeant Robert Cummin Ropson Johnson

# Contents

# Illustrations

# Maps

# Preface

THIS book has its origins in the events of the night of 4/5 October 1944, when my father's crew were killed while mining the River Danube. More immediately, though, it dates from 1985, when, acknowledging a need to rediscover the father whom I scarcely remembered, I tried (and failed) to find any of those who had served with him in 40 Squadron, or earlier in 500 Squadron or at No 1 Air Observer School, and could tell me something about him and his war service. The advertisement I placed in *Airmail*, however, drew a number of letters from former members of 40 Squadron, and it was in response to these, and to their evident pleasure that someone was enquiring about 'their' squadron, that I decided to write this history. It will, I hope, serve as an expression of gratitude to all who served with 40 Squadron, and a way of ensuring that they and their achievements are not forgotten.

It is impossible here to express my thanks individually to the approximately 480 men and women (about three-quarters of them former members of the squadron) who responded so generously to my requests for help and whose names appear in Appendix D (pp. 390–3). With some I had but brief communication. With others the links are enduring, and strong bonds of friendship have developed. To all I owe thanks for the trouble they have gone to in helping me to flesh out the bare bones of the squadron history, derived from the Operational Record Books held at the Public Record Office, Kew, and from the archives at the RAF Museum, Hendon.

Equally it was impossible to include here material from all of the accounts, written or taped, which I now hold—or to publish the nearly 1000 photographs which I borrowed and copied. I can, however, assure all who so generously gave time recalling their memories, or who readily entrusted photographs, logbooks and other mementos to my care, that it was only through their generosity that I acquired the knowledge which enabled me to select the material which has been included. I should add that all the material which I have collected will, in due course, be deposited at the RAF Museum as a permanent record of 40 Squadron and its achievements.

Memory is fallible, and after half a century or more particularly so. Hence not infrequently I have been faced with two or more versions of an incident which I wanted to include in the history. In such cases I have had to make a judgement as to which version to include. I crave the indulgence and understanding of those who remember these events differently. 'Truth' is always in part a matter of perception, as in writing this book I have become acutely aware.

And in craving indulgence on this point, I should seek it also concerning my decision largely (the reasons for the exceptions are clear, I think) to exclude references to decorations. In researching *Sweeping the Skies* I became acutely aware of the disparate criteria applying to such awards at different times, under different commanding officers, and in different commands and theatres of operations. As a result I came to feel that I could not, as I had originally intended, devote an appendix to decorations. This decision should not be taken in any way as disparaging those who were decorated, or belittling the deeds which led the authorities to recommend or approve awards. Rather it reflects my conviction (shared, I know, by many) that quite as many deeds went unrecorded or unrewarded as those that were recognized. *Sweeping the Skies* honours all who served in 40 Squadron, decorated and undecorated.

In tracing former members of the squadron I have received a great deal of help from many quarters, but I would like here to express special thanks to two assiduous '40 hunters', Reg Thackeray and Jo Lancaster. Their success rate proved what detective talents lay untapped during their careers in banking and aviation.

I would also like to express my thanks to the good friends with whom I have stayed during my travels, here in New Zealand and overseas. My thanks, in England, to Doug and Caroline Bagnall, Alec and Hilda Hipperson, Eric and Winneth Laithwaite, Jo Lancaster, Hugh and Bunny Lynch-Blosse, Bill and Dot Moseby, Jo Stevenson, Reg and Kathleen Thackeray, Ron and Vera Thirsk, and Peter Travers-Wakeford and Eileen O'Sullivan; in Scotland to David Gladstone, and Dorothy and the late Bill Goodbrand; in Canada to the late George and Jean Arnott, and Bob Spence; in the USA to Jack and Florence Bellock; and in New Zealand to Grace and the late Alex Greer, Martin and Jill Johnson, and Cec and Joan Rainey.

To the so many former members and their wives and families, who welcomed a visitor full of questions and brandishing a tape recorder, and who were as generous with a meal or tea and refreshments as with their time and their memories, I likewise tender my thanks.

Above all, though, I owe thanks to those who encouraged me to take on the project, and to see it through. There were times when it seemed that it would never be finished (many of my correspondents must have felt that too, though most have been too polite to say so). But for the support that I have received from so many quarters it might never have been.

Outside of the 40 Squadron 'family' I have many other debts of gratitude. Some are institutional; the greatest to my employer, the University of Canterbury, which was broad-minded enough to support a research project well outside the academic discipline (English Literature) in which I teach. My thanks also to Clare Hall, Cambridge, and St. Catherine's College, Oxford, where I held Visiting Fellowships in 1992, and to Massey College, University of Toronto, where I was a Senior Resident during the same year. I am also grateful to Therese Angelo, Archivist at the RNZAF Museum, Wigram, to R. K. Piper and David Wilson of the RAAF Historical Records Branch of the Department of Defence, Canberra, and Carl A. Christie, Senior Research Officer of the General History Branch of National Defence Headquarters, Ottawa; by them and by the Canadian Government Photographic Centre, Ottawa, help was willingly and generously given. My thanks also to Susan Ewing and the staff of the Archival Support Center, National Air and Space Museum, Smithsonian Institution, Washington DC.

In the United Kingdom I owe thanks to the RAF Museum, Hendon, where Peter Murton and Peter Elliott gave me every assistance; to the staff of the RAF Personnel Management Centre, Gloucester, who cheerfully forwarded letters to former members of 40 Squadron; to the Imperial War Museum's Departments of Sound Records (Peter Hart), Photographs (Alan Williams) and Film (Brad. King); and especially to the Air Historical Branch, Ministry of Defence, London, where first Air Commodore Henry Probert and then Group Captain Ian Madelin were tolerant of my repeated enquiries, and where Mr. G. Day answered them promptly and fully. Without his help the casualty lists which are an important part of this history could not have been completed.

I owe thanks, also, to the United Kingdom, Canadian and New Zealand offices of the Commonwealth War Graves Commission, and particularly to its Canadian office, which responded promptly and fully to a series of requests for help, as did the Melbourne office of the Department of Veterans' Affairs in Australia and Steve Harris of the Department of Internal Affairs in Christchurch.

One of my greatest debts is to my good friend Errol Martyn, whose generosity is equalled only by his archives, and by his knowledge of where to find what and (importantly) who to ask. To him, as to my friend and colleague, Vincent Orange, who was ever-generous with his encyclopaedic knowledge of RAF history, my warmest thanks.

Thanks, too, to Richard S. Robinson, who undertook research on my behalf at the Public Record Office, Kew, to my research assistants, Ion Dowman and Donne Medley, who in producing a narrative out of the Operational Record Books made it possible to finish the history this century, to Orma Shaw, who so willingly gave secretarial help, to Michelle Regan who drew the maps, and to Doug Bagnall, Bill Bromley, Jo Lancaster and Jim Steel, who read drafts of a large part of the history, putting me right at a number of points, and making many constructive suggestions for improvement. And my especial thanks to Gwilym Lewis, with whom I discussed the chapters dealing with the First World War, and who has been a constant support and encouragement. For his friendship, as for the many which I have been privileged to experience in the long writing of *Sweeping the Skies*, I express my thanks. That first abortive search for traces of my father brought me riches of which I could never have dreamed.

Map 1. Bases in England and Scotland, 1916–56.

# Beginnings:
# February 1916–February 1917

Forty Squadron, Royal Flying Corps, was formed at Fort Grange, Gosport, Hants, on 26 February, 1916, under the command of Capt G. R. Howard. By 16 March there were 28 pilots on strength, 18 of them under instruction, but Howard had given place as CO to Major L. A. Strange. He was sick, however, and never joined the squadron. The sole Flight Commander, Capt R. Loraine, therefore acted as CO, being confirmed in the posting and rank of Major on 24 May.

Robert Loraine was a man out of the ordinary. A leading West End actor, he was also a pioneer airman, and completed the first crossing of the Irish Sea (under the pseudonym of Jones) in September of that year—though obliged to swim the last 100 yards. He joined the RFC at the outbreak of war and went to France with 3 Squadron as an observer. Badly wounded, he remustered as a pilot and was posted to 5 Squadron, where in September 1915 he commanded B Flight.

Forty was to be a corps reconnaissance squadron, and the pilots began to receive instruction in artillery spotting, signalling (including wireless telegraphy) and photography. As was customary at this time, however, 40 was not only to bring qualified pilots up to operational efficiency but also to train novices to fly. Not surprisingly, this resulted in a lengthy working up.

Flying training methods were, in early 1916, rudimentary, with instruction carried out on the 'older brother' principle, where experienced flying officers instructed the novices. Training was carried out in BE2c and Avro 504 aircraft, and serviceability was a major problem, particularly at first, when at times there were no aircraft airworthy. This delayed flying training considerably, and it was not until 7 April that the first trainee (2/Lt E. B. McManus) went solo.

The tempo of flying activity increased considerably in the second week of April, with more pilots going solo, and the experienced undertaking cross country flights. Lectures on artillery observation continued, though no observers had joined the Squadron, or ever did, for late in May 40 was redesignated a scout squadron, the change signalled by the appearance of the first DH2 single-seat pusher scout on the 27th. Thereafter the numbers of DH2s increased steadily, nine being available on 5 July, with four Henri Farmans for dual instruction on pusher aircraft. Then on 9 July the first of another single-seat pusher scout, the FE8 arrived, and in the next fortnight the Squadron received sufficient to equip A Flight. The FE8 had been intended as the squadron's equipment from the first, but delays in production led to the use of the DH2 for training purposes, and in fact it was used alongside the FE8 until the departure of the squadron for France in August.

The FE8 was the latest of a series of pusher aircraft originating with the Royal Aircraft Factory, Farnborough, of which the most famous and durable was the FE2. A single-seat scout, the FE8 was powered by a 110 hp. Monosoupape rotary engine, and capable of a maximum speed of 94 mph at sea level, and 79 mph at 6,000 feet. Its armament consisted of one Lewis gun on a flexible mounting in the nose. Nimble and responsive, it would undoubtedly have given as good an account of itself as the DH2 did on debut in February 1916 had not production delays occurred.

Given the amateurish training methods, it is not surprising that there were many accidents, or that aircraft were often unserviceable. What was surprising, perhaps, is that in six months only one pilot was killed and two (Lt A. W. Morey and Sgt A. Armstrong) seriously injured. The pilot who died was 2/Lt G. H. E. Rippon, who was killed on 7 June, soon after the Squadron began its conversion to the DH2. According to the Court of Enquiry, the accident was caused by 'improper adjustment of petrol supply, thus causing revolutions of engine to fail'. Rippon then compounded his error by trying to turn back to the aerodrome, the aircraft stalling. There was, the Court concluded, 'No fault in engine or machine'.

Death depleted the pilot ranks by one, but a constant stream of postings to France deprived 40 of almost all its trained pilots. How massive the turn-over was can be seen from the fact that of the twenty-five officers on squadron on 16 March, only the CO, Loraine, and Lt D. O. Mulholland remained at the time the Squadron went to France in August. Besides Loraine and Mulholland, the longest serving pilot was then Sgt F. E. Darvell, who was posted in for training on 10 April.

There was a similar turnover in flight commanders. Capts S. H. Long and J. Valentine provided continuity in June, but the former was posted overseas on 4 July, and Valentine did not accompany the Squadron to France, his place as A Flight Commander being taken by Mulholland, who was promoted to Captain later that month. The other two flight commanders were Capts G. D. Hill, who joined in the second week of July, and F. J. Powell, on 6 August.

Powell's appointment was interesting because he had carried out the operational testing of the FE8 prototype while serving with Robert Loraine in 5 Squadron. Convalescing after a catastrophic attempt to loop off the

1. Officers of 40 Squadron, Gosport, August 1916.
Rear (l to r): ——, 2/Lt J. Hay, ——, ——, 2/Lt C. O. Usborne, 2/Lt H. S. Pell, ——.
Front: 2/Lt E. L. Benbow, 2/Lt H. C. Davis, Capt G. D. Hill, Maj R. Loraine,
Capt D. O. Mulholland, Capt F. J. Powell,, ——. (Chaz. Bowyer.)

2. Capt Powell and pilots, Treizennes, September 1916. (F. J. Powell.)

ground in a Bristol Bullet, Powell received a telegram from Loraine inviting him to command A Flight. Powell wired back an immediate 'yes', and leaving his crutches outside the surgery, sought to convince an RFC doctor that his broken ankle had healed. The trick worked, and Powell was passed fit for service!

The transfer to France followed well established procedures. The motor transport left Fort Grange on 30 July, while the remainder of the ground echelon moved out early on 1 August, with the pilots of A Flight taking off shortly after. With Mulholland were 2/Lts M. Jacks, H. C. Davis, H. A. Rigby and P. V. Tanner, and Sgt Darvell, who had completed his graduation examination just five days earlier. The six pilots flew from Gosport to Folkestone, and thence to St. Omer, before moving on to their base at Treizennes, near Aire, on 2 August.

The sector of the Western Front which 40 Squadron patrolled was held by the British 3rd Army, commanded by General Allenby. Further south, the Battle of the Somme was in its final stages, but around Arras the front had been quiet since the conclusion of the Battle of Loos in October 1915, and was to remain so until April 1917. At Treizennes, 40 was part of 10 Wing, one of its responsibilities being to provide escort for 25 Squadron, flying FE2bs, and later for 43 Squadron, which brought its Sopwith 1½ Strutters to Treizennes in January 1917. Forty was also to carry out line and offensive patrols with the aim of destroying or driving off German reconnaissance aircraft.

From Treizennes members of A Flight flew a first patrol on 4 August 1916. Those on the following day were equally without incident, but 2/Lt Davis was killed in an accident. No details as to what happened appear to have survived. A further loss occurred on 6 August, when 2/Lt Jacks returned ill from a dawn patrol and was hospitalized. The replacements for Davis and Jacks were 2/Lts K. S. Henderson and W. K. M. Britton.

A Flight experienced its share of frustration in the three weeks during which it operated independently. Mist curtailed operations, while forced landings and early returns with engine trouble were common. Moreover it was not until 21 August that contact was made with an enemy aircraft, Henderson coming across one on morning patrol at 11,000 feet but unable to catch it. Mulholland had a similarly frustrating experience on 25 August, sighting an enemy aircraft at 8,000 feet east of Bethune, but losing it in cloud.

B and C Flights moved to France on 19 August, but waited at St. Omer for the transport and mechanics to arrive before joining A Flight at Treizennes on the 25th. There the tempo of operations picked up. Line and offensive patrols were made at up to 13,000 feet, though the FE8s, with an official service ceiling of 15,000 feet, often had difficulty in climbing beyond 11,000. Aircraft were also despatched, usually in pairs, in searches for hostile aircraft—sorties usually fruitless, since the aircraft were generally gone when the FE's arrived, climb to 10,000 feet taking nearly twenty-four minutes. The performance of the FE8 was, indeed, a handicap throughout its squadron service. Early in 1916 the DH2 had enjoyed a period of supremacy over its opponents. The FE8 arrived as the German Air Force regained the initiative, and fought at an increasing disadvantage.

It was on escort duty on 22 September that victories were first obtained. Seeing a Fokker attacking an FE2b, Mulholland dived to assist. The Fokker stalled, and Mulholland followed, firing as it spun, to see it crash in a field west of Douai. A few minutes later, returning from escort duty, 2/Lt J. Hay surprised a biplane, thought to be a Roland two-seater, emptying a drum of ammunition into it from below. The aircraft, its engine dead, glided down but Hay was unable to overtake it because his own engine was misfiring.

The highlight of the last week in September came on the 25th, when 40 escorted a particularly successful series of raids by I Brigade squadrons on railway traffic at Libercourt Station, near Douai. In order to do this without intervention by German aircraft, the aerodromes at Provin, Tourmignies and Phalempin were attacked by pairs of FE2bs of 25 Squadron, each escorted by an FE8 from 40. They dropped phosphorus bombs at intervals shrouding the landing ground in smoke and advertised their presence by occasionally dropping 20-lb bombs. Besides grounding enemy aircraft, the bombing destroyed a hangar at Provin and caused a major fire at Phalempin.

Simultaneously, another formation bombed and strafed two troop trains, derailing one and scattering the troops, while the main force—seven BE2s of 16 Squadron and six FE2bs of 25 Squadron, escorted by FE8s—attacked the railway station at Libercourt, causing severe damage and starting fires. During this highly successful raid only one German aircraft was seen, and it did not attack. The pre-emptive strikes on the three aerodromes had succeeded.

In October poor weather hampered flying, but many escort sorties were flown, and it was on one of these that on the 20th Mulholland brought down his second Fokker, and 2/Lts E. L. Benbow and S. A. Sharpe drove down two Roland scouts. Rolands were again encountered on the following day, when Capt T. G. Mapplebeck, who had joined the Squadron as a supernumerary Flight Commander on 3 October, shot one down into a wood near Ascq, while Lt C. O. Usborne and 2/Lt R. E. Neve claimed two others out of control, Usborne's going down in a spin, smoking.

The 22nd October was a red letter day. Early in the morning the FE8s again clashed with Rolands, John Hay sending one down in flames. Later that morning, Hill, Benbow and Lt R. Gregory went up in search of a hostile aircraft reported by an anti-aircraft battery, and Benbow found an

Albatros C two-seater at 11,000 ft, getting under its tail and firing 25 rounds at point blank range. The Albatros burst into flames, crashing near Vimy. Then, to cap the day's proceedings, Lt H. C. Todd encountered an LVG two-seater while on offensive patrol in mid-afternoon, forcing it to land.

Forty's successes on 22 October did not go unrecognized, for following up a telegram of congratulations, Major-General Trenchard visited the Squadron on the 26th, and in his general communiqué the next day declared himself

> much struck by the . . . extraordinarily fine organization in the Squadron, also by the excellent method and cleanliness in regard to machines, workshop, transport and sheds.[1]

Something which would undoubtedly have taken Trenchard's eye was recalled later by one of the ground crew, F/Sgt Muir:

> On this occasion, all the machines were lined up on the aerodrome, the pilots in their seats, fitters and riggers beside their particular machines. At the sound of a prearranged signal from a klaxon, every machine took off, one after the other. Today [1937] this is less than a commonplace, but *then* it was a wonder. (*Loraine* p. 228)

During the Autumn 40 had other senior RFC visitors, come to view a device invented by 'the gadget king', Canadian Curzon Usborne. Powell recalls:

> Usborne thought of fixing a cylinder above the rudder of his aeroplane, which, at the pressure of a button on his instrument board, would shoot back liquid fire at any Hun who was on his tail. Usborne proved that this liquid fire could not damage his own machine—going at seventy miles an hour he was bound to leave it—all he had to do was to fly straight and his pursuers would automatically come into his line of fire. The gadget seemed fool-proof. We were very excited. (*Loraine* p. 223)

We learn a little more of Usborne's device from a letter by W. T. Bovett, a fitter in C Flight, published in *Popular Flying* (May 1935). Bovett writes (p. 98):

> One of his brain waves was to fix a Roman candle on his tail fin, and when a Hun got on his tail, press the button and pop it off in his face. Well, I rigged it up and off he went. Some time after I was in the Flight Office when an Ack-emma ran in and shouts "The gadget king is back". "Is everything all right?", I asked. "No", says he, "his tail caught fire". "Good God", said I, "anything happen?" "No", he said most mournfully, "the b—— thing went out again".

From Fred Powell we learn that though senior RFC officers visited the Squadron and viewed the device, nothing came of it.

3. Crash of FE8 6379 (Capt G. D. Hill), 1 November 1916. (R. Gregory.)

November opened badly when, while on a flight test on the morning of the 1st, Capt Hill crashed half a mile east of Treizennes. He was seriously injured, and his place as OC B Flight was taken by Robert Gregory until Tom Mapplebeck's return from leave on 8 November.

During early November no combats occurred, but on the 9th there was action aplenty. On an early patrol, Sgt Darvell came across three enemy aircraft over Souchez, emptying a drum of ammunition into an Albatros two-seater, which was seen to crash. Darvell had lost sight of his victim, which is hardly surprising, since in reloading his Lewis he dropped an empty drum, which whipped back into the propeller, breaking off part of one blade, and then into the tail boom of his machine. With the FE8 weakened structurally, Darvell was forced to land, running into a trench system which caused further damage.

Two members of 40 Squadron failed to return that day. Second Lieutenant H. F. Evans was subsequently reported a prisoner of war. So, too, was Tom Mapplebeck, who had been leading the early morning patrol which was so eventful for Darvell. What happened to him deserves to be related in some detail.

Relations between Mapplebeck and his CO had been uneasy from the first, perhaps because Loraine had once been put under open arrest by Lt G. W. Mapplebeck, Tom's elder brother. Matters came to a head when Mapplebeck returned from leave to take command of B Flight. The only available aircraft was, as he recalled, 'a very dud aircraft which was in the back of the hangars'. Obligingly, therefore, his former flight commander, Mulholland, allowed him to fly his old aircraft.

On his return Mapplebeck was met by an irate Loraine, who 'cursed me in front of other ranks (he had no idea of discipline) and told me I had no business to be flying an aircraft from my old Flight—I must fly the dud'. Mapplebeck did so the next morning, to find that it would not climb beyond 5,000 feet. Signalling Gregory to take over, Mapplebeck turned back, deciding to attack a balloon *en route*. He continues:

> I crossed the trenches at 300 feet to come up to a balloon, and I put a drum into the bottom of the balloon where of course there was no gas. So I had to change the drum, come round again, and put more into the top of the balloon, which then went up in flames.

Then attacked by two LVGs, Mapplebeck had a bullet cut his fuel line, and with his engine dead, forced-landed, to be taken prisoner. After the war, with something to get off his chest, he went to the dressing room of the Garrick Theatre in London, where Robert Loraine was playing the title role in Rostand's *Cyrano de Bergerac*, told his former CO what he thought of him, and walked out.

Mapplebeck's judgement of Loraine is harsh, but there is other evidence that he was in many respects a difficult CO. Fred Powell, for instance, recalled that on 5 Squadron, the pilots in Loraine's flight threatened to apply for a transfer *en masse* because of his high-handedness in ordering modifications to their aircraft without informing them. 'If only,' Powell commented later,

> when giving an order, he had not been so autocratic. You felt that the officer was a conception of what he thought the part should be. Loraine, the man, was full of understanding. But outwardly he remained a disciplinarian to the last inch of him. (*Loraine*, p. 218)

Mapplebeck and Evans were not the last casualties in November. On the 13th Darvell was injured in a crash on take off, while two days later Henderson was admitted to hospital when his FE8 also crashed. To set against these losses there was only one confirmed victory—on the 16th, when the newly promoted Lt Benbow caught an Albatros CIII two-seater over Lens, 'got under his tail and fired from fifteen to twenty rounds at a range of twelve to fifty yards'. Benbow reported that the 'machine side-slipped first to left, and then to right, and went down like a dead leaf, striking the ground between PROVIN and ANNOEULLIN', but was 'unable to say, with absolute certainty, that enemy was completely crashed'. Loraine had no doubts, however, and Benbow's second victory was confirmed.

The next victories came on 4 December when, near Arras, Mulholland and Benbow spotted three single-seat biplane scouts of a type they could

4. FE8s being serviced, Treizennes. (R. Gregory.)

not recognize [Albatros DIs], diving on a BE2c. Going to the latter's aid, they caught the German aircraft unawares. Benbow got under the tail of one, firing twenty rounds, whereat it 'turned over on its right wing and went straight to earth in a slow spinning nose-dive'. Mulholland, meanwhile, had fired at a second machine, which 'stalled, side-slipped, and went down completely out of control'. Benbow reported that his victim was 'totally crashed', but Mulholland's attention was diverted by the remaining Albatros, and it was left to Loraine to adjudge the victory 'Certain'.

The only other victory in December, on the 20th, also went to Benbow, now clearly the Squadron's leading scorer. Searching for a hostile aircraft south of Lens, he had his attention drawn by AA fire to a two-seater several thousand feet below him. Diving out of the sun, he 'got under the tail of the Albatros, firing one small drum from a range of seventy feet.' Smoking, it 'dived and crashed into some obstacle just E. of LENS–VIMY railroad'.

In January bad weather continued to curtail flying, so Loraine devised a counter to inactivity—the practice move. F/Sgt Muir recalled:

From the time the signal was sounded on the klaxon horn, everything was to be ready in less than an hour, and was ready. Then, led by the Major [Loraine], we moved off, and did a circuit of about four miles and returned, unpacked and settled on the same ground again. Of course, some of us felt fine fools. The language was awful, and we were all dead beat. It was not a popular event, but as an aid to 100% Efficiency, it could not have been surpassed. I only had to breathe the words, 'practice move', to men after that, for everything to be in apple-pie order. (*Loraine*, p. 227)

Muir added: 'He pushed the men and the officers, I believe, all the time.' Yet though a hard task-master, he was in one crucial respect popular with the rank and file. For as Muir noted,

> he never failed to take an interest in the men's messing and general conditions. He was probably one of the few Field Officers who ever entered the cookhouse at Gosport to inspect and sample the men's food. After that he personally supervised the weekly diet sheet submitted by the Sergeant-cook, and arranged that in spite of the difficulties of obtaining a variety of food, the most varied should be obtained. In France, he ordered a canteen to be opened for the Squadron, the profits from which were used to buy fresh vegetables from the villages nearby, to amplify and vary the men's messing.

'I state emphatically', Muir concluded, 'that no body of men were better fed or looked after than the men of 40 Squadron' (*Loraine* p. 227).

On one occasion Loraine's search for greater efficiency ended farcically, as Fred Powell recalls:

> The Flying Corps had been presented with super-rockets, which the COs were to let off at dusk, to guide stragglers back to the aerodrome. I was coming in from patrol one evening – it was still light in the sky but dark on the ground – when Pfft . . . PFFT, up went one of these rockets. I was furious, more livid than the rocket. Here was I with my Flight hanging hard on my tail, nicknamed 'The Bloke who knows his Way Home', after eighteen months continuous flying in France, actually being shown the way to the aerodrome when I was staring down at it. It was insulting, and just like Loraine's officiousness, I thought, always so occupied was he in being efficient. Couldn't he have remembered it was *me* in the air?

Powell's annoyance was short-lived, however, for

> Suddenly, all over the aerodrome, Pfft . . . pfft . . . PFFT . . . PFFT . . . PFFT . . . ROCKETS, the grandest display of fireworks outside an erupting volcano, at every angle, at every height, along the ground, all ways, with firebells ringing, and a terrific commotion. Loraine had discharged one into a stack of spares. Imagine it, I never laughed so much in my life, the sight was incredible, we were kept five minutes longer in the air, because we couldn't land on ground that was ablaze. That he didn't set the hangars and workshop on fire was his own good fortune. We were quite helpless with laughter when we got down. For days after that Loraine's place at dinner was decorated with crackers, and the lads let off squibs to guide him on his way to Mess. The joke lasted till we had a real fire, one that was frightening. (*Loraine*, pp. 225–6)

The 'real fire' occurred on 27 January 1917, when, with snow thick on the ground:

> a mechanic, who was filling the engines with petrol for the dawn patrol, had his memory numbed by the cold and lit a match to see how much he had put in. There was an explosion, a sheet of flame, so vivid it wakened us before the fire-bell; all the tracer (incendiary) ammunition went off in the aeroplanes, each one firing into the next one's engine and petrol tanks. (*Loraine*, p. 226)

Among those who rushed out to watch the conflagration was Capt H. H. Balfour of 43 Squadron, who gives us a vivid account of Loraine's reaction to the disaster.

> Adjoining the hangar was a lean-to shed which held various mechanic's tools. One little sergeant thought he was being of help by going into the lean-to, which was not yet in flames, and starting to throw out spanners, vices, screw-drivers and other implements. Hardly had he started this somewhat futile task when with a bound Robert Loraine entered within the ring, darted in front of the assembled squadrons, through the glare and into the shed. Seizing the little sergeant by the coat collar he pulled him away and hurled him towards the fire-picket: "Away! If this is anybody's place it is mine", he shouted in a voice of ringing tones which carried right across the aerodrome, and then, in order to show, and quite rightly so, that the destruction of the four burning machines was not irreparable, and that he, as the one responsible, could divert his mind to other matters more mundane, he strode to the middle of the arena and there, in the full glare of the light, performed a perfectly natural function in front of the admiring eyes of the assembled officers and mechanics.[2]

Five aircraft were destroyed, and Loraine drove his men relentlessly to get the Squadron back to full strength. That done, however, not even he was able to keep them employed during the bad weather in January and February 1917. When flying was impossible, the staider members of the Squadron wrote letters, or read, either in their huts or in the Recreation Room. Occasionally, too, there was a 'Cinematographic entertainment' which all ranks were required to attend. But for the officers, the standard recourse was a trip into town. Fred Powell recalls:

> We then used to get into the cars and go off to the various towns, places like Amiens—Abele was too small—and St. Omer. That was good, and that was where most of these boys learnt a little more about life than they would ever have done in normal civil life, because we used to go to the various estaminets, not very popular, and then every town of any size at all had its house of entertainment, which I believe is called a brothel, and so . . . although they were young in years, it wasn't too long before they were quite worldly-wise men.[3]

By the other ranks pleasure had to be sought nearer at hand, and it may be guessed what kind of behaviour was responsible for the statement in Routine Orders on 9 January 1917 that 'the estaminet at the corner of the aerodrome is out of bounds'.

The officers of 40 Squadron had their difficulties with the owner of the château in which their mess and offices were located. Fred Powell again:

> Schatzmann was so interested in his chateau he had no thought of us fighting his confounded war for him. On one occasion one of our boys on the aerodrome, which was on Schatzmann's ground, overshot and ran into the cornfield, where he crashed. I was in the office that morning, and Schatzmann came up and he said, 'Excuse me, major, I understand you have had an accident. One of your planes has landed in the cornfield.' I thought he was being quite decent and so I said, 'Oh thank you Mr. Schatzmann, for your enquiry, but the boy wasn't damaged at all.' And he said, 'I was not thinking of your boy but about my corn'. So you see that Schatzmann was not very popular with us. I am afraid we damaged his chateau terribly, disgracefully.[4]

The Squadron's principal opponent in September and October had been the Roland CII 'Walfisch', a two seater escort and reconnaissance aircraft, equipped with a Spandau machine gun firing forward, and a Parabellum for the observer. The 'Walfisch' was a tough opponent, and slightly faster than the FE8, but 40's pilots held their own through its greater agility, shooting down several Rolands without loss to themselves. It was a different matter, however, with the Albatros DI and DII single-seat scouts, which made their appearance in the first of the specialist fighter units, or *Jagdstaffeln*, in the Autumn of 1916. At first the *Jastas* operated a mixture of types, but late in the year they standardized on the Albatros, and became formidable opponents, well capable of dealing with the DH2 and FE8. The first specialist fighter unit on the Western Front was Oswald Boelcke's *Jasta* 2, but it was *Jasta* 11, commanded by Manfred von Richthofen, which became 40 Squadron's principal opponent in the winter and spring of 1916–17. Aggressively led, they were to exact a grim toll.

Though occasional brushes with German aircraft occurred, there were no conclusive combats until 23 January, when 40 twice encountered *Jasta* 11. The first occasion was during a 9.30 B Flight patrol. John Hay started late, because of plug trouble, and as he hurried to catch up he saw below him an Albatros CIII two seater. Hay reported:

> FE8 dived and coming up the tail of H.A. [Hostile aircraft] opened fire at about 20 yards range. H.A. turned away and nose dived and his wings broke away from his fuselage, which crashed to earth just W. of La Bassée near the Canal.

Hay caught up with the rest of his Flight over Harnes, where they saw six enemy scouts below. The FEs dived to attack but, as Benbow put it, 'enemy turned tail and refused battle'. Benbow noted that the leader of the enemy patrol was flying an aircraft painted entirely red. They had encountered Manfred von Richthofen and *Jasta* 11.

B Flight was again up in the afternoon escorting aircraft of 25 Squadron. Near Lens, Hay was seen by Benbow to attack an enemy aircraft and shoot it down in flames. Then, at about 3.10 pm, the two spotted ten enemy aircraft below them, and dived to attack. Their opponents were once again *Jasta* 11, led by Richthofen in his all-red Albatros. This time, however, they did not refuse fight, and Richthofen sent down Hay's machine in flames. His combat report stated:

> the plane I had singled out caught fire after 150 shots, discharged from 50 metres. The plane fell, burning. Occupant fell out at 500 metres.

John Hay fell in no man's land, and two Canadians crept out, under shell fire, to retrieve his body, one of them later writing to Hay's mother in Australia, saying, 'I had to bring him in alive or dead; he put up such a magnificent fight.'

Two days later 2/Lt H. S. Pell attacked an Albatros two-seater which 'dived steeply and landed near Givenchy', while on 8 February, 2/Lt G. F. Haseler forced down another, which turned over while attempting a landing inside German lines. They were last victories under Loraine's leadership, for on that date Capt L. A. Tilney was posted in, assuming command on 12 February, when Loraine left Treizennes. He had been with the Squadron eleven months, and in that time had built up an efficient fighting force supported by hard-working—and hard driven—groundcrews. He had not flown operationally himself, which was just as well, perhaps, for though courageous, he was, in Fred Powell's opinion, a 'hamfisted' pilot.

Robert Loraine remains in many respects enigmatic. Set apart by his age and social origins, he acted the part of CO, as Harold Balfour recognizes:

> I never saw him other than being Robert Loraine "the pioneer aviator" and Robert Loraine the actor. The whole of his organization was stage-managed with a masterly touch. The Officers' Mess was filled with patent bells and alarm gongs which might go off at any moment, each one indicating some different event such as the start of a patrol, or the sighting of an enemy aeroplane. Always, when one of these went off, it was the custom that not an eyelid should quiver; scarcely altering his tone of conversation he would turn to whomever was concerned: "Gregory—I think there is an enemy around. I think you had better go," and then on with the game of bridge.[5]

A compulsion to act—Loraine's life was lived in larger than life terms–seems to have combined with an inner uncertainty to produce the martinet major of 40 Squadron.

Loraine's subsequent career points up the contradictory elements in his nature. He returned to France a lieutenant colonel, commanding 14 Wing during the German aerial ascendancy which reached its peak in 'Bloody April'. In July, he returned to England to command a training station where, driving hard trainees who he felt showed less than dedication, he, as Winifrid Loraine put it, 'achieved a reputation for sheer unmitigated brutality'. Then, driven, it seems, by the fact that he remained safe while others took the risks for which he was training them, Loraine asked to revert to the rank of major in order to be posted to an operational squadron in France. In May 1918 he took command of 211 Squadron, flying FE2b night bombers, and in July was badly wounded in one knee, and his flying career ended.

Post-war, Loraine resumed his acting career. The war had taken its toll, however, and his health declined, in part, no doubt, because of the damage to his lung done by a bullet in 1914, but more to the stress he had undergone. He died in 1935 at the age of 59.

## Notes

1.  Winifrid Loraine: *Robert Loraine: Actor, Soldier, Airman.* London: Collins, 1938. p. 228. (hereafter abbreviated as *Loraine*).

2.  H. H. Balfour, *An Airman Marches.* London: Hutchinson, 1933. (repr. London: Greenhill Books, 1985) pp. 71–2.

3.  Taped Interview with Wg/Cdr F. J. Powell, Imperial War Museum, Dept of Sound, pp. 25–6.

4.  Powell interview, p. 26.

5.  Balfour, pp. 70–71.

# Mainly Nieuports:
# February–October 1917

L EONARD ARTHUR TILNEY, 40's new CO, was a man different in every respect from his predecessor. An Old Etonian, aged 22, he had qualified as a pilot in March 1915. Accounted 'one of our best pusher pilots' he would bring a new management style to 40, more relaxed and genial, but effective nonetheless.

Two other personnel changes took place on 27 February. One was Fred Powell's posting to Home Establishment. His successor in C Flight was 'the gadget king', Curzon Usborne. The other was the appointment as padre of Capt B. W. Keymer, 1st Leicestershire Regt. For him, more than any other padre in its history, 40 was to feel a great affection.

The first victory for 40 Squadron under its new CO came on 14 February, when Benbow and Usborne attacked one of several Albatros DII scouts near Arras. Neither saw what happened to their victim, but an anti-aircraft battery confirmed that it had crashed. The next day, Benbow sent down another DII out of control—his seventh success.

Bad weather prevented much flying during the latter half of February, and no significant combats occurred until 4 March, when 2/Lt W. B. Hills spotted 'a fast two-seater scout (painted blue)' attacking a Sopwith. Diving, he fired nearly a drum into his opponent at about thirty yards range. The aircraft, perhaps one of the new Albatros CVIIs, went down vertically, apparently out of control, though Hills was unable to see if his victim crashed.

5. Maj L. A. Tilney. (W. A. MacLanachan.)

The same afternoon Usborne, Henderson and Lt W. Morrice had a nasty brush with five or six Halberstadt scouts while escorting Sopwiths of 43 Squadron. Morrice drove off one Halberstadt, but his companions found themselves dealing with tougher opponents. One got on Usborne's tail and he was only saved, he reported, 'by another FE8 (2/Lieut Henderson) attacking at the critical moment'. Even so, Usborne could do nothing but crash land near Béthune. Meanwhile Usborne's tormentor had got on Henderson's tail, 'and being able to turn much faster could not be shaken off'. Henderson spun down to ground level and got away, but his aircraft was badly shot about. The two were lucky to survive, for as Usborne reported, 'the superior speed and extreme handiness of the H.A. gave it at least 25% advantage when fighting'.

The events of 4 March gave the Squadron food for thought, and though a success for Benbow on the 6th, when he sent a Halberstadt down in flames, was encouraging, events on 9 March served to justify their worst fears.

Known thereafter as 'Black Friday', the day began with an offensive patrol over the La Bassée—Bailleul area. Second Lieutenant Lionel Blaxland turned back with engine trouble, and as he did so noticed, high above the patrol, five brightly coloured specks, Albatros DIII scouts of *Jasta* 11, led by Manfred von Richthofen. These dived to attack and a bitter struggle ensued, in which four FE8s were shot down and the remaining aircraft damaged.

6. A4872 (2/Lt G. F. Haseler), shot down 9 March 1917. (R. Gregory.)

The aircraft shot down were those of Lt T. Shepard and 2/Lts Haseler and Hills, all taken prisoner, and Neve, who just made it to Allied lines. With his gun jammed, Neve was 'wounded and had great difficulty in breathing, also a bullet grazed his forehead, but apparently the helmet sheared it off'. His engine then cut and he made as if to land in enemy territory, but finding that the engine restarted on the gravity tank, staggered across the trenches. His report continues:

> FE8's pilot becoming faint decided to land as soon as possible, and seeing three soldiers tried to land near them. Owing to aileron being shot away FE8 made a bad landing, turned over and caught fire. Pilot scrambled out with coat and gloves burning. Pilot rolled over on the ground and soldiers took off their coats and put out the fire on the pilot, and carried him to a safe distance.

The laconic tone of Neve's report cannot disguise a horrifying few minutes, which he was lucky to survive.

All the aircraft which returned to Treizennes were damaged, most of them seriously. It had been a heavy and unmitigated defeat which underscored the fact that FE8s were now incapable of coping with their opponents. It was with relief, therefore, that the Squadron learned that it was to be re-equipped with the Nieuport 17.

French designed and built, the Nieuport 17 had the company's characteristic design features of a single-bay sesquiplane layout, with a single-spar lower wing and V shaped interplane struts. For the RFC the standard armament was a Lewis gun on a Foster mounting on the centre section of the upper wing, firing over the propeller. With a top speed of 107 mph and a service ceiling of 17,400 feet, the Nieuport was a great advance on the FE8, but those used to the latter found the reduced forward vision disturbing at first, and a number of crashes occurred on landing and take off.

Forty's first Nieuports were flown in from St. Omer from 12 March, but patrols continued to be flown on FE8s while the pilots practised with their new mounts, the last operation being on 21 March, when Blaxland, Todd and Lt D. H. de Burgh escorted aircraft of 2 and 16 Squadrons.

On 22 March 2/Lt S. J. Stocks was shot in the stomach during a clash with enemy scouts. Besides his wound he had to cope with a holed petrol tank and a dead engine, but the Nieuport did not catch fire and Stocks was able to forced-land safely. On 30 March another newcomer, Lt D. M. F. Sinclair, was less fortunate. A seven strong patrol led by Gregory tangled with *Jasta* 11, and Sinclair was shot down and killed.

April began inauspiciously, with Sharpe taken prisoner on the 3rd. Yet there were signs of better things to come. For the pilots found their new mounts to be both responsive and capable of reaching (and exceeding) the altitude at which the German scouts were operating. On 31 March, for

7. The first Nieuport, A133, March 1917 (note FE8s at rear). (R. Gregory.)

instance, de Burgh, Benbow and 2/Lt W. T. Walder all reported having having outclimbed opponents, to attack from a height advantage. Saxon Pell reported similarly on 5 April, when at 10,000 feet he encountered six enemy aircraft and found that his 'Nieuport outclimbed them easily'. That evening he scored the first confirmed Nieuport success when he drove down an enemy aircraft which was seen to crash.

On 8 April a British attack at Arras was co-ordinated with a Canadian Corps assault on Vimy Ridge, immediately to the west. These had been planned to distract German attention from an imminent French offensive on the Aisne, but proved highly successful, with Vimy Ridge seized and the Germans pushed back beyond the Hindenburg Line.

The RFC's task was to achieve air superiority, and to that end there began on 4 April a period of intense air activity along the whole British front. During the holocaust of 'Bloody April', when so many corps reconnaissance squadrons were decimated, 40 would at least be flying an aircraft capable of holding its own against the Albatros-equipped *Jastas*. On the other hand, it was to be called on to play a prominent part in what were euphemistically designated 'Special Missions': the dangerous task of balloon busting.

On 4 April, in preparation for the first 'Special Mission', the Squadron practised with Le Prieur rockets, developed for attacks of this kind. Then, on the 6th, it undertook the first of a series of attacks on enemy balloons, employing techniques devised by Major Tilney. These involved a simultaneous

8. Nieuports at Treizennes, Spring 1917. (I. P. R. Napier via Chaz Bowyer.)

attack on all the balloons in the sector by hedge-hopping Nieuports. Accompanying the five rocket carrying machines were three escorts, led by Robert Gregory, whose task was to hold off enemy scouts. The first mission was not particularly successful, with only one balloon destroyed, by Todd, while the Canadian, Pell, was shot down and killed.

Between 4 and 8 April, four new pilots joined the Squadron: 2/Lts A. C. Dunlop, E. Mannock, J. J. Scaramanga and B. B. Lemon. Neither Scaramanga nor Dunlop stayed long, both being injured in crashes, Dunlop seriously. With severe head, back and leg injuries, he lay for more than a week in a coma, and close to death. On 20 April, however, newcomer 'Mick' Mannock recorded in his diary: 'Went to Aire on 17th and 19th to see Dunlop. There's a hope that he'll pull through'.[1] He did, but never rejoined the Squadron.

On 19 April Mannock himself came close to death. His diary reads:

did some gun practice and in one dive from two thousand my right bottom plane broke and fell clean away. Managed to right the machine after desperate efforts with the 'joy stick' and landed slowly and safely about half a mile away from aerodrome. Such a thing has never happened before where the pilot has not been killed or injured by the fall. (*Diary*. pp. 44–7)

The cause was a defective strut socket, and this structural failure was not the first of its kind for 40, or the last. Six days earlier, Benbow's lower port wing had twisted in a dive, while in May Lemon abandoned a diving attack for the same reason. Nor was 40 the only unit to experience these problems. In some cases, the cause was slipshod workmanship, and in others insufficiently seasoned wood. But there was also an inherent weakness in the design of the Nieuport's lower wing, with its single spar vulnerable to deformation or collapse at the point of attachment to the V strut.

Forty's successes since it converted to the Nieuport had been limited. Now at last pilots began to score. One was newcomer, Lt H. E. O. Ellis, who on 13 April, on his first patrol, encountered an Albatros C type and closing, fired twenty rounds. His laconic combat report concluded: 'H.A. cartwheeled, turned over, went down in a spin, and was seen to crash on the ground'.

On 14 April Lts de Burgh and I. P. R. Napier made a diving attack on three Albatros DIIIs, one of which landed in a field, and burst into flames, while 2/Lt L. L. Morgan (nicknamed 'the Air Hog' for his enthusiasm for operational flying) drove down a Halberstadt scout on 21 April and Walder crashed an Albatros C type the following day. On the same day (22 April) Morgan and de Burgh carried out rocket attacks on balloons, but only the latter was successful, the balloon at Sallaumines being hauled down smoking.

The 23rd April was a day of exceptionally heavy aerial fighting, but 40 contributed only a two-seater sent out of control by Lts K. Mackenzie and Ellis. On 24 April, two more two-seaters were attacked, one by the South African, Lt R. N. Hall. This aircraft escaped by diving away, 'the observer . . . seen leaning over limp', but that attacked by Lts J. A. G. Brewis and Napier, a DFW CV, was forced to land undamaged, and the crew taken prisoner. Lt W. A. Bond wrote to his wife the following day:

> A brand new machine, undamaged, and pilot and observer! We collected the machine and it arrived on our aerodrome just before dinner.
> By coincidence the CO had invited the Marine Light Infantry Band to give a concert in the squadron, and so we had them playing in the mess during dinner. It made a celebration.[2]

On 25 April 40 moved from Treizennes to Auchel, Bill Bond writing to his wife:

> We left the old aerodrome for another nearer the line and everything is upset and uncomfortable at present.
> We had breakfast at 6 a.m., and had to have everything packed by 7 a.m. Then the pilots flew their machines here and had to wait in cheerless wooden huts until the lorries with kit and furniture arrived. (*Airman's Wife*, p. 55)

Auchel was only a temporary base, however, for on 29 April the Squadron moved six kilometres south-east, to an aerodrome on the outskirts of the mining town of Bruay. Here it would remain until June 1918.

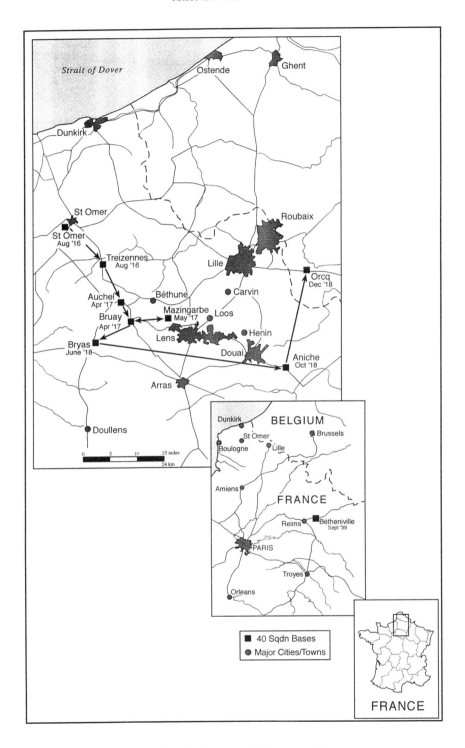

Map 2. Bases in France and Belgium, 1916–39.

On the day of the second shift 40 suffered two losses. One was Brewis, shot down and killed on an early patrol. That evening Capt F. L. Barwell was also shot down after a gallant solo fight of 'almost half an hour', so a German infantry unit reported.[3]

May began auspiciously. On the 1st Capt A. W. Keen, the new C Flight Commander, scored for the first time. Mick Mannock wrote in his diary:

> We were attacked from above, over Douai. I tried my gun before going over the German lines, only to find that it was jammed, so I went over with a revolver only. A Hun in a beautiful yellow and green 'bus' attacked me from behind. I could hear his machine gun cracking away. I wheeled round on him and howled like a dervish (although of course he couldn't hear me) whereat he made off towards old Parry [2/Lt H. R. Parry] and attacked him, with me following, for the moral effect! Another one (a brown speckled one) attacked a Sopwith, and Keen blew the pilot to pieces and the Hun went down spinning from twelve thousand feet to earth. (*Diary*, pp. 57–9)

On 2 May Mackenzie also scored, bringing down one of five enemy scouts attacked near Quiery-la-Motte, but the highlight was a brilliantly successful attack on balloons, carried out by him, Walder, Lemon, Bond, Morgan and 2/Lt S. Thompson. The care that had gone into this 'special mission' is revealed in *RFC Communiqué 86*:

> These pilots had practised low flying, and had learnt how to use trees, houses, and the ground in screening them from infantry and machine gun fire. Artillery co-operated by putting a heavy barrage on the German trenches, leaving the pilots a certain area in which to cross. As a result of the attack four German balloons were destroyed [by Bond, Lemon, Walder and Morgan]. One pilot, who went to within a few feet of the balloon, failed in his attack owing to gun trouble. (p. 6)

The barrage was successful in suppressing small arms fire, the Nieuports not being fired upon until close to their targets. But then the German fire was intense, including machine guns, small arms, AA and 'Flaming Onions', about which Walder reported:

> As far as could be seen Flaming Onions were fired from a species of Mortar 4 or 5 feet long. No sighting apparatus was apparent—a man was seen to stoop down behind the mortar which fired about 12 balls of brilliant light— these spread out and were evidently fired at random.

On 27 April Ellis enjoyed further success when he was set upon by four enemy aircraft, shooting one of them down. The following day he scored again, sending an Aviatik down 'in a vertical nose dive', though unable to observe it crash. Ellis had become a force to be reckoned with, and on 4 May, flew a solo patrol pursuant to the roving commission which Tilney had granted him. His report reads:

Dived on 3 Albatross Scouts S. of Douai at 8000 ft, fired about 40 rounds and drove them down.

One side slipped 500 ft from the ground and then crashed to earth. A second landed on its nose and turned completely over on its back on Douai aerodrome. The third landed O.K. on Douai aerodrome.

Was then attacked from behind by enemy Nieuport—manoeuvred to get under H.A. and gun stopped after 2 or 3 rounds. Sheered off to clear stoppage—Got underneath again and drum ran out.

Fired seven rounds from Colt Automatic pistol, and H.A. nose dived. The left lower wing of H.A.'s bottom plane was seen to fall off, about 2000 ft from the ground. H.A. went down out of control and was seen to land in a pond.

Nor were Ellis's isolated successes, as was demonstrated when on 5 May Walder drove an Albatros two-seater down out of control, while on the 6th the 'Air Hog' (Morgan) sent an Albatros scout down in flames and Gregory, now the longest serving pilot on squadron, crashed an Albatros C type in flames. On the debit side, however, Ellis crashed on landing at the Squadron's Advanced Landing Ground at Mazingarbe, and was seriously concussed. He never flew operationally again.

The Landing Ground at Mazingarbe was opened because from Bruay, eleven miles from the front line, it was difficult to combat the trench-strafing aircraft that the Germans sent across at dawn and dusk. But from Mazingarbe it was only a mile and a half to the front line, and pilots on standby had a chance of interception. A description of the landing ground is provided by a pilot who arrived on squadron in May, 2/Lt W. A. MacLanachan:

The site chosen was a clover field about half a mile behind the village of Bully-Grenay and two miles south of Mazingarbe. Being within easy shelling distance it was not possible to build hangars, but a camouflaged tent, capable of covering two machines, was erected, while a small wood-and-brick hut was built to house the wireless, the telephone, and to act as a 'doss house' for the pilots who were to carry out the patrols.[4]

9. 'The Air Hog', Lt L. L. Morgan. (F. T. Gilbert.)

At first pilots regarded Mazingarbe askance. But when it became clear that it attracted no German interest, the landing ground was favoured, MacLanachan tells us, 'as a picnic place and taking-off pitch for lone flights'.

On 5 May a new flight commander, Capt W. E. Nixon, arrived, and two days later he led Morgan, Hall, Mannock, Parry, and 2/Lts C. W. Cudemore and H. B. Redler, on a 'Special Mission'. The attack was carefully planned with the successful features of that on 2 May further sophisticated, as *RFC Communiqué 87* indicates:

> The pilots crossed the lines at about 20 feet, and as on a previous occasion, artillery put a barrage on the trenches, but on this occasion 12 other aeroplanes crossed the lines at the same time at a considerable height in order to draw the attention of anti-aircraft gunners. (p. 3)

From Bond we learn that the diversionary aircraft were added at Robert Gregory's suggestion.

All seven balloons were destroyed, 3 (Cudemore, Morgan and Hall) catching fire at altitude, 2 (Mannock and Redler) as they were being pulled down, and 2 (Parry and Hall) on the ground. Nixon, however, did not return. Caught at low altitude, he fought fiercely against heavy odds, but was overwhelmed. The others all survived, though badly shot up. Mannock wrote in his diary:

> Hall crashed on home aerodrome, as did Scudamore [*sic*], Parry crashed just our side of the lines at the Canadian H.Q. Redler crashed at Savy, but returned here later and damaged his machine on landing. I was the only one to return properly to the aerodrome, and made a perfect landing. (*Diary*, pp. 69–71)

'My fuselage had bullet holes in it, one very near my head, and the wings were more or less riddled', Mannock went on, adding: 'I don't want to go through such an experience again'.

During late April and early May numerous changes in personnel took place, occasioned both by operational losses (Barwell, Brewis and Nixon) and by postings to Home Establishment (Todd, Benbow, de Burgh, 2/Lt. G. Brown and Capt. McKechnie). Replacing these old hands came a batch of new pilots, including the South African, Redler, and two Canadians—the first on squadron since the death of Saxon Pell—Lt A. B. Raymond and 2/Lt A. E. Godfrey.

'Steve' Godfrey's unconventional behaviour and lurid turns of phrase shocked some, but he won respect as a fighter, and in the months to come was to prove one of the most consistently successful members of the Squadron. The second Canadian, 'Rastus' Raymond, was a man of a different mould, quietly spoken and greatly liked. He acquitted himself well, and on the evening of 12 May assisted Keen in bringing down an Albatros two-seater.

The following morning, however, Keen and Raymond became separated in cloud, and Raymond was shot down and taken prisoner.

During early May fine weather kept 40 busy, but the only success went to Keen, who brought down an Albatros two-seater on the 12th. Bill Bond wrote to his wife the next day: 'the weather refuses to break, and it is oppressively hot. You would love it, I know. But we are longing for a real break. We want a rest from patrols for a day or two.' (*Airman's Wife*, p. 88). The pilots got their break on 16 and 17 May, when very bad weather made flying impossible, with only limited activity on 18th, and none again the following day.

During the fine weather, however, members of the Squadron had been able to enjoy a new amenity of which Bond wrote to his wife:

> Some miles away there is a most topping valley occupied by a chateau and its grounds. A river runs through it and about a week ago the CO and the Odd Man [Padre Keymer] got permission from the people at the chateau to dam the stream . . . in order to form a swimming pool. (*Airman's Wife*, p. 96)

This did last long, however, for Robert Gregory told his mother that 'it attracted such a number of people from the neighbourhood that the owners of the land objected & we have had to take it away'.5

Swimming was not the only amenity developed by Padre Keymer. Within days of the shift to Bruay, Bond wrote to his wife that Keymer was 'working hard trying to level the ground in the middle of our huts to make a tennis court' (*Airman's Wife*, p. 72). By 3 May the court was laid and Keymer had organized a tournament. Later that month MacLanachan, posted in from St. Omer, found a game in progress, creating 'the general impression . . . of a peaceful tennis club at home' (*Fighter Pilot*, p. 5).

From the first the enthusiasm of 'The Air Hog' for air fighting was extraordinary, Bill Bond describing him as 'simply crazy to get Huns' (*Airman's Wife*, p. 95). Morgan scored his first success on 21 April, and his first certain victory on 6 May, when he sent an Albatros DIII down in flames, while the following day he took part in the successful balloon strafe described earlier. By 23 May his score stood at five, but that evening his career with 40 came to an abrupt end when his aircraft was hit at 4,500 feet by a British shell which demolished half the engine. It also left one of Morgan's legs nearly severed, and the other broken at the ankle, but despite this he managed to glide down to a crash-landing. Morgan lost a leg, but returned to active duty, to die in a crash in 1918.

On 8 June Robert Gregory, the last of those who had flown to France in August 1916, was farewelled. Bond wrote to his wife:

> To-night we are having a special celebration dinner. Romney [Gregory], who has been out here a long time, and has brought down many Huns, is going home to-morrow.

We expect he will get a squadron and his majority—in addition to his M.C., and Croix de Guerre. (*Airman's Wife*, p. 127)

Gregory's replacement was Capt W. T. L. Allcock who arrived on 29 May, but survived only briefly, being shot down and killed on 5 June. Pending a replacement Bond took over the Flight.

Between 4 and 8 June six pilots arrived, three of them from the Dominions, 2/Lt G. T. Pettigrew (New Zealand) and Lt H. A. Kennedy and 2/Lt F. W. Rook (Canada). On arrival newcomers undertook practice flights, and like many others Rook found landing a Nieuport difficult and crashed, though without injury. If a newcomer completed these initial practice flights unscathed, he then had to survive his first operational sorties. MacLanachan gives a graphic account in *Fighter Pilot* of his first patrols, when he saw virtually nothing and was lucky to survive. But then he had been given little help or advice, his flight commander, Capt C. L. Bath, merely telling him what course to fly if lost. By Walder, Bath's deputy, he was told that if attacked from behind, 'dive straight underneath the formation—don't wait to let them *get* you', but that was all. For the most part, it seems, it was 'sink or swim' for newcomers, and it is hardly surprising that so many failed to survive their first weeks on operations.

10. 'Five from Forty':
(l to r) 2/Lt H. B. Redler, 2/Lt J. L. Barlow, Lt L. B. Blaxland and Capt I. P. R. Napier. At rear, 2/Lt E. Mannock. Bruay, June 1917.
(W. MacLanachan.)

One who failed to do so was 2/Lt J. W. Shaw, who had been with the Squadron a fortnight, and did not return from a morning offensive patrol on 7 June. To set against Shaw's loss, however, the Squadron chalked up an encouraging number of confirmed victories and 'out of controls'. The most consistently successful pilot during this period was Bond, who was credited with two Albatros DIIIs out of control on 28 May, another destroyed on 5 June, and yet another on the 9th. Steve Godfrey also scored twice—on 1 and 7 June—and on the latter date Mannock also scored his first confirmed success (apart from the balloon), describing it with relish in his diary:

My man gave me an easy mark. I was only ten yards away from him—on top so I couldn't miss! A beautifully coloured insect he was—red, blue, green and yellow. I let him have sixty rounds at that range, so there wasn't much left of him. I saw him go spinning and slipping down from fourteen thousand. Rough luck, but its war, and they're Huns. (*Diary*, p. 105)

On 9 June Bill Bond shot down an Albatros DIII, but the day belonged to 2/Lt J. L. Barlow. He had made an ignominious start with the Squadron, crashing on two consecutive practice flights, but made handsome amends when, diving on an Aviatik, he was attacked 'by 8 Albatross Scouts from above and 4 Aviatiks from below'. Fighting back desperately, he hit an Albatros DIII, which crashed in a field near the trenches, and also brought down an Aviatik two-seater. His Nieuport was severely shot about, however, and he was lucky to make it back to Bruay, as Bill Bond told him:

As his temporary flight commander I strafed him violently for playing the fool, and told him his luck was more than he deserved. But to myself I acknowledged that it was awfully plucky to struggle on as he did. It was his fifth trip over the line and his first scrap—though he had seen one other. He will not attempt to repeat the performance. When his excitement wore off he had a big reaction, and he realizes now what inexperience may do. (*Airman's Wife*, p. 185)

11. 'Air Fighters at Bruay': 2/Lt G. T. Pettigrew, 2/Lt W. A. MacLanachan, Lt L. B. Blaxland, 2/Lt A. E. Godfrey, Lt H. A. Kennedy. Bruay, June 1917. (W. MacLanachan.)

The Squadron's next success came on the evening of 15 June, when Keen sent an Albatros DIII down in flames, repeating his success on 24 June, when his flight attacked a formation of Albatros scouts. Many combats resulted, and Lt G. B. Crole and Blaxland made a joint claim for one out of control, and Pettigrew another. Earlier in the day Godfrey and Rook had also lodged claims for 'out of controls'. The scout Rook claimed what he described as a 'new Albatros—Vee strut, Brownish colour', and it seems likely that this was a DV, which had entered service in May 1917.

By late June Keen and Godfrey were 40's stars, both scoring regularly. On 25 June the scrupulous Keen claimed two Albatros DIIIs 'out of control', though his combat reports indicate a high degree of likelihood that one crashed, and on 2 July another destroyed. That day Godfrey, who had attacked two Albatroses, reported that he had shot one down and that the other had fled, while Crole shot a wing off an Albatros and Blaxland badly damaged another which later crashed.

On 7 July I. P. R. Napier, the B Flight Commander, was posted to RFC HQ. In his place came South African Capt G. L. 'Zulu' Lloyd. Possessed, MacLanachan remarks, of 'a charming manner, a sort of boyish ingenuousness that disarmed any criticism or animosity' (*Fighter Pilot,* p. 57) Lloyd was immediately accepted, and because his previous squadron, 60, was also equipped with Nieuports, found himself drawn into what MacLanachan calls 'dining-table conferences on tactics' involving senior pilots like Bond, Mannock, Godfrey, Redler, Hall and Lemon.

12. Capt E. 'Mick' Mannock.
(RAF Museum.)

The Squadron's next decisive victory went to Mannock, who on 12 July brought down a two-seater DFW CV. This being the first aircraft he had brought down behind the Allied lines, he went to the scene of the crash, later recording his impressions:

> I . . . found the observer being tended by the local M. O. and I gathered a few souvenirs, although the infantry had the first pick. The machine was completely smashed, and rather interesting also was the little black and tan terrier—dead—in the observer's seat. I felt exactly like a murderer. The journey through the trenches was rather nauseating—dead men's legs sticking through

the sides with putties [sic] and boots still on—bits of bones and skulls with the hair peeling off, and tons of equipment and clothing lying about. This sort of thing, together with the strong graveyard stench and the dead and mangled body of the pilot (an NCO) combined to upset me for a few days. (*Diary*, pp. 117–9)

Mannock's victory was followed by another the next day, one of three DFWs he attacked falling completely out of control, while on the 14th, in a clash with four green Albatros scouts of *Jasta* 29 east of Douai, Lloyd, Redler, and Kennedy claimed Albatroses out of control. Second lieutenant Godfrey Davis failed to return from this patrol, but survived to be taken POW.

In mid-July Canadians Godfrey, Rook and Kennedy were joined by 2/Lt W. L. Harrison, who took even longer to be accepted than Godfrey. MacLanachan recalls:

Harrison was an enigma to the rest of us. He was about six feet tall, rather swarthy, and as his bristly hair, which defied all attempts at brushing, stood straight up from his head, his appearance was that of a quarrelsome back-woodsman. (*Fighter Pilot*, p. 61)

Harrison was a rarity on the Squadron, teetotal and a non-smoker. But he was an avid card player, and a poker school was established, the regulars all being 'colonials'—Godfrey, Rook, Harrison and Kennedy from Canada, the New Zealander, Pettigrew, and Hall, the South African.

On 21 July the poker school lost Rook. MacLanachan remembered the 19-year-old as 'a charming boy' whose 'gentle manner and imperishable smile made him a general favourite'. 'Rook was always prepared for a quiet "jape"', MacLanachan writes,

and Barlow, with typical boisterous spirits, was ever ready to turn the jape into a 'rag'. The only difference between them was that Rook treated the war with due seriousness while Barlow treated it as if it were really a 'rag' on a stupendous scale. (*Fighter Pilot*, p. 64)

MacLanachan had first hand experience of the latter's boisterousness when in the course of a 'friendly argument' he was laid out by Barlow with a water jug.

Rook's was one of several deaths that came to be connected with an old piano that stood in the Officers' Mess, there being a superstition that whoever played it would not live a week. MacLanachan, who learned of the super-stition on the evening of Rook's death, writes:

Hall, Steve Godfrey and Redler told me of several pilots who had been killed as justification for the superstition. None of us believed in it, but coincidence had played queer tricks with the Squadron, and continued to play them. (*Fighter Pilot*, p. 81)

Rook, it seems, had played the piano at a dinner a couple of days earlier to celebrate Bill Bond's appointment as A Flight Commander.

There was another loss the next day (22 July) when Bond was killed. A report from an anti-aircraft battery stated that 'at 8.55 am a plane—believed Nieuport—was observed to fall over Sallaumines out of control—right wing blown away by AA gunfire'. MacLanachan recalled:

13. Capt W. A. Bond. (RAF Museum.)

Redler was flying on his right with Kennedy behind him; I was on the left with Tudhope and Harrison behind me. Our speed, at the rate Bond was climbing, dropped to 80 m.p.h. and with unpleasant recollections of the 'heavy gunner' into whose area we were approaching, I began to wonder why Bond was making no effort to mislead the enemy.

We had reached eight thousand feet when the first shells came up, right amongst us.

My machine was blown completely over, and on regaining control I saw that Bond had disappeared. Pieces of aeroplane fabric were whirling crazily in the air amongst the huge black smoke balls of the Archie bursts.

Incredulous I looked around for Bond, but he had gone; all that remained in the air were the stupid, dancing remnants of his planes. (*Fighter Pilot*, p. 83)

The shell nearly claimed Bond's deputy, Redler, also. His aircraft was blown over by the blast, and he only just managed to cross the front line, crashing behind the Allied trenches.

Bond's successor in A Flight was Mannock, which did not go down well with those who harboured suspicions about his willingness to fight. These suspicions, MacLanachan tells us, had resulted in 'dissension in the Squadron during July'. Eventually Lloyd was instructed by Tilney to speak to Mannock, who convinced both that he had mastered his fear. Yet Mannock's growing confidence, which meant that he now spoke out during squadron debates on tactics, fuelled resentments, so that when the promotion came there were still those who accused him of being a 'pandering type who licked the CO's boots'.

Steve Godfrey scored twice in late July, an Albatros DIII out of control on the 22nd being followed by another on the 28th. No further combats took place until 5 August, when *RFC Communiqué 100* reported (p. 1) that Capt Mannock had 'engaged 5 Albatros Scouts near Henin-Lietard. He shot one down out of control, but was unable to see it crash owing to the presence of other enemy machines'. Even if he had seen the aircraft crash, however, there would have been no chance of being credited with a victory unless it were independently confirmed.

On 9 August the first major balloon attack for some time took place, the aim being to blind the enemy's observation posts while the Canadian Corps reinforced their sector prior to an attack on Hill 70 near Lens. Robert Gregory had earlier convinced Major Tilney that no one should take part in more than one 'special mission', hence the task fell to MacLanachan, Pettigrew, Lt J. H. Tudhope, Barlow, Sgt L. A. Herbert, and Harrison. The plan was essentially that of 7 May, whereby a seven strong patrol overflew the trenches at altitude, causing the balloons to be lowered. The balloon strafers, taking off from Mazingarbe, would then attack at low level. On this occasion, however, a sophistication was added in the form of artillery support to suppress trench fire, with safety lanes left for the Nieuports to fly through during the bombardment.

All opted for this approach save MacLanachan, who had 'a horror of meeting a shell in the air', and so took off immediately the bombardment ended. As he did so, he saw the northernmost balloon, Herbert's, going up in flames. Once through the small arms fire from the German trenches, he attacked his balloon, leaving it smoking and deflated. Then, realizing that there was another to the south which had to be brought down, he attacked that also, damaging it sufficiently to ensure that it would not be usable that day.

Last back, MacLanachan was warmly welcomed in bringing confirmation that all the balloons were down. The second balloon he attacked was that assigned to Tudhope, who had run into German telegraph wires, losing the tip of his propeller, and returning with yards of wire around the propeller and undercarriage. MacLanachan himself had only one bullet hole in his Nieuport, but the others had been peppered, Harrison and Kennedy severely.

Arthur Keen had a particularly productive spell in the second week of August. On the 9th he first sent a DFW down in a spin emitting thick smoke, then later that day downed an Albatros DV. On the 12th he also scored twice, crashing an Albatros DV and a DFW, the latter an emphatic victory reported in *RFC Communiqué 101*:

Capt A. W. Keen, No 40 Squadron, when patrolling east of Oppy, observed 3 enemy two-seaters at which he dived. One of the German machines turned and flew towards the Nieuport, so Capt Keen looped over the German machine and opened fire when diving down, and the right hand planes of the E. A. folded back, after which it fell and crashed. (p. 2)

During the same patrol Godfrey and Lloyd each claimed one out of control, while Godfrey followed up his success with an Albatros DIII in flames that evening, and a DFW out of control the following morning.

The 12th also brought Mannock's celebrated victory over a five victory ace, Joachim von Bertrab, who had crossed the lines at low level to attack balloons. Taking off from Mazingarbe, Mannock cut off his retreat, and von Bertrab crashed in the British trenches. Mannock landed, then rushed off in a squadron tender to see for himself the outcome of the combat, later noting:

> I was very pleased that I did not kill him. Right arm broken by a bullet, left arm and left leg deep flesh wounds. His machine, a beauty, just issued (1 June 1917) with a 220 h.p. Mercedes engine, all black with crosses picked out in white lines—turned over on landing and was damaged. Two machine guns with one thousand rounds of ammunition against my single Lewis and three hundred rounds! (*Diary*, p. 129)

The next morning Mannock led Tudhope and Kennedy on an early patrol during which they encountered 'Seven Albatross scouts—long fuselage; various colours, some marked with clubs and crosses. All very fast and good climbers'. The Nieuports attacked but the German patrol gave them a hard time, as MacLanachan recalled:

> Tud's machine was in such a condition that it might have been sent to a flying school to act as an inspiration and a warning to budding fighters. An explosive bullet had burnt through his main spar a few inches from the 'V' strut, one of his top planes had been cut to ribbons by bullets, every one of his instruments was smashed, and a bullet had passed through his coat collar. (*Fighter Pilot*, p. 103)

Kennedy and Mannock had fared better but all were shaken by the incident, the latter feeling (so MacLanachan tells us) his responsibility for what had happened. It was to be a turning point in Mannock's development as a strategist, marking an end to the headstrong behaviour that followed his appointment as Bond's successor.

On 14 August the Canadian Corps attacked at Lens, and on that day two German aircraft were destroyed and three sent down out of control. The first 'certain' went to Hall, who fired on an Albatros DV attacking a British two-seater and watched it crash into some houses in Lens. The other was credited to Keen who sent one of six Albatros DIIIs down in flames and another out of control.

Against the impressive achievements of early August the Squadron had to set two losses, both newcomers. On 12 August Lt W. D. Cullen did not return from an evening patrol led by Zulu Lloyd. He had been on squadron only since 8 August, so this must have been one of his first sorties. He survived to be taken POW. Then on 15 August Capt W. G. Pender did not return from an offensive patrol with Crole, in the course of which they had tangled with five enemy scouts. With four enemy aircraft on his tail and his gun jammed, Crole 'manoeuvred'. Pender was not so fortunate, being shot down and killed.

The next few days brought three victories over two-seaters. Two were DFWs, one brought down on 17 August by Mannock and the other (on the 20th) by MacLanachan. Zulu Lloyd's victim was an Albatros C type, and the circumstances unusual. In recommending the award of the Military Cross Major Tilney reported:

> On August 18th, when patrolling, he observed a 2-seater Albatross upon which he dived. The hostile observer replied with two guns but Capt Lloyd got on the same level as the German machine and fifty yards behind it. The hostile observer continued to fire and his tail plane was observed to break off, the machine going down in a vertical nose dive to crash.[6]

It seems that in a desperate effort to repel Lloyd, the German shot his tail off.

Periodically the Squadron had received some Nieuport 23s, virtually identical to the 17, but in August received a few Nieuport 24s, with a rounded tail unit with a ply covering. Mannock mentions in a diary entry for 31 August that the shape of the new aircraft caused some trouble:

> During the last few weeks, we have been issued with a new type Nieuport machine. The tail plane and rudder are shaped very like a Hun Scout, also the body is fish shaped. These similarities are a source of great concern to our other machines in the air, as we are often mistaken for Huns, and consequently get fired at. (*Diary*, p. 137)

The first Nieuport 24 was brought to Bruay on 15 August, and MacLanachan was very taken with it. The aircraft had been allotted to Godfrey, but he disliked it, and offered it to MacLanachan in exchange for the latter's older model. MacLanachan was delighted with the new machine, and 'The Silver Queen', as he named her, remained his until the Squadron re-equipped with the SE 5a.

The 22nd of August brought another success for Steve Godfrey, who drove a two-seater down out of control, but also the loss of Kennedy. Late in the day HQ ordered a reconnaissance of Dorignies aerodrome. Major Tilney intended sending MacLanachan over solo at ground level, but Mannock persuaded him to provide top cover. The aerodrome found deserted, MacLanachan climbed to join A Flight, which had become embroiled in a dogfight with Albatroses of *Jasta* 30, and

> had almost gained their level when, to my horror, I saw a Nieuport careering downwards in a mad dive, streaks of smoke issuing behind it, while the sun vividly lit up the aluminium-painted fuselage and red, white and blue circles. (*Fighter Pilot*, p. 151)

For MacLanachan, there was particular significance in Kennedy's death. For the latter had confided in him the previous evening, at Mazingarbe:

> "I've got a powerful hunch," he said, "I shall never see my girl again—I'll never last out another day." Then he told me of his university life in Toronto, of his home life and of his fiancée. In conclusion he added: "And in another twenty-four hours, Mac, it'll be all over. What was the use of it?" (*Fighter Pilot*, p. 142)

Struck by Kennedy's intensity, MacLanachan was relieved when the latter returned scatheless from two patrols next morning. After dinner that evening it emerged in discussion with Mannock and Padre Keymer that a couple of nights earlier Kennedy had accompanied Mick (as violinist) on the mess piano, about which so much superstition clung. At that point MacLanachan told the others of Kennedy's hunch, though with no evening patrol scheduled it seemed to have proved false. HQ's demand for information about Dorignies, and Mannock's insistence that MacLanachan be given top cover, changed all that, and Kennedy's death left MacLanachan shaken.

Kennedy's replacement in A Flight was 2/Lt G. E. H. McElroy, of whom MacLanachan writes:

> A new pilot was nearly always a danger to himself and to the others; if he were too cautious he was liable to be left behind to be sniped off by an astute enemy when the flight attacked; or if he were courageous, he was just as liable to be 'downed' in his first scrap because of his ignorance of what was going on around him. In either case, his misdemeanours were likely to incur special dangers for the rest of the flight. McElroy never caused us any anxiety. His attitude towards the war was that of a terrier that has been let loose in a rat infested barn. (*Fighter Pilot*, p. 155)

Born scrapper or not, but McElroy had the usual difficulties in mastering the Nieuport, particularly on landing, crashing twice, on 3 and 19 September. Landings were to remain a problem, for he never became a particularly good aerodrome pilot.

Bad weather in the last week of August forced an almost complete cessation of flying. It was around this time that Major Tilney had the Officers' Mess redesigned. MacLanachan writes:

> A bay window was let into the north wall, an open fireplace of red brick was built between the ante-room and the dining-room, and the mechanics made us some comfortable chairs and a settee, these latter being covered with balloon fabric we were able to 'draw' from Brigade Stores. The fireplace was made in Tudor style, the alcove being panelled in oak with upholstered settles at the sides. (*Fighter Pilot*, p. 160)

'Another improvement', MacLanachan tells us, 'was the provision of a proper bar with a service hatch into the ante-room', while the institution of a shared drinks bill enabled the Squadron to entertain visitors without strain on the finances of any one individual. Enlivened by sporting prints, the Mess 'would have done credit to any shooting-lodge' (*Fighter Pilot*, p. 161).

After a victory to Crole on 23 August, 40 did not score again until 4 September, when Mannock shot down two DFW CVs out of control, one jointly with Herbert. Mannock was also successful on the 6th, when he was set upon by two Albatroses as he attacked a two-seater with Harrison. He reported that he 'swung away, did a sharp turn and got on tail of E. A., firing a whole drum and E. A. went down very steeply' to forced land near Lens. Mannock's run of successes continued on 11 September, when he drove down a DFW out of control, while Lloyd claimed an Albatros DIII out of control on the 12th and MacLanachan another on the 15th.

The Nieuport 17 was highly manoeuverable, with a good rate of climb, but as early as May pilots were complaining about its lack of speed. The Nieuport 24's slightly more powerful engine and its streamlining made it some 3 mph faster, but it still lacked the speed to catch fleeing aircraft. And since the Germans operated defensively, only attacking if they had a good chance of success, the Nieuport's limitations were frustrating.

Manoeuverability requires a measure of instability, and the Nieuport was not an easy aircraft to fly. Most pilots quickly learnt to handle their temperamental mounts, but one who did not was 2/Lt P. W. 'Wylie' Smith. On 24 July, taking off for his first flight in a Nieuport, he was surprised by the swing generated by the torque of the rotary engine, and crashed. Smith himself was unhurt, but after a further series of mishaps Major Tilney was forced, on 2 August, to post him to Candas for 'Further Instruction'. A fortnight later Smith returned to the Squadron, but on 22 September his luck ran out when engine failure necessitated a forced landing, in the course of which he stalled and crashed. Unconscious for six weeks, he made a full recovery, but his service with 40 was over.

On 23 September the cheerful and aggressive John Barlow was not so lucky. The cause of his death is not spelt out in Squadron records, but in his 'Memories of 40 Squadron' (*Popular Flying*, April 1935) F. T. Gilbert recalls:

> I was talking to him on the advanced landing ground one day when he said, "Corporal, I've just completed my 200th roll." I said, "You should not do it, sir, it is too much strain on the wings. Mannock says learn to stunt, but don't do it for pleasure." Next day, his wings folded up at 11,000 feet. It was heartbreaking to see them go like that. (p. 32)

The death of Barlow (the last for five months) deprived the Squadron of one of its most promising younger members, and two days later two stalwarts, Hall and Godfrey, were posted to Home Establishment. They were replaced by two Canadians, 2/Lts J. H. F. Hambley and L. Kert, while Barlow's replacement was a diminutive young man who was to prove as stalwart as Barlow, though less boisterous, 2/Lt H. S. Wolff.

Maclanachan felt that with the departure of such seasoned fighters as Hall and Godfrey 'the Squadron appeared to be breaking up'. But thanks to Mannock (now scoring freely), MacLanachan and Tudhope, the victories continued. On 22 September a five strong patrol led by Mannock engaged four DFWs and four Albatros DVs. Two two-seaters were driven down, and in a fight with the scouts, Tudhope hit one which 'fell over on one side and went down in a series of stalls, dives and spins, to crash near Pont-a-Vendin'. On the following day A Flight scored again when MacLanachan and Mannock each claimed an Albatros destroyed, while on 25 September the latter brought down a Rumpler two-seater.

The most emphatic autumn victory, however, was Tudhope's on 27 September. A German pilot had been carrying out highly successful intrusions, attacking balloons and corps reconnaissance aircraft, and Mannock, MacLanachan and Tudhope, operating from Mazingarbe, took it in turns to watch for the culprit. Two days without success followed, but on 27 September, realizing that the Albatros pilot was timing his attack to coincide with meals, they returned to Mazingarbe at dusk. MacLanachan, patrolling in the semi-darkness, saw a balloon in flames, but was unable to spot the intruder. Mannock meanwhile was at Mazingarbe with engine trouble, and it was left to Tudhope, who had just landed, to take off again and intercept the intruder. He reported:

I . . . fired a burst of about 30 rounds at very close range into E. A. who dived and manoeuvred but was unable to put any distance between himself and Nieuport. I fired two more bursts, almost crashing into E. A. on the second. E. A. immediately turned West and went down very steeply with engine stopped and Nieuport above. E. A. went straight down and crashed alongside the light railway station at SOUCHEZ. Nieuport came right down and circled round E. A., which was immediately surrounded by troops.7

The next day the weather broke, bringing relief which Leonard Tilney expressed in a letter to his mother: 'Thank goodness the weather has broken. I hope it will be dud for a bit. My fellows are dead beat. Six weeks' solid flying.'8 The CO's hopes were fulfilled, since the first week of October brought bad weather, with little flying, and no combats. On 7 October, however, Zulu Lloyd came across an artillery machine guarded by three Albatros DVs, one of which he shot down. It was to be the Squadron's final victory claim on a Nieuport, though not the final incident. These, aptly enough, were two crashes on landing: Harrison on 10 October, and the newly arrived 2/Lt J. W. Wallwork the following day.

At the time of its debut, in July 1916, the Nieuport 17 was a potent force. By the time 40 re-equipped, however, the Albatros DIII was re-establishing

German superiority, while the fast and efficient DFW CV and Rumpler CIV made victories over two-seaters more difficult also. In March and April pilots reported that their new mounts could 'easily outclimb' their opponents. From May onwards, however, combat reports and the SRB [Squadron Record Book] make increasingly frequent reference to the Nieuport's limitations. Brian Lemon gave voice on 16 June to a common frustration: 'Nieuport gave chase but could not overtake'.

By the time 40 exchanged its Nieuports for SE5as in October 1917, then, the little French scout was obsolescent. Because of its responsiveness and manoeuverability, it remained competitive in a dogfight, but it lacked the speed to carry the attack to its German opponents. If they chose not to fight, there was little 40 could do about it. A faster and more up-to-date mount was needed.

# Notes

1. Frederick Oughton (ed.), *The Personal Diary of 'Mick' Mannock*. London: Neville Spearman, 1966. pp. 44–5. All subsequent diary page references are to this edition, abbreviated as *Diary*.

2. [Aimée Constance Bond], *An Airman's Wife*. London: Herbert Jenkins, 1918. p. 54. All subsequent page references to Bond's letters are to this edition, abbreviated as *Airman's Wife*.

3. It was long thought that his victor was Manfred von Richthofen, but it is now clear that this cannot have been so. The single-seater von Richthofen shot down on this date was brought down at 7.40 pm German time. Considering the hour difference between German and British time, it would have been impossible for Barwell to gain height, cross the German Lines, and put up a half-hour battle, all in twenty minutes. William Evans suggests that Richthofen's victim on this date was Sub-Lt A. E. Cuzner, of Naval Eight.

4. 'McScotch' [W. A. MacLanachan], *Fighter Pilot*. London: Routledge & Kegan Paul, 1936. (repr. London: Greenhill Books, 1985. p. 71.) All page references to MacLanachan's recollections are to this edition.

5. Robert Gregory to his mother, Lady Augusta Gregory, late May 1917. Quoted courtesy of the Robert W. Woodruff Library, Emory University, Atlanta, Ga.

6. AIR 1/1411/204/28/40, 18 August 1917.

7. This was Oblt. Hans Waldhausen, an ace of *Jasta* 37. Though the 40 Squadron SRB does not indicate their participation, the victory was shared with F/Cdr. C. D. Booker and F/S/L. J. H. Thompson of Naval Eight.

8. Quoted in 'McScotch', *Fighter Pilot*, p. 175.

# 3

# A Quiet Time:
# October 1917–March 1918

THE SE5a, which replaced 40's Nieuports, was a development by the Royal Aircraft Factory of its SE5, which first flew in November 1916. A classically simple biplane, fitted with a Vickers machine gun firing through the propeller arc and an overwing Lewis gun on a Foster mounting, the SE5 was powered by a 150 hp Hispano-Suiza engine, and capable of 114 mph at 10,000 feet. Shortened span wings and modified aileron controls, accompanied by a move to a 200 hp Hispano, led to the SE5a, which superseded the SE5 during the summer of 1917. With the 200 hp Hispano or its British equivalent, the Wolseley Adder, the SE5a could reach 126 mph at 10,000 feet.

Though the SE's airframe was satisfactory, endless difficulties were experienced with engines, as J. M. Bruce notes:

> In service much difficulty was experienced with the 200 hp Hispano-Suiza engine, especially those made by the Brasirer company, in many of which

14. 2/Lt P. D. Learoyd and ground crew, Bruay. (Chaz Bowyer.)

the reduction gears and airscrew shaft were imperfectly hardened. The Wolseley-built geared Hispano-Suiza (Wolseley W.4B Adder) was no better, and the basic engine design suffered from lubrication problems.[1]

The 200 hp Sunbeam Arab proved an unsuccessful alternative, so recourse was made to the Hispano-Suiza and Wolseley Adder, until a Wolseley derivative of the Hispano, the ungeared 200 hp Viper, was introduced. By the end of the war all but two of the eleven squadrons operating the SE5a on the Western Front were equipped with this model.

Forty did not fly the SE5a operationally until 29 October, when an offensive patrol was flown by eleven pilots. Of those first weeks MacLanachan later wrote:

> The particular engines with which they were fitted were so unreliable that within a fortnight our pilots had over twenty forced landings through engine failure, my own record for one week being four.
> For nearly three weeks we experimented with the SE5s, machine-gun practice, formation flying, and stunting, with only occasional patrols, nearly all of which were split up because of engine failures. (*Fighter Pilot*, p. 186)

Nor were unreliable engines the only problem, since the Vickers machine guns were prone to jamming, and the Constantinesco interrupter gears often malfunctioned. So bad was the situation that late in October General Trenchard visited the Squadron to discuss the difficulties. Shortly afterwards a gunnery expert was sent to advise on the working of the Constantinesco gear, and this and the efforts of the Gunnery Officer, 2/Lt W. A. Douglas, resolved the problems with the Vickers.

Despite its inauspicious beginnings with 40 Squadron, the SE5a was soon highly regarded. For though less manoeuvrable than the Nieuport, it was more robust, and considerably faster. It was also easier to fly and a more stable gun platform. The four months without a fatality which followed its introduction to 40 may have been largely due to a low level of aerial activity, but also reflected the SE5a's tractability and high performance.

Forty's first success with its SEs occurred on 31 October, when a patrol led by MacLanachan sent a two-seater down out of control. The patrol was then attacked from above and a brief dogfight followed. MacLanachan had briefed the inexperienced Wolff to stay close to him, and this 'Little Sampson' had done most faithfully:

> Throughout the fight young Wolff had almost literally 'stuck to me', and even on the worst turns and twists I had been reassured to see him following only fifteen or twenty feet distant from my wing-tip. (*Fighter Pilot*, p. 192)

Later it transpired that Wolff had not realized that the flight had been attacked and had thought that MacLanachan was stunting! Even more surprising were the fifty bullet holes in Wolff's machine.

The first three weeks in November were quiet. The 20th November, however, saw the start of the Battle of Cambrai, an assault on the Hindenburg Line revolutionary in that it involved a co-ordinated attack by tanks and infantry. Forty operated on the northern periphery of the battle, and during the next ten days flew many Special Missions, observing train and troop movements, and (as opportunity offered) attacking troops.

Under normal circumstances the low cloud and mist experienced on the morning of 20 November would have ruled out operations, but the need to support the British attack was imperative, and so, as *RFC Communiqué 115* put it:

> Eighteen scouts of the 1st Brigade left the ground under most unfavourable weather conditions in order to reconnoitre certain areas, and Capt E. Mannock, No. 40 Squadron, returned first with valuable information, while many other machines brought back information that was of considerable use. (p. 1)

Over the next three days, the Squadron was active whenever the weather allowed, but on 23 November it deteriorated further, and the few reconnaissance flights achieved little. The next three days were worse still, gales and low cloud bringing 40's involvement in the Battle of Cambrai to an end, though the Battle itself continued, with the Germans counter-attacking on 30 November, eventually driving the British back more or less to their starting point.

During October and November the Squadron had been fairly stable, personnel-wise, the only changes involving postings to Home Establishment. A number of new pilots were posted in, included some, like 2/Lts C. O. Rusden and W. E. Warden, soon to join Harrison, 2/Lt. C. W. Usher, Herbert and Wallwork as the new core of competence in the Squadron. Early in December, several further changes took place, the most significant involving Keen and Lloyd, who were posted home. The flight commanders by mid December were thus Mannock (A Flight), Tudhope (C), and newcomer, Capt G. H. Lewis (B).

Gwilym Lewis, who replaced Zulu Lloyd, came to the Squadron from the Central Flying School, where he commanded the SE5a Flight. His first impressions of the Officers' Mess, recorded in a letter to his parents, conveys a relaxed atmosphere:

> About eight of us are in a tin hut, sitting round a very comfortable fire. Some are reading and puffing pipes, others are talking and making noises, another fellow is playing with a pup, while another (dare I say it?) is making a violin squeal (that doesn't mean to say you are to send mine out!). People let fly some nasty language with reference to the Huns, but apparently the fire is too comfortable to move from. The dog still plays and the violin still squeals! [2]

Throughout early December the bad weather continued, though whenever possible patrols were flown in support of the ground forces attempting to beat back the German counter-attack at Cambrai. Few combats resulted, and the only successes were Albatros DIIIs 'out of control' for 2/Lt R. C. Wade and Tudhope on 15 December, and for Tudhope, Lewis and Warden on the 19th.

Christmas Day 1917 was celebrated in high style, according to Gwilym Lewis:

> I remember I went down to the men's Mess and found them hard at work with a very excellent meal. The officers of each Flight had somewhat contributed towards the success of this in so far as we had done our best to place them all in a complete state of inebriation, and then give them smoker's throat! . . . .
>
> Our meal was sumptuous; of course turkey and sticky pudding were the backbone of the whole show, but there were all sorts of other things flying about. I sat down with a fixed determination to consume everything I could lay hands on . . . .
>
> After this horrible orgy the officers en bloc proceeded to the men's quarters again, and then took place what was called a 'concert'. Sometimes it was and sometimes it wasn't. When it wasn't, it developed into a sort of competitive noise between officers and men, the Major spending his time vainly striving to keep irresponsible young officers in order, with only moderate success.
> (*Wings*, p. 124)

On 28 December there occurred an event more auspicious than anyone could have realized at the time. George McElroy's combat report reads:

> Observed E. A. at about 4000' approaching our lines. Dived down evidently unobserved, and fired about 100 rounds at 50 yds range. E.A. went down out of control. In dive SE overshot falling E.A. but in turning round observed machine at rest on ground, and evidently crashed.

MacLanachan's account of the incident shows that the outcome could have been fatal for McElroy. For the German formation they attacked was in Flights at two levels, and MacLanachan had only intended to attack the upper. But when McElroy dived through and attacked the lower he had to lead the rest of the patrol after him, a mêlée ensuing in which they were lucky to escape without loss.

One of the drawbacks to the Foster mounting with which both the SE5a and the Nieuport were fitted was that if the Lewis gun were not properly secured, it could slide back to hit the pilot on the head. This had happened to Major Tilney during the summer, and on 28 December it happened to Wallwork, who had just driven an enemy aircraft down out of control. The casualty report notes that the pilot was 'partially stunned by Lewis gun falling on his head' and 'admitted to hospital with bruises to face and body and suffering from slight concussion'. The 'out of control' was Wallwork's first claim, and on the same day Capt. O. Horsley, a supernumerary flight commander, scored his first victory, driving down an enemy aircraft which crashed near Lens.

As 1917 drew near to an end, 40 was starting to exploit the SE5a's potential. Engine failures still occurred, but the problems with the guns had been solved, and it had been found that manoeuverability and climb rate could be improved by reducing the dihedral on the wings. On New Year's Day Tudhope carried out tests to determine how successful these modifications had been, and found that his aircraft would reach 10,000 feet in seventeen minutes, and 15,000 feet in forty minutes.

The year 1918 began with victories for Rusden and Herbert, who sent down an two-seater out of control, and for Mannock, who shared in the destruction of an Hannoveraner. This was Mannock's first success with the SE5a and his last with the Squadron, as his posting to Home Establishment had come through a few days earlier, along with MacLanachan's. On 1 January the customary farewell dinner was held, and their send off the next day was an emotional one, as MacLanachan recalls:

> When we left, the whole ground personnel of the Squadron lined the aerodrome to bid us farewell. They cheered lustily as the tender passed, and looking back at them, I felt a wave of emotion surge over me. Our cheery family, 'A' Flight, had been my school; the mechanics and NCOs had done everything possible to make 'their' pilots safe and happy; Davidge and Biggs would, the next day, be attending to another pilot's machine, my SE5. (*Fighter Pilot*, p. 233)

With 40 Mannock had claimed 23 victories, including 6 aircraft and one balloon destroyed, 14 out of control, and 2 forced to land, making him the Squadron's top-scoring pilot to date.[3] His replacement as A Flight Commander was 'Naps' Napier, who returned after a period as RFC Liaison Officer at French Army GHQ.

Snow and low cloud during the first weeks of 1918 allowed little operational flying. Moreover the German Air Force was little to be seen, as Gwilym Lewis commented in a letter home: 'It is very seldom we spot an Albatros scout. Nearly all their work is being done by two-seaters either round about the Lines or very high up' (*Wings*, p. 127). In the absence of aerial opposition, 40 used its SEs for ground attack, carrying four 25-lb Cooper bombs on the racks, which had been fitted during October.

In mid-January the pace of aerial combat picked up, with two-seaters claimed on 13 January by Tudhope and McElroy. Six days later this tally was exceeded when Lewis and Harrison claimed 'out of controls' and McElroy a DFW which he sent down out of control with 'a burst of about 60 rds . . . from underneath at about 10 yds range'. McElroy followed, firing, and watched his victim crash. Yet another DFW fell to McElroy on the 24th, while the next day 2/Lt H. M. Hutton claimed an Albatros out of control, and Hambley a two-seater.

Like Steve Godfrey, Hambley was a rough diamond, as Gwilym Lewis explained to his parents:

> Old Hambley is a very bad Canadian, and if I wasn't out here I should have difficulty in seeing any good in him at all. As a matter of fact, he is one of my best 'comics'. (Usher is my best.) He used to pull the Major's leg and say things to him that a subaltern does *not* say to a CO. He was uncouth, used to bring terrible Canadians into the Mess, and the Major wanted me to get rid of him at one time, but I said I would rather not. Worst of all he drinks too much, wears side-whiskers and sometimes a dirty stock. Really he is a splendid fellow, and I had the utmost confidence in him over the Lines. Best of all, though he used to pull my leg a bit (everyone does), he would do just anything I asked him to, and never worried me in the slightest. (*Wings*, p. 137)

Hambley's success augured well, but on 26 January, in misty conditions, he crashed, his injuries ending his flying career, and leaving him in indifferent health for the rest of his life.

January 1918 had been a good month for 40, and it ended positively when on the 28th Hutton and Woolf made 'out of control' claims. It also brought a hint of things to come when Oswald Horsley saw the Squadron's first Fokker Triplane. There would be many more.

Successes in the air depend on efficiency on the ground. Forty had a skilled and loyal team of riggers, mechanics, coppersmiths, carpenters, sail-makers and the rest, and men like Gilbert, Biggs, Davidge and Bovett, NCOs with skill and experience, took an immense pride in their work, in the Squadron, and in 'their' pilot and his aircraft. Even so, things did not always go smoothly, and Gwilym Lewis found it necessary to remedy deficiencies in B Flight, as he explained to his parents at the end of January:

> The working part of my Flight is now in excellent working order. When I first arrived I nearly went off my head. I only just restrained myself from having half of them shot. I have now sacked the Flight Sergeant, and put a junior man in his place. I sometimes shriek at myself the things I say to these men, some of whom are very skilled labour. I told the ex-Flight Sergeant why I was fed up with him and what I thought his shortcomings were. Then I let his successor know what I required of him. (*Wings*, p. 139)

Scoring began in February with 'out of control' claims by McElroy (a two-seater on the 2nd) and Horsley (an Albatros scout the following day). Then on the 5th McElroy scored twice. He reported:

> When at 8000' saw a green camouflaged DFW crossing our lines in company with 3 other E.A. Singled out the DFW, which was the most Easterly of the four and, after diving steeply, got in a burst of about 100 rds from at 100 yds

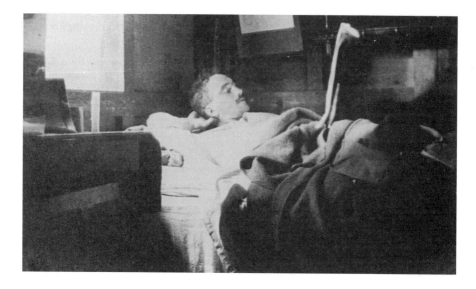

15. George McElroy relaxes. (G. H. Lewis.)

range. Then got underneath E.A. and fired a second burst of 100 rds, on completion of which saw pieces flying off E.A.'s tail or fuselage. E.A. went down in a slow spin, and finally crashed near WINGLES.

Later McElroy was alerted to the presence of a second DFW by AA fire and sent it down in flames with a single burst from the Vickers.

On 16 February, the first fine day for some time, McElroy scored again, a single burst of fire sufficing to send yet another DFW 'down in a slow irregular spin, obviously out of control', while Lewis and Usher were credited with a Pfalz DIII 'out of control'. The following day both Wade and McElroy scored twice. Wade's victims were Pfalz DIIIs, one of which he sent down in flames. McElroy's first victim was also a Pfalz. He reported:

> Whilst on escort duty to DH 4s observed E.A. scout dive on a DH. SE dived on E.A. and he drew away from DH turning under SE, which still turned round and kept on his tail. Opened fire from close range from both guns until E.A. commenced to go down in a slow irregular spiral out of control. Kept E.A. under observation and observed him crash completely on the Eastern outskirts of LILLE.

The second victim was a two-seater which McElroy found at 8,000 feet near Lens. The aircraft dived to prevent him making an attack from beneath, but at 1,000 feet he was able to get beneath it, reporting that 'SE opened with both guns and set E.A. smoking very quickly. E.A. then went down (SE then being over OPPY at about 400' ) and hit ground heavily, turning over crashed and still burning'.

On 18 February McElroy was again successful, picking off an Albatros DV attacking a Camel, but others had a harder time. For Lewis, Herbert and Usher, returning from an escort mission, engaged an eleven strong enemy formation led by a bright red aircraft. Lewis's aim was to make just one pass, but

> this wasn't Herbert's intention. Away he went back again, and started a full-out scrap with a green and white striped fellow. Of course *I* had to go back, and this brought green-and-white's friends back too. I was just getting started with Herb when up came my red friend, with a tartan and one other. I had proper wind-up, but old Herb would go on! The red fellow got into me, and I went down all over the shop, engine well on. Then old Herb took it in the neck and got properly shot up. However he got away whole in body and dropped into an advanced landing ground. (*Wings*, p. 146)

On 21 February came news of George McElroy's posting. Gwilym Lewis wrote home:

> McElroy as usual came to the front and has now got 12 perfectly good Huns in under two months. Suddenly got his eye in and gone right ahead. Never touched a Hun in his first three months. Now they have taken him away from us and given him a Flight in Edmund's old squadron (24) who are away down south, and are still in the engine trouble period. Rather bad luck on us though, as a lad like that means a lot. (*Wings*, p. 142)

The loss of McElroy was followed by two others. On 24 February the experienced and aggressive Herbert was wounded, while two days later Richard Wade was shot down and killed — the first fatality since Barlow on 23 September, and though the Squadron could not know it, the precursor of high losses during the desperate fighting of the German spring offensive.

On 4 March there was posted in a pilot, Capt R. L. Tipton, who was something of a celebrity. Serving in Egypt, 'Tiny' Tipton had forced landed in enemy territory in June 1916, to be captured by the Turks. Fourteen months later he escaped with three army officers, eventually reaching Russia. On returning to Britain he was lionized, and (at the latter's request) met the King.[3] He was offered leave, but declined in favour of a posting to the Western Front.

Tipton undertook his first Offensive Patrol on 6 March, and was at once successful, shooting down a Pfalz DIIIa. In the same engagement, which the SRB described as 'the first real dog-fight since the previous summer', Wallwork, Harrison and Napier all claimed Albatros DVs shot down, while Tudhope and Harrison put in 'out of control' claims.

That the air battle on 6 March was not an isolated incident, but marked the resumption of large scale German air activity, was demonstrated on the 9th. A morning clash with Albatros scouts went exceptionally well, a nine strong patrol, led by Tudhope, claiming one aircraft crashed and five out of control. The 'certain' went to Tudhope, who reported:

> Patrol engaged 7 Albatross Scout[s] E. of LENS. At second attack on E.A., got to 30 yards range on its tail and opened fire with both guns. E.A. fell down sideways, eventually spinning to earth where it crashed and burst into flames.

'Out of control' claims were made by Wolff, Harrison, Tudhope, Rusden and Wallwork.

After the morning's triumphs high hopes for the afternoon were tragically misplaced. For though further successes were scored, Lt R. E. Bion, Tipton, and Wallwork claiming 'out of controls', one pilot was killed, another mortally wounded, and a third taken prisoner. The latter was newcomer, 2/Lt P. LaT. Foster; the mortal wound suffered by Tiny Tipton; the death that of the CO.

Knowing Tipton's impetuosity, Gwilym Lewis had, before going on leave, ordered him not to venture over the lines. But this order went unheeded, and Tipton, having sent the rearmost machine in a German formation down out of control, was himself hit. What followed is recorded in a report filled in on Tipton's behalf by Sgt A. G. Adams of C Battery, AA:

> At about 4–45pm on 9/3/18 I saw an SE5 coming in very low from direction of LENS. He circled over CALONNE ROAD and made a good landing behind our billet. I received orders to mount a guard and take charge of the machine. I found Capt Tinton [Tipton], the pilot, was badly hit in the abdomen but was conscious. He gave me the number of his Squadron and said he didn't mind much, because he got the Hun who hit him, and was quite cheerful owing to that fact. I did not question him as he appeared very weak.

Returning from leave, Lewis visited Tipton in hospital and found him conscious, later writing home:

> Tipton, who escaped from Turkey, got a bullet in his abdomen and died a few days later, like the hero he was. I never expect again to see a fellow lying halfway between life and death, knowing it, and yet showing such wonderful pluck. (*Wings*, p. 148)

How Major Tilney died is uncertain. The Germans credited Lt Paul Billik of *Jasta* 52, but the SRB states that Tilney's SE was last seen diving on an enemy aircraft, and (noting Wallwork's report of an SE5a breaking up in a dive) was believed to have broken up in the air. Gwilym Lewis commented later that he thought that Tilney's participation in an Offensive Patrol—his first in more than a year as CO—perhaps sprang from enthusiasm over the Squadron's success that morning. What is clear is that he was not really prepared for the dog-fight in which he was killed. For although he had frequently undertaken line patrols, and occasionally engaged enemy aircraft, he had never been involved in a mêlée of the kind that developed on 9 March.

As a CO Leonard Tilney was efficient and considerate. There is ample testimony to his concern for the comfort and well-being of those under him, and to the efforts he made to ensure that Treizennes and Bruay were comfortable and well-equipped. Of Tilney the man we get brief but telling glimpses. MacLanachan's first impression was of the informality of a 'rather florid-faced youth' who waved his racquet at the newcomer from across the tennis court, saying "You the new pilot? See you later when we've won this set" (*Fighter Pilot*, p. 5). This impression of cheerfulness and vigour is supported by Bond's description of the CO stunting joyously on an early morning line patrol. But alongside this may be set the picture of the sensitive soul who blushed when the Matron of a nearby Hospital seemed about to learn that the Squadron cat was named 'Piddle'.

Neither charismatic, like his successor, nor authoritarian, like his predecessor, Leonard Tilney was a popular and effective CO, under whom 40 Squadron went from strength to strength. If the quality of the flight commanders—men like Mannock, Keen, Napier, Lloyd, Tudhope and Lewis—had more to do with the forging of the unit into a formidable fighting force than had the CO himself, nonetheless he provided the environment in which *esprit de corps* flourished.

## Notes

1. J. M. Bruce, *The Aircraft of the Royal Flying Corps*. London: Putnam, 1982. pp. 476–7.
2. G. H. Lewis, *Wings Over the Somme*. London: William Kimber, 1976, p. 117. [Hereafter referred to as *Wings*]
3. On Tipton's adventures, see Capt E. H. Keeling, 'An Escape From Turkey in Asia', *Blackwood's Magazine*, Vol. CCIII, No. MCCXXXI (May 1918), pp. 561–92.

4

# A Squadron at its Peak:
# March–May 1918

L EONARD TILNEY's death on 9 March 1918 occurred a year to the day
since 'Black Friday', when 40 had lost three pilots and four aircraft at
the hands of Manfred von Richthofen's *Jasta* 11. It also coincided with
the beginning of a new phase in the air war on the Western Front,
in which large forces would be deployed on both sides, and patrols by
squadrons, or even by pairs of squadrons, become commonplace. The
quiet that 40 had enjoyed for six months had ended. Now it would
find itself operating intensively, and suffering considerable losses.
During this period of trial, however, it would rise to a peak of achievement, with a reputation as one of the finest fighter squadrons on the
Western Front.

16. At ease: Lt C. W. Usher, Maj R. S. Dallas, Napier and Capt C. O. Rusden.
Spring 1918, Bruay. (G. H. Lewis.)

Tilney's successor, who arrived on 15 March, was Squadron Commander R. S. Dallas, and the appointment was epoch-making, since he was the first RNAS (Royal Naval Air Service) officer to command a RFC squadron. That such an event occurred at all was due to the fact that the decision had been taken to amalgamate the RNAS and the RFC, creating on 1 April 1918 an autonomous entity, the Royal Air Force.

The man appointed to command 40, Roderic Stanley Dallas, was an Australian, born in 1891. Enlisting in the Australian Imperial Forces at the outbreak of war, he had transferrred to the RNAS, qualifying as a pilot in August 1915. Posted in November to 1 Squadron, RNAS, he became a flight commander and, in June 1917, CO. He came to 40 with twenty-three victories, second amongst RNAS pilots.[1]

Dismayed by the news that an RNAS officer was to command them, the Squadron awaited Dallas's arrival with curiosity and scepticism. It took only a few days, however, for their views to change, as Cecil Usher indicates:

> Breguet had not been with us a week before a vast change came over the scene. People began saying 'My God—if that's the RNAS why haven't we got more of them?' Never had we seen such quiet and competent leadership. Like many really big men he had a gentle voice and his words came slowly, but were well weighed and carried instant and great effect. At once we all fell under his spell and counted ourselves the most fortunate Squadron of the whole newly-formed RAF.[2]

Dallas's arrival was timely. For the battles of 6 and 9 March were the forerunners of the large-scale clashes which were to occur throughout the Second Battle of the Somme and thereafter. Moreover during the battle the *Deutschen Luftstreitkraft* [German Air Force] would, for the first time, be able to draw on greater numbers of aircraft than the British. On 21 March, the RFC and RNAS had a total of 579 serviceable aircraft in the battle area, 261 of them single-seat scouts. Against them were deployed 730 aircraft, of which 326 were scouts. Dallas's inspirational leadership was going to be needed.

For 40 there was an additional problem: the number of inexperienced pilots. In the week prior to the opening of the battle, there were six new arrivals: Capt J. L. Middleton (as a supernumerary flight commander) and 2/Lts L. H. Sutton, D. F. Murman, I. F. Hind, H. H. Wood and F. C. B. Wedgwood. In this situation the burden of responsibility fell heavily on those who, like the flight commanders, Lewis, Tudhope and Napier, were experienced: Wallwork, Warden, Rusden, Horsley, Wolff, Usher and Harrison. Of the latter Mick Mannock had remarked, 'Heaven help the Germans when Harrie gets bloodthirsty'. After destroying a balloon on 9 August 1917, Harrison did not score again until 13 January 1918, when he was awarded an 'out of control'. In March, however, he claimed three enemy aircraft

destroyed in twelve days. The second, on 11 March, was also claimed by
an AA battery, but Harrison's combat report makes it clear that the two-seater
was his:

> Whilst on patrol observed an E.A. 2-seater pointed out by A.A. fire. Ap-
> proached and fired 1 drum of Lewis into it from medium range, but without
> apparent effect. E.A. turned, and did a large circuit round LA BASSEE finally
> returning across lines S. W. of LA BASSEE, where it was again fired on by
> A.A., all the bursts being behind it. S.E. dived on E.A., and fired a complete
> drum from 50/25 yards range, tracers being observed to enter E.A., which
> heeled over and went down out of control, finally crashing alongside the
> canal and West of LA BASSEE.

On 18 March Harrison scored again, sending another two-seater down in
flames with a single burst of fire. Clearly he had now mastered the art of
aerial combat.

At 4.45 am on 21 March, the Germans launched their attack on the 3rd
and 5th Armies. The Allied commanders had predicted the attack, but
underestimated it, for on a fifty-four mile front between the Sensée and the
Oise rivers fifty-six German divisions were waiting, with a further twelve
in reserve. The RFC's primary task was to harass advancing enemy units.
How effective this could be is evident in a report by the German 73rd
Regiment:

> The English got valuable support from their aircraft which attacked regardless
> of consequences. The Squadrons, flying very low, found profitable targets, for
> bomb and machine-gun, in the thickly concentrated masses of the 111th and
> 2nd Guards Reserve Divisions. Our own airmen were absent. (*War*, p. 301)

At the northern end of the front, 40 was called on to assist the 3rd Army
squadrons, but on the first three days bad weather severely limited flying.
There were few contacts with enemy aircraft, but on the 23rd Tudhope
surprised a DFW two-seater, 'approaching below out of the mist' and brought
it down with a short burst. The following day there were more enemy
aircraft about, and both Horsley (Albatros DV) and Wallwork (Fokker DrI)
were credited with 'out of controls', while Harrison shot down an Albatros
C type.

Routine orders for 24 March state that until further notice no leave is
to be granted to officers or other ranks excepting pilots. For the explanation
for this draconian measure we have a clue in the number of forced landings
and crashes during intensive low-level operations—Gwilym Lewis and 2/Lt
W. H. Smith on 21 March, 2/Lt P. D. Learoyd two days later, and
Wedgwood on the 24th. In the case of Smith, the SRB gives no cause: he
simply 'crashed'. In the other cases, however, engine failure was involved,
and this was undoubtedly a major element in the dislike most pilots had for

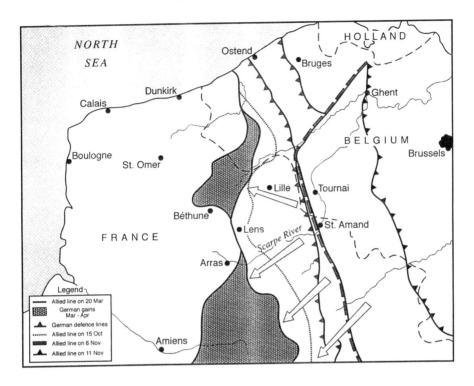

Map 3. Allied and German Offensives, 1918.

the low-level flying which the German offensive forced on them. For a few, however, the excitement outweighed the risks of engine failure at twenty or thirty feet. One was Warden, and another Rusden, whom the SRB notes had taken to attacking enemy columns with gusto.

The German attack on the Somme produced some intense air fighting. On 26 March, for instance, Harrison and Learoyd both claimed enemy aircraft out of control, while Warden spotted a formation of Albatros scouts which, joining forces with two Sopwith Dolphins, he attacked. He reported:

> Selected 1 E.A. and endeavoured to engage but E.A. dived away. S.E. followed E.A. and fired 200 rounds from both guns at a range of 100/50 yards. Shots were observed to enter E.A.'s fuselage and pieces began to fly off E.A. which went down out of control. At this point S.E. was obliged to turn off to help a Dolphin, driving E.A. off it, and was in consequence, unable to see E.A. crash.

It was a busy day at ground level also, where 40 assisted with patrols around Bapaume. In one such Warden, Tudhope and Horsley fired 1,700 rounds at troops coming up to reinforce the German lines, while the enthusiastic Rusden reported that while patrolling 'between Nurlu and

Manancourt at 5/800′ saw columns of enemy on march with field Arty., dived to 200′ and fired on enemy all along the column. Men scattered and horses stampeded.'

Hitherto, the main thrust of the German assault had been to the south, but on 28 March the Germans attacked at Arras. The Squadrons of I Brigade were now defending their own sector, and concentrated on attacking the advancing German troops:

> S.E. 5A pilots of No. 40 Squadron, who left at 1.30 p.m. to patrol the area of Arras, found the main Arras-Cambrai road and most of the side roads full of troops and transport, with the Douai main roads similarly congested. These targets were attacked from heights down to 300 feet and panic and stampedes were reported. (*War*, p. 337)

On the 30th 40 carried out further ground attacks, but the highlight was a reconnaissance flight at dusk by Tudhope, Napier, Harrison and Warden, which drew congratulations from GOC 1st Brigade 'on the very fine flight carried out by them last night in the face of extremely adverse weather conditions'. The 31st March saw a return on both sides to patrolling at altitude, but with the likelihood of further low level strafing attacks, since the Germans were shifting large numbers of lorries and guns northwards towards La Bassée in preparation, it was thought, for an attack.

On 1 April the Royal Air Force came into existence, with Roderic Dallas now a major. The only victory to mark the event went to Harrison, who crashed a two-seater near Izel,[3] since the first three days of April were given over mainly to flying cover for the Camels of 4 Squadron, Australian Flying Corps. With its twin Vickers machine-guns and an engine more reliable and less vulnerable to ground fire, the Camel was well suited to ground attack, and the SE5a, with its better altitude performance, for covering patrols.

At Bruay 3 April brought the first American pilot to serve with 40, Lt Reed Landis. He later recalled:

> I was the first of the this bunch to get out [to No. 40 Squadron] and I was an oddity. People were very nice to me, but it was obvious that I was a "queer" thing to them. But the word that I roomed alone had gotten ahead of me and I was assigned a little tar paper hut that offered more bunks in it and I was there all alone.[4]

In the circumstances it is not surprising that Landis was drawn to Dallas, because (as Landis saw it) being an Australian, Dallas was an 'outcast in the English outfit' also. This, clearly, was a massive misreading of the situation, since what the latter took for fellow-feeling was presumably an awareness on Dallas's part that the American might feel out of it.

Between 21 March and 1 April German assaults on the Somme were renewed daily. The absence of an attack on 2 April heralded the end of the

German offensive, attention shifting to the Arras-La Bassée-Armentières area, where reconnaissance suggested an offensive might be imminent. Accordingly 40 and other I Brigade squadrons resumed patrolling their sector of the front.

The 6th of April was particularly busy. Patrols reported large numbers of enemy aircraft, and many indecisive combats. Three victories were recorded, one of them a 'first' for Canadian, Lt. H. Carnegie, who brought down an Albatros DV. The others both went to 'Naps' Napier, who had his most successful day ever. Both his victims were caught unawares, the first, an Albatros DV, 'glid[ing] down with steam issuing from it and with propeller stopped'. The second victim was a two-seater, which Napier attacked out of the sun, probably killing the observer. The aircraft dived, Napier following, and further bursts from his Vickers sent his victim crashing into houses near Brebieres.

Gwilym Lewis had a less happy time:

> I was contour-chasing home with my patrol; had just passed over a favourite CCS [Casualty Clearing Station], and was about three feet off the ground ready to zoom a light railway embankment, when my engine cut dead out through lack of petrol. (*Wings*, p. 154)

With his Flight in close line abreast, he had no chance to turn aside, so he attempted a high speed crash landing, in the course of which he

> touched the ground with my wingtip, with the disastrous result that I turned some four or five somersaults on the ground, ending up head down, with the tail alongside the engine, and the Lewis gun prattling merrily. (*Wings*, p. 154)

Fortunately the SE did not catch fire, and Lewis extricated himself from the wreckage with nothing worse than cuts and bruises.

At this time the Squadron was rebuilding after a series of personnel changes, Gwilym Lewis noting in a letter of 8 April: 'My Flight has changed considerably, but though it is not quite so strong as it used to be, it is shaping itself into a very fine style'. 'Really', he added,

> I have nothing to be anything but very proud of. Wallwork (my 'second'), Usher and Rusden form a very fine fighting head. All have done very good work and take a lot of beating. Then come three new lads—Hind, Captain Middleton and Murman. Middleton will be very stout, Hind is good but lacks individuality for the time being; Murman is disappointing.

Lewis's opinion of Murman changed, however, as he explained in a letter to the author:

> He [Murman] wasn't up to it—he was holding back in combats—I decided he must go. Dallas had a long and friendly talk with him. The boy was transformed. Rather than holding back, he went into the forefront of attack.

It was in such as this that Dallas's leadership made all the difference.

On 9 April the Battle of the Lys, the anticipated offensive in the Arras area, began, the Germans attacking the weakest point in the line—that held by a Portuguese division. The resulting chaos made communication over the battle area difficult, and fog prevented flying until 2 pm, when 40 attacked infantry with bombs and machine-gun fire. The bad weather persisted on the second and third days of the battle, but when possible the squadrons of I Brigade were used intensively for ground attack, 40 playing its full part, with pilots going out more than once, and Cecil Usher, for example, flying three patrols on the morning of the 10th.

Such intensive activity brought losses, with Lt Rupert Bion killed on the opening day of the battle, and Harry Carnegie wounded on the second. Aerial combat was not sought, but occasional enemy aircraft were encountered, Rusden crashing a two-seater on the 9th, while Tudhope claimed an Albatros DV out of control on the 10th and he and Lewis each shot down a Fokker Triplane near Lens the following day, when Dallas also scored, downing a DFW whose observer was foolish enough to attract his attention by firing on him from below.

The 12th of April was critical. British reinforcements were on the way, but until they arrived the line had to be held by exhausted and outnumbered troops. The RAF strove to stem the advance towards Hazebrouck, aided by what Gwilym Lewis described as 'the most wonderful day I have ever seen in France'. 'In the morning', Lewis writes,

> Napier had his Flight up and I lent him Hind. Most of them were new pilots so the 'Admiral' went up too. They got into about a dozen Huns, and Hind pushed one down. Five of these Huns on being attacked played their usual trick of climbing. Dallas therefore climbed alongside them just out of range, and so kept them from diving down. This probably saved a couple of young pilots! (*Wings*, p. 156)

Later in the day Lewis led a successful B Flight patrol during which he, Wallwork, Middleton, and Usher sent enemy aircraft down out of control. Then, to round off the day, Horsley and Dallas went up in the evening. Gwilym Lewis wrote home:

> They attacked seven Huns [Albatros DVs], and Shorty shot at one which he forced to land. The others ran away, except one which went down to about 5,000 and watched his friend land. The 'Admiral' dropped down and crashed him into a hedge a few fields from his friend. Some lad, isn't he? (*Wings*, p. 156)

On 13 April 40 continued its low-level attacks, most pilots flying two patrols, and on the 14th, with the Allied defences stabilizing, the Squadron was given an assignment whose importance can be measured by those who flew it:

Major R. S. Dallas, Capts I. P. R. Napier, G. H. Lewis and O. Horsley carried out a special reconnaissance of the battlefield at the junction of the 1st and 2nd Armies to determine the situation which had been reported to be obscure. In spite of the most unfavourable weather conditions, they returned with much valuable information. Major Dallas was wounded by machine gun fire from the ground early in the operation but continued to fulfill his mission until he was again wounded, when he successfully reached his aerodrome.
[Air 1/692]

Dallas's foot wound was not serious, and in a little over a week he returned to the Squadron to recuperate, Napier acting as CO in his absence.

As the German offensive abated, 40 was as active as weather would allow. Low-level attacks remained the priority, though occasional clashes with German aircraft occurred, in one of which, on 15 April, 'Pusher' Usher shot down an aircraft whose crash was confirmed by an AA battery. A lull in fighting, beginning on the 18th, lasted a week, but during that time the Squadron lost one of its stoutest fighters, Capt Tudhope. With 40 since July 1917, 'Tud' had proved a skilled and courageous fighter, scoring ten victories. He was exhausted, though, after eleven months operational flying, for Gwilym Lewis commented in a letter home: 'He is a great loss, but it was full time he went home. He nearly fainted in the air' (Wings, p. 159). He was replaced as C Flight Commander by Oswald Horsley, while the consequent vacancy was filled by Lt D. S. Poler, the second American to serve with 40 Squadron. His arrival must have given 'outsider' Reed Landis considerable pleasure.

On 14 April Gwilym Lewis had told his parents that despite the German advance there was, as yet, no move to withdraw from Bruay. On the 24th he wrote:

We spend most of our nights trembling in every nerve while high velocity shells pitch within a few hundred yards of us. Most of them pitch in a little valley just the other end of the aerodrome, but at other times they drop them around the town. They make an enormous noise and cause great damage.
(Wings, p. 159)

The shelling was preparatory to the German offensive renewed on 25 April. Forty responded by bombing Estaires, but thereafter there was little it could do, since bad weather prevented flying until the 29th, when Napier, Sutton and Learoyd forced a DFW CV down behind the Allied lines.

The Battle of the Lys ended that day, and 40 resumed a more ordered and leisurely existence, taking the opportunity on 1 May, for instance, to resume target practice. The next day poor weather restricted flying, but did not stop Roderic Dallas from carrying out the famous 'boots' incident.

Inactive himself, on a walking stick and with his bandaged foot in a carpet slipper, Dallas was disgusted by German inactivity, and flew to the

17. Officers of 40 Squadron, Bruay, May 1918.
(l to r) Lt W. L. Harrison, Lt H. Carnegie, Lt G. A. B. Weldon, Lt H. S. Cameron, Capt
J. H. Tudhope, Lt J. W. Wallwork, Capt O. Horsley, Lt C. W. Usher, Maj R. S. Dallas,
Capt B. W. Keymer, Lt L. H. Sutton. (G. H. Lewis.)

aerodrome at La Breayelle, 'fired on hangars on South side of Aerodome to attract attention' and dropped a parcel which contained a pair of boots and a note saying: 'If you won't come up here and fight, herewith one pair of boots for work on the ground, pilots for the use of'. Climbing into the mist he circled until the Germans had gathered around the parcel and then, diving, dropped two bombs and fired 100 rounds at them. 'General panic ensued', the report concludes. To cap it all, Dallas then shot down one of two Albatros DVs which 'got in my way' on the return journey.

However satisfying, the boots episode hardly galvanized 40's opponents. Indeed, pilots encountered little opposition in the days which followed, and the only success went to Napier, who on 3 May shot down a DFW near the Bois de Pacaut. On 8 May, however, there was more action, with three victories over Pfalz DIIIs, two 'out of controls' to Dallas and Landis, whose victim 'did a series of stalls, dives and side-slips till lost in mist at about 1000 feet'. A third Pfalz, certainly destroyed, was brought down by newcomer, Lt L. J. Seymour. Further successes followed on the 13th, when Napier shot down a DFW near Lacouture, and on the 14th, when Murman and Hind claimed 'out of controls', while Rusden crashed an LVG near the Arras–Cambrai road.

The 15th of May was again busy and successful. In one engagement Usher attacked an Albatros and a Pfalz, flying in company near the Scarpe, and shot the Albatros down. He then engaged the Pfalz, but found its pilot a far tougher proposition. The Squadron Record Book notes:

Pilot of Phalz, which was new type. with Albatross Scout tail [i.e. a DIIIa], was exceedingly good. Attacked without effect, This machine was attacked by 3 other S.E.s of the patrol and forced right down to 200' where he contour chased across to LA BRAYELLE. S.E.s finished at 2,000' & returned heavily archied.

On another patrol, Napier and three members of his Flight, Lt H. H. Wood, and 2/Lts G. Watson and W. L. Andrew, attacked a DFW CV, Wood stopping its engine and possibly wounding the pilot. From this patrol, however, Andrew failed to return, and was later reported a prisoner of war. He had been with the Squadron three weeks.

Within a few days two more junior members of the Squadron were lost. On 17 May it was Seymour, who had been with the Squadron a month, and was (in Gwilym Lewis's words) 'a perfect topper. Very, very keen and doing very well'. Fortunately he survived to be taken prisoner of war. That day Watson was credited with one enemy aircraft crashed and another out of control. But on the 20th he was shot down near Hinges, dying of his wounds shortly after being taken prisoner.

Two victories at this time exemplify Dallas's mastery of air fighting. On 15 May he observed a two-seater Albatros 'and proceeded to stalk him through the low-lying mist'. The Albatros was surprised, and before the observer could respond Dallas had hit it with half a drum of Lewis and 50 rounds of Vickers. An AA battery saw the Albatros falling out of control, though mist prevented it observing the crash. The second victory, three days later, was over a high-flying Rumpler. The combat report reads:

Left aerodrome to meet high flying E.A. crossing lines. First saw E.A. at about 10-30am climbing over his own lines so S.E. proceeded to get height. S.E. was unable to get E.A.'s height so hid below E.A.'s tail and followed for an hour. A Camel passed below E.A. which E.A. mistook for S.E. breaking off combat. Thinking he was no longer pursued E.A. started to lose height over LILLE when S.E. fired a drum of Lewis without a stoppage into E.A. A great volume of smoke came from below sump and a red flame was seen, E.A. being on fire. Having exhausted petrol S.E. returned home.

Dallas's victory was one of several during the third week of May. On the 19th Hind claimed a Pfalz DIII out of control, while Landis and Rusden crashed two others near Provin. Then the next day a patrol led by Lewis sent a Pfalz DIII down out of control, credit being shared. On 21 April the successes continued, with Lewis shooting down a Pfalz. He reported:

Led patrol into action with 12 E.A. who were below S.E.s. E.A. were at once reinforced by the arrival of a further 8 E.A. A dog fight ensued between the whole of the two formations. Pilot dived on Phaltz Scout which was endeavouring to close up with other E.A. Fired 100 rounds from both guns with marked effect. E.A. spun for 4000′ out of control and on coming out of spin fell over sideways and crashed.

During the same fight Warden and Murman made 'out of control' claims, and Gwilym Lewis recorded his pleasure in a letter home:

> I always like having everyone in the Flight with a Hun to his credit. They have all been bringing them down lately, 'Pusher', Rusden, Hind, Middleton, 'Bolo' and Murman. (*Wings*, p. 161)

Murman, so a note on the combat report reads, 'returned to aerodrome with machine so badly shot about as to necessitate repair at a depot'. Dallas's talk had certainly done the trick.

The 20th of May saw the end of Oswald Horsley's service with 40 when, on patrol, his hands swelled up and his legs became almost paralysed. He managed to land his SE, but was at once grounded. The cause was presumably altitude sickness or stress (or both). Gwilym Lewis commented many years later:

> When visiting a RFC unit overseas, on its aerodrome, the infantryman would be amazed at the comparative comfort of living standards—and rightly so, although casualty lists were high. But there was of course stress and strain which challenged the nervous system. Basically the job was subject to the great contrast of enjoying a swim or a game of tennis and in the next hour fighting for one's life or that of the enemy at say 15000 ft.[5]

With Horsley's departure, Rusden was promoted to command C Flight, while Usher took Rusden's place as Lewis's deputy.

Mid-May was a time of considerable changes in personnel, five new pilots arriving between the 14th and 23rd: 2/Lts H. W. Clarke, G. V. O. Russell and R. A. Whitten, and Lts P. V. Burwell and G. J. Strange. Burwell was the third American to join the Squadron, and on 24th there came a fourth, Major M. F. Davis. Unlike the others, Davis was a career aviator, and was posted in from 84 Squadron for operational experience prior to forming US pursuit squadrons. On 28 June he would, accordingly, be posted out, joining the USAAS 3rd Aviation Instructional Centre.

Another who joined the Squadron during May was Guy Symonds, the new Armaments Officer. In his unpublished memoirs he recalled the acute embarrassment of his first encounter with Oswald Horsley and Gwilym Lewis:

> I was walking down the lane from the living quarters to the hangar and aerodrome when I met two chaps in flying gear obviously just back from

work, and stopped to introduce myself. They were two flight commanders, Capts Oswald [Horsley] and Lewis. Then of all the stupid remarks to make I said the obvious, "Great weather we're having isn't it?" The two looked at each other for a few seconds without speaking till Oswald said, "Well, some say one thing and some another." Long before then I had realized my faux pas. The previous months had seen an all out attempt by the Germans to penetrate the line and 40 Squadron had been doing ground strafing on infantry support, one of the most dangerous jobs the fighter pilot can be called upon to do. They didn't want 'great weather'. They were praying for some dud weather so that they could get a bit of rest and a chance to have their aircraft serviced.[6]

18. Americans with 40 Sqn. (l to r) Lts
D. S. Poler and P. V. Burwell,
Maj M. F. Davis. (G. H. Lewis.)

Forty was indeed in need of a break. Fine weather in the second half of May did not provide it, but someone discovered a pond near the aerodrome. Gwilym Lewis wrote home:

> We have found a pretty priceless pond to bathe in! It looks like a large crater. Anyway, it is about 200 feet deep, so with the help of rafts, planks, a canoe, a football, and a few elementary swimming strokes, we have the very best of fun. (*Wings*, p. 164)

The swimming pool provided the relaxation needed if pilots were to remain in good physical and psychological condition, but Lewis had no doubt about what made 40 such a happy squadron:

> The spirit of this squadron is simply wonderful now. All due to the 'Admiral', or the 'Old Fool' as we sometimes call him. Everyone adores him and everyone is full out to bring down Huns as a result. (*Wings* p. 160)

In fostering squadron spirit Dallas not only stressed the interdependence of all that 40 did, on the ground and in the air, but put it into practice, personally thanking the ground crews whenever the pilots achieved note-worthy results. He also ensured that these results were acknowledged by listing the victories of the previous day in Routine Orders. A small innovation, it was symptomatic of an approach to the running of the Squadron which generated remarkable *élan*.

In the air Dallas was also an inspiration, adding to his score while providing leadership and support. On 22 May he was credited with a Pfalz out of control, while Wood, Usher and Sutton shared a DFW, and he scored again on the 27th, one of three (with Lewis and Hind) to do so during a scrap between eleven SE5as (led by Lewis) and eight Pfalz DIIIs. Lewis wrote home:

> I got onto the tail of one stupid lad who didn't seem to quite know what to do. I gave him a good deluge with both guns and he went down in flames. Hind picked up another, which we all saw crash as it burst into flames as soon as it hit the ground. The 'Admiral' cut across from another quarter of the heavens, swearing he was not going to miss the show, and crashed one lad, and sent another out of control. A Bristol Fighter then got another, so I don't think those fellows had a very enjoyable patrol. (*Wings*, p. 168)

May ended with 40 at a peak of confidence. On 1 June, however, the unthinkable happened when Roderic Dallas was killed. An eyewitness, Harold Rayner, described in the 1970s how he died:

> I happened to be stationed with the Royal Engineers near the Red Chateaux of Rollericourt when Dallas was shot down and saw the whole episode from beginning to end.
>
> First I saw a lone British biplane flying on the outer edge of a very large black storm cloud. Next I saw three German planes come out of the cloud.

19. Capt G. H. Lewis and 'The Artful Dodger'. (G. H. Lewis.)

The English pilot must have seen them because he turned away from them— and then, before I had realized quite what was happening, the British biplane was plummeting earthwards. It had been shot down by the centre of the three German aircraft.[7]

The news of the CO's death was received with shock and disbelief. Gwilym Lewis' reaction in a letter home is typical:

The world is upside down. I don't know where to start. In the first place Dallas has been killed; I can't think why, but he has been. Too good for this world, I suppose . . . .
We simply couldn't believe our ears when we first got the news, but all the same it was true. It wasn't a matter of admiring the 'old fool'; we simply adored him. He must have had a most wonderful influence because the Squadron has had awfully bad luck, and a very large element of new pilots. Yet the spirit has been wonderful. There never was such a happy bunch of lads. (*Wings*, p. 166)

For Lewis, too, there was the feeling that he had 'lost a very good friend as well as a CO'. He wrote:

Since I returned from leave we got to know each other awfully well, and had all sorts of discussions on the Squadron and pilots in it. He had got everyone summed up properly, and knew everything worth knowing about the lads. He seldom, if ever, said or seemed to think anything but nice things about everybody. (*Wings*, p. 166–7)

Guy Symonds, writing seventy years later, drew particular attention to Dallas's role as a mentor for new pilots:

It was a rare day indeed that did not see the Admiral in the air, generally in company with someone who by reason of a dud engine or other affliction had been unable to do his job that day. Anyone who had been in that unfortunate situation was expected to join the Admiral in an offensive patrol usually after dinner that night. If there was no one else he would go alone.[8]

Dallas's penchant for patrolling alone worried his flight commanders, and they tackled him about it a week before his death, urging him never to go up without a companion. Sadly, their advice went unheeded.
C. G. Grey wrote:

Roderic Dallas . . . was a pilot of quite extraordinary skill, a fighting man of astonishing gallantry, a humorist of a high order, and black and white artist of unusual ability. But, above and beyond all this, he was a great leader of men. To be in Dallas's squadron was quite one of the highest honours open to a young fighting pilot of the RNAS, and the high reputation held by certain of the RNAS squadrons operating with the RFC during the past year or two has been largely due to the training, example and leadership of Roderic Dallas.[9]

Dallas's tally of victories was thirty-two, enough in itself to ensure an honoured place in aviation history. But this is not how those who served under him would wish him remembered. For them 'the Admiral', 'the Old Fool'—the names speak volumes—was a peerless leader and a fine human being. Those who served under him in 40 Squadron counted themselves lucky indeed.

## Notes

1. Dallas inspired at least three nicknames: 'Breguet' (or 'Breggy'), 'the Admiral' and 'the Old Fool'—the latter after his escapade with the boots. By his Australian friends he was known as 'Stan', but in the RNAS and RAF as Roderic. See two *Cross and Cockade* (GB) articles: Douglass Whetton, 'Roderic Dallas: Forgotten Ace'. Vol. 2, no. 1 (1971), pp. 1–10, and Norman Franks, 'Dallas'. Vol. 3, no. 4 (1972), pp. 147–54.

2. Letter of October 1975 to Neil ?, p. 1.

3. It was to be Harrison's last with 40. On 11 April he was promoted captain, and posted to command a Flight on 1 Squadron. There he scored one more victory before being wounded, bringing his total to twelve.

4. James J. Hudson, 'Interview with Reed Landis'. *Over the Front*, Vol. 5, no. 1 (Spring 1990), p. 9.

5. Gwilym Lewis to the author, 30. 10. 86, p. 13.

6. Extract from Guy Symonds, 'The Chap in the Back Seat' (unpublished), via Stewart Taylor.

7. *Flying Review*, date unknown.

8. 'The Chap in the Back Seat', extract via Stewart Taylor.

9. *The Aeroplane*, 3 July 1918.

5

# A Good Keen Squadron:
# June–August 1918

FINDING a successor to the charismatic Roderic Dallas was not easy, clearly, but Arthur Keen was a good choice, rapidly endorsed by the Squadron. Born in 1895, Keen gained his wings in January 1916, and served with 70 Squadron before joining 40 in April 1917 as a flight commander. Credited with twelve victories before returning to England to instruct, Keen was well-placed to fill the post of CO, but that he succeeded so well was due to qualities that Gwilym Lewis noted in a letter home:

> He is a fine Hun strafer, and though a younger type of squadron commander, is possessed of a very striking and independent personality. (*Wings*, p. 168)

On 3 June the Squadron acquired a new CO; the next day a new base. Since the spring offensive Bruay had been uncomfortably close to the front, and within range of German heavy artillery. No shells hit the aerodrome,

20. Capt P. C. O. Riddell (Recording Officer), ——,
Maj A. W. Keen. Bryas, June 1918. (G. H. Lewis.)

but they fell in Bruay itself, and this and nocturnal visits by German bombers led on 4 June to a shift to Bryas, some five miles to the west.

The first two weeks of June were quiet, but on the 11th 40 encountered for the first time the redoubtable Fokker DVII. Not particularly fast—an SE5a could outpace it low down, and match it at altitude—the DVII it had qualities which more than compensated for this:

> The success of the Fokker DVII was attributable to the fact that it was a fairly easy, yet responsive, machine to fly, with an apparent ability to make a good pilot out of mediocre material; also it retained extreme controllability at its ceiling. With these points went an ability to "hang on its prop" to shoot at an opponent when other machines would have stalled into a spin.[1]

Competently handled, the SE5a could hold its own against this latest Fokker, but the margin of superiority over the Albatros DV and Pfalz DIIIa was gone.

On 10 June Capt Rusden, the C Flight Commander, was admitted to hospital, and in his place the Squadron welcomed back George McElroy. In February he had been posted to 24 Squadron as a flight commander, scoring a further sixteen victories before being posted to Home Establishment. Gwilym Lewis wrote home:

> we have McElroy back with us again. He is a wild youngster, went home and refused to instruct and quarrelled with most people, and soon applied to come overseas again. (*Wings,* p. 172)

In the weeks ahead, he was to do more than anyone else to maintain 40's considerable reputation.

The return to the Squadron, on 19 June, of 2/Lt I. L. Roy must have seemed of less import. Son of a Calcutta lawyer, Roy was at public school in England when war broke out, and, precluded by race from obtaining a commission in the Army, he joined the RFC, with his first posting to 56 Squadron. Sent back to England for further training, in April 1918 he was posted to 40 as Gunnery Officer, but a month later was admitted to hospital, then posted to Home Establishment. Persuading a Medical Board that he was fit to fly, he returned to 40 and flew his first patrol with McElroy on 25 June. Under the latter's tutelage he was to undergo a remarkable transformation.

On 26 June McElroy scored 40's first victory since Keen became CO when he dived on a DFW, opening fire 'at 400 yards, continuing in bursts up to 150 yards when E.A. fell over on right wing tip, then dived steeply, and crashed about 500 yards S. E. of ANNAY'. He was successful again on 28 June, bringing down one of three balloons he attacked during a solo patrol, while on 30 June, he led Strange and Whitten in a successful attack on the balloon at Annay, and the following day brought down another at Harnes in a solo attack carried out to point blank range, the observer baling out as the balloon burst into flames. A second balloon was brought down by Don Poler, who had told

Gwilym Lewis that as he [Poler] was about to go on leave, and had not yet scored a victory, he had better go and do something for King and Country.

On 30 June Arthur Keen scored his first success since rejoining the Squadron. His report details how he observed three triplanes at 18,000 feet over La Bassée, and 'fired three very short bursts at extremely long range' to entice them to turn and fight. One turned back briefly, firing a short burst at Keen before turning to follow his companions. It was a fatal error, since Keen was able to close and open fire with both guns. The triplane turned tightly to try to get on his tail, but Keen looped and placed himself above and behind his opponent. He then fired a series of short bursts at very close range until his opponent stalled and spun, the end coming when 'the E.A. collapsed in the air and wings were seen to fall off'.

On 11 July Gwilym Lewis wrote to his parents: 'McElroy has been going absolutely full-out. He is quite mad and seldom returns without having brought something down' (*Wings*, p. 174). His run of successes in July had begun on the 2nd when he downed two DFWs. After the first, he landed at Mazingarbe with a minor engine problem, then took off again on 'a solo low patrol in the area of the FORET de NIEPPE'. Having scattered a working party standing around the machine shot down in the morning, McElroy surprised another DFW, three short bursts proving sufficient to send it into a spin, to crash near Lestrem.

On the 5th McElroy led C Flight to three 'out of control' claims, two joint, and the third (a DFW) his own. A noteworthy feature of the latter was the range (500 yards) at which he opened fire. For most pilots this would have been a waste of ammunition. With McElroy it was often decisive. The next day he scored twice more. In the first combat he and his patrol cut off two Hannoveraner two-seaters, which dived steeply to escape. Opening fire at 200 yards, McElroy silenced the observer in one, and with a second burst the two seater 'spiralled slowly, still engaged by S.E. and fell straight to earth, left wing down and crashed'. The second encounter also began with an accurate attack at 200 yards, silencing the observer. McElroy then 'zoomed up and cleared gun stoppage and then got position 100 yards behind E.A. and fired about 50 rounds. E.A. went down out of control in slow spins and crashed 3 miles E of LA BASSEE'.

Others were also successful at this time. Napier, after a scoreless six weeks, shot down a Pfalz DIII and a Rumpler on 1 July, and claimed a Fokker DVII out of control on the 4th, while on the 7th Lewis and Hind forced an LVG CV to land behind Allied lines. On the debit side, however, Lt Clarke was wounded. Lewis recalled in a letter home that

> I managed to frighten a couple of biplanes off Clarke's tail, and saw him across the Lines, but unfortunately they had hit him in such a way that he won't be able to sit down comfortably for some time. (*Wings*, p. 172)

That day, 8 July, George McElroy shared a Hannoveraner out of control with Strange and Roy. For the latter this victory was a turning point, for an hour later he claimed as out of control one of four Fokker DVIIs that the patrol ambushed south-east of Douai. It was the start of a brief but meteoric career.

On 11 July McElroy again brought down a Hannoveraner. Opening fire at 200 yards, he had fired only ten rounds when his gun jammed. Even so it was enough, for 'On zooming to clear stoppage saw E.A. fall on to its left wing tip, and crash into a wood just S. of the SCARPE and just W. of VITRY'. Though a tough opponent might take 100 rounds, McElroy often scored now with 20 or less.

On 13 July C Flight had a remarkable morning, with five claims from an early patrol. The first of these was yet another Hannoveraner, brought down jointly by McElroy, Roy, Strange and South African, Lt F. H. Knobel. Later the patrol surprised four scouts—an Albatros and three Pfalz—claiming all of them, three certain. The latter went to McElroy, who hit a Pfalz with 90 rounds, causing it to dive vertically and crash near Vitry, to Roy, whose Pfalz 'crashed straight into the ground' between Vitry and Brebières, and to Strange, who closed on the third Pfalz, firing more than 200 rounds. He continues:

> By this time E.A. had started to go down in a long dive, which turned later into an uncontrolled side slip.
> When nearing the ground E.A. began to roll, and fell from side to side.
> E.A. finally crashed just E. of BREBIERES.

The fourth success went to the Canadian, Whitten, who attacked the only Albatros in the formation, firing 300 rounds at medium to close range. His report continues, in a slightly puzzled vein:

> E.A. just kept on diving away, and made no apparent effort to turn on to S.E. which overtook E.A. at about 8,000 ft, and followed it down to 2,200 feet.
> When last seen E.A. was seen diving steeply at 800 feet and emitting smoke. At this point S.E. lost sight of E.A. and was unable to pick it up again, but E.A. was already out of control.

Napier, as acting CO, annotated the report thus:

> Patrol leader thinks this E.A. was almost certainly crashed, as neither he nor any other of his pilots saw any of the four original E.A. escape.

It had been a remarkable success; the only occasion when 40 downed an entire German patrol.

McElroy's run of successes continued on 14 July, when he scored twice. The second victory was incomplete because, having stopped a two-seater's engine with two 10-round bursts, he ran out of ammunition, but the first was clear cut, his victim diving into the ground north of Drocourt. The next day both he and Roy scored twice when, spotting a large formation of Fokker DVIIs, McElroy took his patrol towards them, at a lower altitude, to induce them to attack. This they did, two of them continuing their dive down through C Flight. McElroy immediately got on the tail of one, firing several bursts at 'very short range'. The outcome was inevitable: 'At 2,000' E.A. was on its back, and finally crashed N.E. of Hill 70. McElroy then attacked the second Fokker, 'firing two bursts of over 50 rounds each at from 150/100 yards range'. His victim, McElroy reported, 'went down in a side stall and fell out of control until lost sight of'.

Roy's combat report demonstrates both coolness and accurate shooting:

Whilst returning from patrol and near lines in LOOS SALIENT saw a large formation of Fokkers above and behind.

Upon E.A. starting to dive S.E. turned and opened fire on leading E.A. when Vickers gun jammed. S.E. dived vertically for 5000' and pulled out with Fokker still on tail and firing on S.E.

S.E. turned underneath, E.A. gradually lost height till on same level as S.E. S.E. and E.A. went round each other in right hand circles, S.E. turned inside getting long bursts at opponent at about 20 to 30 yards range, Fokker suddenly swerved and side-slipped to left and crashed into the ground.

Another Fokker now dived and fired a short burst but turned East. S.E. followed firing a long burst, whereupon Fokker went down in vertical dive turning slowly and out of control.

On 18 July it was Roy's turn once more when, after two members of C Flight had made diving attacks on a DFW, he himself fired a long burst from above and behind. Continuing his dive, he came up under the two-seater and fired another burst, 'upon which', Roy reported, 'E.A. dived vertically into ground near an avenue of trees SE of ARRAS'. On 19 July both McElroy and Roy scored: Roy an 'out of control' and McElroy a certain. The latter's report underlines the economy of ammunition that he had now achieved: three bursts totalling forty-five rounds sufficing to destroy an Albatros DV.

By 20 July C Flight had accounted for 20 enemy aircraft that month. Of these, McElroy had brought down 12 and shared in 4 others, while Roy had brought down 3 and shared in 2. As a team they seemed invincible, but on 20 July there were the first signs that things could go wrong when McElroy's aircraft caught fire after a connecting rod broke. In forced-landing, he jumped clear to escape the flames, and miraculously got away with only a few bruises. Then on the 22nd Roy was shot down in combat with Fokker DVIIs. Since returning to the Squadron a month earlier, he had flown with skill and courage, scoring ten victories. A posthumous DFC, gazetted in September, was richly deserved.

On 21 July Gwilym Lewis was posted. He explained in a letter home that 'I knew I could get home any time I liked, as I have been feeling a pretty good physical wreck lately, so I got an MO to examine me, and he stopped me flying' (*Wings*, p. 175). But though glad to leave operational flying behind him, he felt some regret:

> This is a great squadron, and I am awfully sorry to leave. I have had the happiest times of my life out here, and now that McElroy is back with us, we are easily top squadron in the Brigade. (*Wings*, p. 176)

The customary farewell dinner was held on the eve of his departure, and Lewis told his parents about it:

> Mick Mannock was there with two of his Flight commanders [from 85 Squadron], and also several members of the Brigade. It was a great binge. I feel awfully rotten leaving my priceless Flight. I am awfully pleased that I have had the luck not to lose a single fellow while I have been here, though two went down when I was on leave. (*Wings*, p. 176)

Lewis's success in not losing a member of his Flight owed much to his decision to put newcomers alongside him, protected by more experienced pilots, rather than at the outside of the formation, where they were more vulnerable. As an air fighter he could not match George McElroy, but as a flight commander he was perhaps superior, providing tactical leadership where McElroy provided example.[2]

In late May Reed Landis had been admitted to hospital. He returned to the Squadron early in July, and began to score once more. His first victory came on 14 July when he shot down a Pfalz DIII near Epinoy, and a second on the 22nd, when his patrol was attacked by four Fokker DVIIs north of Carvin, and 'a general engagement ensued' in which he 'selected an individual opponent' and 'Fired about 300 rounds down to close range from above and behind'. The 'E.A. spiralled down very steeply, side-slipping at intervals, and was observed to crash in the vicinity of CARVIN'. In the same fight Ben Strange brought down his second victim, which he attacked from above, firing about fifty rounds as he closed to point blank range. The enemy aircraft spun down on its back, and an AA battery confirmed the crash.

At this time there were three Americans on squadron, Landis, Poler and Burwell. On 23 July they were joined by two more, Lts L. Bennett and R. A. Anderson. The latter had joined the Aviation Section of the US Signal Corps, but Louis Bennett had made his way into the RFC through enlistment in Canada. Bennett was assigned to C Flight, replacing Roy. He was to prove as fiercely aggressive, and to have as brief a career.

July 25th was a good day for 40, with claims for four enemy aircraft destroyed. Two Hannoveraners went to George McElroy, who sent one spinning down to crash near Neuve Chappelle, and later in the same patrol caught another. He reported:

> S.E. secured position behind tail of E.A. and fired 100 rounds from 200 down to 100 yards range. E.A. went into a steep dive, pulled out temporarily at about 1000' but then seemed to stall and spin, and finally crash just W of BOIS D'EPINOY.

The other two aircraft fell to B Flight, led by Hind, which surprised five Fokker DVIIs. Murman and Burwell lodged a joint claim for one, the aircraft they had hit spiralling into the ground and bursting into flames, while the other fell to Hind, whose laconic combat report reads:

> S.E. selected nearest E.A. and dived getting to within 50 yards, and fired a burst of about 50 rounds. E.A. turned over to the left and dived at a very steep angle and burst into flames, the right hand planes falling off after E.A. had gone down about 1000'.

After these successes came nearly a fortnight of bad weather with little operational flying, and during which the Squadron had to cope with two items of devastatingly bad news. The first, on the 26th, was that Mick Mannock had been brought down by ground fire, and killed. This was felt badly in 40 Squadron, where several, including Keen, knew him personally, and where he had recently been a guest at Gwilym Lewis's farewell dinner.[3]

Five days later George McElroy failed to return from a solo patrol. A German note dropped several days later explained that he had been brought down by ground fire near Laventie after shooting down one of their aircraft. This can scarcely have come as a surprise, since on his own he tended to work at low level. Moreover, as Gwilym Lewis told his parents, 'if he [McElroy] decides to get a Hun, he always gets it because if it runs away he goes right down to the ground after it'. Following a victim down was a high-risk option which McElroy chose to take.

George McElroy was a slow starter. It was four months before he claimed a victory, but when he did, on 28 December 1917, it was the start of a remarkable run of successes. He became the undisputed master of the art of shooting down two-seaters, but as his record with 24 Squadron indicates, he was equally adept at shooting down single-seaters.

McElroy was an average pilot, but became a superb shot, and his victories were won with a growing economy of ammunition, ten or fifteen rounds sometimes sufficing to despatch an opponent. He was also given to opening fire at long range, partly because he was such a good shot, and partly because he knew that this would, if he missed, convey the impression that he was a novice, and lull his opponent into a false sense of security. And this points to another factor in his success: his capacity for stalking and outwitting an opponent. At first impetuous, he became a cool and crafty fighter who rarely settled for anything less than the destruction of his opponent.

F. T. Gilbert, his fitter, began 'McElroy of "Forty"', published in *Popular Flying* in June 1936, thus: 'Frankly, this article had to be written. The writer's conscience would give him no peace till he had put before the public this, the saga of a little-known, but truly heroic British war pilot' (p. 132). George McElroy is still the least known of the leading RFC and RNAS aces, despite his forty-seven victories.

McElroy's successor in C Flight was a Canadian, Capt George Dixon, who was posted to 40 from 85 Squadron a few days before McElroy's death, presumably to command B Flight, which Ivan Hind, promoted Captain, now took over.

The first week of August was quiet, with few combats, and the only claim an LVG out of control by Landis. Then on 8 August 1918 the British and French attacked along a fifteen mile front east of Amiens. Supported by 430 British tanks they had, that evening, pushed the German forces back up to seven miles in places. The RAF squadrons detailed for low level support work sustained heavy losses, and 40 was fortunate to be patrolling at altitude, claims being made for two enemy aircraft out control (by Strange and Hind), and four destroyed. One of these went to Murman, who dived on a Fokker DVII, firing about 200 rounds, and sending his victim down vertically to crash near Don.

The other three victories went to Landis in the course of one patrol. He reported:

> In a general engagement between S.E.s, Bristols, Fokker Triplanes, Fokker Biplanes & Phaltz Scouts W. of DOUAI, S.E. got in a short burst from point blank range at a Triplane.
>
> E.A. immediately dived, stalled, and, after emitting a great burst of smoke several yards in diameter, went into a vertical nose dive, trailing a huge stream of smoke from the vicinity of the cockpit, and evidently on fire.
>
> At this juncture S.E.'s engine cut out, and pilot turned towards lines, but later engine started again low over VITRY.
>
> Whilst diving on VITRY balloon, observed a DFW at about 1,000' diving East. Attacked EA. instead, and fired a long burst from above and in front upon which E.A. stalled, went into a dive, and eventually a partial spin, finally crashing on the Southern edge of the village of VITRY-en-ARTOIS.
>
> Resumed attack on balloon almost immediately, as E.A. was disposed of in single burst. Attacked from very close range and saw one observer make parachute descent. Balloon speedily caught fire and fell to the ground in flames.

Landis's reference to his engine cutting out is a reminder that the SE5a's engine problems remained. The day before, for instance, Don Poler had forced-landed after engine failure, while on the 9th Paul Burwell crashed after his engine cut, though without injury.

On the second day of the offensive, an attempt was made to destroy bridges over the Somme and trap retreating German units. Forty flew covering patrols, and it was on one of these that Keen scored the only victory that day. Sighting a Pfalz through a gap in clouds, he 'Dived through the gap and attacked E.A. from behind and above, firing about 30 rounds from a range of 100/50 yards'. His aim was good, for the Pfalz 'burst into flames and fell near the bridge across the SOMME'.

For the next two days 40 flew patrols without result, and it was not until the 12th, on its own sector of the front, that further combats were reported. Sadly they brought the loss of two of the Squadron's experienced pilots, Ivan Hind killed and Lt Wood POW. To set against these losses they had only a victory by Landis, who despatched a Fokker DVII with two bursts of fire near Mons. The following day he scored again, an 'out of control' with all the appearance of a 'certain', when over Lens he dived on four Fokkers, three DrIs and a DVII, sending the latter 'down in a slow spin on its back, out of control'.

The same day, however, 40 suffered two more crash landings because of engine trouble. Neither Murman nor 2/Lt W. V. Trubshawe were seriously injured, but both SEs were written off. In a third crash, two days later, Arthur Keen was not so lucky. The casualty report reads:

> Pilot left aerodrome to visit 70 Sqdn at 5–30 pm. Landed at 70 Sqdn & during return journey did a stall turn low down near BRUAY, striking a bank about 9–30 pm. Machine crashed heavily & burst into flames. Pilot admitted to hospital suffering from burns to face & legs & severe concussion.

Why Keen attempted a stall turn at such a low level is perhaps explained by Laurie Field, who had joined 40 as a 2/Lt the previous day:

> Major Keen the CO visited a drome to see a friend of his and, after dining (perhaps too well) he took off to return to us and crashed doing a few stunts too near ground level.

On 2 September, after seventeen days of intense suffering, he died.

Arthur Keen was CO of 40 Squadron for only six weeks, but it was long enough to reveal his capacity for leadership. MacLanachan, who describes him as 'the best type of Englishman; courageous, modest, clever, yet with that aloofness which many people mistook for superciliousness', also felt he was 'quiet and shy', yet he had done remarkably well in succeeding a charismatic predecessor. And with fourteen victories, thirteen of them with 40, he had established himself as one of its leading aces. On the roll of 40 Squadron's COs, Arthur William Keen, whose period of command was briefer than any save J. G. Llewellyn's in 1940, has an honoured place.

# Notes

1.  Peter Gray and Owen Thetford, *German Aircraft of the First World War*. London: Putnam, 1970, p. 107.
2.  Lewis scored a total of 12 victories with 32 and 40 Squadrons.
3.  When his VC was gazetted, Mannock was credited with 59 victories. Research has subsequently assessed his score at 61, Shores *et al.* noting that the percentage of verifiable victories is higher in Mannock's case than that of almost any other of the leading British aces (See *Above the Trenches*. London: Grub Street Books, 1990. pp. 255–7.

# 6

# The Final Phase:
# August 1918–July 1919

ARTHUR KEEN's crash came at a time of transition for 40. With the death of George McElroy on 31 July, command of C Flight had passed to George Dixon, while that of Hind on 12 August brought the promotion of Middleton, his deputy. Napier still commanded A Flight, though about to be posted to 5 Brigade HQ, and he handed over to the new CO, Major Compston, on 20 August.

During the ten day lull following the abandonment of the Amiens offensive on 11 August, 40 resumed its customary mix of line and offensive patrols and escort duties. It was on an offensive patrol on 15 August that Lt Louis Bennett claimed a Fokker DVII out of control, the first of a dazzling series of victories in the next nine days.

The second and third were registered on the 17th, when Bennett shared with Franz Knobel the destruction of an LVG two-seater. After a fight lasting several minutes, during which Knobel 'succeeded in getting several good bursts with both guns' and Bennett 'opened attack from all directions, firing bursts from close range whenever opportunity offered', the LVG crashed. Knobel landed with engine trouble, but Bennett returned to the aerodrome to reload his guns and then attacked a balloon, sending it down in flames.

On 19 August Bennett, delayed in starting the morning patrol, was unable to catch up with his Flight, and when he saw balloons being raised decided to attack them. Diving on the first, he 'fired about ¾ drum of flat nosed Buckingham into the balloon, which burst into flames, one observer making a parachute descent'. He then attacked a second balloon, which burst into flames almost instantly: both victories being confirmed by AA batteries. Then, after returning to Bryas to refuel and reload, he went up again. At 1.40 pm he sighted another balloon, which he sent down in flames before turning his attention to a second that was being hauled down. Bennett had fired only half a drum of Buckingham before his gun jammed, but the balloon was seen to be on fire on the ground. He had now scored seven victories in four days.

Bennett's approach was rash. Not so that of Reed Landis, who displayed both skill and circumspection in scoring two victories that day. His combat report reads:

Observed 6 E.A. E. of LA BASSEE about 1,000' above S.E. formation. Climbed towards Béthune firing red lights to attract attention of Bristol Fighters & other S.E.s which had been seen earlier in patrol, as S.E. formation was inferior in numbers. Upon arrival of other Allied machines S.E.s turned and engaged E.A. W. of SECLIN.

A general engagement ensued in which S.E. selected an opponent (Fokker Biplane), and got in a long burst from above and behind. E.A. half rolled, did a few turns of a slow spin and was observed to crash about half way between SECLIN and LA BASSEE.

At this juncture several triplanes dived into the fight from above. S.E. observed a triplane on the the the tail of Bristol Fighter, whose observer had apparently ceased fire. S.E. zoomed up beneath and behind E.A. and fired a short burst at point blank range.

E.A. stalled, dived vertically and crashed just W. of SECLIN. A portion of E.A. fell off in the dive, probably a plane.

Landis's decision to await reinforcements paid off handsomely. So did his accurate shooting. His victories rarely involved more than one burst of fire.

21. [Maj] R. J. O. Compston.
(C. W. Usher via O. A. Sater.)

On 20 August the new CO, Major Compston, arrived at Bryas. Born in 1898, Robert John Orton Compston (known as Robin) joined the RNAS in August 1915, and was posted in October 1916 to Naval Eight, with which he flew without a break, save for leave and recuperation after being wounded, for seventeen months. Posted to Home Establishment at the end of February 1918, he had by then twenty-five victories, and had been awarded the DSC and two bars.

Another arrival on 20 August was Capt R. L. Chidlaw-Roberts, who replaced Napier as OC A Flight. Born in 1896, he joined the RFC in May 1915, serving as an observer with 2 Squadron and then as a pilot with 18 and 60 Squadrons. With the latter he was a participant, on

23 September 1917, in the last fight
of Werner Voss, and on 9 January
1918 shared in the downing of Max
Muller, CO of *Jasta* 'Boelcke'. In the
months ahead 'Chiddles' would be a
crucial member of 40 Squadron.

On 21 August the British
launched an assault in the vicinity of
the Arras-Albert railway, supported
by tanks and what assistance the RAF
could provide in poor weather. Forty
flew line and offensive patrols, during which Dixon sent a Fokker DVII
down out of control near Cambrai,
and early next morning carried out
a bombing raid on Gondercourt
aerodrome. On the way home several balloons were spotted and three
shot down. One went to Dixon; the
others, almost inevitably, to Bennett.

22. Lt Louis Bennett Jr.
(University of West Virginia Library.)

August 23rd saw the launching of
the Battle of Bapaume. The RAF's role was, as before, infantry support,
bombing enemy positions, providing information about events on the ground
and denying it to German reconnaissance aircraft. A dawn patrol led by
Dixon did just that when it encountered three LVGs, and Bennett brought
one down. He reported that he 'fired 300 rounds following E.A. from 3000
feet to 500 feet. The cockpit was observed to be full of smoke and the
observer had disappeared'.

Bennett had now downed ten aircraft and balloons in eight days. On 24
August he set out to improve on that figure, attacking a balloon near Provin,
and setting it on fire before flying towards Hantay, where the Germans were
lowering a second balloon, and setting it too on fire. The German defences
were accurate, however, and with his aircraft on fire, Bennett crashed near
Marquillas. Dragged from the wreckage, he died of his injuries soon after.

Louis Bennett was with 40 Squadron only a month, and had scored
so quickly that there had been no time for Robin Compston to recommend him for a decoration. His twelve victories in only twenty-five sorties
was perhaps the most rapid rate of scoring by any Allied pilot in World
War One.

On 26 August the British 1st Army struck at Arras with the object of
turning the enemy positions on the northern Somme, and the following
day 40 was heavily engaged in flying covering patrols for strafing single-seaters

and corps reconnaissance aircraft directing fire on German positions. One pilot was lost, the American, 'Andy' Anderson, failing to return from a C Flight patrol which had attacked five Fokker DVIIs. Anderson recalls that after a diving pass

> I had a Fokker on my tail, firing from about 200 yards and I decided that I didn't want any more of that without giving something back. I turned and went straight for him, firing head on. At this point I was pretty sure that I'd gotten into more than I could handle and thinking that since I was probably in for it, I'd hold my course—if he did, too, then we'd finish up together.

Anderson had indeed taken on more than he could handle. Wounded, he 'went into a vertical dive but quickly saw that I had no altitude to work with. I pulled out just above ground level and there was nothing to do but put it down just where I was'.[1] His wounds were not severe, and he escaped from a German POW camp on 26 September, reaching neutral Holland.

Having exhausted the possibilities at Arras, the British switched to Bapaume, where the 1st and 3rd Armies attacked on 2 September, gaining considerable ground during the first two days. A new role arising from the mobility of the attacking force involved watching for German air attacks on an armoured car force ranging along the Cambrai road. Forty were heavily engaged on 2 September, a two flight patrol being engaged by twelve enemy aircraft. The Squadron lost 2/Lt Clarke, shot down and killed, but recorded an 'out of control' for Dixon.

Another loss that day was Lts Landis, Burwell and Poler, all posted to the USAAC 3rd Aviation Instructional Centre. Reed Landis subsequently commanded the American 25th Squadron, where Burwell and Poler joined him, but the Squadron never flew operationally, so none of the three added to their RAF scores. Landis had been particularly successful, with twelve victories, but all three had proved 'stout', and were sorely missed.

Bad weather during the second week of September prevented much operational flying, and there were no combats. From the 14th, however, the weather improved, and patrols encountered enemy aircraft once more. On 16 September this brought the wounding of George Dixon. He had led C Flight with courage and flair, adding a further five victories to the four he had on arrival. His Flight was taken over by Lt Strange, his deputy.

During September, the German Air Force made one last attempt at aerial dominance, and the Squadron found itself engaged in heavy though intermittent aerial fighting, climaxing on 18 September, when 40 was caught up in fifteen individual combats between Douai and Cambrai. Two enemy aircraft were claimed destroyed and two out of control, and Robin Compston annotated the combat reports with the comment that 'Owing to the intensity of the fighting it is impossible to credit any one individual with these successes.' In this fight 2/Lt L. C. Band was wounded, his loss following that of a newcomer, 2/Lt F. W. King, taken POW the previous day, and preceding that of Capt G. J. Strange, killed on 24 September. Younger brother of Major L. A. Strange, who had been intended to command 40 in February 1916, Ben Strange had become one of the Squadron's experienced core during the hard summer fighting, and his appointment as OC C Flight had been a popular one. Prior to 24 September he had been credited with six victories, three of them shared. During his last fight he brought down a Fokker DVII, but was then himself shot down. During the same action a Fokker DVII was brought down in flames by a newcomer, Lt G. S. Smith, who was to prove 40's most successful pilot in the last weeks of the war.

Another pilot who began scoring during this period was Lt A. T. Drinkwater, who forced a Fokker DVII down out of control on 17 September. An Australian, Drinkwater had joined the RFC in November 1916, and flew DH4s with 57 Squadron. When he joined 40 he had six victories to his credit. His 'out of control' now would be one of three added to his tally before the war ended.

On 26 September eleven aircraft bombed and strafed Lieu St. Amand aerodrome, setting planes and hangars on fire. This was part of preparations for an attack on the Hindenburg Line next day by the 1st and 3rd Armies. The squadrons of 1 Brigade were ordered to operate at low level, destroying balloons and harassing German troops. It was in carrying out these tasks that the 40 had one of its worst days of the war. For though Fokker DVIIs were brought down by Middleton and Smith, two pilots died (Lt P. B. Myers and 2/Lt G. M. J. Morton), a third was taken POW (Lt N. D. Willis), and a fourth wounded (Lt R. Mooney). Myers, Morton and Mooney were newcomers, but Willis had been with the Squadron since mid-April, with two victories to his credit. Fortunately, SE5a squadrons were not used for ground attack the following day, but reverted to offensive patrols and balloon suppression, meeting little enemy opposition.

By the end of September the Hindenburg Line had been breached. The RAF's job now was to assist in keeping the momentum going, and in carrying out these duties 40 met only occasional resistance, for the German Air Force had been seriously weakened during August and September, and air battles became increasingly rare as the war drew to its close.

In these circumstances, most of the few victories which came 40's way were over balloons. On 29 September Chidlaw-Roberts, Smith and Field brought one down in flames near Cambrai. Two days later Chidlaw-Roberts attacked two more, reporting that the observer jumped from the first and that the second was driven down, while on 9 October he, Smith and Field again shared in the destruction of a *drachen*, attacking it in what Chidlaw-Roberts would later refer to as 'the old man's way', line abreast and firing

simultaneously from a distance of 500 yards. The only successes against aircraft
went to Drinkwater, with a Halberstadt two seater in flames on 1 October
and another out of control on the 10th, and to an American, Lt R. R.
Spafford, who claimed a Fokker DVII 'out of control' the same day. His
report begins, 'After dropping my bombs I found myself amongst an E.A.
formation'. Clearly not dismayed, he 'picked one out and fired 150 rounds,
pulling out when within 50' of E.A., which went down out of control in a
vertical dive'. Spafford's laconic account concludes: 'Three Fokkers were
now diving on S.E., no final result could, therefore, be observed'.

The only losses at this time were 2/Lts Trubshawe and W. D. Archer,
wounded on 9 and 11 October. Little is known about the circumstances of
Trubshawe's wounding, save that he came down in no man's land, but that
of the American, Wesley Archer, is thoroughly documented, largely because
of the controversy that later surrounded his book, *Death in the Air*.[2] With
40 less than three weeks, Archer was hit by two bullets, forced-landed and
was admitted to hospital. Robin Compston wrote to him

> I was extraordinarily pleased with the way you got on in so short a time here
> and I wish to thank you personally for the work you did, and the interest
> you took in the work. You will always get on if you take a similar interest
> in anything.

'I was coming to see you', Compston added, 'but I have rather a lot of
work on hand, as we are shortly going to move to a more forward
Aerodrome.'[3]

Compston's letter was written on 16 September. On the 24th the move
to which he alluded took place, the Squadron shifting from Bryas to Aniche,
on the Douai-Denain road, not far from the former home of the Richthofen
Circus, and closer to the front line.

During 28–30 October the German Air Force made a last effort to counter
roving Allied aircraft, and major battles resulted. For 40, however, the only
major engagement during its first week at Aniche was on the 26th, when
a two flight patrol encountered a formation of 25 Fokker DVII and Pfalz
DXII scouts near Valenciennes, and in the mêlée which followed lost Lt
T. H. Turnbull, killed. Two days later, Lt P. G. Greenwood brought a
balloon down, and on the 30th added a Fokker DVII in flames near
Valenciennes. The usual form of offensive activity now, however, was
bombing and machine-gunning targets of opportunity.

On 30 October 40 suffered its last fatality when Lt E. H. Mulley crashed
at Aniche. Recalling that Mulley 'had just joined the Squadron and had
gone up on a familiarization flight', Guy Symonds adds:

> As he passed over the aerodrome very low indeed, about 500 feet, I looked
> up and to my horror saw him pull the kite over on to its back in a half roll.

At that height he had no hope and just as I crossed the threshold of a little hut at the edge of the aerodrome I heard him hit the ground.[4]

The 1st November brought 40's last victory when Stewart Smith shot down an enemy aircraft near Valenciennes. It was his fifth victory (two of them shared with Chidlaw-Roberts and Field), and established him as the Squadron's leading scorer during the last weeks of the war. Only Greenwood, who scored twice in the five weeks he was with 40, came near him, though Chidlaw-Roberts, Drinkwater and Compston had larger total scores.

From 1 November air combats were infrequent, and even ground targets became scarce. The only event of note, indeed, was the loss of Greenwood on 3 November. Fortunately, he survived to be taken prisoner: scarcely a privation with the end of hostilities at hand.

Early in November a RAF circular warned against 'insidious rumours' and 'unfounded peace talk' which undermined concentration on winning the war. How much this stifled rumour is an open question, but what is clear is that amongst 40 Squadron personnel there was no strong sense, as late as the 10th, that it was about to end. Chidlaw-Roberts' account of how he heard the news clearly demonstrates this:

The First Army ran very good pierrot troupe called the Rouge et Noir, and they had a concert near our aerodrome—so most of us went there. Halfway through the show an officer came onto the platform and said, "Gentlemen, I have an announcement to make. The war is going to be over tomorrow at 11 o'clock." We all laughed like hell—we thought it was part of a joke and clapped. When we got back to the aerodrome we were told, seriously, that it was quite right—no more fighting after 11 o'clock. Of course we all went up at 11 o'clock, just to see what it was like.

The Armistice brought many changes, of which the greatest was that from a busy regimen of operational flying, and the repair, maintenance and administrative work that made it possible, to a situation in which there was little flying and therefore little else to do. Chidlaw-Roberts later recalled:

'Compass course flying', 'compass course flying, Aniche to Orcq'. At that time you would be doing very little flying at all except occasional direction-finding, navigational flying.

How was the free time spent? Concerning the NCOs and other ranks we have no record, though no doubt attempts were made to 'keep the men busy' with organized sports and unnecessary cleaning and maintenance. About the recreation of the officers we do not know a great deal either, though Laurie Field recalls horses kept for the officers' use, while earlier references to tennis and polo suggest that they must have had less difficulty than the men in filling in their time, particularly since they had access to motor transport, and were more easily able to visit local towns when off duty. 'We prowled around the countryside', Guy Symonds writes.

Two other activities can perhaps be deduced from Routine Orders for 28 November, which warns officers to watch out for 'revolutionary literature' (if read, presumably, by the other ranks), and introduces a strict prohibition against low flying or stunting over towns, villages, casualty clearing stations and the like.

Not all the Squadron's aircraft were flyable. Because of a shortage of hangarage at Aniche, some were left in the open for days at a time, and the cold and wet wrought havoc, as with E3946, which on 21 December Major Compston reported should be declared 'unfit for further service in the field', adding: 'This machine no doubt suffered through being left in the open for about a week recently, owing to lack of hangars'. As in numerous other cases, permission was given to strike the aircraft off charge.

The move from Aniche to Orcq, near Tournai, in Belgium, was made on 29 December, in the depths of a harsh winter. There were compensations, however, at least for the officers, who were billeted in a nearby château, the home of a marquise. Laurie Field recalls:

She had lived all through the hostilities with troops and officers billeted there. The building was square with three of its sides standing in a moat. Whilst there we had a fortnight of severe frost and we purchased what skates the shopkeeper had left. Several days we played ice hockey in the morning, and without removing skates awkwardly went up the steps and into lunch, resuming with an afternoon session.

23. Capt R. L. Chidlaw Roberts, Orcq, Winter 1918–19. (W. L. Field.)

Though hours were by now severely curtailed, some flying continued, as is evidenced by casualty reports or requests for aircraft to be struck off charge. On 7 January 2/Lt L. A. Brais crashed into the château moat. Brais, who was injured and admitted to hospital, suffered engine failure on take-off. This was also the cause of a crash on 20 January, when Stuart Smith forced-landed southwest of Lille. He seems to have escaped without injury, but the machine was written off. To the end, SEs were plagued by unreliable engines.

During January 1919 the Squadron was steadily run down, with two officers and fifty-three NCOs and other ranks struck off strength in the last fortnight, and others demobilized while on leave in Britain. By early February 40 was a shadow of its former self, shorn of its aircraft, which had been ferried to Marquis for disposal about 20 January, and with a greatly reduced complement of officers and men. Reduction to cadre status took place on 13 February, when Robin Compston handed over command to Chidlaw-Roberts, and all but the latter, the Equipment Officer, Lt G. A. B. Wheldon, and ten men, under a sergeant, were posted to other units, or to demobilization centres.

Robin Compston relinquished command on admission to hospital, perhaps for routine tests, but more likely ill, since his health was not robust. Chidlaw-Roberts recalls that Compston 'never looked very fit', and Guy Symonds recalls an occasion when he and the Recording Officer (Capt P. C. O. Riddell) felt it necessary to intervene when the CO was exhausted. But despite Robin Compston's fragile health, he was liked and respected, Laurie Field recalling a man who was 'very genial and very everyday', and Chidlaw-Roberts one 'distinctly quieter than the ordinary RFC chap.' 'He was not a mixer', Chidlaw-Roberts adds, 'He didn't stand aloof or anything like that, but he was naturally a quiet type.'

Laurie Field's recollection that 'we kept a Camel on the Squadron because Compston always flew a Camel—even when we went on patrol he'd come in the Camel' suggests a pattern of activity akin to that of Dallas, who often flew near by when a patrol was up, particularly if it contained inexperienced pilots. Yet it is the understanding of Robin Compston's family that he was told, when posted to command 40, that he was not to fly operationally, because the Squadron had lost two COs that way. His logbook certainly contains no entries relating to operational flying, and he did not add to his score of twenty-five RNAS kills.

Admired and respected, Chidlaw-Roberts was an appropriate choice as 40 Squadron's last CO. Laurie Field recalls an ideal flight commander, who led his men with courage, skill, and circumspection, while Guy Symonds eulogizes him thus:

> Completely fearless, very skilful, self-effacing, his gentle smile and manner made the most spectacular action look and sound insignificant.[5]

Reduction to cadre status was the first step towards disbandment; the second return to a base in the United Kingdom. For 40, this was Tangmere, in Sussex, which the cadre shared with numerous others, and where, Chidlaw-Roberts recalls, they did 'absolutely nothing'. It must have been something of a relief, therefore, when on 4 July 1919 the unit was disbanded.

# Notes

1. See Patrick Mallahan, 'Shot with Luck: The Story of Robert Alexander Anderson', *Over the Front*, Vol. 5, no. 2 (Summer 1990), pp. 154–165, from which the quotations are taken.

2. In 1933 Archer and his wife, Gladys Maud Garrett, perpetrated a most successful hoax, publishing *Death in the Air*. Purporting to be based on letters and photographs by the deceased fighter pilot husband of one Gladys Maud Cockburn-Lange, the book became famous not for its text, but for its photographs of dog fights between German and Allied aircraft. Though some, including most notably C. G. Grey, Editor of *The Aeroplane*, suspected the authenticity of the photographs, it was not until 1985 that there was proof that they were of models made by Archer. The book and photographs earned Archer and his wife some $30,000. See *Cross and Cockade* (GB), Vol. 16, no. 4., pp. 145–67.

3. R. J. O. Compston's letter is quoted by courtesy of the National Air and Space Museum, Smithsonian Institution, in whose archives the Archer papers are held.

4. From Guy Symonds' unpublished biography, 'The Chap in the Back Seat', courtesy Stewart Taylor.

5. *Ibid.*

# Epilogue

At the war's end 40 Squadron had, in twenty-seven months on the Western Front, claimed 350 victories, the fourth highest total of any scout squadron. In achieving this these successes, however, the Squadron had lost 31 pilots killed or died of wounds, and 19 as prisoners of war. A further 17 had been wounded and 15 injured during non-combat flying.

The following scored five or more victories while serving with 40 Squadron. (The figure in brackets indicates total victories with all squadrons. Ranks are those attained while with 40.)[1]

| | | |
|---|---|---|
| Capt. G. E. H. McElroy | 31 | (47) |
| Capt. E. Mannock | 16 | (61) |
| Lt. A. E. Godfrey | 13 | (14) |
| Maj. A. W. Keen | 13 | (14) |
| Lt. L. Bennett Jr. | 12 | |
| Lt. R. G. Landis | 12 | |
| Capt. I. P. R. Napier | 12 | |
| Lt. W. L. Harrison | 11 | (12) |
| Capt. G. H. Lewis | 10 | (12) |
| 2/Lt. I. L. Roy | 10 | |
| Capt. J. H. Tudhope | 10 | |
| Maj. R. S. Dallas | 9 | (32) |
| Lt. E. L. Benbow | 8 | |
| Lt. H. E. O. Ellis | 7 | |
| Lt. W. McLanachan | 7 | |
| Capt. G. J. Strange | 7 | |
| Lt. J. L. Barlow | 6 | |
| Capt. W. A. Bond | 5 | |
| Lt. G. B. Crole | 5 | |
| Capt. G. C. Dixon | 5 | (9) |
| Lt. R. N. Hall | 5 | |
| Lt. D. F. Murman | 5 | |
| Lt. J. W. Wallwork | 5 | |

The following pilots who served in 40 Squadron scored more than 5 victories in total (40 Squadron victories, where scored, are given in brackets: the rank is that finally attained).

| | | |
|---|---|---|
| Maj. R. J. O. Compston | 25 | |
| Capt. A. Hepburn | 16 | |
| Capt. C. W. Cudemore | 15 | |
| Capt. R. L. Chidlaw-Roberts | 10 | (2) |
| Lt. H. B. Redler | 10 | (3) |
| Capt. A. T. Drinkwater | 9 | (3) |
| Capt. G. L. Lloyd | 8 | (4) |
| Maj. J. B. Quested | 8 | |
| Capt. H. A. Rigby | 6 | |

# Note

1.    This data is drawn from Shores *et al*, *Above the Trenches*.

# 7

# Halcyon Years:
## April 1931–August 1939

IMMEDIATELY following the Great War, the British government reduced the Royal Air Force from a peak of 280 squadrons to a force one-tenth that size, mostly stationed abroad. Yet the future of even this remnant seemed uncertain, and that the RAF survived may be put down to circumstance and to the sympathy and prescience of Winston Churchill, the Minister responsible for demobilization, Viscount Weir, the Secretary of State, and General Trenchard, the founder of the RAF.

Two sets of circumstances provided a strong case for the retention of the RAF. One was the cost of policing the Empire, and another, closer to home, the defence of Great Britain. During 1920–22 deteriorating Anglo-French relations led Lloyd George to announce the Government's intention to raise the strength of the Home Defence Air Force tenfold, to 500 machines. Electoral defeat for Lloyd George threw all into doubt, but the Salisbury Committee came down in favour of expansion, and in June 1923 a new programme ordered that fifty-two squadrons be created for home defence, with a ratio of two to one in favour of bombers over fighters.

The 1923 expansion scheme was to be completed by 1928, but financial stringencies, a strong peace lobby, and international developments, most notably the 1925 Locarno Treaty, led the Cabinet to delay completion by five years. Consequently by 1932, only forty-two out of the fifty-two units envisaged had been formed. Of those one was 40 Squadron.

The expansion programme included new aerodromes, and it was at one of these, Upper Heyford in Oxfordshire, that on 1 April 1931 No 40 (Bomber) Squadron came into being under the command of Sqn/Ldr M. L. Taylor, AFC. Malcolm Taylor was a First World War pilot, and one of his first acts was to ask the RAF Air Historical Branch to supply information on the Squadron during the Great War. On learning of its association with Mick Mannock, Taylor obtained the combat report of Mannock's victory over von Bertrab on 12 August 1917, having it framed and hung in the Squadron crew room. In 1937, at the time of the Squadron's 21st birthday celebrations, this combat report was to be the founding item of a collection of memorabilia.

A sense of the Squadron's past was also evident in the trophies which were early presented to the Squadron:

> One prized possession of the Squadron is a trophy for inter-flight bombing at Catfoss. It takes the form of a silver model of a 'Gordon', and the pedestal is inscribed 'Presented to the Officers of No. 40 (Bomber) Squadron, R.A.F., by C. R. Fairey, esq., M.B.E., in memory of those officers who lost their lives whilst serving in the Great War.' Mr. J. D. Siddeley is giving another trophy, for inter-flight gunnery, and Col. Robert Lorraine [sic], the first C.O. of the Squadron, has also promised to present a trophy.[1]

The aircraft the Squadron was to fly was the Fairey Gordon, 40 being the first unit so equipped. A large twin bay biplane, based on the successful Fairey IIIF, the Gordon differed from its predecessor in its radial engine, the Armstrong Siddeley Panther IIA of 525 hp, this conferring a top speed of 145 mph, a range of 600 miles, and a service ceiling of 22,000 feet. Cruising at between 110 and 120 mph, carrying a 460-lb bomb load, and provided with a forward firing Vickers machine gun, and a Lewis gun for rear defence, the Gordon carried a crew of two, pilot and air gunner.

Forty was established as a three flight squadron, and the Flight Commanders were F/Lts J. E. L. Drabble (A Flight), C. C. Edwards (B), and R. J. H. Holland (C)—all veterans of the First World War. Tom Sayers, then a fitter in A Flight, recalls that Drabble had an artificial leg, and 'when the hinge needed oiling his cry for "Herman", his fitter, could be heard throughout the hangar'.

The Station Commander at Upper Heyford was, Sayers recalls, a sports fanatic who

> decided that inter-Flight sport was better than Station sport. It gave more people a chance of taking part. Once a month of a Friday afternoon a cross-country run was held. Every person fit, under 35, and not on duty, had to take part, officers and other ranks. A short cut through the hedge was soon found but was closed by RAF police the next time. A number cooled their feet in the canal. The Station Commander came in well up the list. On the Station morning parade on the following Monday, as S/Ldr Taylor hobbled on he was heard to exclaim loudly, "What the hell are you laughing at, Drabble?".

Sayers continues:

> The inter-Flight sport was a success. My friend, LAC Carter, was the undefeated heavyweight boxing champion. He was never opposed, fortunately, as he hadn't a clue about boxing! We had several RAF boxers on the station but they were excluded from the inter-Flight games, which was just as well.

Malcolm Taylor seems to have been an austere man, fair-minded but humourless. He ran a tight ship, and when Major F. A. de V. Robertson

24. Pilots of 40 Squadron, Upper Heyford, April 1932. (l to r) Sgts Elmy, Harris, Pattenden, Sowden, Evans; F/O D. G. Morris; Flt/Lts J. E. L. Drabble, C. C. Edwards, R. J. H. Holland; (behind) F/O N. C. M. Styche; Sqdn/Ldr M. L. Taylor; (behind) P/O O. P. E. Williams; F/O H. V. L'Amy; P/O Taylor; F/Os H. P. Wilson, G. Calvert; Sgt J. W. E. Christian; P/O G. W. Montagu; Sgt O'Brien; P/O R. H. Page; Sgt Avent; F/O L. F. H. Orr; P/O W. H. N. Turner. ('Flight' photo via T. G. B. Sayers.)

visited Upper Heyford, in April 1932, to gather material for an article on 40 in a *Flight* series, he was impressed:

> It does not take very much experience of regular fighting units to enable a spectator to see when a squadron or regiment is well disciplined. One quickly spots accuracy in details of all sorts, from the correct alignment of machines in front of the hangars to the speed with which each order is carried out. When one notices in addition that every officer and man looks cheerful and jumps to do his job as though he enjoyed doing it, one can be sure that one is watching a first-class squadron. And such is No. 40 (Bomber) Squadron of the Royal Air Force.[2]

The Fairey Gordon was staid and cumbersome, but devoid of nasty surprises. This was just as well, since in the 1930s new pilots were expected, on their first squadron posting, to receive the instruction which later became the responsibility of Operational Training Units. After a familiarization flight with an experienced pilot, newcomers engaged in the standard programme of take-offs and landings, formation flying, local and cross country navigational flights, and practice bombing on the Otmoor range, north-east of Oxford. The latter was done at heights of up to 16,000 feet, and with no heating crews often returned to base half-frozen despite their Sidcot flying suits.

On 31 July 1932 the Squadron left Upper Heyford for annual exercises at No. 1 Armament Training Camp, Catfoss. Generally lasting a month, during which personnel lived under canvas, armament camps were a pleasant change from routine. Crews flew regularly, practising air to ground firing with the front gun and air to air firing at drogues with the Lewis in the rear cockpit, as well as bombing and formation flying.

At the time of 40's re-formation, Upper Heyford was home to 99 Squadron, equipped with Handley Page Hinaidi night bombers. This was not an ideal pairing, and it was envisaged that 40 would shift as soon as feasible to RAF Abingdon, then under construction. The records are silent on the point, but it appears that the Squadron remained under canvas at Catfoss until it moved to Abingdon, on 8 October 1932. It was to remain there until the outbreak of war.

One of the fine RAF stations built to designs by Sir Edwin Lutyens, Abingdon was regarded as one of the most desirable of all pre-war RAF postings. Eight miles from Oxford, it lay in rolling country whose villages contained attractive and welcoming public houses: 'quite the best pub-crawling district I have come across in England', it seemed to Hugh le Good, who joined the Squadron as a pilot officer in August 1933.

When 40 arrived at Abingdon, there was only a small Station staff in residence. Shortly afterwards, a Station Flight arrived from Upper Heyford (its CO a Flt/Lt E. C. Barlow, of whom 40 was in time to see much more),

25. The newly-completed Abingdon, 1932. (G. A. Mills.)

and later the Oxford University Air Squadron, but until XV Squadron
re-formed on 1 June 1934, 40 had the capacious messes, accommodation
and hangarage largely to itself. Those at Abingdon then recall empty rooms
and echoing hangars.

What was the social structure of the Squadron which moved to Abingdon
in October 1932? A description requires some understanding of the ways
by which men entered the RAF at that time.[3] Pilots fell into three categories.
A few in the Officers' Mess were Cranwell graduates, whose families had
been able to afford the £350 fees plus living expenses for two years at the
RAF College. These were career officers with a guarantee of promotion to
Squadron Leader. Serving alongside them, however, were those, more
numerous, who had entered the RAF on short service commissions, involving four years active service followed by six years in the reserve. For these
men, nicknamed 'Sainsburys Boys' or 'Butter Slappers', promotion to Flying
Officer was all that could be expected unless they were re-engaged for a
further four years active service.

The third category of pilots were sergeants, analogous to officers on
short-service commissions, since they were committed to flying for five years,
after which they returned to their ground trades. Usually ex-apprentices,

they shared the Sergeants' Mess with long-serving ground trade sergeants: men with whom they had little in common in age or outlook.

With the other ranks career prospects were again determined largely by the mode of entry. The élite were the ex-apprentices, those who had won entry to Halton (training as fitters or riggers) or Cranwell (as wireless mechanics). After three years training these young men looked forward to ten years regular service, and two in the reserve. The remaining tradesmen were recruits who, after basic training at Uxbridge, went to The School of Technical Training at Manston for instruction as, e.g., driver, fabric worker, vulcanizer or general fitter. These men might at best expect to rise to the rank of LAC. Halton and Cranwell 'Brats' could expect promotion (eventually) to sergeant.

At Abingdon, 40's training programme had pilots flying most weekdays, though rarely for more than an hour or so. Typically, indeed, they spent much of the day in the hangars, the officers in the flight offices and the sergeant pilots in the crew room, except during briefing, when all gathered in the latter. For the other ranks who volunteered as air gunners there were no such opportunities to talk shop: they were busy about their duties as armourers, riggers or whatever. Their sixpence a day additional flying pay was hard-earned.

The 1933 Armaments Camp, at Montrose, ended in fatalities. Bob Penwarn, then a sergeant pilot, later recalled:

All was completed on the Friday, and the unit was to fly back to Abingdon on the following Tuesday [26 September 1933]

At the time I owned a 1932 Morris Cowley—a two seater with a dickie—and coachbuilt. I was very proud of it. A Flight Sergeant friend had driven it up to Montrose. He had to return by air on the Friday, leaving me with the worry of how to get both aircraft and car back to Abingdon.

During the time at Montrose, we had another Sergeant Pilot posted to us. All of the crews had been operating as crews, so the new arrival, F/Sgt. Christian, did not get in much flying time. This saved the day for me, I considered. Chris., as we called him, was jumping for joy, as he could get some flying in and was due to be married the following Saturday.

On Tuesday I set off in the Morris early in the morning and the weather thickened terribly, and soon it got worse still—one of those North Sea fogs that plagued the east coast. Unknown to me it also covered the Midlands and southern England. The result was chaos.[4]

Hugh le Good, newly arrived at Abingdon, remembers the Gordons returning in ones and twos. Two aircraft did not return at all, however. One (Sgt J. W. E. Christian) crashed into the sea off Hartlepool. One of the Gordon's wheels was found on the shoreline, as (later) was the pilot's body, but of the gunner, Cpl A. C. Lewis, no trace was found. The other Gordon,

(F/O N. C. M. Styche) also crashed while trying to forced-land near Bamborough, and Styche and his gunner, AC1 M. A. C. White, were killed.

On 1 April 1934 Malcolm Taylor completed his term as CO. Remembered with respect rather than affection, he had built an efficient unit with pride in itself and its traditions. His successor, Sqn/Ldr E. I. Bussell, who commanded 40 for sixteen months, continued the good work, but has left no personal impression on those who served under him. What little can be said about his period at CO, therefore, is limited to incidents which took place during his term of command.

One of these was an accident which ended a promising career. On 3 September 1934 AC2 F. W. Holland was standing by a Gordon, using arm and hand signals, when his right hand was struck and amputated by the propeller. Holland, it was adjudged, was injured not because of negligence but because 'lack of experience and zeal' had led him to place himself too close to the aircraft.

In June 1934, the Squadron left Abingdon for an armaments training camp, at North Coates in Lincolnshire, the ground party travelling in a convoy of ancient lorries. The officer in charge was P/O Geoffrey Mills, and he, impatient at the 15 mph at which the convoy was moving, went on ahead to visit a girlfriend. It was a mistake, for the lorries broke down one by one as they processed funereally up the Great North Road. A carpetting by the CO resulted.

Bombing was not a precise art at this period, and it is indicative of how imprecise it was that armourer Vic. Lilley remembers vividly a success scored during the armaments camp at North Coates:

we practised bombing on an armoured motor boat off Bridlington. We were not told the speed of the boat (we estimated this by studying the wake) and Sgt Woods and his AG, LAC Waugh, actually hit the boat with their first bomb.

Forty did not only bomb motor launches, however. Another annual exercise took them to coastal aerodromes such as Tangmere to practice bombing HMS *Centurion*, a dreadnought converted to a radio-controlled target ship.

Most practice bombing from Abingdon was carried out at Otmoor, and it was while engaged in one of these exercises on 5 October 1934 that Sgt Blackler, with Vic. Lilley in the rear cockpit, had the disconcerting experience of watching the propeller fly off. Gliding down, Blackler was able to find a field large enough for him to carry out a dead-stick landing.

During Sqn/Ldr Bussell's term as CO there was only one major innovation, an open day at RAF Abingdon marking the first Empire Air Day, 24 May 1934. As part of this consciousness-raising and public relations exercise, the Station was open from 1400 to 1900 hrs, over 2,000 adults and children being admitted at a charge of one shilling per adult and sixpence per child. The money raised went to the RAF Benevolent Fund, and the crowd viewed static exhibits, and was treated to a flying display. The Empire Air Day displays were a great success, and the following year Abingdon playing host to a crowd of nearly 2,800. The static and flying displays were much as in 1934, but innovations were the sale of programmes and a recruiting bureau.

On 6 August 1935 Sqn/Ldr Bussell handed over to Sqn/Ldr E. P. Ledger MBE, who was to lead 40 until the last day of 1936, and in the process see it through two re-equipment programmes whereby the Fairey Gordons gave place to Hawker Harts, and these to the very similar Hinds.

The Hart, with which 40 re-equipped in November 1935, was not a new type, having entered service in 1930. Forty, indeed, was the last United Kingdom-based unit to be equipped with the type, and the only one to receive the Hart (Special), which was powered by a de-rated Kestrel X engine of 510 hp, and fitted with a tropical radiator, desert equipment, heavy duty tyres and a braked undercarriage. Yet though the Hart itself was about to be superseded in squadron service by the Hind, it represented a considerable advance over the Gordon. A biplane with a crew of two, an engine of much the same power, fitted with the same defensive armament, and carrying a slightly larger 500-lb bomb load, the Hart was smaller, more agile, and vastly more streamlined. The result was a top speed of 184 mph, as against 145 mph for the Gordon, as well as a greatly enhanced rate of climb.

It was, perhaps, the difference in performance which led, on 9 November 1935, to the worst accident which befell 40 Squadron between the wars. Hugh le Good recalls:

> We had taken some pilots and aircrew up in Gordons to Cardington and were returning with the Harts. On this occasion we had a leading formation of Harts in V formation, followed by three Gordons, which we had used to take up the crews, following behind. And over the aerodrome, on breaking up the formation in order to land, one of the Harts turned very sharply and collided with the wing of one of the Gordons. The Hart was flown by a P/O Ross, who was a great buddy of mine. Unfortunately he had with him as his aircrew a very nice lad called LAC Waugh, who had flown a considerable number of times with me. The sergeant pilot who was flying the Gordon [Sgt W. Park] was also killed.

An enquiry concluded that the fault lay with Ross, who on the break-up of the formation 'climbed and dived (contrary to regulations) and turned 180 degrees, and flew into an aircraft of the second flight'. The enquiry noted that the flight commander had contravened Squadron Standing Orders in not breaking up the formation before reaching the circuit, but concluded that this was not a contributory factor.

The Hart (Special) was issued to 40 as an interim measure, and in March 1936 was replaced by the Hawker Hind. In most respects identical, the Hind

26. 40 Sqn Hinds in flight. (W. G. Moseby.)

was powered by a fully supercharged Kestrel V engine of 640 hp, had a cut-away gunner's cockpit and a tailwheel in place of the skid fitted to the Hart. Maximum speed was only marginally increased—to 186 mph—but take-off and altitude performance noticeably improved, as Dick Maling, who joined the Squadron at this time, recalls:

> Pushing through the throttle gate the extra horsepower came in with a wallop, and resulted in a spectacular take off and climb when compared with the normally aspirated Hart.

The tail wheel was also an improvement, but Dick Maling recalls that it had disadvantages too, notably 'a decided tendency to swing when taxying in strong wind conditions'. This apart, however, the Hind, (like the Hart), was regarded with great affection as fun to fly, aerobatic, reliable, fairly viceless and for its time, modern and fast.

Maling arrived at Abingdon in January 1936 on his first posting, and Abingdon and 40 Squadron made a great impression, not least the strict social protocols:

> Pilot officers and flying officers were referred to as 'Mister', and their calling cards were so worded. Flight lieutenants and above were always referred to by their rank.

Calling on officers was punctiliously observed by every junior officer upon being posted to a new station. Cards had to be of regulation size and engraved, *not* printed.

Within a few weeks of arrival an officer dropped cards on the Station Commander, squadron and flight commanders and all married officers. Usually the operation meant dropping the cards in a small metal box outside each house—invariably the box had the owner's name and rank, and the words 'Not at home', painted on the front. The box was left in place even when the house was occupied.

Correct dress for dropping cards was a lounge suit, and the time between four and five p.m. It was unusual for the resident officer to invite junior officers in (F/Lt Jones was an exception to this rule). The procedure was cut and dried. The calling officer dropped two cards (one for the husband and one for his wife) and later the husband would return the call by placing one of his cards in the caller's letter rack in the Mess.

Dress was equally strictly prescribed. Save on Sunday evening, when supper was provided, and mufti permitted, dining required a dinner jacket, but on Dining In nights (held every week) and Guest nights (about twice a month) blue mess kit was *de rigueur*. Attendance at formal dinners was obligatory, but officers could sign out for others.

Within this structure, the gap between junior officers and their CO was considerable, and many who served with the Squadron at this time comment on how remote he seemed, rarely dining in, and not often spoken to, since day to day transactions were undertaken through the flight commanders. When 40 was re-formed these men were veterans of WWI, expecting to see out their time as flight lieutenants. By early 1936, RAF expansion meant that many of them had been posted away on promotion, while others had retired. Their successors were younger men who had entered the service in the late twenties and early thirties. The C Flight Commander, however, Flt/Lt A. A. Jones, was one of the old school, remembered by Dick Maling as 'an unassuming, gentle introvert; fatherly, and popular with younger officers'.

The formation of new squadrons under Expansion Scheme F was accomplished largely by detaching flights from existing units. The first detachment, for 40, occurred in January 1936, when C Flight became 104 Squadron. Of cadre strength, with four Harts and three pilots besides Flt/Lt Jones, 104 moved from Abingdon to Hucknall in mid-November. Appropriately, it was to spend much of the war operating alongside 40 in the Mediterranean.

By the time war broke out, two further squadrons had been hived off—B Flight as 62 Squadron on 12 April 1937, and B Flight (again) as 185 Squadron on 1 June 1938. On each occasion the Flight was reconstituted, but after the detachment of C Flight, 40 ceased to be a three-flight squadron. Shortages of men and machines made such an arrangement impractical.

27. Officers of 40 Squadron, January 1936.
Rear (l to r): P/O F. L. Newall, P/O A. G. G. Baird, P/O J. R. Maling, P/O Bayley, P/O B. V. Robinson. Front: F/O H. J. F. Le Good, Flt/Lt A. A. Jones, Sqn/Ldr A. P. Ledger, F/O W. J. Smail, P/O J. W. Haythorn. (F. L. Newall.)

The year 1936 brought the usual armament camps during the summer and early autumn, and the Empire Air Day Pageant, with a further enlarged programme of exhibits and activities, the former including several RAF aircraft types not in service at Abingdon. A Recruiting Enquiries Bureau was also set up.

July 1936 saw the Squadron participating in Observer Corps exercises, giving the new organization practice in aircraft recognition and in plotting the height, distance, and numbers of incoming aircraft. Just prior to that, however, on 8 July, 40 had been involved in a far grander event: a Royal Review at Mildenhall. inspected by Edward VIII and his brother, the Duke of York (afterwards George VI). R. A. Bain, one of the first direct entry air observers, remembers:

All ashine in bright aluminium, 40 Squadron was selected to represent the Light Bomber Force at the front of rows of heavy green/brown bombers. Pilot and rear seat occupant stood either side of the nose of the aircraft, dressed in sparkling white overalls, sidecaps and shiny black footwear. To

ensure that the new white overalls stayed so they were carried by transport
and not issued till the last moment; unluckily an oil drum on the wagon
had leaked, and the overalls were yellow spotted. Not unresourceful, the
CO sent to the kitchen for some of the whitewash they used on their pipes
and drains. This applied to the spots was reasonably effective, and he and
the flight commanders completed the job with sticks of chalk. H.M. flew
himself in dead on time, took the Royal Salute and was led to the right
of the line where the C.O. was presented. He in turn accompanied H.M.
along our front, stopping to present the flight commanders. H.M. cracked
a few jokes and then raised a number of pertinent queries regarding our
training, fitness and competence. H.M. was accompanied by his brother later
K.G.VI, the smartest person I had seen in R.A.F. uniform. Whilst H.M.
was conversing with the flight commander, the Duke of York spent his
time inspecting me minutely, I am sure he saw through the whitewash and
even to the holes in my boots.

Until 1935 the RAF relied, in filling the rear cockpit, on part-timers
drawn from the ground trades. New and faster aircraft, however, required
specialist aircrew, and in March 1936 No. 1 Air Observers School opened
at North Coates. The course involved the theory and practice of both guns
and bomb aiming, as well as, R. A. Bain recalls, 'navigation at the Educational
Test level, high falutin' stuff including astral and the solution of P.Z.X.
triangles for position finding'. There was, however, 'nothing practical. I
hadn't even seen a sextant.' He continues:

> In June I was posted to No. 40 Squadron. As an Observer I was appointed
> to the lead aircraft in A Flight, provided with a chart board and map of
> England; a pocket watch; a course and distance calculator; a calculator for
> true wind and air speed and height, and I was let loose.
>
> We were flying from grass airfields surrounded by hedges. My pilot, the
> Flight Commander, was hard of hearing. Drawing attention to the Gosport
> tubes, flexible aluminium piping between the two cockpits with a mouthpiece
> at one end and earpieces at the other, he said they were useless, adding that
> if you want me to go to the right, tap me on the right shoulder, to the left
> on the left, and if we are all right, just leave me alone. He did, however,
> have very keen eyesight, and could see the aerodrome we were seeking as
> soon as it broke the horizon.
>
> Two days later I found myself aloft at the front of a formation engaged in
> a triangular cross country flight. I had gleaned what information I could from
> other air gunners, marked the desired track on the face of the chartboard and
> places I would need to identify to establish my actual track. I also noted the
> ETA for each turning point. In the event as we crossed the hedge I was lost.
> I stayed lost. At the appropriate time I gave the pilot a chitty with the new
> course to follow and lo and behold at the appointed time approached the
> River Thames and the aerodrome came into sight. We landed, I was called to
> the Adjutant, he asked for my logbook—he too had been in the formation—it

was as blank as my mind. I got more than a mild rocketing. I kept my position, and slowly improved.

Arthur Ledger, whose term as CO ended on the first day of 1937, is remembered as pleasant and quiet-spoken, and Cecil Barlow apart, he was certainly the most approachable of the pre-war COs. His successor was Sqn/Ldr A. H. H. MacDonald, whom Douglas Wilson, then fresh from Cranwell, recalls as

> in his late thirties, a great character, with outside interests and moving in somewhat august society. He was very much the CO, but very fair, very loyal and very understanding. He had a dry sense of humour, and one of my first memories was of his taking a flight of six Hinds, putting us in line astern and flying very low over George Bernard Shaw's house—No 6 in stepped down formation being virtually on the ground! Later he told us that G.B.S. thoroughly enjoyed the show and was "most amused".

On 25 February 1937 MacDonald presided at the most significant event since the refounding of the Squadron: the 21st anniversary of its formation. Bad weather forced the abandonment of a formation flight to Gosport, but there was an all ranks dinner and dance, at which the 160 guests

28. 21st Anniversary All Ranks Dinner, 25 February 1937.
('Aeroplane' via R. F. Richardson.)

included 11 who served with 40 during World War One—de Burgh, Middleton, Wolff, and MacLanachan amongst them. The main speaker was MacLanachan, whose *Fighter Pilot* had been published in 1936. The evening was a great success, and *The Aeroplane*, reporting the event (17 March, p. 323), concluded that 'other units who are planning celebrations of the twenty-first anniversary of their formation would be well advised to use a similar programme'.

In his speech Sqn/Ldr MacDonald announced that a collection of memorabilia had been established, with gifts from MacLanachan (photos of men and machines), flight commander's streamers (Middleton), Mannock's prop tip (Kay), a canvas side from a 40 Squadron Nieuport (Stuart-Smith), F. E. 8 prop tip (de Burgh), and programme of entertainment from France (Muir). The collection was displayed in the crew rooms at Abingdon, Wyton and Alconbury, but vanished after the Home Echelon became 156 Squadron in February 1942.

The Squadron's coming of age was marked in another way, too, as fitter John Corser recalls:

> The CO obtained special permision for us airmen to be issued with the new uniform—slacks instead of britches and puttees, jackets instead of tunics, shoes instead of boots, and collars and ties—in advance of the rest of the Air Force so that we could wear it at the celebration functions.

Photographs show the men resplendent in their new uniforms, and point up one of the results of the changes: a reduction in the visual differences between officers and other ranks. This did not indicate a change in the social structure of the RAF: the gap between officers and other ranks remained wide and deep. But in a sense the change was a forerunner of the move to battledress taken during the war—a change which narrowed still further the gap between officers' uniforms and those of other ranks.

How wide the gap was in the RAF in the 1930s is recalled by the then Cpl Algy Jane:

> One couldn't approach an officer without filling in a form for a formal interview, no matter what the subject. You had to fill in a formal application and await the outcome of the application which would be at the convenience of the Flight Commander, you couldn't tell when. And then for this interview you would be formally marched in and stand to attention in front of him. There was no relaxed atmosphere of talking or being able to relate any personal or confidential matters, so it was hardly surprising officers didn't get to know their men.

On 20 April 1937 the Squadron was presented with a new crest by Air Chief Marshal Sir John Steel. When reformed, 40 had adopted a crest showing a 250-lb bomb between two wings, and supported by the motto

29. Officers and men of 40 Squadron, 25 February 1937.

The front row is ——, Flt/Sgt Morris, Sgt Scrace, Sgt Boyce, Sgt Edwards, Flt/Sgt Green, W/O C. F. Glenn, P/O L. D. Wilson, P/O L. E. Abel, F/O C. F. Sarsby, Sqn/Ldr A. H. H. MacDonald, F/O J. W. Haythorn, P/O T. N. Partridge, Sgt McArdle, ——, ——, ——, Sgt Haytor, ——, Flt/Sgt Carter.
(J. Cornelius.)

*Fiat justitia coelum ruat* [Let justice be done, though the heavens fall]. How or by whom this unofficial crest was chosen is not clear. Nor is it apparent why the decision was made to replace it with another. But the new crest, showing a broom over the motto, *Hostem a coelo expellere* [To drive the enemy from the skies], was certainly more in keeping with the Squadron's traditions in alluding to Mick Mannock's admonition to his pilots to 'sweep the ———— from the skies'. XV Squadron might make wisecracks about lavatory cleaning brushes, but 40 had a crest both distinctive and appropriate.

These major events over, 40 resumed the familiar pattern of activities, the highlights being the Abingdon Empire Air Day display—which in 1937 attracted 6,000 people—and the month spent at the Armament Training Camp at Catfoss. Flying accidents with the Hind were few, the only ones of note being on 28 April, when Sgt W. B. Confan suffered engine failure during a low flying exercise, and in avoiding high tension cables hit the ground heavily, turning the aircraft over, and on 16 June, when P/O L. E. Abel suffered engine failure on take-off and in a valiant effort to land crosswind, dropped a wing, which hit the ground, causing the Hind to cartwheel. Neither accident resulted in serious injury.

On 21 February 1938, Sqn/Ldr MacDonald was posted to Prague as Air Attaché. His successor was Sqn/Ldr H. C. Parker, a contrast in almost every respect. MacDonald was a tall, thin man of considerable presence, Parker shorter, and plump. MacDonald did not fly often—none of the COs did—but enjoyed doing so. Parker, however, showed less enthusiasm for flying, and this (a cardinal offence in the eyes of officers and men alike) was one reason for his unpopularity, another being that he lost contact with those serving under him, including his flight commanders.

Though Parker's remoteness did nothing to enhance his popularity, it did not significantly affect the running of the Squadron, since the crucial individuals were the flight commanders and the SNCOs to whom they delegated day to day responsibility for the running of the Flights. For the Flight was the crucial unit. As fitter Eric Taylor puts it:

> Pride in being one of the Sqdn. came naturally, and was universal throughout the members, whatever their trade or calling. But one thing that perhaps was a little more important was being a member of your *flight*. The Sqdn. was everything, but your 'flight' was something else. A family within a family. The important thing was we got on together.

Important it was, and when a flight commander was felt to be remote or unsympathetic—as with one in 1937 nicknamed 'doggy' (i.e. dogmatic)—difficulties arose, not only for the rank and file, but also for the NCOs who stood between the Flight Commander and the other ranks.

During 1937 the two Flight Sergeants were Thompson and McArdle, men highly respected. When the latter was promoted to warrant officer engineer, however, his place in B Flight was taken by Flt/Sgt Goble, of whom many have less happy memories. Gordon Ogden, arriving at Abingdon with fellow Halton Brats, reported to B Flight office:

> Goble asked us who the hell we were, and when we replied that we were fitters fresh from Halton he said, 'Well, go back there, you are no bloody good to me'. We all turned to go away and he said, 'Where do you lot think you are going?', and I foolishly replied, 'Back to Halton'. He gave me a withering look and said, "Oh, so we've got a comedian here, have we. Well, do any of you know what the Squadron Crest is?' After a pause I summoned up courage and said, 'Yes, F/Sgt, the Squadron's crest is a broom'. He said, 'That's right. You'll find four big ones in the corner. Now grab hold of them and sweep the hangar out.' It appeared that F/Sgt Goble did not like ex-apprentices. Personally I don't think he liked anybody.

From Algy Jane, however, we learn of Goble the family man, and of the pressure that he was working under, carrying out the directives of a flight commander who operated on the 'upstairs, downstairs' principle. One member of the Flight remembers Goble coming out of the Flight Commander's office and hurling a mug across the hangar in rage and frustration, and Algy Jane, in the midst of a tense confrontation with his Flight Commander, during which he was accused of mutiny, recalls Goble appearing in the door of the office, in response to a shouted summons, his face white as a sheet.

Early in 1938 it was announced that 40 was to begin night flying training. The Hind was unsuited to night flying (the flames from the unshrouded stub exhausts interfering with the pilot's night vision) and Abingdon was ill-equipped for it, the flare path being a single row of goose-neck flares, similar to an oil can with a wick in the spout, and fuelled by paraffin. R. F. Richardson, detailed to be at the landing end of the flare path, recalls that the CO had a chair brought out, and sat there for an hour or so, assessing the different pilots' performances, adding: 'Our position was at times quite precarious: one minute you would detect the exhaust flames, the next a wing would pass so low that one had to duck to avoid it'.

David Green, newly arrived from Halton, found himself tending the beacon which flashed out the airfield code, enabling the pilots to identify the base. 'A mini-lighthouse like structure high on wooden stilts' it was fuelled by acetylene, and driven by clockwork. Unfortunately the mechanism tended to stick, and when it did Green had to set it going once more. He writes:

> When the mechanism stuck the situation was that the pilot light remained alight while gas leaked slowly but inexorably into the burning chamber. Thus, when I set off on my bike I knew very well what would happen. I would climb the portable ladder very cautiously and open the access window very slowly. Then, either immediately or within a few seconds, the trapped gas

would explode and blow me off the ladder onto the ground six feet below. The crisis would then be over until the next time.

Night flying was not greatly enjoyed. In daylight, however, the Squadron was in its element, and the pilots could express their *joie de vivre* during cross-country exercises. Eric Taylor recalls that

> the mechanic often flew with the pilot so one had quite a few hours in the air. One often found oneself beating up an express train on the Paddington-Bristol-South Wales route, to be told on one's return: 'If anyone should ask, we were doing rate one turns in cloud'.

In May 1938, after a period deployed to the grass strip at Weston-on-the-Green, 40 took its Hinds up to West Freugh for the annual Armaments Camp. For David Green the Camp—the last before the Munich Crisis—was idyllic:

> We enjoyed the increased tempo of flying and the challenge of keeping the aircraft serviceable 'in the field' without the luxury of hangars etc. The weather was marvellous, spirits were at their highest, and in the deep Scottish countryside, although we were practising for war, this was the last thought in our minds.

Back at Abingdon 40 was involved in the 1938 Empire Air Day, the most elaborate yet. The range of service aircraft on display included a stripped down and war-ready Hind. It was to be the type's last appearance at Abingdon, for the RAF was replacing it with the service's first monoplane day bomber, the Fairey Battle. When B Flight became 185 Squadron at the beginning of June, it was equipped with Battles. Re-equipment for 40 could only be weeks away.

Though unavoidable, the departure of the Hind was regretted. David Green recalls that

> to us the Hind was thing of beauty with its silver airframe and its sleek, polished nose pointing upwards with a certain modest arrogance. As befitted thoroughbreds they were kept in mint condition. Saturday mornings were devoted to a thorough 'grooming', when we scrubbed the silver fabric with soft soap while the pilots set to with Brasso until the aluminium nose cowlings shone like mirrors.

Green took every opportunity to fly, and the joy of flights in the Squadron's Hinds remains vivid:

> There was something about flying in those open cockpits that was lost forever once cockpit canopies were introduced. For a start we flew standing up in the rear cockpit with just a 'monkey chain' attached to one's harness for security. This, coupled with the tremendous force of the slipstream, the lovely crackle of the Rolls Royce Kestrel engine, the high-pitched hum of the flying wires and the smell of exhaust fumes made it an experience to be remembered and repeated as often as one could get away with it.

The Fairey Battle, with which the Squadron re-equipped in August 1938, was a low wing monoplane of stressed skin construction, powered by a Rolls Royce Merlin engine of 1,030 hp. Carrying a 1,000-lb bomb load twice as far as the Hind, and at a maximum speed of 241 mph, it represented a major technical advance. Yet even before it entered service with 40 it was recognized that the aircraft was underpowered and (with one forward and one rear gun) poorly defended. The Chief of Air Staff sought to cancel further orders, but to enable RAF expansion to continue, and to keep the new shadow factories busy, production continued.

Pilots found the Battle stable, if heavy, and good for formation flying. Observers were less impressed, since their accommodation provided them with no view upwards or to the side unless they joined the WOp/AG at the rear of the long glasshouse, and downwards vision only through a panel in the floor which was often fouled by glycol or oil. John Holmes writes:

> The bomb aiming position was immediately behind the radiator and oil cooler and was unbearably hot if the power was put on the engine, even having the effect of melting the chinagraph in the bomb sight pencil. It also resulted in the Air Observer becoming the focus point for all oil leaks; goggles were essential.

Re-equipment with the Battle marks a watershed in the history of 40 Squadron, since the moment when biplanes gave place to monoplanes was also when the Squadron began to be reorganized along more modern lines. As David Green remarks:

> Not only did we have to master new techniques and skills, but more, and different, trades had to be introduced. Our trusty Fitter's Mates had to go, and in their place we fitters were assisted by two new tradesmen grades—semi-skilled Flight Mechanics for the engines and Flight Riggers for the airframes. Such an increase in establishment called for increases in the numbers of NCOs and, thus, more promotions. And so the new order began.

One aspect of the 'new order' was a breaking down of traditional promotion expectations. It took Algy Jane seven years to attain the rank of corporal. Less than two years later, David Green and his friend David Chapman, eighteen months out of Halton, and LACs for a month, were corporals also. 'Our embarrassment', says David Green, 'was so acute that we didn't dare show our faces in the Corporals' Club for weeks afterwards'.

There was also a change in personnel, as David Green notes:

> Not only had we lost many of the familiar faces of colleagues and friends to the new squadrons but the new faces of their replacements were added to by the influx of many more ancillary tradesmen such as armourers and wireless mechanics/operators, and a whole new breed of short-service Sergeant Pilots and, to our horror, Sergeant Observers in barely worn uniforms and bright

new brevets. Add to these the many Wireless Operator/Air Gunners needed
to make up the requisite crews of three per aircraft and the increase in our
numbers was considerable.

The first two specialist WOp/AGs on Squadron, ACIs S. Jones and
H. W. Oxley, had joined prior to the departure of the Hinds, but they and
one or two specialist observers apart, the rear cockpits were still occupied
by volunteers. The Battle, however, required a specialist three-man crew
(pilot, observer and wireless operator/air gunner). Some were drawn by
remustering from the ranks of the part-time aircrew, and some posted in.
But most needed further training, and Jones and Oxley found themselves
engaged in introducing air gunners to the intricacies of the latest in wireless
equipment, the TR 1082/1083. For young men recently qualified, it was a
daunting task. And since WOp/AGs were also expected to service their
equipment, their working days were full indeed.

Even so, there was opportunity for relaxation. For Bill Oxley

> Sunday morning was the best day of the week. No compulsory Church parade,
> lie in bed till about eight a.m. if you wanted to go to breakfast; later, if you
> didn't fancy going to breakfast. The wireless set tuned to Radio Luxemburg
> and the card games would start.

For some, Abingdon offered superb walking or cycling in idyllic countryside,
as well as the quiet delights of Oxford, but for Bill the highlight of the
week was

> the weekly dance at the Abingdon Liberal Club. The Libs we used to call it,
> and every Saturday night you could find 40 Sqdn WOp/AGs there in force.
> I don't think there were more than four or five who didn't go. In fact that
> was the only day of the week we used to fraternise with the bods of XV
> Sqdn who were stationed at Abingdon with us.

For Alan Cody, one of the 'Sergeant Observers in barely worn uniforms
and bright new brevets', one of the strongest memories is of the Sergeants'
Mess, and the protocol attaching to it:

> Peace-time protocol was in force and discipline was strict. The tradition of
> buying drinks all round for wearing one's hat in the Mess was strictly enforced,
> and the Station Warrant Officer was all-powerful; nobody, but nobody, sat
> in his chair.
>
> One morning a friend and I were, quite legitimately, alone in the Mess,
> playing snooker when a practice gas alert alarm sounded. The drill was to
> don one's gas mask whatever the circumstances; this we did and continued
> with the game. The S.W.O. entered the room, unexpectedly, and ordered
> us to remove the masks. When I said, 'But Sir, there's a gas attack', he replied,
> 'NOT in the Sergeant's Mess!'

An officer's life was leisurely, as Bill Bromley, who joined 40 in June 1938, remembers:

> We had a particular time to be down at the hangars, but the timetable wasn't too onerous, and we enjoyed most magnificent breakfasts, as indeed all meals. There was the Maitre d' standing by the silver dishes and covers, asking: 'What would you like this morning, Sir? Mushrooms and bacon? There are some very nice kidneys, some fried eggs, scrambled eggs?' You name it, and there it was. We were really a pampered lot.
>
> At lunch we would wander back to the mess and have a most magnificent lunch. Wednesday afternoon was sports afternoon. Weekends we were off, and usually went the 60 miles from Abingdon into London. A few chaps would have a car, and we would have a lovely weekend there, and usually end up in Piccadilly Circus at the pilot officer's paradise, which was called the Brasserie Universelle.

Bill also recalls the juxtaposition of formality at dinner and high jinks afterwards:

> On dining in nights, we dressed up in mess kit, with tables beautifully set with candelabra and silverware. One would order one's own choice of wine and that would go on the mess bill. Port would be passed and really people were feeling pretty mellow at the end of the dinner. From there we would go in to the ante-room, all a bit high-spirited, have a pint or two of beer and get down to stupid mess games.

These games were not to everyone's taste, and some officers developed the habit of going to their rooms, and locking their doors. Others regarded this as anti-social, and one evening Bromley led a group which burst open the locked doors, carried the occupants off and doused them in cold baths. For this and an earlier misdemeanour he was brought before the Station Commander, Wg/Cdr H. S. P. Walmsley, and given a severe dressing-down. This was followed, though, by off-the-record approval of the way the young New Zealander had reacted against those who did not 'join in'.

Hugh Walmsley was no doubt less understanding when two young officers, walking home from their usual haunt, The Dog House, Frilford Heath, found a steamroller, still fired up, on the side of the road. They got it moving and headed back to Abingdon, where, Bill Bromley recalls, they smashed through the balance arm at the gate, and ended up 'right in the middle of Hugh Walmsley's pride and joy', the rose garden in front of the Mess.

The Dog House was the site of an elaborate practical joke, played by F/Os Hugh Smeddle and Bob Batt, as Hugh recalls:

> One evening Bob Batt and I decided to have a little fun at the expense of the local gathering. We pretended to have a flaming row, and the height of

the fracas I drew a revolver and shot him twice in the stomach, the blanks
making a most satisfactory noise in the enclosed space. Bob did his dying act,
and I picked up one of his legs and dragged him out of the room, sliding
quite easily on the parquet floor, remarking en route that it served him right,
walked back to the bar and ordered a pint. Bob soon appeared and joined
me at the bar without saying a word, to the evident relief and rather forced
laughter of our captive audience.

During the summer of 1938 international tension rose over German
territorial demands in the Sudetenland. Mobilization plans required No. 1
Group, Bomber Command, to proceed to France as part of an Advanced
Air Striking Force, and squadrons had been warned to be fit for service
with the AASF by 1 October. But early in September, advice was received
that 40 and XV Squadrons should be ready by 15 September. This caused
difficulties, as the Abingdon Station ORB indicates:

This warning came at a time when these squadrons were engaged in the
process of forming their second Flights and re-equipping their original flights
after 'throwing off' Flights to form the nucleus of Nos 106 and 185 (B)
squadrons. Progress in preparation for war was therefore considerably hampered
and made extremely difficult owing to large deficiencies in the normal peace
time basis in addition to the extra requirements for mobilization.
On Sunday, 24 September, events became extremely grave and on that day
orders came from the Air Ministry establishing continuous Point-to-Point
watches. That same evening orders came for the immediate recall of all ranks
from leave.

The following three days were spent making all possible preparations, including the 'painting of aircraft with war markings and obliterating wing
identification letters and numbers'.

By September 27th mobilization seemed inevitable, and that evening a
Station Commander's conference was held to settle the details of such items
as the reception of Reservists, but the following day, when the Prime
Minister, Neville Chamberlain, met Adolf Hitler, tension eased, and by the
end of the first week in October, the Station ORB notes, 'routine had
practically returned to normal'.

In preparation for the move to France, the Station Medical Officer, assisted
by medical orderlies, gave everyone on the station their 'overseas jabs'. David
Green recalls what followed:

We were awakened in the middle of the night by a highly excited NCO
who was accompanied by a Medical Orderly demanding to know if anyone
was suffering from head-aches or felt unwell. The short answer was unanimous
and fairly ribald to the effect that that to be awakened at that time of night
in that fashion was a certain way to ensure that we all had head-aches. Our
jocularity was replaced by stunned disbelief when we learned that the Adjutant

was dead. P/O Macfarlane was one of the very few married officers who lived in Quarters on the station with his wife and two children. He was such a big, healthy-looking man that it was impossible to believe that a few innoculations had killed him. But they had.

In fact Macfarlane, who died in his sleep, was killed by an air embolism. In the rush to innoculate one of the orderlies assisting the MO had not excluded all the air from the hypodermic syringe. The Squadron's first 'war' casualty had been entirely avoidable.

The Munich crisis past, the Squadron resumed training, though with greater intensity, as can be deduced from the fact that 40 held an Armaments Camp at West Freugh in January 1939. Hitherto such visits had been made only between May and October. On 6 April 40 took its Battles to Evanton, on the Firth of Cromarty, for a further camp. Bill Oxley remembers the flight north not only because, unusually, all crew members were called to the briefing, but for what followed:

> The orders were that Sqn/Ldr Parker would take off first with A Flight, followed fifteen minutes later by Flt/Lt W. G. Moseby with three aircraft of B Flight. The brief was to make our way to Evanton via the coast, avoiding the mountains inland when we crossed the Scottish border. Just before take off Flt/Lt Moseby took me on one side and asked what the possibilities were of obtaining bearings from Leuchars shortly after take off. I told him that if it was possible I'd get them as early as I could. It was one of those days when everything went right. We couldn't have been airborne more than five minutes before I contacted Leuchars with a good signal and obtained a first class bearing.

Bill Moseby then took B Flight direct to Evanton, crossing the Grampians and landing well ahead of the CO and A Flight. 'Sam' Parker summoned Moseby and his crew to demand an explanation for this deviation from the briefed course, barely restraining himself in the presence of Sgt J. A. D. Beattie (the observer) and Oxley, and venting his feelings when they were dismissed. Yet ironically, it was Moseby who led the Squadron back from Evanton on 22 April—via the direct route!

The inclusion of the WOp/AGs in the briefing prior to the flight to Evanton marked a further step towards recognition of their standing as members of a team. How recently they had been regarded as little more than ballast can be seen from the fact that prior to September 1938 they were not expected to record their flights, and that those who did so for their own satisfaction used a notebook of their own. In September notebooks were made available, but not until May 1939 were flying logbooks issued.

In April 1939 changes were made to the Squadron establishment, raising the Commanding Officer's rank to Wing Commander. This brought a new CO, E. C. Barlow, Sqn/Ldr Parker remaining as OC Flying and A Flight

30. A Fairey Battle crew. West Freugh, January 1939.
(l to r) Sgt J. H. Higgins, Sgt B. L. 'Cappy' Harris, LAC W. Furby. (G. Furby.)

Commander, with Bill Moseby commanding B Flight. Bill comments that
'Cecky Barlow was the first CO I had who actually joined in our flying
and other activities and "got to know" his officers and men and gave them
encouragement and occasionally a pat on the back'.

Amongst the NCO pilots there were now two modes of entry. For
alongside the original Sergeant Pilot scheme there was now direct entry, as
for observers, the first of these pilots on squadron being Sgt. J. H. Higgins
in February 1938. In July 1940 Jim Higgins would be the first of 40's sergeant
pilots commissioned, and in September the last pre-war pilot on squadron.

The Battle being a stable and forgiving aircraft, and powered by a first-class
(if overworked) engine, there were comparatively few accidents in the
fourteen months prior to the outbreak of war, and none resulting in fatalities.
The most spectacular was a forced landing on 14 July 1939, during a mock
war exercise, when a Battle piloted by P/O J. E. Edwards suffered an engine
coolant leak. The leak became progressively worse until the coolant tank
collapsed completely and hot glycol poured over the engine. Bill Oxley
writes:

> The smoke was so bad that we couldn't see each other and the other two
> lads in the formation told me afterwards that they could swear we were on
> fire. The fumes were obviously affecting the pilot as well and he looked for
> somewhere to put down. As it turned out the only place he could find was

31. Battles in formation. (R. W. Huntley.)

a reservoir near Naseby. My mate who was flying in No. 2 said we did a perfect crash landing. Wheels up, flaps down, coarse pitch and *hit*!!

Bill Oxley continues:

Beat. [Sgt Beattie] was flung out of the aircraft and disappeared under the port wing. I was going through the procedures for a ditching, and when I looked up, he was clinging to the wing blowing like porpoise. His harness had caught in the pitot tube and he had just managed to extricate himself. Now comes the interesting part. We expected the aircraft to sink completely, but it didn't. The nose sank and then stopped as the prop hit solid ground under the water. The rest of the aircraft sank only so far and eventually all three of us were standing on the fuselage hanging on to the fixed aerial.

How lucky they were, they learned when their rescuer informed them that they had landed on the only shallow area in the reservoir.

Customarily, formation flying had been undertaken in sections, or at most in flights. But during 1939 larger formations of Battles were essayed, with 40 and XV undertaking several Wing formation flights, usually over France. Known colloquially as 'Balbos' (an allusion to the long distance flights undertaken by Marshal Balbo's *Regia Aeronautica* formations), these served primarily to reassure the French. But even those aware of the Battle's defects as a fighting machine could be moved by the sight of eighteen or more of them in close formation.

The large formations of Battles indicate one aspect of official thinking on how the bombers might be employed in the coming war. Another was the dive bombing practice undertaken during the early summer of 1939. A third, more sinister, though conjectural, was the delivery of a quantity of torpedo-shaped wing tanks. David Green recalls a rumour that they were liquid poison gas dispensers, adding

> Credence was given to this theory when we were required to fit them to an aircraft for trials. The tanks were filled with a fairly viscous fluid and one of the pilots flew backwards and forwards across the airfield emitting a fine spray which clearly drenched those areas affected.

What the tanks were for was never explained. The Squadron took them to France, but they were never fitted to the aircraft.

Those who serviced the Battles were pleased with their new charges, though the Merlin engines, worked hard because of the heavy airframe, tended to give trouble. David Green comments:

> Sparking plug changes were a too frequent occurrence and, as time went on, deterioration in cylinder compressions demanded a much higher rate of cylinder block changes than we were accustomed to. But perhaps the greatest problem was that the starting system depended on an external 'trolley acc.'. The slowness with which this turned the engine was only adequate to ensure a quick start if air temperatures were moderate and engine compressions good. This presented no great problem at Abingdon, where trolley accs were in good supply and Station workshops could overhaul below-par cylinder blocks in short order. But it did not augur well for operations from airstrips or during detachments to dispersed bases.

As the tempo of training increased, exercises in operating from dispersed bases became more frequent, and one from Weston-on-the-Green during the early summer proved memorable for David Green:

> One unforgettable day we were required to turn round the aircraft, including refuelling and rearming, wearing full gas kit—ie. gas mask, oilskin cape, overboots and head covering—all on a broiling hot day in full sun. I prayed that we would never again have to undergo such torture whether in practice or for real.

Good relations between RAF Stations and the communities in which they were situated was always considered important, and on 14 June 1939 the links between RAF Abingdon and the town were formalized when, in accordance with the Municipal Liaison Scheme, 40 Squadron affiliated to the Borough of Abingdon. The event was marked by a special meeting of the Council, attended by Cecil Barlow. Henceforth 40 would be 'Abingdon's Own'.

August 1939 brought glorious weather, and many took summer leave to enjoy it, only to receive 'Return immediately' telegrams. Back at Abingdon they found that this was not a rerun of the Munich crisis, but much more serious. David Green recalls that 'one of the first things we had to do was to pack up all our civilian clothes and personal possessions and despatch them to our homes with no communication of any sort'. Not everyone's arrived. Percy Panting, a wireless mechanic with 40 just a week, recalls that he 'lost civilian clothing and quite a few personal and sentimental items' when his suitcase and belongings never reached his parents. Nor could everything be sent home. When all ranks were confined to camp, on 1 September, Algy Jane was unable to take his 'very attractive' AJS motorcycle to a nearby garage for safe-keeping. 'I just had to abandon it'.

During those last hectic days, much advice was given on how to prepare for what lay ahead. David Green recalls that '"Chiefy" Thompson, now Engineer Officer for the Wing, addressed us in our rooms and, as an old sweat of the Great War, proceeded to give us sage advice on how to survive reasonably comfortably "in the field"', while Bill Bromley remembers a talk in which Hugh Walmsley announced

> that he had been instructed by Air Ministry to tell us that our average expectation of life was two weeks and consequently we had to straighten up our financial affairs; we had to make wills and we had to make peace with girlfriends.

Bill Moseby and Hugh Smeddle took the injunction seriously, marrying their fiancées in a joint service at which the Station padre officiated and each couple acted as best man and bridesmaid for the other. For the other ranks, too, there were girlfriends to deal with, and Bill Oxley recalls that, with the connivance of sympathetic service policemen, there were 'many tearful farewells on the road outside the camp'.

On Friday, 1 September 1939, a small fleet of civil aircraft arrived at Abingdon, including several Imperial Airways aircraft. Resplendent in their silver livery, they had to be camouflaged. Algy Jane recalls working on a pair of Handley Page HP42s:

> They were biplanes with interplane struts and engines mounted on the struts. Our first task was to camouflage these beautiful glistening silver aircraft. So we climbed all over the thing, which was no mean feat as we had no ground equipment to facilitate this sort of thing, and we hoisted five gallon drums of camouflage dope, that is the earth and green colours. We just poured this stuff over the main planes and using enormous platform brooms, which we normally usually used for sweeping out the hangars, we shunted the dope around until we covered the complete surface. You can imagine the ghastly mess and the dope dripping off the trailing edges of the mainplanes. The Imperial Airways crews, still dressed in their immaculate uniforms, were almost reduced to tears when they saw the state of their aircraft.

All was now ready. David Green writes:

As dusk fell on the evening of 1st September 1939 we dispersed all the aircraft to the outer perimeter of the airfield. It was a beautiful and balmy summer's evening. The pink afterglow of the sun as it disappeared over the horizon, the smell of the recently cut grass and the absolute quiet should have evoked the ultimate feeling of peace. But as we walked the mile across the airfield back to the hangars our minds were miles away. Not a word was spoken until Jimmy Higgins voiced the thoughts of us all. 'I don't know about you', he said, 'but I'm bloody scared'. Which was not the truth, as we well knew. But it served to unleash our unspoken thoughts. The truth was that we were undeniably apprehensive about what was going to happen, yet at the same time we were excited at the adventure to come. For in the morning we were to start on our way to France.

# Notes

1. F. A. de Vere Robertson, 'No. 40 (Bomber) Squadron'. *Flight* (13 May 1932), p. 412.
2. Ibid, p. 411.
3. For an excellent account of the social make-up of the RAF in the 1920s and 1930s see John James, *The Paladins*. London: Macdonald, 1990.
4. Robert Penwarn, 'Ages of an Airman', *Flypast* (December 1988), p. 47.

# 8

# Champagne Country:
# September–December 1939

ON 2 September 1939 40 and XV Squadrons moved to France as 71 Wing, Advance Air Striking Force, under the command of Gp/Cpt Walmsley. Initially, these squadrons remained part of Bomber Command, but this was soon found unsatisfactory, and the AASF was established as an autonomous command under Air-Vice Marshal P. Playfair, with his Headquarters in Rheims.

The base for 71 Wing was Betheniville, fifteen miles north-east of Rheims, and thither 40 despatched a Forward Air Party [FAP] by civil aircraft, followed by sixteen Battles and their crews. The bulk of the ground crews, however, were to travel by land and sea, arriving on 3 September, with a small Rear Party following several days later. It was a simple scheme which at Abingdon went like clockwork. At Betheniville, it did not.

The FAP took off at 9.40 am, one member of the Party, wireless mechanic Percy Panting, experiencing an ironic moment as they crossed the English Channel:

> In the aircraft I read that day's copy of *The Daily Mail* which clearly stated that no person under 20 would be going with the Expeditionary Force to France. I was 19 on July 5th 1939.

In brilliantly sunny weather, sixteen Battles followed, led by Cecky Barlow. His WOp/AG was Bill Oxley, who writes:

> I shall never forget the incident before we embarked. His wife had come out to see us off, and before we entered the aircraft she not only kissed her husband, but myself and Sgt. Beattie, the Observer, as well, and wished us luck.

Only fifteen Battles reached France, Bill Moseby's suffering engine failure over the Channel and ditching close to a cross channel ferry, by which he and his crew, Sgt Cody and AC1 W. Furby, were rescued. Deposited at Dieppe, the crew returned to Newhaven next day, where Moseby was admitted to hospital with concussion, not returning to the Squadron for nearly a month. His crew reached Betheniville four days later.

Over Betheniville, crews were, Jim Higgins writes, 'fortunate to recognise the so-called airfield surrounded by turnip fields and clearly not used for flying operations since W.W.I.' He continues: 'Our arrival can only be described as a shambles. Fifteen Fairey Battles milling around. Not the slightest preparation or a single person to advise or direct us'. A 'shambles' it was. The French army were supposed to assist and to feed RAF personnel prior to the arrival of their field kitchens, but the *Armée de l'Air* Corporal and six airmen guarding the airfield petrol dump were unaware that the RAF were coming.

Faced with chaos, the CO caught a bus into Betheniville, and sought the Mayor's help. The pilots and observers likewise went into Betheniville, but the air gunners joined the ground crew in servicing the aircraft and picketing them for the night before marching into the village.

Just as there had been no preparations at the airfield, so there had been none concerning accommodation. Nor were there many options, since Betheniville was a small village. The hotel was taken over as an Officers' Mess, while the SNCOs occupied a large farmhouse, but there was no accommodation for other ranks. Algy Jane writes:

> we scouted around the village and came across a small cinema which hadn't been used for that purpose since the First World War. It still bore the wartime damage, shellholes and so on in the walls, and was completely empty. As there was a curfew to be exercised by the evening, we decided to sleep in this place. To get all the airmen in we organized them in shoulder width strips on the concrete floor, where they deposited all their worldly possession, the possessions in their kitbag, and laid out their brown blankets.

Most decided that the time had come to sample French village night life, and adjourned to the *estaminet*, Bill Oxley among them:

> It was my first encounter with French champagne (domestic, of course, and very cheap) and I'm afraid the rest of the evening after about 9pm is a closed book to me.

Bill Oxley may not have remembered what happened, but Algy Jane does, vividly.

> At the time of the curfew we got all the airmen off and into the cinema. The French beer had a remarkable effect in that no matter how much one relieved oneself before going to bed, it was necessary, about 2 or 3 in the morning, to repeat the process, for which chaps were going into the dark outside. The problem was that coming back in, faced with this sea of brown blankets with such narrow spaces allocated to each person, there was pandemonium with people trying to find their own kit, their own bedding and so on, and they kept stepping on each other's faces, people lighting matches, and cigarette lighters to try to see—you can imagine some of the language. The worst of it was that those who had perhaps too much champagne were then incapable of getting out of their beds and in some cases were violently

ill, and this was running down the sloping floor of the cinema, much to the disgust of the people further down the slope.

The drunkenness was exacerbated by hunger, for Gordon Ogden recalls that on leaving Abingdon the FAP had been issued rations consisting of a tin of bully beef, a packet of hard tack biscuits, and an apple or orange, but not told that this was a forty-eight hour ration. Hence most ate theirs on the aircraft or shortly after landing, and had nothing for the rest of the day except (courtesy of the locals) some apples.

Sunday, 3 September, brought the declaration of war, which aircrew heard over their earphones on stand by in their aircraft, while for ground crew, Percy Panting recalls, 'at 6 pm. the Station Adjutant came into the Cinema and said that we were at war, since France had declared war on Germany at around 5.30pm. He then read extracts from Air Council Instructions giving additional penalties to which we were now liable, being at war.'

The RAF field kitchens not being expected for several days, the CO made arrangements for messing with a small French cavalry unit. Jo (F/O J. C.) Stevenson remembers 'an amazing French field kitchen, like a tank, but belching smoke and flames', and Algy Jane the food:

> It was basically horse flesh, boiled in galvanized buckets with big white haricot beans and potato bread. Potato bread was baked once a fortnight, and 24 hours after baking it set like concrete. It was later to become the cause of a lot of dental problems.[1]

There was however, a compensation which Gordon Ogden appreciated:

> we were also given a generous ration of rough red wine. There was huge barrel of it in the barn we used as a dining hall, and we could just help ourselves. A lot of the chaps didn't like it, so I and people like me had a fair old share.

While the FAP was sampling French army cuisine, the Main Party was on its way from Abingdon, which it had left on the morning of 2 September in a convoy of buses and lorries. At Southampton they boarded the Southern Railways ferry, *Isle of Thanet*, which sailed that night for Le Havre, docking in the early hours of the 3rd amidst an industrial dispute which forced the airmen to do their own off-loading from the ferry and loading on to flat railway waggons. The train then set off for Paris, David Green having been appointed OC train guard: 'Six airmen and myself were issued with 50 rounds of .303 ammunition each and allocated a box car at the very end of the train, following the flat cars carrying the stores and equipment'.

About midday on the 3rd, the train arrived in sidings north of Paris, where French civilians and army personnel supplied lunches. They also brought the news that war had been declared. At Rheims that evening the majority of the Main Party went off by bus, while David Green was left

with a handling party to unload the stores and equipment into a huge diesel
lorry. He recalls:

> Hours later, dirty, tired, cold and hungry, we had just about finished our task
> when a bustling little Flight Lieutenant appeared at the trot, shouting, 'Come
> along, get moving; the enemy always strikes at dawn'.

Exhausted, they boarded the juggernaut and set off—only the French driver
knowing whither they were bound.

Dawn brought a typical September morning, with mist which cleared as
the sun rose. The lorry halted, and the airmen found themselves in a small
village. David Green writes:

> Just across the road the women were already doing their laundry from floating
> wooden platforms tethered to the bank. Some looked up and waved. Others,
> the older ones, looked up and either averted their eyes or, in true peasant
> fashion, flung their aprons over their heads.

This first glimpse of a rural French community was followed by an encounter
with one of its delights. For the lorry had stopped outside the village bakery,
where 'the proprietor and his jolly assistants were overjoyed to serve us
delicious baguettes, still warm from the oven, with two fried eggs inside'.

Gradually the situation at Betheniville improved. The messing problem
was solved when the field kitchens arrived (the cinema becoming the other
ranks mess hall) though Bob Mullins recalls that many 'augmented [their]
food intake with delicious buns, cakes and confectionery from the village
patisserie'. For the officers, who after a few meals of horsemeat had fed at
the *estaminet*, the situation had been less desperate, but there was pleasure
when soup with bread floating in it was replaced by such delicacies as fried
rabbit.

Accommodation remained a problem, with two squadrons and Wing HQ
crowding into a small village, but most of the officers were moved out into
billets. The SNCOs also fared quite well, taking over the upper floor of a
large barn, which they made comfortable, despite the stench from the animals
tethered below. Some corporals took over an empty garage, but the majority
of the other ranks, moved from the cinema, were first accommodated in
the school and then, when term started, installed in part of a local flax linen
factory, damaged during the World War One. Algy Jane recalls that

> we filled the holes in the walls with 4 gallon petrol cans that we cut up and
> rivetted together, and filled up the holes so that we could have a light at
> night time and avoid any blackout problems.

Furniture was improvised, using the wooden boxes in which fuel was
transported, two four-gallon tins per box. David Green and his companions
in the garage, for instance, having provided themselves with 'bedside lockers,

wardrobes, tables and endless shelving', prevailed on the local blacksmith-cum-carpenter to make them bed frames for their straw-filled palliasses. 'Somewhat to our surprise', he comments, 'we found ourselves living with greater personal convenience than in our modern billets at home'. Many of the SNCOs also had beds, courtesy of the officers, who turned over their official issue camp bed kits to them.

There remained sanitation and hygiene problems. At the school there was a row of typical French toilets, wooden cubicles with each of which was a concrete slab with a couple of footprints and a strategically placed hole. But this system became overloaded, and all ranks turned to to dig trench latrines out of the chalk. Long pits with two poles, one for sitting on and the other for leaning against, such latrines were efficient, though on one occasion disaster struck, as Hugh Smeddle recalls:

> One early morning I took a Battle to test the practicability of dropping a bomb with a very short fuse setting from a low altitude. All went well and the bomb duly exploded, but when I returned I was met by Sergeant Duckworth, who had been sitting on the bottom log when it became dislodged by the explosion, with consequent dire results.

'I must say', Hugh adds, 'the Sergeant took it with a grin'.

Bathing was carried out in the river, David Green commenting that 'it was not much fun stripping off to one's underpants in the crisp cold of September mornings and standing knee-deep in the weeds of the fast-flowing river under the solemn gaze of a dozen washer-women'. There was compensation, however, in weekly trips into Rheims, where, though the public bath house was, in Algy Jane's opinion, 'a fairly squalid, ancient and Dickensian place', there was limitless hot water. Refreshed, the airmen would then buy a meal and go out on the town, B Flight gunners feeling particularly privileged to have amongst their number LAC Gerry Quinn, who spoke fluent French.

Betheniville was ill-prepared to receive two squadrons of Battles. An L-shaped strip, it had an underground petrol storage tank, from which fuel was extracted by a manually operated pump, but nothing else. One of the first tasks undertaken was the digging of slit trenches. Another, using tarpaulins and small marquees, supplemented by saplings from a nearby wood, was the erection of temporary storage and accommodation facilities. It was in the process of cutting saplings that an eerie discovery was made, as David Green relates:

> The graceful, swaying silver birch and beech trees concealed a German trench system which appeared to have been untouched since 1918. There was equipment and paraphernalia everywhere—some half buried in rotted leaves, but much completely exposed. No arms, but gas masks, water bottles, webbing,

32. By-play at Betheniville: F/O Smeddle about to be assaulted by Flt/Sgt Goble (?) outside the B Flight office. (H. F. Smeddle.)

and (stacked in one corner) the rusted remains of what had apparently been a food store.

'It was difficult not to be moved in some way', David Green adds, 'rather like being caught disturbing a grave. We avoided that part of the wood thereafter.'

Though 40's Battles were bombed and refuelled in readiness from the morning of 3 September, war brought no action until the 9th, when an operational sortie was undertaken by six aircraft from B Flight. One of the pilots was Jim Higgins:

> My first operational flight was in a Battle, K9309, doing a reconnaissance of the Franco-German border (9/9/39). Base—THIONVILLE—METZ—SARREBOURG -VERDUN—Base—No incident.

This was to be a pattern repeated frequently during 40's stay in France. For theirs was to be as phoney a war as that of any RAF unit during 1939, no aircraft firing a gun in anger, or encountering enemy aircraft. Other squadrons were less lucky.

As originally deployed, a total of nine AASF squadrons, all equipped with Battles, was based around Rheims. Many airfields were overcrowded, however, and plans were drawn up for further dispersal, with most pairs of squadrons split up. On 12 September, accordingly, XV Squadron moved to Condé-Vraux, while 71 Wing moved into Betheniville itself. With further accommodation available in the village, rearrangements could also be made to billeting, as Bill Bromley recalls:

> I was billeted with an elderly couple. [He was] a retired schoolmaster who had gone back to teaching because of the war, and they vacated their main bedroom and I was given preferential treatment which I didn't want, and their bedroom and their double bed, complete with family po underneath, which I was very reluctant to use.

In one respect the Squadron did remarkably well from the first, for Hugh Walmsley ensured that contacts were established with the local champagne growers. Bill Bromley comments:

> This worked like a charm; the Renault van would arrive and crates of champagne would be unloaded and the senior representative of Moet et Chandon or whatever would front up in the evening. Talk about waste of quality stuff! In those days we didn't have the proper champagne glasses and we used to drink the beautiful champagne vintage stuff out of half-pint NAAFI glasses; talk about pearls before swine.

Nor was it only the officers who thus indulged, Jim Higgins commenting that 'it was Champagne for breakfast, lunch and dinner. I've had the taste ever since but now lack the wherewithall to indulge on such a grand scale.'

On 16 September the redeployment was completed with the arrival of the Rear Main Party (F/O R. M. Burns, and P/Os P. F. T. Wakeford and K. Bell). A rearrangement of other ranks accommodation was carried out, with personnel now arranged in billets according to their trades. Jim Higgins recalls:

> Gradually things got better. The hay-loft was cleaned up and a local pub-keeper was contracted to feed the SNCOs—three meals a day. When the rear party arrived the airmen were accommodated in the disused factory.

On 15 September six aircraft of A Flight carried out the Squadron's second operational sortie, reconnoitring the Verdun and Nancy area without incident. Further reconnaissance flights on the 17th and 20th likewise passed peacefully, though on the latter there were difficulties in locating the German frontier, and it was considered likely that the Battles overflew German airspace. In this 40 was fortunate, for that day 88 Squadron lost two of three Battles attacked by Messerschmitt 109s. These losses exposed not only the Battle's shortcomings, but also the fallacy that 'the bomber will always get through'. Yet AASF Headquarters still sent out Battles unescorted, the only concession being an instruction that reconnaissance flights should be made at two section strength.

On 21 September six aircraft reconnoitred the Merzig and Losheim districts of Germany. No fighters were encountered, but flak was, surprising the crews, who had been told that German AA could not predict above 16,000 feet. Bill Bromley recalls:

> We were stooging along with cameras turning when all of a sudden, woomph, woomph, woomph, heavy ack ack at 20,000 feet. So we climbed a bit more and I think we got to about 22,000 feet and the predicted heavy flak followed us, no trouble at all.

As the first RAF aircraft hit by German flak, 40's Battles attracted great interest, AVM Playfair himself paying a visit. Aircrew, feeling themselves 'blooded', marked the event in the *estaminet*, singing to Algy Jane's accordion, 'Here's a toast to the dead already, three cheers to the next one to die'.

In the next six days, 40 flew five reconnaissance sorties, luckily without encountering fighters. Flak, however, was met with, particularly on 25 September, when, during a photo reconnaissance of the Thionville–St. Avold area, there was an ironic follow-up to a reprimand Cecil Barlow had administered on 20 September, after the unwitting penetration of German air space. Then the CO had said that 'he would do the next reconnaissance and get the right results'. Jim Higgins comments:

> There were 3 aircraft led by Wg/Cdr Barlow. We got partially lost and strayed 20 miles or so into German territory to experience our baptism of fire. Over Kaiserlauten we were subjected to a barrage of anti-aircraft fire. Wg/Cdr Barlow & his No 2 were hit but I got off scot free.

Clearly, navigation was more difficult than Cecky Barlow had imagined.

While 40's luck held, other squadrons were less fortunate, the worst hit being 150 Squadron on 30 September, when five Battles were attacked by Me 109s over Saarbrucken, with four shot down and the fifth burnt out after crash landing. Clearly, unescorted Battles were incapable of surviving determined fighter attacks, and henceforth reconnaissance became the responsibility of Blenheim squadrons, with the Battles temporarily redundant.

What was their role to be? HQ was undecided, and 40 did virtually no flying until 9 October, when it began to practice dive-bombing, the ORB noting that this was the method 'it is understood this Squadron will be required to employ when attacking enemy targets'. In the event of an offensive, it seems, the AASF was thinking of using its Battles to destroy pontoon bridges, railways, roads, barracks and airfields over a thirty to forty mile front, with Blenheims penetrating deeper behind enemy lines.

Dive bombing practice continued throughout October, though without urgency, since there was no flying on eight days that month, and dive bombing practice only on six. The rest of the time flying was restricted to engine tests and, late in the month, to taking a mosaic of the aerodrome and surrounding district.

With operational sorties effectively at an end, it became possible to allow personnel off base more frequently. For Bill Bromley, one of the attractions in Rheims was prosaic:

> We would go along to Le Lion d'Or, where we would have a bath comparatively cheaply and then have a few drinks and an excellent 4-star dinner and go out on the town and see what delights could be found.

One of those 'delights' was

> a champagne bar which had beautiful tiled walls with French mottos in the porcelain. You would sit on a half-barrel and sit around a whole barrel, beautifully done, and there was nothing on that menu except various brands of champagne at 6d per glass.

Another of the attractions in Rheims was a photographer, whom the Squadron patronized on a number of occasions. Of a photo of the Squadron officers no copy seems to have survived, but there is ample surviving evidence of another photographic session, when many of the officers, including Cecky Barlow and Sam Parker, adopted exaggerated poses. Some of these photos, taken for fun and intended for the sitters and their families and friends at home, achieved notoriety subsequently, published for propaganda purposes first in a German magazine and then in *Picture Post*.[2]

A steady stream of RAF and Army visitors came to Betheniville, the first being AVM Playfair, on 3 September, and the most distinguished the C-in-C of the British Expeditionary Force, Lord Gort, and ACM Sir Robert Brooke-Popham. To these, however, were added French visitors drawn from nearby regiments, units with which Cecil Barlow and Hugh Walmsley cultivated good relations. There were visits, also, by celebrity groups touring BEF and AASF units, and members of the Squadron recall the visits of a concert party led by actor Sir Seymour Hicks, and a concert by the expatriate American cabaret singer, Josephine Baker.

Nor was all the entertainment imported. At Abingdon Bob Batt, one-time secretary-manager to pianist Charlie Kunz, had formed a Station Band. At Betheniville this grew into a concert party, and the extent to which this was given official support is demonstrated by the fact that fitter Jack Atkinson was transferred to 40, when XV moved to Vraux, because he was a talented cornet and trumpet player. Another who played a significant part in the concert party was Algy Jane, whose accordion playing was much admired.

The first concert, which save for a French soldier, an operatic tenor in civilian life, was entirely a 40 Squadron affair, was held in the cinema on 7 October, the Adjutant adjudging the performance 'excellent'. A week later a 71 Wing Concert Party, in which 40 Squadron members figured largely, gave a performance in Chalons-sur-Marne, repeating the performance in Epernay on the 30th, and in Betheniville on 18 November. The most important concert, however, was held the Betheniville cinema on 21 October before an audience which included ACM Brooke-Popham, AM Burnett, AVM Playfair and AASF HQ staff. The visitors were making an official visit to the Squadron, and were entertained to dinner in the Officers' Mess prior to the concert.

On 1 November the Squadron was visited by Press representatives and cameramen, who saw the CO briefing crews and took photographs of three A Flight aircraft taking off on an 'operational sortie'. Photographs were also taken of Battles dive-bombing the aerodrome, and of an aircraft shooting up a gun emplacement.

From 7 November onwards, crews carried out low-level bombing exercises, sometimes involving mock attacks on the aerodrome and at others dropping live 250-lb bombs at the Moronvilliers bombing range. As the month went on, however, the weather deteriorated markedly, with rain, low cloud, fog and finally snow preventing flying on fourteen days.

Bad weather meant discomfort and difficulty for the ground crews, who had to service the Battles in the open. Particular problems were experienced in starting the Merlin engines, and David Green recalls that the 'situation worsened to the point where we could no longer guarantee to get a whole flight off on time unless we began starting up a ridiculous time before take-off'. The solution? David explains:

> As always there was someone around with an answer: and the solution was to 'swing' the propeller in order to produce that extra bit of compression in the cylinders. One look at the enormous propellor on the Battle was enough to rule such a proposition right out; until Cpl Sherwood produced his long length of sturdy rope to one end of which he had spliced a canvas bag just big enough to make a loose fit around the tip of the propeller. The procedure was simple if somewhat hilarious. The canvas bag was fitted snugly on the tip of one of the propeller blades, and the propellor then rotated until that blade was just before top-dead-centre, with a cylinder on compression. Half a dozen erks would then hold the rope as in a tug-of-war. The occupant of the cockpit, having primed the engine very carefully, would then poise himself to press the starter button while the erk manning the trolley acc. would be ready to press the contact switch. On a given signal they all sprang into action, those on the rope running like mad while the 'starter' in the cockpit kept one hand on the starter button to keep the 'spark' going, while priming the ki-gas primer madly with the other. The results were miraculous. First time starts became the order of the day: and never a take-off time was missed.

During September armour plate had been fitted to give crews a measure of personal protection against fighter attack. But additional fire power was also needed, particularly against attack from below, and during early November the Battles were fitted with a Vickers Gas-Operated K gun in the bombing aperture. Described as giving 'an excellent field of fire both fore and aft' beneath the fuselage, the gun had a second set of sights on its underside, since when it was trained aft it was inverted. Observers were given rudimentary training in handling the gun, followed by ground and air firing. And though no one was convinced that the gun provided a significant increase in protection, at least the observer had something to retaliate with when under attack.

On 6 and 9 November the Squadron liaised with *Armée de l'air* units, taking aircraft to Chantilly and Beauvais 'to acquaint the French with the Battle', as the ORB puts it, and practising co-operation with French fighter units. Bill Bromley recalls:

> They were learning tactics, so were we, and later on I was able to avail myself of the lessons we had learned in these exercises, which did quite a lot of good.

Liaison with the French also took place when, from the beginning of November, aircrew were rostered for weekend leave. Bill Bromley was one of the first to go:

> To relieve the boredom with not much flying going on, they said: 'Right you chaps, pick a chum and go off to Paris. We'll give you a first class rail warrant but you support yourselves while you are in Paris', which we did. I went with a mate, a Canadian, George Hill, and a good deal could be written on the adventures we got up to.

Jo Stevenson also recalls Paris leave, and particularly the moment when he and his companions went into Madame Merotte's restaurant bar at the 'Hotel Ambassadeur', to be greeted by Madame herself with 'Ah! Les premiers aviateurs anglais depuis 1918'. The 'English aviators' were in fact an Australian, a Canadian and a Scot, but the service was marvellous, and when they left at 11 pm, she gave them a bottle of brandy.

Nor were these long weekends the prerogative only of the officer aircrew, as Jim Higgins remembers:

> It didn't seem like we were in a war. Trips to Paris became frequent; these were tremendous because our Pound went so far in those days. On a Sgt/Pilot's pay we could live like aristocrats in Paris.

Relations with the locals in Betheniville were also cordial, and Percy Panting recalls that 'there were two equivalents of Pubs in the village, and while we were [billetted] at the Cinema and School we patronised one, and when we went to the Factory we patronized the other'.

With a policy of fraternal contact with French army and air force units, an official interpreter was provided, and useful contacts established. Hugh Smeddle writes:

> We made contact with a French cavalry squadron stationed in a large farm 2 to 3 miles away from the airfield. Bob Batt and I gave some of them a few

trips when doing local flying and in return we made use of their horses whenever available. One night a few of us were invited to their mess for dinner and it was staged with typical gallic verve.

Jo Stevenson remembers the cavalry songs after dinner, '"Une a droite, une a gauche. Deux a droite" etc., standing at the trestle table, tapping with the appropriate number of fingers', but for Hugh the vivid memory is of 'bottles of champagne being opened by being decapitated with a sabre and a change of course signalled by a shot from the revolver into the ceiling'. At Betheniville numerous bottles of champagne were wasted as attempts were made to emulate the cavalrymen's technique.

November was frustrating. No operational sorties were flown, for though 40 and XV Squadrons took turns to be at readiness for two hours from noon, nothing happened. Then during the last week in November the weather took a turn for the worse, Squadron records describing the 24th as 'intensely cold'. Snow fell, bringing sub-zero temperatures which issue blankets could not adequately withstand, but the prospects of even worse weather was tempered by the knowledge that 40 was to return to England to re-equip with Bristol Blenheims.

Forty's shift to Wyton, in Huntingdonshire, began on the 30th November, when the Advance Party got away. The Battles left on the 2nd, by which time, Peter Wakeford recalls, Blenheims of the replacement squadrons, 114 and 139, had already arrived, and the entire operation was complete by 4 December. The ORB records the planning that went into this move. It does not mention unofficial arrangements. Jim Higgins recalls that 'the Squadron arrived at Wyton loaded with contraband; cigarettes, brandy, wine etc', while Bill Bromley fills in the details as to how the contraband was carried:

> Our SNCO ground staff said: 'Now why don't we solder a couple of 4-gallon petrol tins together, put a wire across the top and these can hook onto bomb releases and we can fill the cans with liqueurs and whatever grog you want to take back?' This was a great idea, and when we flew back to Wyton we had every Battle laden with these 8-gallon containers full of liqueurs and champers.

At Wyton, Bill Oxley recalls, customs officers were deterred from searching the incoming Battles by the CO's pointing out that they were bombed up, and a green Very light signalled that it was safe to taxi up to the tarmac for unloading.[3] Bill Bromley remembers what followed:

> When Percy Rowan [P/O P. J. H. Rowan] unloaded his petrol cans, he had an airman or two waiting under the port wing, but unfortunately released the starboard bombload, which crashed onto the tarmac, smashing all the bottles.

Forty's excursion to France was over.

# Notes

1.  Fitter George Reddy also recalls the horsemeat and the buckets. He and another airman were sent down to a farmhouse to collect the FAP's cooked meal. They went into the walled farmyard to find French soldiers helping the farmer to shovel manure. George and his companion made it understood that they had come for the meal, whereupon the soldiers emptied two buckets of their manure, rinsed them cursorily under a tap, and filled one with spaghetti and the other horsemeat stew. The two airmen just managed to leave the farmyard before throwing up.

2.  After the German occupation of Rheims, some of the photos fell into their hands, and one of F/O. G. W. C. 'Gerry' Gleed, Bob Batt, Hugh Smeddle, Sam Parker and Cecky Barlow was published in the German paper, *Schwarze Korps*, as part of an 'Answer to Bishop Partridge', Bishop of Portsmouth, who had denounced German pilots as 'flying Huns with lustful maniacal faces, out of a lunatic asylum'. The photo, in which all five assume grossly exaggerated poses, could have been a considerable embarrassment had not the Germans gilded the lily by publishing obviously touched up separate photos of the individuals, enabling *Picture Post* (7 November 1940, pp. 20–21) to dismiss all the photos as fakes.

33. The spoof photo taken at Rouen (see also rear cover). Rear (l to r): Gerry Gleed, Bob Batt, Hugh Smeddle. Front: Sam Parker and Cecky Barlow. (H. F. Smeddle.)

3.  George Reddy recalls, however, that when his HP42, 'Hannibal', arrived at Wyton, one kitbag was leaking cognac from what must have been a broken bottle. The customs officer merely observed, with a smile, that there seemed to be a lot of broken eggs!

9

# Waiting at Wyton:
# December 1939–May 1940

FORTY received its first ten Blenheims on 3 December. Six more followed three days later, though flying did not begin until the 6th because on arrival at Wyton personnel were granted forty-eight hours' leave.

The Blenheim IV, to which the Squadron was now converting, represented in many respects an advance on the Fairey Battle. With two Bristol Mercury engines of 920 hp, and capable of 266 mph at 11,800 feet, it was also more agile and possessed a power-operated turret for rear defence. Even so, the Blenheim was undergunned (its only other weapon was, as on the Battle, a single wing-mounted machine gun) and serious thought was being given to how its defences might be enhanced. It was also acknowledged that the Blenheim, designed to outrun enemy fighters, could no longer do so.

On 6 December pilots received their first instruction, Sqn/Ldr W. S. Steadman training two or three pilots, who in turn trained the remainder, all of whom Steadman then checked. The first pilots went solo on the 7th, and the last on the 13th. Four days later air gunners were taken up for practice in handling the power-operated turret, while what the ORB termed 'fairly long cross-country flights' took place on 20 and 21 December, the aim being, to 'acquaint A/Os with the navigational facilities' of the Blenheim.

The weather during January was often bad, but a substantial programme was completed on the 25th, when the Squadron flew navigational flights over the Irish Sea, and practised bombing and air to ground firing on markers dropped in the sea.

During January and February, steps were taken to improve the Blenheim's operational viability. One was the installation of self-sealing tanks, a tricky and time-consuming business, as David Green recalls:

The tanks—four of them—were buried in the wings behind panels held by hundreds of screws. These existing tanks had to be removed from the aircraft and then from the panels to which they were attached. The new self-sealing tanks were larger, and so new retaining straps had to be made up, new pipe joints made and then the whole lot refitted into the wings—a very tight fit and rather like doing a jigsaw blindfold.

6

For each aircraft this job, which Algy Jane recalls invoked 'a tremendous amount of swearing, pushing, pulling, hammering and so on', involved a thirteen hour day for three men.

A second attempt to improve the Blenheim's viability involved rubbing down and repainting the aircraft. David Green writes:

> Every aircraft had first to be rubbed down—every square inch of the fuselage, wings, tail, and fin—with fine wet and dry paper and soft soap. Every lap joint of the metal skin had then to be chamfered off with a paste and the joints covered with strips of the finest medaplin material. Finally the entire aircraft had to be resprayed with a glossy finish cellulose. All this effort was calculated to add 5 mph to the top speed of the Blenheim, and maybe save its crew.

'To this day', he adds, 'my idea of purgatory is working in an unheated hangar at 2 o'clock on a freezing winter's morning with one's hands almost constantly immersed in a bucket of ice-cold water.'

A third modification, begun in February, was the fitting of an undergun, fired by the observer. This modification, involving the replacement of the escape hatch in the nose floor with an aft-firing gun mounted on a gimbal, and aimed by mirrors, was complex, and it was not until 16 March that the first conversion was completed, with sufficient aircraft modified by 29 March to enable observers to practice at Wainfleet.

During February bad weather frequently prevented flying (though Peter Wakeford recalls 'lots of low flying up and down the Bedford River that stood us in good stead later'), but the Squadron was not idle. Indeed, it was frenziedly active following notification, on 15 February, that 40 was to be posted overseas (Malta and Finland were the rumoured destinations). As part of this process there was an enlarged Establishment, inward postings doubling the Squadron size. There were also changes, of which the most significant was probably that signalled by the arrival of P/Os W. G. Edwards and L. H. Ewels as Flight Gunnery Leaders, joining P/O Miller, the Squadron Gunnery Officer. Both Edwards and Ewels were commissioned from the ranks, and the rapidity of the latter's promotion—from Corporal WOp/AG to Pilot Officer in four months—indicates the sudden recognition that aircrew had to be specialists. This was completed when, at the end of May, it was decreed that the minimum rank for aircrew should be that of sergeant.

Amid this hustle and bustle, an order came from Group to the effect that eight Blenheims from Wyton were to be repainted for ferrying to Finland, then fighting the Winter War with the Soviet Union. The four 40 Squadron machines were drawn from B Flight, and Bill Moseby recalls feeling 'disappointed and surprised at this sudden depleting of squadron aircraft just when we needed them'. Squadron crews were called upon to fly the Blenheims to the ferry departure point, RAF Hendon, and this led to an

embarrassing error on the part of Sqn/Ldr Eric Springall, the B Flight
Commander, who got lost, so that eight Blenheims, swastikas flashing in
the morning sun, found themselves circling over the fighter base at Duxford,
in Cambridgeshire. Unfortunately, word of the débâcle reached official ears,
and Springall was posted, to return to 40 later that year.

On 12 March Bill Moseby was informed that for the forthcoming move
he was to command an Advance Party consisting of a sergeant and three
other ranks. The Movement Order gave no clue as to the destination, and
Bill recalls that he and the CO guessed it was 'the shores of the Black Sea',
in support of Turkey. They were never to find out, however, for on 17
March the Squadron was 'given to understand' that it would not after all
be moving overseas, and that it would be reduced to its original size, as by
early April it was.

Flying during the second half of March consisted mainly of navigation
and bombing exercises, and (beginning on 23 March) practice sweeps over
the North Sea. These were by now a regular 2 Group activity, their purpose
being to restrict German naval operations, though specific reconnaissances
were also carried out to locate flak ships and monitor the movement of
capital ships. Forty flew three of these sweeps at up to squadron strength
during the last week of March, each without incident.

On 1 April 40's first air-to-air combat occurred when Bill Moseby, on
North Sea reconnaissance, emerged from a rainstorm to find a Ju 88 ahead
of him. What followed was summarized by Bomber Command Routine
Orders the following day:

> Flight Lieutenant Moseby opened fire with his front gun, and three bursts
> appeared to hit the port wing of the enemy aircraft near the fuselage. This
> fire was replied to by the rear gunner of the enemy aircraft. Flight Lieutenant
> Moseby then attempted to turn on the enemy's tail, and his rear gunner [LAC
> A. E. Millard] who continued the fire, is confident that the enemy aircraft
> was once again hit and disabled. It was later confirmed by a British warship
> that the enemy aircraft was forced to land in the sea, and was destroyed.

April 1940 brought the German invasion of Denmark and Norway.
Despite a 2 Group Operational Order calling for enemy activity over and
around Norway to be reduced to a minimum, the RAF achieved little, and
40 virtually nothing, the only operations flown being a reconnaissance of
Wilhelmshaven by Flt/Lt L. D. Wilson on 8 April, and an unsuccessful
search for enemy warships on the 12th.

Between 13 and 17 April 40 had twelve crews standing by continuously
to look for enemy shipping, though no operations were flown except for a
reconnaissance of Wilhelmshaven by F/Os Stevenson and Hill on the 16th.
They were told that if cloud cover ran out they were to return to base.
Near Heligoland, Hill did so, but Stevenson, noting cloud over the land,

took a chance and kept going. Over Wilhelmshaven, dodging in and out of the cloud base, he was able to give his observer, Sgt Usher, opportunity to study the *Tirpitz*, then fitting out. On their return the cloud ran out at Borkum, but, remarkably, they were not troubled by fighters or by flak.

This reconnaissance had an unpleasant conclusion, when at debriefing Gp/Cpt Lawrence, the Station Commander, questioned whether they had actually gone to Wilhelmshaven, Jo Stevenson recalling that only the thought of a court martial prevented him from responding to the insinuation with violence. Lawrence was widely disliked, and there was general satisfaction when in May he was replaced by Gp/Cpt 'Pussy' Foster, a man of a very different ilk.

Setting aside Lawrence's insinuations, there was a problem with cloud cover operations, where the instruction to turn back if the cloud cover was insufficient often left crews feeling damned if they did and damned if they didn't. George Hill decided to turn back. Jo Stevenson pressed on. Had he been killed, his decision would have been branded foolhardy. As it happened, it paid off. Over the next few months crews were to find themselves in this dilemma constantly.

During early April the entire squadron was often on stand by from 0530 until dusk, and this began to affect morale. Bill Bromley recalls:

> Nearly every morning we were given an early call. We would have breakfast in the mess, walk up to our crew rooms and even have lunch brought up there so that we could be airborne as soon as possible when we got the operational call. Sometimes we would be sitting in the crew room all day, waiting for that call to come through, and the telephone would be going from time to time for legitimate enquiries: 'Is F/O So-and-so there?' or 'P/O So-and-so there?'

Eventually it was pointed out to the CO that this was bad for morale, and the point was taken, but considerable damage had been done. Bill Moseby recalls the days spent at readiness as

> like standing in the rain on a cold day on the top of a diving board, without any bathing trunks on, waiting for the umpire to blow the whistle!

A more humane system was evolved, whereby a squadron spent a day on stand by at one hour's notice from 0530, and a second at three hours' notice, followed by two days' stand down. Along with the new rotational system also went seventy-two hour leave for aircrew.

On 14 April, there occurred an extraordinary incident. A group of XV and 40 Squadron officers walking back to the hangars after lunch observed a Blenheim making a very poor take-off. At the controls was AC2 J. F. B. Lewis, who had been on guard duty when he started the machine and took off. It was rumoured that he had had elementary flying training in Canada and, having been rejected for pilot training, had somehow obtained a copy of the Pilot's Notes for the Blenheim IV, and was intent on demonstrating that he was pilot material. Whatever the truth, the outcome was tragic: Lewis died when his Blenheim spun into the Thames.

During April several significant personnel changes took place. On 20 April three senior members of the Squadron were posted away. One was 'Sam' Parker, appointed to command 226 Squadron, AASF; the others Bill Moseby and Douglas Wilson, whose postings are explained by the latter:

> In March 1940 the structure of command was altered to meet the responsibilities of the larger twin-engine squadron. Thus the Flight Commanders' posts were to be upgraded to Sqn/Ldr rank. Both Bill Moseby (two years Flight Commander) and self (one year) were told we were too young to hold the rank and Wg/Cdr. Barlow, very fairly, told Bill and me that we could stay if we wished under new 'imported' squadron leaders, or, in consideration of our considerable time in the Squadron, could, with assistance, seek other employment.

There was a significant promotion also, in the commissioning (on 6 May) of 'Chiefy' Thompson, the Warrant Officer Engineer. Both his appointment to F/O rank (appropriate under the new War Establishment order) and his retention on squadron—hitherto unheard of where promotions from the ranks occurred—point to the changes that were taking place in the RAF under the pressure of war.

During the first nine days of May no operations took place, though the Squadron was on stand by. On the 9th, however, Sqn/Ldr B. Paddon and F/O Burns were briefed for a reconnaissance of the Dutch-German border the following morning, to check on German troop movements. For 40 the war was about to begin in earnest.

# 10

# The Battle of France:
# May–June 1940

W HEN at dawn on 10 May 1940 the long-awaited German attack in
the west began, the 40 Squadron reconnaissance became the first 2
Group response to it. Brian Paddon and Robbie Burns took off at 0905,
crossed the North Sea at sea level, and near Rotterdam saw parachutes and
columns of smoke. Paddon was attacked by a Ju 88 after crossing the Dutch
coast and, faced with the obvious, returned rather than attempt further
reconnaissance. One engine caught fire as the Blenheim landed, but it was
quickly extinguished, and no one was injured.

What happened to the second crew is related by Jim Brooker, the observer:

> On reaching the Venlow area light flak was encountered. This continued
> on the Enshede leg and the aircraft was seen to have a number of holes
> in the wings. I received some shrapnel in my arm. A few minutes later
> the port engine caught fire and F/O Burns decided to make a wheels-up
> forced landing. This occurred in a field of cows beside the Rhine near
> Wesel, Germany. I suffered eleven broken ribs and concussion and the Air
> Gunner [Cpl Geoff Hurford] a broken leg. F/O Burns escaped with minor
> injuries.

After nine months of war, 40 had suffered its first loss.

After the departure of the two reconnaissance aircraft, 40 received Operations Instruction No. 31, which anticipated that the role of 2 Group
would be to locate and attack advancing enemy columns. But these plans
were foiled by the speed of the *Wehrmacht* advance, and the RAF's response
to the Blitzkreig had to be improvised, 2 Group beginning with raids on
Dutch airfields to prevent their use by the Germans. These attacks began
badly, with five out of six fighter Blenheims of 600 Squadron shot down.
XV Squadron fared better in an attack on Ju 52s at Waalhaven, all aircraft
returning safely. Then it was 40's turn, with Ypenburg aerodrome, at The
Hague, as the target.

Twelve aircraft were detailed to attack in sections at (fatal error) five
minute intervals, and Bill Bromley, flying as No. 2 to Bob Batt, remembers
the briefing as casual by later standards. Their section bombed successfully,
Bromley's bombs exploding in a hangar. He continues:

I thought I'd go down the line of Ju 52s which we had seen on the foreshore on the North Sea coast, as we were running in. I weaved and increased speed and dived, so as to have a run along the Ju 52s. From about the fourth or fifth aircraft some fellow in a grey uniform jumped out and started running up the dry sand towards the sandhills. Having just been shot at I was entering into the spirit of the thing and I gave him my front gun. It was like something from a Foreign Legion film. One could see where every shot went by the spurt of dry sand and I think I hit this poor fellow, because he went spreadeagled, and it looked too realistic to be faked.

Afterwards, coming out, I thought, 'Well damn it, you have killed some poor so-and-so in cold blood'.

Gerry Gleed's section also bombed unhindered, but the third and fourth sections ran into enemy fighters, and lost three aircraft, with a fourth damaged. Hugh Smeddle saw his No. 2, Percy Rowan, go down in flames and his No. 3, Sgt. I. L. Thomas, shot down also, while Jo Stevenson, who led the fourth section, recalls:

I led the last vic of three with a Sergeant Pilot [A. J. Robertson] as No. 2 and Pete Wakeford as No. 3. Crossing the coast (all on radio silence; our briefing was stupid), we changed over to 100 octane (outer tanks only), and climbed to 1,000 feet to bomb. The airfield was littered with parachutes and gliders. 'Bombs gone', and then it was 180° to nought feet. We shot over lawns in front of a magnificent brick building on the the east side, over an ack-ack gun, with a Dutch crew running to it, sleeves rolled up, capless; they stopped, recognizing us. Then out over the sea, hotly pursued. There was no sign of the No. 2 [Peter Wakeford recalls seeing it go down in flames on the run up to the target], but Pete was away to port. LAC Corney instructed us on evasive action and called to Usher [the observer] when he was replacing his empty 60 round pan on the V.G.O. Usher then fired blind (we were at nought feet). Twin cannon shell splashes appeared and I caught a glimpse of 'our' 110, which eventually broke off. Despite Corney's assurance, we remained at nought feet until near the English coast.

Peter Wakeford, also harried by an Me 110, likewise escaped by jinking violently at low level, returning to base without injury to the crew. It was realized what a close shave they had had, however, when it was revealed that a cannon shell had gone through the wing main spar. Hugh Smeddle, meanwhile, was struggling home in a damaged aircraft, the compass out of action, he and the observer, Sgt B. H. Wooldridge wounded, and the gunner, LAC G. D. P. Quinn, holding off enemy fighters. David Green writes:

It was not until Hugh Smeddle parked that we realized all was not well. Gerry Quinn was standing up in the rear turret, impassive as ever. Then Sgt. Wooldridge stood up in the front. The pained look on his face coincided with the arrival of the ambulance. We could then see that they had been shot up and both pilot and observer wounded. As they were taken off in the

THE BATTLE OF FRANCE

ambulance Gerry told us he had got one of the Me 109s. There was no jubilation in his voice. Neither was there jubilation in the faces of any of the other survivors as they climbed out of their aircraft.

For his skill and courage, Hugh Smeddle was awarded 40's first DFC of the war, while Wooldridge and Quinn received the DFM.

The losses of 10 May were traumatic. David Green went back to his barrack room to be confronted by empty beds, and the arrival of four new crews in the next few days underlined what had happened to a squadron hitherto exempt the losses suffered by other units.

On 12 May XV Squadron lost six out of twelve aircraft attacking Maastricht bridges. On 15 May, therefore, 40 supplied nine of twelve Blenheims detailed to attack and block roads in Dinant. The raid was led by Cecky Barlow, and included three others (F/O Edwards, Sgt Higgins and P/O F. R. McAuliffe), not on the Ypenburg raid. Jim Higgins recalls:

> There were 3 of us, Wg/Cdr Barlow leading, F/O Edwards as No 2 and myself as No 3. I have vivid memories of flying east through squadrons of German bombers flying west until we got near our target. Wg/Cdr Barlow was obviously lost for a while in the vicinity of the target, and we spent several precious minutes milling about until he and his navigator found the target. The weather was fine. About the same time as dropping our bomb loads I saw approaching us what appeared to be a black cloud of giant insects, later to be identified as Me 109s.
>
> The 109s pounced on us from the starboard quarter. All three of us dived for the ground & in doing so broke formation. It was each one for himself. We of course stood a better chance of denying them a rear attack from under the stern by flying as low as possible. I turned due south into the sun and fortunately found myself over a huge forest with wide fire breaks. I got into the fire breaks below the level of the tree-tops with 3 Me 109s harrying me. Of course it wasn't long before we were running out of forest but it was a start & long enough. At ground level my gunner, LAC Furby (later killed) was able to give almost as much as we were getting. In the end the Me's broke off & we returned safely to base. I never saw what happened to Wg/Cdr Barlow or to F/O Edwards.

In fact both crews had been shot down, and killed.

The death of Cecky Barlow came as a great shock. Bill Moseby recalls him as the first CO who mixed easily with those he commanded, and others his readiness to praise. Lawrence Ewels found him a 'kindly, humorous man', and his capacity for fun was certainly in evidence in his participation in the spoof photographs taken in Rheims. His loss on his first Blenheim operation must no doubt be put down primarily to bad luck, but it is worth noting that, heavily burdened with administration, he flew much less than any of his pilots, and a parallel with Leonard Tilney's loss in March 1918 seems appropriate.

With the death of Wg/Cdr Barlow, Brian Paddon assumed temporary command of the Squadron, and on 18 May he led six aircraft from 40 and six from XV in an attack on enemy troops and transport at Landrecies. Jo Stevenson recalls that fighter protection took the form of three Gladiators. One aircraft was attacked by Me 109s but these were driven off. No 40 Squadron aircraft were lost, though XV lost three.

On 19 May night flying exercises had been carried out at short notice, fitter Joe Raybould noting in his diary that men were sent into Huntingdon to round up those needed, and the following night six aircraft were detailed for an attack on German armoured columns at Aderard. One aircraft bombed a column of motor transport, and the others roads and the railway in the area. No aircraft were lost, but it seems that this new tactic was not successful, since it was not repeated until mid-July.

On 21 May three aircraft, together with six from XV Squadron, attacked armoured vehicles and motor transport in the vicinity of Abbéville. All returned safely, though Lawrence Ewels, Bob Batt's WOp/AG, was wounded in the leg by ground fire, and admitted to hospital. Next day 40 returned to the scene, three sections again bombing without loss. On 23 May, however,

it was a different story. Two sections, led by the newly arrived CO, Wg/Cdr J. G. Llewellyn, were detailed to attack German columns near Arras, in company with two from XV Squadron. Low cloud prevented this, so motorized columns near Boulogne were bombed. Two 40 Squadron aircraft and one from XV were lost, neither John Llewellyn nor F/O Ralph Jacoby returning. The latter survived, though the other crew members were killed. From Llewellyn's aircraft only the observer (Sgt Beattie) escaped, returning to the Squadron several days later. A story circulating amongst ground crew, and recalled by Joe Raybould, is that Llewellyn's aircraft caught fire, and he was seen trying to open the sliding hatch above his head. Joe gives credence to this, since the CO's aircraft had a hatch which was notoriously hard to open.

34. Wg/Cdr J. G. Llewellyn.
(XV Squadron.)

With the death of a second CO in eight days, Brian Paddon resumed command, as the RAF in an all-out effort began to support the BEF, penned in at Calais and Dunkirk. On the afternoon of 24 May, two sections attacked German armoured columns near Calais without loss, but an attack on a motorized column near Guines the next day met fierce light flak, one aircraft being shot down, and four others damaged. Of Sgt S. I. Tonks' crew only he survived.

On 26 May the Dunkirk evacuation began, and 40 supplied six aircraft for a major attack on targets around Courtrai. A fighter escort was provided, and no 40 Squadron aircraft were lost. Two escorted operations the next day were also flown without loss, as was an afternoon raid on the 28th, when nine aircraft attacked German columns north of St. Omer, scoring hits on tanks and machine gunning motor transport.

On 29 May bad weather hindered an attack on targets between Ostend and Nieuport, though lorries were bombed, while the next day low cloud both prevented half of a combined 40/XV Squadron force bombing troops and transport on the Dixmude-Roulers road. On the morning of 31 May six Blenheims attacked enemy transport and armoured columns near Dixmude, troops and horse-drawn artillery being bombed and machine gunned, while in the afternoon bridges near Nieuport were the target of another six. No Blenheims were lost then, or on 1 June, when twelve aircraft attacked enemy troop and vehicle concentrations around Hondeschoote, hits on motor vehicles being reported.

From 30 May all aircrew were of sergeant rank or above. This was not merely a matter of status or pay. It also had important consequences for POWs, since those below sergeant rank were assigned to work camps. There was another change, too, an end to a situation explained by Barclay 'Curly' Baker, who found himself a sergeant at the ripe age of 18:

> In those days we came back from ops and the gun had to be dismounted, taken into the armoury, cleaned, replaced in the aircraft, and the round cans of ammo had to be refurbished, which meant that it could be anything up to two and a half hours before you could go for a meal, and if the airmen's mess was closed at that time, that was too bad. You borrowed money and went to the Naafi and bought your bun and cup of tea.

Henceforth WOp/AGs would be treated as specialist aircrew, like observers and pilots, and the servicing of guns and wireless would be the responsibility of armourers and wireless mechanics.

The Dunkirk evacuation ended on 3 June. Save on the last two days the Squadron had operated once and sometimes twice a day, and though no aircraft had been lost, the crews were exhausted. Nor was the absence of operations a respite. For except on 4 June, when the Squadron was stood down, sections were on stand by at one to three hours' notice, and the

35. Wg/Cdr D. H. F. Barnett.
(P. Barnett.)

hours of inactivity were particularly difficult. For ground crews, on the other hand, the first days of June brought a respite from the long hours—on occasion twenty out of twenty-four—needed to keep the Blenheims operational.

On 4 June Wg/Cdr D. H. F. Barnett, a New Zealander, assumed command of 40 Squadron, and next day he was shown round by Brian Paddon, and introduced to members of the Squadron. Then on the 6th Paddon failed to return, along with four other crews. It was a sobering introduction to the Squadron, and it was perhaps fortunate for Denis Barnett that he himself was not immediately able to operate, since he was short of a gunner.

The operation on 6 June followed dawn reconnaissance flights by Jo Stevenson and Bob Batt. The latter's Blenheim was attacked by three Me 109s, one of which was claimed shot down. Jo Stevenson's flight was equally eventful:

We reached the Canal de la Somme and turned along it for the coast at nought feet, below tree level. I saw an island ahead, with a post on it, and dipped the starboard wing to avoid it, having had to climb a little. There was a horrendous noise and the starboard engine stopped, the prop. flailing. There had been a cable attached to the post, and the starboard wing was damaged. With less lift and a dead engine I could not maintain height, or prevent the aircraft turning starboard towards the shore. Then Usher came to the rescue, switching over from the outer tanks (100 octane for recce) to the main, and the engine picked up. I made a mental note that I must jettison the bombs, and make a fast approach to retain lift on the starboard wing. However, I forgot both and the starboard wing kissed the grass as the landing was completed firstly on the starboard wheel, then on both wheels. Fortunately the aircraft ran straight.

Twelve aircraft, led by Sqn/Ldr Gleed, took off at 0830 to bomb an enemy concentration near Abbéville. Three hours later, seven returned. That most of the missing had survived, and four would return to Wyton, was not yet known. What was obvious were the fifteen empty beds that night.

36. Blenheim L4908 (F/O P. F. T. Wakeford) en route for Abbeville, 22 May 1940.
(J. C. Stevenson.)

The five Blenheims brought down succumbed to a combination of flak and fighters. P/O B. B. James, inexperienced, dropped back and was shot down, the crew perishing, but all the others survived, some injured. Sgt D. J. Rice's crew, and Brian Paddon's, were taken prisoner.[1] P/O V. G. W. Engstrom's observer (Sgt M. R. Chouler) and gunner (Sgt D. Liddle) suffered a similar fate when their Blenheim crash landed just ahead of the advancing German forces, Engstrom escaping capture because he had, though injured, gone for help for the others. Peter Wakeford also crash-landed his aircraft, in circumstances recalled by Bertie Wallace, his observer:

We were hit by pom-pom shells in the first instance; we lost an engine and all three of us were sprayed with shrapnel. We were then finished off by Me 109's. Wakeford did a magnificent job in crash-landing our damaged aircraft despite his own wounds, and I have thought, over the years, that had his conduct and bearing been observed by people a little older than Curly Baker and me (neither of us yet 19 years old) he must surely have been considered for a bravery award.

Wallace had a shrapnel wound; Wakeford a broken arm, and Curly Baker, shrapnel in his back, and a bullet in his leg. Peter Wakeford recalls:

> We were taken in hand by a French farmer and his wife, who poured some stuff down us—it must have been eau de vie. I remember choking and being sick, but it seemed to help Curly.

All three were taken to Rouen for treatment, Wallace managing to get away with refugees fleeing westward and returning by boat, while Peter Wakeford hitched a ride in a Blenheim night fighter. Baker also returned by boat after an extraordinary series of events which included capture and treatment by the Germans, escape from a field hospital in the back of a truck driven by a British soldier, travel to St. Nazaire with the help of French civilians, and smuggling out to sea in a rubbish barge. His account concludes:

> I felt the motion of this tug going, and away we went and many hours later there was a shout and the tarpaulin pulled back and these barges were full of people, soldiers, sailors, and airmen; hundreds. And I would say that to get from the barge to climb aboard this hospital ship (I believe it was called the *Dorchester*) I would say that I had to cross 10 to 20 other craft. And my last glimpse as I went over the side was of boats coming from all directions: canoes, yachts, everything.

Baker did not to return to the Squadron for many weeks. When he did, he found scarcely anyone whom he knew.

The losses of 6 June meant five new crews and a new Flight Commander, Hugh Smeddle, back from hospital, assuming command of A Flight, with Jo Stevenson, promoted to flight lieutenant, as his deputy.

What it felt like on squadron at this time can be gauged from Bertie Wallace's recollection not only of 'the empty bed-spaces in the large barrack-room which I shared with other NCO aircrew', but also 'the line of small cars awaiting disposal—most of them of the sporty type'.

On 7 June, two sections attacked motor transport in the village of Miannay, and the following day two more bombed tanks near Poix. Fighter escort was provided, and all returned safely. The pattern was repeated on 9 June, when two sections bombed armoured vehicles and transport near Neufchatel and on the 10th, when the target was armoured vehicles around Rouen. All returned safely, reporting that they had attacked convoys in the area, scoring direct hits. On 11 June, again without loss, three sections attacked enemy troops in the Seine valley, scoring some hits.

Several features of the operations during this period stand out. One is the length of time during which crews were held on stand by. On 9 June, for instance, two sections on stand by from 0900 finally took off at 1540, while the previous day they were on stand by from 0900 and took off at 1430. Not all this time was spent in the Crew Room. For when on two hour stand by, crews might be given permission to drive to nearby Houghton, for a swim in the River Ouse. Nonetheless, the stress was considerable, greater for most than operational flying itself.

Occasionally a day's stand down was announced, and Curly Baker recalls that

> you'd tear back to the billet to change, and hope you could get on the back of somebody's motor bike, or a lift in a car and all go down to The Jolly Butcher in Houghton—a favourite aircrew haunt—or The Cricketers in St. Ives. The reason The Cricketers was a favourite was because the publican had played for England and he had two gorgeous daughters.

Others favoured The Market Inn in Huntingdon, where George and Eve Ashpole were kindly hosts, while officers tended to congregate at The George, in Huntingdon, or The Red Lion in St. Ives.

Also noteworthy is the high proportion of new crews operating. Of six crews up on 10 June, for instance, two were on their first operation, with two out of nine the following day also operational for the first time. Some of these became veterans themselves—P/O W. M. Lewis, for instance, and P/O F. A. Bowler—but others survived only briefly. Sgt C. W. D. Bartlam was shot down on what was effectively his first op., while P/O James had been with the Squadron ten days, and Sgt Tonks a week. 'New boys started dropping back over enemy territory', Jim Higgins writes, 'purely through insufficient training, and the moment they dropped back if there was a fighter about, they would get picked off. It was harrowing.'

On 12 June two sections attacked a battery firing at evacuation beaches at St. Valery, but the target was covered in low cloud, and only Bill Bromley's section located the guns, claiming one hit. However, Sgt Bartlam's aircraft was hit by flak, and though he and the Wop/Ag (Sgt E. Rodgers) escaped by parachute, the observer (Sgt D. L. Dorris) was killed. Similar difficulties in locating targets were experienced on 13 June, when three sections set out to attack motor transport in the Forêt de Bizy, only five of the nine crews bombing. Two crews (Sgts W. B. Cowman and K. Newton) searched for forty-five minutes before abandoning the task.

The 14th of June brought the Fall of Paris, and with it the virtual end of French resistance. For 40 it also brought the worst losses since 6 June. Three sections were briefed to attack targets in the Eure Valley around Breteuil, but only the the third was successful, the second section returning with their bombs, and the first encountering flak so accurate that one aircraft (P/O Bowler) was forced to turn back, its oil tank holed, and two (Sqn/Ldr Gleed and P/O Lewis) were shot down. Lewis, one engine on fire, gave the order to 'Abandon aircraft'. His observer, Bob Currie, recalls:

> I jettisoned the bombload, then the escape hatch and blister gun before heading back out of the nose to get my parachute pack on. Then there was a difference of opinion with the pilot. Butch seemed to think that I had decided not to bale out, so put a foot on my chest and began pushing me out. I waved like mad and got him to see that I hadn't got my pack on. After that I quickly clipped on my chute, knelt on the edge of the escape hatch, noticed the altimeter showing 1000 feet and rolled out, forgetting to take off my helmet. Whilst getting my chute I had seen the WOp/AG still removing the camera mounting to get at his escape hatch. I pulled my ripcord fairly quickly, the chute opened, I saw the Blenheim going into the ground in a trail of smoke and flame, then I touched down, standing up, very gently as there was no wind. I heard the aircraft's fuel tanks explode, noticed a lot of soldiers in grey uniforms staring at the wreckage, so quickly got rid of my chute and headed for a ditch.

Currie soon found that the troops were Belgian, and was able to use his schoolboy French to convince them of his nationality, and that of Lewis, whom he found near by, 'shouting loudly in English, so the foreigners would understand that he was RAF'. Lewis had baled out at 300 feet, his parachute barely opening in time. The WOp/AG (Sgt S. W. Johnson) had been less fortunate, and perished in the crash.

The adventures that befell Lewis and Currie *en route* back to England would grace a novel of derring-do. Having hitched a ride with a Belgian general as far as Tours, they stayed overnight with a French fighter unit, then hitched a further ride in a Bloch bomber—Lewis as co-pilot and Currie as gunner—and at Nantes joined the personnel of a Hurricane squadron about to fly out their last serviceable machines. Currie was told to join ground crew who were about to be evacuated by lorry to St. Nazaire, thence by the *Lancastria* to England, but they had just left (fortunately, since the *Lancastria* was bombed, and sank with heavy loss of life) and he was smuggled aboard a Handley-Page Harrow about to be flown back to Heston with a load of parachutes—'smuggled' because the Station Commander had decreed, imbecilically, that no one was to be evacuated by air, and had only let Lewis fly with the Harrow's pilot because he lacked a co-pilot or navigator. In the event, Currie ended up navigating for the two, who had no maps, and brought them safely to Heston.

Gerry Gleed, all of whose crew perished, was a great loss to the Squadron. Promoted to flight commander on the departure of Eric Springall, he had, in the bloody battles since 10 May, led by example, coolly courageous. Bill Oxley, who flew with him occasionally pre-war, remembers:

> a quiet unassuming officer and a very good pilot. He never seemed to raise his voice and always seemed to be in control of any situation. I have very

fond memories of him not only for his piloting but for his efforts [as Adjutant, pre-war] for the well-being of *all* members of the Squadron.

Gleed was succeeded as B Flight commander by Bob Batt, George Hill becoming his deputy.

Mercifully, after the losses of 14 June, the Squadron had four days without operating. When the Squadron was next up, on 19 June, their target was a German-occupied aerodrome. It was the beginning of a new operational phase both for 40 Squadron and for 2 Group. The Battle of France was over, and as Winston Churchill prophesied, the Battle of Britain was about to begin.

# Note

1.  Terry Foreman, Brian Paddon's WOp/AG, writes:

    We were shot down by Me 109s. I and the other two crew escaped by parachute. My pilot, Sqn/Ldr Paddon, escaped from the well known punishment camp Colditz in 1942. On his return he was made Group Captain and commanded a station. My observer, Sgt Salvage, escaped from the train on our way to the POW camp and I never heard from him again.

    Salvage was in fact recaptured, and spent the rest of the war as a POW. Concerning Brian Paddon's career as an escaper, see P. R. Reid, *Colditz: The Full Story*. London: Macmillan, 1984. Sqn/Ldr Paddon's account of his capture, imprisonment and escape is contained in PRO file WO 208/3310.

# 11

# The Battle of Britain: June–October 1940

WHEN after a four day break 40 resumed operational flying on 19 June, it was in a new role. Hitherto the majority of targets had been enemy columns, but for the next month the characteristic mix would be weather and photographic reconnaissance and attacks on aerodromes, with occasional sorties to Germany and night operations. Two Group's primary task was now to bomb the *Luftwaffe*'s bases in France and the Low Countries, and thereby assist Fighter Command, engaged in the opening phases of the Battle of Britain. At first these attacks were at two section strength, but later harassment raids were by single sections, and often by single aircraft. Fighter escort being a luxury, cloud cover was generally used, and hence many operations were, during the beautiful summer of 1940, abandoned.

On 19 June, Boos and Amiens aerodromes were attacked, with direct hits claimed, and at Amiens aircraft damaged and set on fire, but lack of cloud cover led to the abandonment of three morning reconnaissances in the next week, while four of the six Blenheims which took off in the late afternoon of the 25th to attack Waalhaven airfield turned back for the same reasons.

On 27 June 2 Group scheduled two escorted photographic reconnaissances by 40 of the coast from St. Valery-en-Caux to Le Crotoy (i.e., twenty-five miles either side of Dieppe) to discover the extent of a build up of land forces and shipping for an invasion of England. Using six aircraft taking line overlaps, it was hoped that a comprehensive record of German activity could be obtained.

The morning reconnaissance went without incident, protected by a strong force of Hurricanes. The afternoon operation was not so lucky. For halfway across the Channel the fighter escort left, low on fuel, and the rear section was jumped by Me 109s. Bill Bromley recalls that his WOp/AG (Sgt J. A. Gamble) was transmitting a message to Wyton, reporting the successful completion of the reconnaissance, when 'all of a sudden the whole of hell let loose'. Three 20-mm shells had hit the aircraft, one exploding in the cockpit, a second on the radio, and a third passing without exploding through the starboard oil tank. The shell that burst in the cockpit had put most of the instruments out of action, and damaged the hydraulics, while a piece of shrapnel had penetrated Bromley's headset, embedding itself in the earphone. Bill writes:

Gamble had a 20mm shell explode very close to him on his equipment. Despite severe leg wounds, he crawled forward to tell me that the intercom was out of action, which was absolutely heroic of him.

I had been doing quite a lot of things while he had been crawling forward. I looked around and my No 2 was OK but my No 3 [Sgt J. L. Morton] was nowhere to be seen; he had already spun into the Channel. I thought the starboard engine was on fire, but it was in fact oil from the oil tank vapourising, and at the speed we were going it looked like black smoke. I feinted by dummying a spin to low level, and feathered the engine on the way down.

I managed to hold her on one engine, although the air speed indicator had gone, and got down as close as I could to the ground before I pulled out of this deliberate spiral dive. I pulled up at the cliffs, and fortunately there was Hawkinge airfield straight ahead. I dispensed with the niceties of finding out which way the wind was blowing and managed to put the Blenheim down on one undercarriage leg (on the other the hydraulics had gone) so though we touched down all right, we did a ground loop at the end of the run. I nipped out with my navigator and we got Ginger Gamble out of the back, into an ambulance and away. As soon as I made contact with base I strongly recommended that he be awarded an instant Distinguished Flying Medal.

Still in a wheelchair, John Gamble joined Sgts F. G. Nevill and Wooldridge in receiving his DFM at Wyton from Air Marshal Sir Charles Portal, on 29 July.

Because only vital Blenheim operations could be given fighter support, much depended on the weather, and on thirteen days during July reconnaissance sorties had to be abandoned and sections on stand by stood down. On a number of other occasions, moreover, raids were either aborted when cloud ran out, or alternative targets attacked. And here again the order that a sortie should continue only if cloud cover was 7/10ths or more caused problems. Old hands did the sensible thing, but new crews sometimes flew on when conditions did not warrant it. P/O Peter Billyeald persisted in an attack on Caen airfield on 9 July when the other two crews turned back, and recalls that

on my return to base I was met on the tarmac by a worried CO who informed me that the other—more experienced—pilots had aborted their sorties because they had assessed the cloud-cover as inadequate. I was mildly rebuked because the briefing had stressed the importance of 'adequate' cloud cover.

Some of the most difficult ops were the dawn weather and photo-reconnaissance sorties. Flown by experienced crews, they involved solo flights as far afield as Kiel and Bremen, and imposed particular pressures

because the day's bombing operations frequently depended on their outcome. On 7 July Hugh Smeddle abandoned a reconnaissance of Kiel
because of insufficient cloud. Two days later Bob Batt, on a mission to
Lisieux, failed to return. Later his body, and that of his WOp/AG (Sgt
P. E. Johnson), were picked up in the English Channel by a destroyer,
and buried at sea. Bill Bromley recalls a story that circulated to the effect
that 'the fellow who pulled Bob Batt out of the water was an old friend
of ours who knew Bob well from Abingdon days, when we used to drink
at The Dog House'.

Bob Batt was one of 40 Squadron's 'characters'. An ebullient individual,
he cultivated a degree of eccentricity, and was always to the fore in squadron
activities, as in the formation of the band. He was also a fine pilot who
took his flying seriously, and Lawrence Ewels recalls that 'one of his practices
when returning from a quiet mission was to throttle back the engines at
about 3000 feet and make a landing without using them again!'. 'It was a
bit hairy', he continues, 'but he had in mind the possibility of coming back
damaged one day and of being able to land first time regardless of a faulty
engine or other problems'. Bob Batt's death came as a shock. If he could
not survive, who could?

To aircrew with 40 since the Blitzkreig began, this was a question of
some significance. Of eighteen pilots on 10 May, only five were now left:
Hugh Smeddle, Jo Stevenson, George Hill, Peter Wakeford and Jim Higgins.
For them, and for the groundcrew, who had taken such a pride in 'their'
aircraft and 'their' crew, the loss of so many familiar faces—and of many
unfamiliar ones—generated a sadness which Bob Batt's death intensified.

Only one operation was flown during the six days from 10 July, and that
(13 July) was only a partial success. A section led by Flt/Lt Paine was detailed
to attack Brussels aerodrome using cloud cover. The usual problems of
defining 'adequate' led Paine to abandon the operation, and P/O G. Parker
to bomb barges near Bruges, but Sgt Johnson pressed on to Brussels and
bombed.

On 17 July three crews were detailed for night ops. This had occurred
once before, as a response to devastating losses on daylight operations. This
raid, however, marked a first, tentative outcome of discussions at 2 Group
HQ, and two more would be scheduled before, on 12 August, night bombing
began on a sustained basis, with daylight operations flown only rarely
thereafter.

The first night ops. were not particularly successful. Of three crews
operating on 17 July only one (P/O W. R. Evans) bombed the aerodrome
at Lannion, but on the return journey he was driven off course by storms,
and forced-landed on Exmoor. On 25 July the results were not much better.
For though most of the crews bombed aerodromes in Flanders, they were

unable to observe results. Moreover, Sgt P. H. Steele's crew did not return. Their aircraft crippled by flak, they had baled out, the WOp/AG (Sgt R. Peacock) so low that he was saved only when the updraft from the exploding Blenheim gave his parachute time to deploy fully.

Two sections were on stand by most days in the last fortnight of July, but only one major operation was flown, on the evening of 18 July, when three sections attacked shipping at Boulogne, reporting hits on ships and warehouses. This raid was significant as a first by on invasion ports. During August these attacks on harbours and shipping would occur rarely, and only when aerodromes were not located. From September onwards, however, they become the primary objectives.

One other event in July deserves mention: the visit to Wyton of a team filming for the popular *March of Time* series. Ground crews were filmed bombing up 40's Blenheims, and aircrew being briefed, and then driven out to their machines. The Squadron then took off, to be filmed in formation over eastern England. In fact the whole 'operation' was faked, Joe Raybould recalling that ground crew were called upon to rock a Blenheim, simulating flight, while the camera team photographed the observer and pilot through the nose of the stationary machine. For the aerial filming the cameraman flew in Jo Stevenson's aircraft, and the latter recalls how when 'on return to base, I flew over Flying Control and then stuffed the nose down. Sadly, the poor man, sitting in the right hand seat, was violently sick.' Observer Frank Fitton remembers that when the Blenheims did a dummy bombing run on the drome with $11\frac{1}{2}$-lb practice bombs, 'the CO didn't allow for the starboard vic being near the hangars, and on the signal to bomb, the big wigs sitting on the tarmac were running all over the place'.

During early August, 40 was still operating by day, but brilliantly fine weather meant that only on the 2nd was an operation completed, five aircraft attacking aerodromes and one (Sgt Johnson) hitting barges and a lockgate and bridge at Leimuiden. Otherwise, until 12 August the entries in the ORB are largely a catalogue of stand bys, abandoned operations and stand downs. On 9 August, however, there is an entry of considerable significance: 'Sgt HIGGINS granted commission as P/O and reported for duty'. The significance lies not just in the commissioning of a sergeant pilot, very rare pre-war, but in the fact that he remained on squadron. Six months earlier this would have been unthinkable.

On 12 August three aircraft carried out a night attack on the aerodrome at Dinard, P/O Goodman starting fires, and Sgt Johnson's crew, though unable to observe the results of their own bombing, noted that 'someone had been there before, one hangar being on fire'. It was an operation noteworthy in only one respect: that it marked the beginning of a campaign

37. Bombing up, Wyton, 22 July 1940.
(Chaz Bowyer.)

38. Preparing to take-off, Wyton, 25 July 1940.
(Imperial War Museum.)

of night bombing to be sustained until the war's end. Henceforth, daylight ops would be a rare exception.

From the 12th to the end of August 40 Squadron operated intensively, aerodromes in Brittany, Normandy and the Channel Islands receiving particular attention. Generally two sections operated, with the aircraft sent to different 'dromes for maximum disruption. The results varied greatly: a typical night's work, on 23 August, resulting in two crews reporting large fires; three others that bombs were dropped without significant results; and one that the target could not be identified, so an AA battery was attacked.

Despite the shift to night ops, five crews were lost during the second half of August. On the 15th two crews failed to return from an attack on the airfield at Chartres. P/O Parker's crew survived, he as a POW and the others (the observer, Sgt G. H. Easton and the WOp/AG, (Sgt E. G. Watson) evading, and reaching Spain, returning via Gibraltar to England and (in Watson's case) to the Squadron. Sgt Newton's crew survived also when their aircraft was crippled by coastal AA batteries near Cherbourg and ditched, with Newton himself seriously wounded.

Two out of three crews were lost on 25 August, when only Jim Higgins returned after a successful diving attack on Le Treport Aerodrome. The other two (Sqn/Ldr F. G. R. Thomas and Sgt C. P. Riley) perished. Both were newcomers, Thomas (appointed OC B Flight on 21 August) on his second operation, and Riley on his fourth.

The fifth aircraft lost was that of P/O Evans, who crashed on take-off on the 30th, all three crew members being killed. The accident card states that the Blenheim 'crashed immediately after turning left and losing height on take-off', noting that the 'Pilot [was] dependent on visual aids only on night take-off with no horizon'. That this was felt to be unsatisfactory is suggested by the endorsement by the AOC 2 Group: 'Additional aids are now in use'.

September 2nd brought further losses when Flt/Sgt R. B. Broadhurst failed to return from an attack on Nordenham, and P/O R. V. Whitehead crashed on landing. Jim Robbins, the WOp/AG, recalls:

Due to weather conditions we couldn't make Wyton and I vaguely remember approaching my old airfield of West Raynham. I think that we hit a tree and I was extremely fortunate as I was crouched down messing around with the radio. One of the ammunition pans sprang off and hit me on the head, and when I came to it was pitch black and I was on my own, the aircraft having been severed just ahead of the turret. I fell out backwards into a ploughed field, but saw no sign of the rest of the aircraft so, having no broken bones, started walking. Near a hedge I came across a main wheel and half way over the next field I came across another, and so I just followed bits of wreckage until I came to the main part of the aircraft.

Robbins climbed into the wrecked Blenheim, to find the pilot, dead he thought, in front of the control column, and located Paddy Coburn, the observer, some twenty yards in front of the wreckage. Coburn was indeed dead, killed instantly when flung through the nose of the aircraft, but Whitehead survived to return to operations with 40. Jim Robbins also resumed operational flying, only to be seriously injured in May 1941.

During the first week of September a mix of aerodrome and shipping targets was attacked, but from the 7th 40 focussed exclusively on harbours and shipping, as Britain faced the threat of sea-borne invasion. On 8 September nine aircraft went to Ostend, one (Sgt L. F. S. Patrick, on his second operation) failing to return. Also up that night was Jim Higgins:

> My final operational raid, on barges deployed in the OSTEND canals, was on 8 Sept 1940. I was fully aware that it was to be my last raid. Therefore I was extremely apprehensive, particularly since Two Gun Cody [Sgt. A Cody, the observer] demanded 3 dummy runs over the target before dropping the bombs, and also because we were at fairly low level, coned by searchlights, & seeing tracer shooting up like incandescent fire hoses. Never was I so thankful to get back to terra-firma.

Very much 'the linchpin of the NCO aircrew complement' in Denis Barnett's opinion, Jim Higgins was the last of the pilots who had served with 40 Squadron since the outbreak of war. For during July Bill Bromley, Peter Wakeford and Jo Stevenson had been posted, and in August George Hill and Hugh Smeddle.

Hill's departure was part of a programme which the Squadron had been told about a week previously: delivering Blenheims to the Middle East. The first crews, who left Wyton for Thorney Island and Malta on 17 August, were those of Flt/Lts Hill and Bush, and P/O Lewis. Three more (Flt/Lt Paine and P/Os Traill-Smith and Goodman) were to leave on 11 September.[1]

Between 10th September and the end of the month, nine ops were flown against harbour facilities and shipping at Ostend, Boulogne and Calais. The most successful was probably on the 21st, when large fires were started, and 'a terrific explosion'. No aircraft were lost during this period, though the flak was intense at times, and one crew, at least, had a brush with a night fighter, P/O Winstone-Smith's gunner (Sgt Shawyer) claiming a victory on 30 September.

The same night P/O A. D. Greer RNZAF had a close shave over Boulogne. Alex Greer writes:

> The squadron was sent some anti-icing spark plugs—experimental ones— and we were supposed to go out and find some ice clouds and try them out. My Blenheim had them fitted in one engine (port). However, we were put on ops that night, and someone forgot to put back the usual plugs. It was a

crystal clear night over the target and about −30° outside temperature. It was a theory of some of the 'Know alls' that by imitating the off-beat throb of most German aircraft we could probably fool the German AA and Searchlights into thinking it was one of theirs. So as we were on our bombing run I had the port throttle slightly back to give my engines the 'German sound'. However, just as we let our bombs go we were coned, so I opened the port throttle for more power to jink out of trouble, and instead of picking up the port engine stopped dead and we flipped into a vicious left hand spin. I pulled out of that and must have over-corrected, for we whipped into a right hand spin which I got out of at under 500 feet over the docks, where our bombs were going off. The warm atmosphere—and the spin no doubt—had started up the port engine, and I screamed out to sea, followed by an Me110 night fighter as we left the coast. I lost him out over the Channel when we went through a 2000 feet layer of cloud, levelling out about 1000 feet above the sea. The bombsight was wrenched off the mounting by the spin and the wireless set pitched up in Sgt. Hobbs' lap.

The first fortnight of October brought further raids on harbours and shipping, though deteriorating weather meant that only five were completed. None were particularly successful, and that on Antwerp on 2 October, an almost complete failure. Of the six crews detailed, only one (Sgt R. E. Finlayson RNZAF) who made a low-level attack, positively identified where their bombs had fallen. Three others made high-level attacks, with bombs falling 'in the target area', but 'results not observed', while a fifth carried out a high-level attack 'on the Flushing area', and the last failed to find either target.

Something of how it felt on squadron at this time can be gained from a letter written on 10 October by Monty Coe to fellow observer Frank Fitton. It reads, in part:

> We're still on night trips but have lost six kites since Ken [Newton] went down:- Reilly [sic] (Sgt. Pilot) and crew; that new B Flight Commander, Sqn/Ldr Thomas; Chiefy Broadhurst, Marsden, and Jock Burns; Evans, Frank Little and Jock Watts; Alf Coburn was killed in a crash at Raynham when Whitehead pulled his flaps up instead of his undercart after overshooting— Robins [sic] (A.G.) was hurt but both he and Whitehead will be okay after a spell in hospital. You don't know the others, they're all new blokes.
>
> By the way I fly with 'Ginger' Johnson and 'Paddy' Morrison these days and on Monday night coming back from Ostend we ran into an electric storm. My Christ!! We fell about 5,000 ft. in stops and starts and bumps and bangs and little blue devils were dancing all round the instruments, the prop-tips and the aerial; it was a shaky do alright.

Weather affected the operations flown during October, Battle Orders being posted only eight times in the last seventeen days, and operations completed on only five, two night ops being cancelled before take-off, and a daylight attack on Den Helder, Rotterdam and Flushing on 19 October—

the last until July 1941—being abandoned when (surprise) cloud cover ran out. During this period there is evidence of a shift in targets. The attacks on Calais, Rotterdam and Antwerp continued, but mixed with German targets such as Krefeldt, Essen and Köln. Not much was achieved, for weather and navigational difficulties prevented most crews finding their targets, though the five aircraft which went to Antwerp on 26 October returned with clear accounts of bombs bursting on the docks.

On 28 October 40 flew its last Blenheim op, eight aircraft attacking targets in Holland and Germany. All bombed their primary targets, though the only specific account of results came from P/O Winstone-Smith, who reported that he had attacked the Dutch aerodrome at Waalhaven, where flying was in progress, and that the bombs had fallen in the middle of the flarepath. From the others came general accounts of fires and bombs dropped in the target area, but not of specific damage. It was an outcome typical of Bomber Command operations at this time, and of 40 Squadron's experience when bombing beyond the Channel Ports and Ostend.

On 29 October the ORB noted that F/O S. Palmer, the Squadron Gunnery Officer, was attached to 75 Squadron at Feltwell 'for three days' instruction in Wellington aircraft'. It is the first mention of a re-equipment programme which took 40 off operations for almost two months, and out of 2 Group. Before it handed over its Blenheims, however, there occurred an incident which made a fitting end to the Squadron's operational employment of the type. It occurred on 30 October, when Sqn/Ldr E. J. Little, the B Flight Commander, on a training flight, encountered a Ju 88. The Wyton ORB reports that 'The enemy aircraft was engaged with both front and rear guns, and was seen to be hit in the port wing and fuselage. Black smoke was coming from one engine, but the enemy was lost sight of in the mist'. The 88 was in fact brought down, and the crew taken prisoner. Forty's experience with the Blenheim had not on the whole been a happy one, but it certainly began (with Bill Moseby's victory on 1 April) and ended spectacularly.

As a flying machine the Blenheim was praised, but as a fighting machine it was too slow and inadequately armed. It was also badly designed, ergonometrically, one of the major causes of accidents on take-offs and landings arising from the placing of the undercarriage and flap levers so close to one another that on overshooting the inexperienced pilot could easily make the fatal mistake of raising the flaps. Nor was it only the pilot who had problems, as Jim Robbins recalls:

The equipment for the WOp/AG was pathetic. A 1082/1083 transmitter and re-ceiver were situated down by your knees in a tiny turret amidships. There was a single Vickers gas-operated gun on a central column but hydraulically operated, and fed by pans of ammunition holding about 100 rounds. Spare pans were spring clipped below the turret. To change wavelength, coils had to be changed and

I found that if one was about 50 miles from the station they could be heard, but not much beyond. To operate the set at night was awkward, as the receiver had to be brought off oscillation, which meant taking off your glove, wetting your finger and tapping a metal point on the set. No wonder we called ourselves 'The Grand Antediluvian Order of Lickers and Tappers'.

Another problem was that the Blenheim had no heating system, and at times crews endured intense cold, which undoubtedly impaired their operational efficiency.

On 1 November 40 Squadron received this signal from AVM Robb, AOC 2 Group:

> Now that Wyton, with Nos 15 and 40 Squadrons, is leaving 2 Group, I wish to express my warmest appreciation of the splendid manner in which all ranks have upheld the highest traditions of our service.
>
> The well executed and determined bombing by the flying crews and the high standard of serviceability of the Wyton aircraft have been deserving of special praise. I wish you all good luck and trust that your good fortune will always be with you.

However well-meant, the message hardly reflected reality when it referred to 'your good fortune'. For though 40 suffered no more severely than many other squadrons in 2 Group, and was spared the massacre which attended AASF Battle squadrons in France, it nonetheless sustained decimating losses during May and June. By the end of July only a handful of crews remained from the palmy days of pre-war Abingdon, and by mid-August these, too, were gone, and a new era had begun, with (save among the ground crews, where there was a high degree of continuity) members of the RAFVR now predominating. The autumn, too, saw the arrival of Dominion aircrew, at first mainly from New Zealand. For the rest of the war, Dominion aircrew would form a significant and sometimes dominant part of the Squadron.

During the Blitzkreig morale undoubtedly suffered, the loss of two COs bringing the Squadron to its lowest ebb. Nor was the situation helped by the situation at Wyton, Group Captain Lawrence being regarded as insensitive and overbearing, and the Station Adjutant unhelpful. Under the firm but sympathetic command of Denis Barnett, however, morale recovered, while Wyton became a pleasanter place under Lawrence's successor, Gp/Cpt 'Pussy' Foster. By the end of October, when 40 relinquished its Blenheims, it was in good heart. During the dark months of 1941, it needed to be.

# Note

1.  Navigational error led P/O Goodman to land on the Italian island of Pantelleria. He eventually made his way back to Britain via neutral territory, but his crew (P/O K. E. Grey and Sgt R. B. W. Shaw) were taken prisoner.

# 12

# Operations with 3 Group:
# November 1940–October 1941

W HEN 40 Squadron joined 3 Group it was in the process of shifting from Wyton to the satellite aerodrome at Alconbury, where B Flight, under Sqn/Ldr Little, functioned autonomously. 'Daddy' Little (as he was widely known) was a devout man, and Bertie Wallace recalls that

> he maintained close associations with the Church, and demonstrated them publicly at Alconbury where, as CO of B flight, he was the 'station commander' as well, by requiring the officers to take lunch and dinner together, whenever possible, and starting the meals by saying grace, much to the amusement of his junior officers.

Others recall the unwelcome solicitude with which he would call in at the local pub, about 9 pm, to suggest that the men consider making their way back to Alconbury because 'You've got to be fit for this job'.

On 3 November P/O M. W. Hartford was posted in to convert pilots to the Wellington, using a dual control aircraft, and on the 5th Flt/Lt E. H. Lynch-Blosse converted to the type and flew to Aldergrove to collect the first of the Squadron's Ics. By 15 November the flying programme was based exclusively on the Wellington, and on the 26th the last Blenheim left.

The Vickers Wellington Ic, with which 40 was now equipped, was a medium bomber with a crew of six. Powered by two Bristol Pegasus engines of 1,050 hp, and with a maximum speed of 235 mph at 15,500 feet, and a service ceiling of 18,000 feet, the Ic had a maximum range of 2,550 miles at 180 mph. The armament consisted of twin-gun nose and tail turrets, and beam guns, and a maximum bomb load of 4,500 lbs could be carried over a short distance. With its immensely strong geodetic structure, the Wellington had a reputation for being able to absorb punishment, though its fabric covering burnt readily.

Late November was spent on familiarization, and on formation and cross-country flights, circuits and landings, and air firing. During the first half of December the conversion programme continued, with single engine practice, height tests and day bombing practice followed by night flying. The conversion programme went well, with only one mishap, on 12 December, when Sqn/Ldr R. G. C. Arnold, who had replaced Eric Springall as OC A Flight, swung on take-off, the Wellington ending up in a field adjoining the aerodrome. Two crew were injured.

On 15 December four aircraft were detailed for operations, but weather forced the cancellation of this and three more ops before aircraft were despatched to Antwerp on 21 December. All three returned safely, two (Sqn/Ldr Little and P/O Whitehead) reporting that they had 'Bombed close to target', while the third (Sgt Johnson) had bombed Flushing. Three more operations were flown before the end of the year: all with mediocre results. It was an undistinguished end to a year in which so much had been attempted, and at such cost.

Two days before Christmas Wg/Cdr E. J. P. Davy succeeded Wg/Cdr Barnett as CO. Denis Barnett had done an outstanding job, taking command when 40 was at a low ebb, and rebuilding morale through strong but understanding leadership. His style was low-key, and stories about him are few. Typical, though, is one which Jim Higgins tells about an incident in late July 1940, when his commission recommendation was in train. Taxiing a repaired Blenheim to dispersal, he ran into another when the brakes failed. He writes:

> My immediate thought was, there goes my commission—a Sgt/Pilot for evermore & more than likely on a serious charge. I hardly slept that night. Next morning I reported as usual to the Squadron HQ. The adjutant opened his window as I approached the hangar entrance and shouted, 'Sgt Higgins, the Wg/Cdr [Barnett] has said the cock-up you made last night will make no difference to your recommendation for a commission'. I never heard another word about the incident.

The winter of 1940–41 was severe, and this is reflected in the fact that in January 1941 Battle Orders were posted only nine times, with five of those cancelled. Moreover, three of the four operations which were flown were disappointing, weather making target identification difficult, as over Wilhelmshaven on the 16th, when one aircraft (Sgt A. E. Jones) failed to return. It was 40's first loss in four months.

On 16 January Roy Arnold was posted to command 9 Squadron, his successor as a flight commander being his deputy, Hugh Lynch-Blosse. Another posted at this time was the Adjutant, Flt/Lt L. E. Provis, who had been with the Squadron since May 1940. His successor, P/O John Hutton, nicknamed 'Tom Tit' because of his diminutive but portly build, was to prove one of the Squadron characters, serving with 40 for nearly two years.

On 1 February A Flight and the Squadron Offices moved to Alconbury 'for the greater efficiency of the Squadron', as the ORB put it. The shift involved both profit and loss. Operationally, Alconbury was far superior, its concrete runways offering all-weather serviceability, where Wyton was still a grass field. On the other hand, as Charles Goodridge recalls,

> Alconbury had no hangars. It was only a landing strip, and if any major repairs wanted doing in a hangar then we had to go to Wyton to do it. In fact I was at Wyton most of the time.

Moreover there was little accommodation for ground crews at Alconbury, George Reddy commenting that though some were billetted in huts there, others commuted each day from Wyton.

Aircrew did not have to commute, being housed locally in two large mansions. Upton House, for the officers, was not uncomfortable, but Dick Broadbent, an RNZAF sergeant pilot who had arrived on squadron in November, recalls 'a disappointing lowering in accommodation and messing standards'. He adds:

> From being quartered in peacetime arrangements at Wyton, the aircrew NCOs on the Squadron were quartered at Alconbury house, a large, barnlike Victorian mansion, stripped of all its furnishings, and offering minimal comfort. It was about a 500 yard walk from the A Flight dispersal hut to Alconbury House, and a further three or four hundred yards down the hill to the NCO's mess.

'However,' Dick says, 'these were only minor snags compared with the very cold, snow-laden winter of 1940–41, which remains in my memory to this day'.

39. Final approach, Alconbury, Summer 1941. (J. O. Lancaster.)

Hugh Lynch-Blosse has equally vivid memories of that bitter winter, and of the inadequacies of the Wellington's heating system, which adequately warmed only the wireless operator. He also remembers

> the everhot bags perched on the knees. They were rubber pouches filled with lime, to which water was added just before take off. The reaction within the pouch released warmth and they certainly helped.

If the pilots were cold, however, the gunners were freezing, and it was to counter what New Zealander Harry Corrin remembers as 'the terrible cold' that the first electrically heated flying suits were issued. He writes:

> The idea was excellent except in practice, and I was surprised that the RAF got so far as issuing them to squadrons, because the ones we had were replaced or rejected and I had a very bad experience with mine.
> It was on the way home from a trip, over Holland, when I noticed that my right hand glove had got hot. I opened my palm and it was on fire, right in the palm of my hand. I tried to put it out, and couldn't, so finally I had to take it off, fearful of any other thing happening with it because that broke the circuit. On the Frazer Nash turrets there was a small door on the side of the turret, only about 150mm x 150 mm or so, and it went out that door into the slipstream, and finished up in somebody's paddock, no doubt.

There was an ironic sequel to this incident when Harry went next day to stores at Wyton for a new pair, to be told that regulations required him to hand in both gloves. He reverted to the Sidcot gear.

In January 1941 the Air Ministry directed Air Marshal Sir Richard Pierse, C-in-C Bomber Command, to attack German synthetic oil plants, but bad weather delayed the start of the campaign until 10 February, when Pierse prefaced it with one of Bomber Command's most ambitious operations to date, sending 222 aircraft to Hanover. Forty despatched ten crews, eight reporting that they had bombed the primary target. The ORB labelled the results 'highly satisfactory', and 3 Group HQ felt the raid as reflected 'the greatest credit on all members of Units composing the group'.

No operations were flown again until 15 February, when ten crews attacked the oil plant at Sterkrade, near Duisberg. The raid was not a success, for only three crews considered they had bombed the target, three others bombing the 'estimated position of primary target'. Given what is now known of navigational shortcomings at the time, it seems unlikely that they were within miles of the target.

After Duisberg there was no operational flying until the 23rd, and the weather was so bad that little could be done by way of alternate employment for aircrew except on 21 February, when a heavy fall of snow was followed by a clear day, and 'Rugby and Soccer matches, and a cross-country run were arranged for the flying crews, Officers and NCOs taking part'. These were the brainchild of Daddy Little, who clearly believed in the value of physical activity in a snowy landscape.

Early on 23 February, eight aircraft took off to attack the *Hipper* at Brest. The raid was a rank failure, as was an attack on Dusseldorf on the 25th, when cloud forced many crews to bomb on dead reckoning. The next two operations went no better. On 1 March seven crews attempted without success to bomb the *Tirpitz* at Wilhelmshaven, while on 3 March cloud thwarted nine crews over Cologne, though not for want of trying. Sgt Johnson, for instance, reported that his crew had

> spent 29 minutes over the target area after centre of COLOGNE was seen through a gap in the clouds. Results not seen owing to searchlight dazzle, but medium sized fires seen after leaving the area. Very heavy and intense accurate Flak caused damage to both sides of tailplane and fuselage.

It was on this night, Peter Billyeald recalls, that his aircraft first carried a camera: the beginnings of a concerted effort to determine how accurately crews were bombing. The results would demonstrate that results fell far short of what, in good faith, was claimed.

On 12 March fourteen crews were detailed for operations. One of three 'Freshman' crews, (Sgt D. W. Gough RNZAF) was shot down in flames over Boulogne, one of the supposedly soft targets used to give new crews targets involving only shallow penetration of enemy air space. One crew failed to return, also, from 40's first raid on Berlin. Flak damage left Hugh Lynch-Blosse's Wellington with one engine dead, the co-pilot (P/O H. Heaton) wounded, and the front turret damaged, and when the remaining engine began to surge uncontrollably, he and his crew baled out, to begin four years as POWs.

The raid on Berlin was unsuccessful, and the bombing scattered. The attack on the Focke-Wulf factory in Bremen went better, with the factory hit, though production was little affected. But excellent results were achieved the next night in an attack on Gelsenkirchen oil refinery, crews reporting fires visible up to ninety miles away, with P/O Sanders' crew noting a blue flash, followed by a shock wave which lifted their Wellington bodily, even at 11,000 feet. The Hydriewerk Scholven oil plant was badly damaged, and production temporarily halted.

Between 18 March and the end of the month, 40 operated against Bremen, Cologne (twice), and Berlin, though without much success. No losses were sustained, though on 23 March one crew had a narrow escape. Peter Billyeald writes that when they were hit by flak over Berlin,

> the damage was confined to the hydraulic system. Although we could lower the undercarriage manually, the flaps were inoperative. I misjudged my approach and landing, ran out of runway and finished up by crashing into the back of the gun testing range.

40. The end of R1166, 24 March 1941. (P. Billyeald.)

The ORB amplifies in stating that 'the aircraft overshot the flarepath on the second try, hit a wooden hut and an office trailer, and came to rest against a large mound of earth.' Three men were injured, and the crew was declared 'tour expired', having completed 29 of its 30 operations.

The figure of thirty operational sorties had finally been determined upon by Bomber Command after a period, in 1939–40, when there was no set tour. On the other hand, operational methods still retained much of their earlier casualness, as Dick Broadbent notes:

> The target for the night was usually announced by mid morning; the navigators then got together and decided how they would get to the target, picking out individual routes to conform with their own previous experience—maybe of places to be avoided, or just simply going on hearsay—as to what would be the best way to get there and back. Met. forecasting was not as sophisticated as it was to become later on, and weather conditions, particularly wind strengths and direction, were largely an unknown quantity. Time on target was usually given as within a two or three hour span, but of course the constraints of shorter hours of darkness in summer and the bad weather in the winter were major factors in determining an individual crew's takeoff time and tactics en route.

During April the results achieved over Germany were much as they had been in March. The successes were two raids on Kiel (7 and 8 April). On the 7th 13 aircraft were part of a force totalling 229 (the largest sent to one target to date). One (Sgt T. Gamble) was lost, but the damage inflicted on Kiel was severe:

> In good visibility, the raid lasted 5 hours, causing the failure of KIEL's electric light supply, starting several fires needing reinforcement of the local fire-fighting services, and widespread damage to naval, industrial, and civilian housing. Night shifts at Deutsche Werke and Germania Werft (U-Boat manufactories) were sent home during the raid, and both yards were out of action for several days. 88 people were killed and 184 injured.[1]

Just as successful was a raid the following night, when damage was concentrated in the town, with 425 people killed or injured, and 8,300 civilians and naval personnel bombed out. No 40 Squadron aircraft were lost.

Two attempts to follow up these successes with further raids on Kiel later in the month, did no more than scattered damage. Nor were other German targets hard hit. A raid on Mannheim, in which six crews took part, caused only very modest damage, while haze prevented concentrated bombing over Berlin on the 17th. Returning from the latter one crew (Sgt K. Jenner RNZAF) had navigation problems, and crashed on a hillside near Combe Martin, in Devon. Ken Jenner gave his crew the option of baling out or remaining with the aircraft. The rear gunner (Sgt J. Griffin) baled out, but his parachute failed to deploy fully, and he was killed. The others stayed with Jenner, who brought off a remarkable landing on a steep hillside, wrecking the aircraft, but without serious injury to the crew.

Two raids on French targets were flown in April. On the 3rd eleven crews took part in an unsuccessful attack on the *Scharnhorst* and *Gneisenau* at Brest. Then a week later 40 raided the air base at Merignac, near Bordeaux, the ORB describing the attack as 'of major importance, being against the base from which enemy aircraft were operating against our shipping in the Atlantic'. The raid was most successful, Dick Broadbent recalling that 'we bombed from a relatively low altitude—about 8000 feet—and we departed with a row of hangars on fire as a result of our efforts'.

Merignac involved an eight hour flight, so crews were instructed to land at Chivenor or St. Eval to refuel before returning to Alconbury. Two aircraft found themselves in trouble. One (Sgt Finlayson RNZAF) had the starboard engine fail fifty miles from the target, jettisoned its bombs and turned for home. There followed a nightmare forty-five minutes during which, losing height, the crew jettisoned everything possible in order to lighten the aircraft. Eventually Finlayson succeeded in restarting the engine, and the aircraft made it to Chivenor. Flt/Lt Bowler's crew was less fortunate. They ditched in the English Channel, and though they radio'd their position, searches failed to locate them. Subsequently it was learned that all but the rear gunner (P/O J. P. L. Branson) had been rescued by the Germans.

On 20 April two Merlin-engined Mk. II Wellingtons arrived at Alconbury. Able, as the Ics were not, to carry the new 4,000-lb blast bomb, or 'cookie', they were allocated one to each Flight, and used operationally when attacks on cities were ordered, as against Dusseldorf on 2 June, when P/O A. B. Baird RNZAF (one of the captains who regularly flew the Mk. IIs) brought back the 4,000-lb bomb because haze obscured the target.

During May 40 operated every other night until the 12th, but only twice during the second half of the month, when the weather deteriorated. Germany was targeted on six of the eight nights, but only three raids were successful, one of these on Mannheim and Ludwigshaven on the 9th. Forty Squadron contributed 10 crews, 7 of whom bombed successfully, 2 others attacking channel ports, and 1 (P/O F. J. Steel RNZAF) jettisoning his bombs when carburettor icing caused both engines to cut briefly near Trier.

Of the four attacks made on Hamburg during May, only two (on 8 and 11 May) were successful. Earlier, on 2 and 6 May crews had claimed good results, but the Hamburg authorities reported little or no damage. On the 8th, however, their reports bore out Bomber Command claims, the 188 aircraft (including 10 from 40) taking part starting 83 fires, and killing 185 people, the highest German fatality figure so far.

The fourth attack on Hamburg, on 11 May, was also successful, though costly for 40 Squadron, which lost two crews (Sgts. F. T. Luscombe and Finlayson), while a third (P/O R. M. Smith) was lucky to get back. The wireless operator, Jim Robbins, recalls:

> The front gunner reported a Me 110 coming in from the starboard bow and then he came in from the rear and killed the rear gunner [Sgt K. B. Martin]. He then came in from the port bow and, sitting on the arm of my chair so that I could get at my parachute if needed I just had time to pull back the curtain and see the tracers coming for us, and then I remember no more. I believe I came to on the 13th attack, when the fighter ran out of ammunition. The door between me and the cockpit was peppered with large cannon shell holes and there was a large hole in the starboard side of the fuselage. One engine was gone and one wheel was hanging down.
>
> I knew that I had been hit in the jaw as I couldn't speak, and I automatically used my left hand when using the radio as I thought that I had bumped my funny bone in my right arm. I didn't realize at the time that a bullet had gone through my jaw and a cannon shell had blown away my right clavicle and gone through my scapula. Fortunately it exploded afterwards, giving me bits of shrapnel in my knee and neck.

P/O Smith was awarded the DFC, and Robbins the DFM, while on 13 May all aircrew were required to attend lectures on First Aid given by the Squadron Medical Officer, Flt/Lt Lawrence.

41. P/O R. M. Smith and crew, Alconbury, February 1941.
(l to r) Sgt Ison, Sgt J. E. Robbins, Sgt K. Williams, Sgt Bowers, Sgt Gardner
(or Sgt R. D. Hesketh), P/O Smith. (J. E. Robbins.)

Two other operations in May deserve comment. The first, on the 4th, was another attack on the *Scharnhorst* and *Gneisenau* at Brest. Eleven crews operated, and claimed hits, though these are not confirmed by German records. Then on 27 May ten crews were part of a force searching in daylight for the *Prinz Eugen*. Dick Broadbent writes:

> We set off from Alconbury with myself as the lead aircraft in a Vic of three—a very loose formation indeed, since we had never practised formation flying prior to this. Somewhere south of Land's End in heavy cumulus cloud the formation broke up and we were all somewhat surprised to see each other again when we landed back at St. Eval in Cornwall after some six and a half hours of dodging our own aircraft and seeing nothing whatever.

A raid on Dusseldorf on 11 May went no better, with none of the seven crews sure where their bombs had fallen, and the only highlight the dropping of some tea to the Dutch by Sgt J. Taylor and his crew. Two aircraft did not return. P/O R. F. Payne's crew perished, and Jack Rettie, a rear gunner in another crew, recalls that earlier that evening Martin Soames, Payne's second pilot, had told him, 'I am not coming back tonight'.

What happened to Sqn/Ldr M. E. Redgrave's crew is recounted by Bob Alldrick, the Canadian front gunner, who recalls that when they were coned

42. Down in the Scheldte: R1312 (Sqn/Ldr M. E. Redgrave), 13 June 1941.
(R. Alldrick.)


Redgrave took violent evasive action, diving clear of the lights. Then searchlights caught them again, and at probably no more than 1,000 feet Redgrave again took evasive action. Bob writes:

> I believe we were descending in a curve to the right so that the first contact with the water was made by the starboard wingtip, then the a/c slewed around sharply to the right. The nose and turret were next to strike and as the turret came apart I was thrown out, just beyond the port wingtip. I came to knee deep in water but free of the turret.

They were in the Scheldt estuary, 'on a sand bar 18″ deep with ½ mile of water on either side, and sizzling noises coming from the aircraft'. With the dinghy useless, and two crew members injured, they could only wait to be rescued, and taken POW.[2]

On 15 May eight crews were despatched to Hannover as part of a force of 101 aircraft. One of the two Wellingtons lost during what was an unsuccessful raid was that of Sgt W. E. Moore. Only the rear gunner (Sgt P. Addison) survived to be taken POW.

Bad weather prevented 40 from operating on the last four days in May, and during the first ten in June there was operational flying only on the

2nd, when ten crews took part in an unsuccessful raid on Düsseldorf. To add to the night's woes, Sgt P. D. Sargent crashed on landing at Alconbury, killing all on board except the rear gunner (Sgt R. C. Hillebrandt) who was seriously injured. It seems that the aircraft stalled after overshooting.

On 12 June one of two freshman crews raiding Rotterdam (Sgt M. Evans RNZAF) was attacked by an Me 110, the second pilot (Sgt A. C. Shilletto) and front gunner (Sgt F. Lowrey) being slightly wounded. The rear gunner (Sgt J. Hoban) returned the fire as the night fighter closed to about fifty yards before breaking away. On landing the undercarriage collapsed, but no further injuries were sustained. For his skill and courage on his first operation as captain, Evans was awarded the DFM.

Late in June the weather improved, and 40 operated regularly, though only one of the six operations, on 29 June, was a success. Cologne was visited three times but little was achieved, while on the third occasion (26 June) one crew (P/O D. R. Horrocks) failed to return, and another (Sgt H. T. Bagnall RNZAF) which had turned back with the intercom system u/s, encountered an Me 110. It seems that the night fighter did not see the Wellington, since it was only fifty yards astern, slightly above, and overtaking. The rear gunner (Sgt Orr) fired three bursts before Bagnall realized what was happening, and dived for cover in cloud. A 'kill' may well have resulted, since Orr 'saw a large flame reflected in the clouds, as though the E/A had blown up'.

Raids on Düsseldorf and Kiel on 17 and 20 June were no more successful, the latter, when 9 crews were part of a force of 119 despatched to attack the *Tirpitz*, proving a thoroughgoing failure, few bombers even locating the town.

The one success for the month was on 29 June, when 40 sent two crews to Hamburg, and seven to Bremen. The latter reported satisfactory results, but the success of the night was the twenty-eight strong force which attacked Hamburg, causing a great deal of damage. The cost to the attackers was also considerable, however, with seven bombers lost, one of which was captained by the newly-promoted Flt/Lt Baird. Interestingly, only the Squadron's two MkIIs were involved.

During the first week of July, 40 raided Germany three times. The least successful of the raids was probably Bremen on the 2nd, when only Sgt Ebsworth's crew identified the shipyards. Four days later crews found Münster only lightly defended, but only eight of the twelve bombed, while one (P/O J. McK. Steeds RNZAF) was shot down over the Dutch coast. The Wireless Operator, Angus MacAskill, recalls that on its first pass a night fighter knocked out the intercom and broke open the escape hatch. Having managed to close the hatch, Macaskill returned to his position beside the pilot, to be hit in the shoulder and back when the fighter attacked a second time. He continues:

> The aircraft was now well on fire and John Steeds was indicating furiously towards the escape hatch, which I took to mean that he wished to abandon

the aircraft. The Observer had not moved and I assume that he must have been hit; the front gunner was out of his turret. I, therefore, put on my parachute and jumped.

The only survivor, MacAskill landed on the island of Texel, the Wellington falling in flames in the distance.

The third of the raids, Cologne on the 7th, was the most successful. 114 Wellingtons attacked in perfect weather, and good bombing resulted in Cologne's heaviest raid for 1941. Though 40 suffered no losses, the raid had its unsatisfactory features, since of the thirteen aircraft detailed two failed to take off, two returned early, and one which could not climb above 9,000 feet (Sqn/Ldr R. G. Weighill, the new OC B Flight) bombed Ostend. On the plus side, however, Sgt J. O. Lancaster's observer, Sgt G. Leitch RCAF, placed their bomb load accurately across a rail bridge.

On 22 June the German invasion of the Soviet Union removed the threat of a sea-borne landing in Britain, and the Air Staff were able to reconsider their priorities. Since attacks on oil refineries had not achieved the results hoped for, Bomber Command was now instructed to direct its main effort 'towards dislocating the German transportation system and to destroying the morale of the civil population as a whole and of the industrial workers in particular'. In pursuit of what was, essentially, an area bombing programme, Bomber Command would, over the next four months, step up the tempo of its attacks. So would the German night fighters.

The first raids in which 40 Squadron participated following this new directive—Osnabruck (9th), Bremen (13th) and Hamburg (16th)—were all failures, the last two because of bad weather, conditions on the 13th being so severe that every crew turned back and one (F/O G. C. Conran) failed to return. Likewise when 40 visited Hamburg on the 16th, icing and heavy cloud meant that only one crew (Sgt R. Broadbent RNZAF) bombed the primary target, and two of the nine did not return. One (Sgt A. W. P. Bird RNZAF) radio'd routinely as it crossed the Dutch coast on the way back, but was not heard from again, only the observer (Sgt J. R. Jamieson RCAF) surviving a night fighter attack. From Sqn/Ldr Weighill's crew there were no survivors. Flying at 400 feet, the crew were dazzled by searchlights near Great Yarmouth, and the Wellington dived into the ground.[3]

Three more operations were flown to Germany in late July: to Mannheim on the 22nd, Kiel on the 24th, and Cologne on the 30th. The dismal results achieved against Cologne could be attributed to the weather. Nearly as dismal results over Kiel on 24 July could not, for the three crews who bombed reported good visibility. The raid, indeed, exemplifies the deficiencies of Bomber Command's campaign at this time: both in locating targets and reporting damage.

On 4 July 40 contributed ten crews to yet another attack on the *Scharnhorst* and *Gneisenau* at Brest, but though the weather was good, smokescreens prevented accurate bombing. Later in the month came a bolder attempt to deal with the vessels, a sophisticated plan for a daylight raid by 150 aircraft. This plan, however, had to be modified when it was discovered that the *Scharnhorst* was at La Pallice, and it was a 100 strong force which targeted the *Gneisenau* on 24 July.

Under the plan, 3 Fortresses were to draw up German fighters, 18 Hampdens, escorted by 3 squadrons of Spitfires, completing the process. A main bombing force of 79 Wellingtons (unescorted) would then attack the *Gneisenau*. In fine weather the operation went as planned, but German fighter opposition proved stronger and more prolonged than anticipated, 2 Hampdens being shot down, and 10 Wellingtons, 1 of them from 40 Squadron.

Having spent ninety minutes the previous day practising formation flying,[4] the Wellingtons from Alconbury operated in two sections, Sqn/Ldr L. J. Stickley leading P/O Greer and Sgt Evans, and Sgt L. J. Morris, Sgts. Lancaster and Bagnall. In the run up to the target, Pat Pattison, Bagnall's Wireless Operator recalls,

> it looked as if we were heading for hundreds of barrage balloons, which I knew was not possible at 11,000 feet, but as we got closer we realized that

43. En route to Brest, 24 July 1941: 'C' (Sgt Morris) and 'R' (Sgt Bagnall).
(J. O. Lancaster.)

this was AA fire. Flak was frightening enough at night with a flash and thump thump, but in daytime the black menacing cloud which followed each flash was terrifying in itself and seemed to envelope the whole formation.

The flak was accurate, and Bagnall's and Evans' aircraft were hit, the latter going down in flames. Then, after the others had bombed, and cleared the flak zone, German fighters attacked. In the intact rear section, Sgt Lancaster's gunners (rear, front and beam) engaged an Me 109 which dived past to attack a Wellington in a formation below, firing at it again when it pulled up on the port side. The fighter turned on its back and spun down, the pilot baling out, and it may have been this 109 which approached Sgt Morris's aircraft, and which the front gunner hit.

The 109 which approached the rear vic did not fire at them. Alex Greer, ahead, was less lucky. After bombing, he and Laurie Stickley became separated, and Greer found himself alone and under attack by an Me 109. In the first pass it raked the Wellington with cannon and machine gun fire, the rear gunner (Sgt T. Gould) returning the fire until the turret was hit, the guns put out of action and he himself wounded. During the same attack the second pilot (Sgt M. E. Holliday RAAF) whom Greer had sent to what he judged to be safety amidships, was killed. Two passes were then made from starboard, of which one, from ahead, was ineffective, and countered by three bursts of fire from the front gunner (Sgt Davey) but the other, from the starboard beam and above, resulted in further damage to the Wellington.

The enemy fighter's next pass was made from the port bow, the front and beam gunners returning the fire and forcing the 109 to break away. During this pass the the Wireless Operator (Sgt J. Hobbs), who was manning the beam guns, was wounded in the head and legs, and knocked out. A further starboard beam attack followed, the fighter closing to fifty yards, but his fire going wide. Finally the fighter attacked from the port bow, and Greer, turning towards the 109, gave his front gunner the opportunity to get in three bursts, as a result of which the fighter burst into flames.

With the hydraulics damaged, wheels and flaps down, and bomb doors open, Alex Greer nursed his Wellington back to St. Eval, where he landed without further injury or damage. It had been a close thing, with the crew showing courage and skill in repelling attacks, particularly when the aircraft was so badly damaged.

The results of the raid were disappointing. Neither the *Gneisenau* nor the *Prinz Eugen* were damaged significantly, though Laurie Stickley's crew claimed that the last part of a stick of seven 500-lb bombs fell near the stern of the battle-cruiser. One possible reason for the mediocre results is suggested by the ORB's comment on the bombing of Sgt Lancaster: 'Bombs fell in the town itself, this a/c being on the left of the formation'. In open formation there was no way that most of the aircraft could target the ships they had come to sink. In this, as in so much else about this raid, there is evidence of insufficient thought.

Whatever the outcome, the powers-that-be professed themselves highly satisfied, and on 8 August there came the announcement of awards, made at an all ranks 'cinema entertainment which included *Target for Tonight*, the Bomber Command film in which several scenes were shot at a 3 Group station and in which many 3 Group officers appeared'. DFCs had been awarded to Laurie Stickley, and to P/O Duncan, his observer, and DFMs to Sgts. Gould and Morris.

On 2 August Hamburg was raided without success, but the next two German targets brought good results. On the 5th five crews took part in a successful attack on Mannheim, Sgt Ebsworth's bombs dropping 'plumb in the centre of the town', while two days later nine crews bombed the great marshalling yards at Hamm. Large fires were started, with smoke rising to 11,000 feet.

An attack on Hanover on 12 August was not a success, and on the return journey P/O A. R. Fitch and his crew were surprised by a Ju 88 near Nijmegen, the first attack, from astern and below, putting the rear turret out of action, and wounding the second pilot, P/O D. F. Hutt. In subsequent attacks both the front and rear gunners (Sgts J. C. Beauchamp and W. P. Hudson) were also wounded. Three attacks were made in all, Fitch taking avoiding action by turning into the attacks and diving for cloud cover.

Earlier, another aircraft (Sgt Stephens) had lost an engine to flak over Holland, and turned back, bombing the flarepath at Nijmegen *en route*. Losing height, the aircraft crossed the English coast, only to be warned that Alconbury and Wyton were under attack. Suddenly a Ju 88 closed, and with a short burst disabled the remaining engine. Pat Pattison writes:

> At this time I estimated our height at around 1500 feet and we were in a dive heading for the town of Huntingdon. The skipper shouted 'Brace yourselves for a crash-landing, there's a large meadow almost directly below us'. I unplugged my intercom and and scrambled back to my position at the wireless desk. The front gunner crawled out of his turret and standing in the gangway held on to a strap on my right and braced his feet against the geodetic structure. The silence was frightening; only the swish of the aircraft gliding down and occasional heavy breathing over the intercom. I could hear prayers being murmured and I joined in. Then a bump, a blinding flash and we hit the deck, heaps of earth ploughed into the aircraft as we bellied along for what seemed an eternity, then suddenly we had stopped.

Unharmed, the crew ran clear, then turned to look back, to see the Wimpy 'majestic on her belly, but miraculously in one piece': so much so, indeed, that it was recovered from Portholm meadow a week later, repaired and returned to service.

What followed had elements of farce about it:

> Through the gloom we saw a squad car heading across the field towards us. It stopped about 10 yards in front of us, and three or four helmeted soldiers jumped out with rifles trained on us, an officer stepped forward with a pistol pointed at us, and shouted 'Achtung. Hands above your heads'. We all started to laugh and the skipper tried to explain that we were RAF, but the officer was not convinced even when we pointed to our faithful old Wimpy displaying the RAF roundels.

It took a phone call to Alconbury from the police station to convince their Home Guard captors, who then plied the crew with hot tea and rum.

How was life at Alconbury in the spring and summer of 1941? John Tipton, a sergeant observer, comments:

> We lived a strangely rural existence. The buildings on the airfield consisted of a wooden hut, housing the Squadron offices, and the briefing or plotting room, and some barns around the farmyard in the middle of which there was a pond where we used to sit and watch the dragonflies play while we speculated on what if anything would be in store for us that night, and tried to guess by the loads on the bomb trolleys what the distance and nature of the target might be.

Alconbury house remained comfortless, Bob Alldrick recalling that 'the entrance hall below was always open to the elements, but was also the location of an old table spread with bread chunks, cheese and sliced onions'. 'Other "food"', he adds, 'was supplied by a mobile kitchen parked along the driveway to the house—just one look at the ladle full of ———— was enough to put you right off.' On the other hand if you were crewed with Dominion aircrew, you could do well, as Jo (Ollie) Lancaster recalls:

> Keith Coleman (rear gunner) used to receive from NZ abundant supplies of tinned butter and tins of Nescafe ready mixed with condensed milk. Glenn Leitch and Bill Harris (RCAF) received from Canada tins of peanut butter and hundreds of cigarettes. We all smoked heavily, and cigarettes were in short supply on the home market, so Canada kept us all well supplied, while all we needed for supper was a loaf of bread and some hot water!

Jo adds:

> My pay as a Sergeant Pilot was £8. 8. 0 per fortnight. We were all on much the same scale, but we managed to maintain a very full social life on this without too much difficulty. As a crew, whenever the opportunity presented itself, we made forays into Huntingdon, Cambridge, London, or Coventry (my old stamping ground) and invariably managed to have a hilarious time.

44. Sunbathing outside Alconbury House, Summer 1941. The group includes (1st and 3rd from left), Trevor Bagnall (2nd pilot), Ken Jenner and his Observer, Sgt C. D. Noble RCAF. (K. Jenner.)

45. Sir Archibald Sinclair speaking at a briefing on 16 August 1941. On his left Wg/Cdr E. J. P. Davy (half obscured) and Flt/Lt A. D. Greer. (IWM CH3229.)

On 12 July there had been a visit to Wyton by Lord Trenchard, and all aircrew from Alconbury had paraded there to hear him speak. On 16 August it was Alconbury's turn to receive the Secretary of State for Air, Sir Archibald Sinclair and AVM. Seely, AOC 3 Group. They attended the briefing, dined in the Mess at Upton House, saw the crews take off and returned for the interrogation on an eventful night. Two crews (P/O J. E. King and Sgt G. Byrne) had successfully carried out freshman attacks on Rotterdam, while nine others went to Duisberg, reporting large fires. Fighters had been active, three crews reporting contacts, and Flt/Lt R. Healey, P/O Cowsill's rear gunner, shooting down an Me 110.

On 19 August a Guest Night was held in the Officers' Mess at Upton House, to mark Wg/Cdr Davy's posting to the Air Ministry and the award of the DFC to Sqn/Ldr Stickley, who was to succeed him. On the 23rd Davy left after nearly nine months as CO. Very much the regular RAF officer, he had a style which did not go down well with some, but Hugh Lynch-Blosse recalls him as helpful and sympathetic, while Jim Steel comments:

> Wg/Cdr Davy was pretty aloof and we didn't see a lot of him apart from briefing and debriefing. He had quite a good sense of humour when he relaxed. I think he went very much by the book, but he was fair. In retrospect he could have been somewhat shy.

Operations during the remainder of August were mostly failures. On the 22nd seven crews bombed Mannheim, reporting fires, but the authorities recorded only six high explosive bombs in the city. On 25 August the target was Karlsruhe. Eleven crews were detailed, but only one (Sgt Byrne) bombed the primary, electrical storms and thick cloud defeating the remainder. Two crews (Sqn/Ldr A. C. Martin, the B Flight Commander, and Sgt D. F. Youldon) were lost, Martin's unusual in that it contained four officers. Alan Martin himself was a career RAF officer who had been one of the pilots who flew the Gladiators, 'Faith', 'Hope' and 'Charity', on Malta in 1940.

The most successful raid in late August was on the 28th, when 40 sent all nine trained crews to Duisberg. Six bombed in the face of intense flak and searchlights, and one (Sgt Stephens) was coned and badly damaged, while another (P/O King) failed to return. On the 31st, by contrast, though all crews returned safely from Cologne, bad weather prevented accurate bombing, only a few bomb loads landing on the city. August thus ended, as it began, in failure.

September began no better, with few bombs hitting Frankfurt-am-Main, and one crew (P/O Fitch) ditching in the North Sea after engine failure. Four men were picked up by a trawler and returned to England, but Fitch drowned, and (to quote the ORB) 'the Wireless Operator, Sgt Robertson, who had displayed great courage and who stayed at his post on the set

46. T2701 'S-Sugar' at dispersal, Summer 1941. (J. O. Lancaster.)

sending out Wireless messages right up to the moment of impact, also lost his life'. A second Wellington (P/O M. Baker RAAF) was destroyed when it overshot on landing, crashed and burnt out. The crew escaped unhurt, the ORB noting that 'Great heroism and devotion to duty was displayed by AC2 RIDEN, a member of the crash party in his attempts at rescue'.

Fog prevented 40 operating again until 7 September, when three crews were despatched to Berlin and to Kiel with satisfying results. This was far from the case on the 10th, however, when 40 operated for the first time against Italy. Eight aircraft were on the Battle Order, Wg/Cdr Stickley flying his first op as CO. Bomber Command claimed good results, but for 40,

> This raid was the most disappointing one ever undertaken by the Squadron, no less than seven crews returning to Base without having reached the target, all complaining of aircraft defects of one sort or another. The only Pilot to reach and bomb the target was Sqn/Ldr Kirby-Green, who reported a successful raid.

The statement is not quite accurate, for Sgt K. G. Edis also bombed. But the raid *was* a failure, with crews reporting a catalogue of problems. Newly commissioned P/O Lancaster had to abandon a crossing of the Alps when his aircraft would not climb above 11,000 feet, while Mervyn Baker turned back with an unserviceable gyro compass, Laurie Stickley with aileron trouble, P/O I. M. V. Field RNZAF with intercom failure, and both Sgt Byrne and Sqn/Ldr J. C. Atkins had engines cut when they switched to overload tanks. Not surprisingly, the next day was devoted to an investigation into the causes of the failures.

On 12 September nine crews were despatched to Frankfurt, and despite thick cloud inflicted considerable damage on Frankfurt, nearby Offenbach—and Mainz, twenty miles away! Sqn/Ldr Atkins did not return, ditching in the North Sea after engine failure. All save Atkins himself, and the observer (P/O R. M. Ryder RAAF), survived to be taken prisoner.

In clear conditions an attack on Hamburg on the 15th also caused much damage. Three crews bombed the alternative target, Bremen, and the following day the Squadron ORB found it 'noteworthy to mention that not one aircraft of the whole Group turned back before reaching either the primary or the alternative target'. To crown a good night, three crews had participated in a successful freshman raid on Le Havre.

After an unsatisfactory raid on Karlsruhe on the 17th, fog—or the threat of it—prevented operations until 29 September, when nine crews went to Stettin, and three to Hamburg, reporting success in each case. All returned safely. It was from Stettin, Jo Lancaster recalls, that Sqn/Ldr Kirby-Green's wireless operator (F/Sgt P. L. Hennigan), who had previously been upbraided for not maintaining routine W/T contact, 'tapped out a request for a QDM (course to steer for base). This', Jo comments,

> would normally be requested when within about 100 miles of home. On receipt of his QDM he acknowledged, and added that he would call again in four hours, which caused a lot of mystification.

The first operation in October was on the 3rd, when a record twelve crews went to Rotterdam. Heavy mist was forecast in the early hours of the morning, so crews were despatched very early, the ORB reporting that 'all a/crews had returned safely by 2345, in very high spirits after extremely successful raids'. Three crews also completed freshman raids on Dunkirk, Sgt J. R. Hiscock surviving an attack by a Ju 88.

The next raid saw a new record set when thirteen crews were detailed for Emden. Adverse weather conditions made target identification difficult, however, and bombing was scattered. Both freshman and experienced crews had been included in the Battle Order, presumably because it was not much further distant than the ports in France and the Low Countries which were the staple targets for new crews. The following night the three new crews went to Bremen, while nine others tackled the lengthy trip to Nüremberg. Neither target was attacked successfully. Heavy cloud over Bremen forced crews to bomb by dead reckoning or (in the case of Sqn/Ldr W. J. C. Craigen, the new A Flight Commander) astronavigation, and without observing results. One crew (Sgt G. F. Bateman) failed to return.

The Nüremberg raid was also a failure. Few crews bombed the city, and of the nine from 40 Squadron one failed to take off, three turned back, and one (P/O Field) was shot down. The Operational Record Book noted that Field was 'one of the Squadron's best pilots, and his navigator P/O Sugg, was particularly able'. A follow-up raid on the Nüremberg raid two nights later went even worse. The twelve crews encountered severe weather conditions, and jettisoned their bombs or attacked targets from Frankfurt to Dunkirk. Fighters were also encountered, and three crews (Sgt Edis, P/O G. B. Buse and Sgt Hiscock) failed to return. There were no survivors.

Five crews had now been lost on two failed operations. Yet another went missing on 16 October, when nine crews carried out searchlight suppression flights around Duisberg. How Sqn/Ldr Kirby-Green's crew was lost is not known: though the fact that only the captain survived suggests that the aircraft may have exploded.5 Night fighters were certainly active, for Sgt H. W. Garvin's aircraft was attacked by a Ju 88, but took evasive action, the fighter disappearing before the gunners could return fire. Sgt F. Sunley's aircraft was also approached, by an Me 110. Sunley dived, the fighter following, though lost to view for a time. When contact was re-established the 110 was forty yards away, and the rear gunner (Sgt S. Shepherdson) fired a long burst before it broke away. He continued firing, and the second pilot (Sgt M. Ashpitel) saw the Messerschmitt hit the sea and explode. It had not fired a shot.

Forty now had just eight trained crews and two freshmen. This deficit of six became a matter of urgency when on 16 October notification came through that the Squadron would be moving to Malta on a two month tour of special operational duty. Besides sixteen operationally fit crews, the Commanding Officer, Adjutant, and Navigation and Engineering Officers were to proceed by air, together with sixty-four maintenance personnel listed in the Operational Record Book thus:

> 1 F/O Engineer; 1 F/S and 6 Sgt Fitters; 1 Sgt and 8 Cpl Fitter II; 2 Cpl Fitter AE; 1 Cpl and 8 AC Fitters E; 2 Cpl and 10 Airman Fitters A; F/S and 2 Cpl Electrician I, 1 Electrician II, 1 Cpl and 1 Airman Instrument Repair; 1 W.O., 1 Sgt, 1 Cpl Fitter Armourer; 1 Sgt and 2 Cpls Armourers; 2 Airman Armourer B; 1 F/S, and 1 Sgt Wireless Electrical Mechanic; 2 Cpls, Wireless Mechanic; 1 Sgt ACH/P.P. ; 1 Cpl Clk/CD.

No further operations were flown, and all efforts were directed towards preparing men and machines for the trip. Aircraft were fitted with long range tanks, and crews innoculated and, after leave, kitted out. Six crews also arrived to bring the operational strength up to sixteen: P/O G. C. R. Saunders RCAF, Sgt Lowe, Sgt R. C. Munro RNZAF, Sgt J. D. Paine, Sgt T. W. Parker, and Flt/Lt F. J. Steel RNZAF—the latter returning after instructing at No. 15 OTU, Harwell.

The move to Malta was supposed to be a closely guarded secret, but as John Tipton recalls, 'those who entered the bar of The George on the day after the Duisberg operation were greeted with "Have you had your jabs yet?" The Huntingdon intelligence network never failed.'

Customarily, Wellingtons went to Malta via Gibraltar, but 104 Squadron had just taken its Mk. IIs directly to the island, and this no doubt influenced the decision to send 40 direct also. Instructions stated that the Squadron would proceed to Malta by Flights, eight aircraft taking off on 23 October, weather permitting, and the rest the following day.

At 1500 hours on the 23rd, eight crews were briefed, and an hour later the AOC 3 Group arrived and addressed them. At 2110 hours, led by Wg/Cdr Stickley, and the new B Flight Commander, Sqn/Ldr Greer, all eight aircraft took off in a manner which the ORB described as 'very impressive'. The following morning arrangements were completed for the departure of A Flight, but this was postponed, crews being told that the journey would probably now be via Gibraltar, presumably because of the difficulties experienced by B Flight.

On 25 October A Flight, led by Sqn/Ldr Craigen, flew to Hampstead Norris, but on landing his aircraft

47. Wg/Cdr L. J. Stickley. (F. J. Steel.)

damaged its elevator, and instructions were received for the other seven to take off for Gibraltar between midnight and 1 am on the 26th, with Craigen to follow as soon as possible. The departure was postponed until 0300, when two aircraft took off safely. Fitter Jack Wey recalls:

Trying to fly out of this tiny OTU field proved as disastrous as flying direct, as the first two of the heavily laden Wellingtons were damaged by the hedgerows and small trees at the end of the take-off run. Both managed to stagger into the air and continue on their way.

Disaster struck the third. Bill Craigen recalls that 'on take-off P/O Saunders kept her down very low to get up good speed, and caught his pitot head on the barbed wire fence at the far side of the airfield and tore it off'. With no indication of airspeed, Saunders attempted a circuit of the airfield, but the Wimpy clipped a tree, crashed and exploded, killing all ten men aboard.

Further light is shed on the incident by the Accident Card, which carries the AOC's comment:

> Primary cause obscure, but is of the opinion that the runway in use was quite unsuitable for the take off of a Wellington Ic loaded to all-up weight.

This must have convinced those responsible, for it was decided to despatch the five remaining Wellingtons from Portreath. There bad weather delayed departure, and it was not until the morning of 30 October that they left, landing at Gibraltar after flights of between five and seven hours.

While at Portreath, Bill Craigen recalls, he undertook an unusual errand:

> The night we went off I got a signal from Air Ministry to go into Redruth and pick up all the Sanatogen [a nerve tonic] that I could possibly lay my hands on for the Governor of Malta—Dobbie. So we had to pinch a vehicle and drive into Redruth and knock up all the chemists and get them out of bed, and buy out their complete stock of Sanatogen and load it up in the van. And we took that off with us to Malta.

Thus are wars won.

# Notes

1. Martin Middlebrook and Chris Everitt: *The Bomber Command War Diaries*. (London: Viking, 1985), p. 142. Information on German damage reports quoted elsewhere in this chapter is drawn from this source.

2. For another account of this crash see Cyril Rofe, *Against the Wind* (London: Hodder & Stoughton, 1956), pp. 9–12. Rofe, the observer, exchanged identities with a Palestinian soldier, and was sent to a work camp from which he escaped three times, finally linking up with Ukrainian partisans and reaching Soviet lines. He was awarded the Military Medal for his exploits.

3. This operation, and in particular the loss of Weighill's Wellington, is written up in the November 1985 issue of *Flypast*. See Bob Collis, 'The Saga of "H for Harry"', pp. 28–31.

4. So the ORB asserts. But Jo Lancaster's crew, at least, had no practice at all for the raid.

5. Kirby-Green was one of fifty Air Force officers shot by the Gestapo in the aftermath of 'The Great Escape' from Stalag Luft III in March 1944.

13

# The Home Echelon:
# October 1941–February 1942

THE departure of the entire operational strength of 40 Squadron for Malta, together with sixty-four maintenance and administrative personnel, left Alconbury semi-deserted, and on 3 November the ORB reported only two officers in the Mess. The first sign of a rebuilding came on 6 November, when Sqn/Ldr Spence, of 218 Sqn, was appointed to command. Gradually crews arrived, and on 22 November flying took place, with Spence, P/O J. D. N. Bain RCAF and Sgt Griffith carrying out night flying, circuits and landings.

On 26 November a new CO, Wg/Cdr P. G. R. Heath, arrived, and the following night two freshman crews (Sgts J. Swain and Griffith) successfully attacked Ostend. Swain and Griffith were experienced pilots, and Swain close to completing his tour, which he did on 14 January.

Fog grounded the Squadron 2–4 December, and when the weather cleared there was little flying because of a simulated attack on Alconbury by a 'German' invading force. The exercise, involving the RAF defences and army units, resulted in many 'Germans' being captured and interrogated in the Crew Room on the 6th, and further prisoners and 100 vehicles taken on the following day. 'The attack on the aerodrome', the ORB notes, 'was completely broken up'.

Invaders repelled, life at Alconbury resumed its customary pattern of air tests, ferrying in new aircraft and cross-country exercises. Few of the crews were operationally fit, however, and it was again Swain and Griffith who flew the Home Echelon's second operation on 7/8 December, against Aachen. The target was cloud covered, and though Griffith bombed hopefully, Swain bombed Boulogne. Further freshman ops on 11 and 15 December were followed, on th 17th, by a raid on the *Scharnhorst*, *Gneisenau*, and *Prinz Eugen* at Brest. Two crews bombed, but neither claimed to have sighted, let alone hit, the German ships, and return visits on 23 and 27 December were equally unrewarding.

Brest apart, one of the hardest winters in years meant there were no operations between 23rd December 1941 and 6 January 1942. The weather, indeed, remained severe throughout most of January, being at its worst in the middle of the month, when XV Sqn operated from Alconbury, since Wyton, with its grass runways, was unusable.

January was also difficult in personnel terms, with crews and individuals coming and going constantly. In part the changes were due to the departure of Canadian aircrew to 419 Squadron at Mildenhall, and of New Zealanders to 75 (NZ) Squadron at Feltwell. But there were also a number of crews posted to 215 Sqn in the Far East. These changes cannot have helped Wg/Cdr Heath build up a squadron at two Flight strength, as required in a message received on the last day of 1941.

Operations in 1942 began on 6 January with an abortive attack on Cherbourg, while at Brest three nights later, only two of the six crews (the most put up since the Malta Echelon left) identified the target visually. Success also eluded five crews who went to Wilhelmshaven on 10 January. The German authorities reported a small raid, which suggests that few bombloads fell in the town, though crews thought that they had bombed the primary. One aircraft (P/O P. S. Sanders) did not return, and it was later learned that he and three others had been rescued from the sea, and taken prisoner.

An attack on Hamburg on the 14th was also a failure, very bad weather preventing target identification, and again one (P/O E. G. Broad RAAF) of five aircraft failed to return. The following morning the CO and P/O Parker flew sweeps over the North Sea in the hope of finding the missing crew, but without success. Of Broad and his crew nothing more was heard.

During the following week heavy snow prevented operational flying, but on 20 January three crews took part in a small scale attack on Emden, while on the 22nd two crews bombed Münster, one reporting that its bombs burst close to the railway station. A return visit on 28 January was a thoroughgoing failure, two crews bringing their bombs back, and the third bombing hopefully on ETA.

Apart from Münster, severe weather permitted only two raids between 22 January and 10 February. On 26 January four crews attacked Brest without observable results, while on the 31st an attack on Le Havre by P/O Bain was distinguished only by the skill shown in bringing back his Wellington on one engine, and with the ailerons locked. The ORB, noting Bain's 'exceedingly good work', added:

> The other members of the crew were all ready to bale out over Le Havre, and one Sergeant said the only thing that stopped him doing so was that his Commission had not come through.

On 31 December a signal was received from the Air Ministry stating that the Malta Echelon was to become 156 Squadron, while the Home Echelon would retain its original number. For reasons explained hereafter, this proposal was later rescinded, and the Home Echelon was advised that on 14 February it would become 156 Squadron, while 'the old Squadron in Malta would retain the nomenclature 40 Squadron'.

In the three days remaining the Home Echelon operated twice. On 11 February, four freshman crews were sent to Le Havre, and two experienced crews to Mannheim, one of whom bombed successfully. The other (P/O L. J. Ackland) ran into trouble when an engine failed soon after take-off. Fortunately, he was flying a Mk. II, and was able to coax the aircraft to the coast and jettison the 4,000-lb 'cookie' before attempting to return to base. With the aircraft rapidly losing height, the crew baled out. All landed safely, though the second pilot (Sgt P. L. Hall) was injured and admitted to hospital.

The last operation undertaken by 40 from Alconbury, on 12 February, was (though a failure) fitting in its way. For the Squadron had visited Brest often enough to make appropriate participation in the search for the *Scharnhorst*, *Gneisenau* and *Prinz Eugen*, which had left the port on what became known as 'The Channel Dash'. The Germans had timed their departure well, and in bad weather they succeeded in avoiding interception by all but a handful of the 242 RAF and Fleet Air Arm sorties flown during the day.

Five 40 Squadron aircraft took part in the search, fruitlessly, but not without incident, for one (P/O Bain) jettisoned its bombs when an Me 110 approached, circled, and fortunately left without attacking, while another (F/O Barr) turned back with the front turret unserviceable, only to be fired on by coastal AA batteries. With the rear gunner wounded, Barr landed at Lakenheath, whence P/O Leavett was taken to Ely Hospital.

On 13 February 1942 the 40 Squadron Adjutant made the final entry for the Home Echelon: '6 crews of B Flight did Air Tests and 2 of A, night flying' Then he added: 'This concludes the Operations Record Book of No. 40 Squadron at Alconbury. As from to-morrow the good work will be carried on by No. 156 Squadron.' And so it was, for in August 1942 156 Squadron became a founding unit of the Pathfinder Force, with which it operated with distinction—and heavy losses—until the end of the war.[1]

## Note

1.  For the history of 156 Squadron after it joined the PFF in August 1942 see Michael P. Wadsworth, *They Led the Way: the Story of Pathfinder Squadron 156*. Beverley: Highgate Publications, 1992.

# 14

# The Malta Echelon:
# October 1941–February 1942

A T dawn on 24 October 1941, the first of the Wellingtons of B Flight (captained by Harry Garvin) landed at Luqa airfield, Malta, followed within an hour by four others. Three more were still airborne. One (Sgt Munro) found itself at daylight off the north-west tip of Sicily, landing at Luqa after nine and a half hours. Another, piloted by fellow New Zealander Flt/Lt Jim Steel was in a more difficult predicament when, at dawn, the crew were 'well north of Sicily, with more than 200 miles to go to Malta'. 'It was', Jim adds, 'a horribly clear morning with no sign of cloud on the route ahead.' With fuel low there was no option but to fly over Sicily, which they did at low level, following a road from Termini to Licata. They landed at Luqa after eleven hours in the air, with only fifty gallons of fuel left.

The problems that Steel and Munro had encountered—unforecast beam and head winds on the second half of the flight—were presumably responsible for the loss of the eighth Wellington (Sgt Paine), which was either shot down or ditched out of fuel near the Island of Stromboli. All aboard died.

48. 40 Squadron crew room, Luqa, Autumn 1941. (J. E. Tipton.)

When 40 arrived, there were two Wellington squadrons, 38 and 104, operating from Luqa, as well as two Blenheim squadrons, a Flight of ASV MkVII Wellingtons, and photo-reconnaissance Marylands. 104 with its MkII Wellingtons, had only recently arrived, but 38 was about to return to Egypt.

Forty arrived at a good time. Food, ammunition and fuel were in adequate supply, and the *Regia Aeronautica*'s raids were scarcely more than a nuisance.[1] Hence the RAF and Fleet Air Arm units were able to operate with freedom, the Wellingtons complementing the Blenheims, which operated by day.

Forty's Wellingtons were dispersed to the east of the airfield along the Safi Strip, a meandering taxiway extending (at this time) half a mile or so, with disperal bays along its length. The Squadron Office was a wooden building close to the Station HQ, but the Operations Room was underground, while maintenance facilities were located in large caves off the eastern end of the main runway. The officers and ground crew were accommodated on the airfield, the former in huts close to the Squadron Office, and ground personnel in tents.[2] NCO aircrew, however, were billeted in 'The Poor House', owned by an order of nuns, fifteen minutes walk away on the Valetta road. Ken Rees, who had flown a part tour with 40 at Alconbury before volunteering for the Middle East, and who now, along with another former 40 Squadron pilot, Sgt G. H. Easton RNZAF, rejoined at the invitation of Wg/Cdr Stickley, recalls that The Poor House was 'really primitive': cold, damp and uncomfortable. The food was also poor, Ken Rees recalling the 'shortage of veg. and bread and the ubiquitous hard tack biscuits', and pilot Frank Haden 'the [tinned] Bacon (which no one seemed to be able to fry until it was crisp and palatable), tinned butter or margarine, tinned corned beef and tinned stew'.

Forty began operating on 28 October, when six crews carried out a nuisance raid on Tripoli harbour. Ken Rees comments:

> We didn't much like 'nuisance raids'. We would be sent on a target, and had to spend about an hour or an hour and a half over it, dropping our bombs singly, moving away and coming in again, dropping another bomb; the idea being to keep the Italians in their air raid shelters. It meant that, although the defences were not as concentrated as they were in Northern Europe, we were in the danger area quite a long time.

The next night the same six crews operated, in company with twelve from 104 Squadron, disrupting work in the Tripoli marshalling yards, while on the 31st five went to Naples and Palermo. All returned safely. B Flight was away to a good start.

On 1 November only two aircraft operated, Sgt Rees and F/O Hutt (the first A Flight arrival) making nuisances of themselves over Naples. The next night, however, twelve crews were up for an attack on the airfield at Castel Benito, in Tripolitania. They went in at low level after bombing, strafing aircraft and buildings, and Bob Andrews, Wg/Cdr Stickley's front gunner, recalls the satisfaction that his crew felt on returning to base. One aircraft (Sgt G. D. Colville) failed to return, however.

During the next week 40 operated on five nights at strengths of three to eleven aircraft. Twice, on 5 and 7 November, the Squadron bombed single targets (Castel Benito and Brindisi), but the remainder were nuisance raids, with two to four aircraft despatched to a range of targets. No losses were sustained. Then on 11 November nineteen Wellingtons (a maximum effort for 40 and 104) were despatched to the Royal Dockyard, Naples. All ten from 40 bombed safely, but on the return journey Sqn/Ldr Greer lost an engine, and ditched thirty miles short of Malta. Five of the crew survived the ditching, but two drowned when their dinghy twice capsized during a severe storm. Blenheims searched for Greer's crew next day, but rain and low cloud prevented a sighting, and the dinghy was blown towards Sicily, the three survivors being picked up after four and a half days.

The bad weather which prevented Alex Greer's rescue also prevented operational flying until 14 November, when twelve aircraft raided Catania, in Sicily. One of the crews operating that night was a new one. En route to the Middle East, it had been 'retained' as a replacement for Sgt Colville, and given a new captain, Sgt C. A. Armstrong RNZAF. This process, characteristic of AVM Lloyd, the AOC Malta, was the only means by which the operational strength of the Wellington squadrons could be maintained.

Bad weather prevented 40 operating again until 18 November, when ten Wellingtons were despatched on nuisance raids to Brindisi, Tripoli and Naples. Another nuisance raid the next night was followed on the 21st by a new experience, when south of the Straits of Messina, twelve crews attacked an Axis convoy. The trip was rated 'easy', and it was, in that the anti-aircraft defences were concentrating on FAA Swordfish, but not easy at all to score hits. The most that could be claimed, Jim Steel comments, was that 'we scattered the convoy and separated escorts from the merchantmen, allowing our submarines, assisted by our flares, to bag the odd ship'.

The 22nd of November brought another 'first', an attack on Berka aerodrome, near Benghazi. The six crews were told that Benghazi had never been raided from Malta, and that a hot reception should be expected, but the searchlights and flak proved ineffectual. On the 24th 40 returned to Benghazi, bombing harbour installations. The defences were again weak, and the only anxiety was provided by the weather. En route, crews had been buffeted by a cold front which on the return journey was so bad that diarist Bruce Holloway, in the front turret of Sgt Armstrong's aircraft, noted that 'We were thrown about all over the place and we all honestly thought our end had come'. The storm may have been a factor in the loss of Sgt Parker's crew, though the primary cause was wireless failure, which prevented them receiving navigational fixes. They ditched, but only Parker and his second pilot (Sgt E. I. Cooper) survived to be taken prisoner after five days in a dinghy.

Back at Luqa there was further misfortune when two armourers (Sgt W. Shearsby and AC1 T. McCann) were killed, and four others injured when an anti-personnel bomb, lying on the bomb doors of X9662, dropped out when they were opened.

Bad weather prevented 40 operating again until 27 November, when twelve crews went to Naples. Guided by the volcanoes of Stromboli and Vesuvius, they found the city without difficulty, and against weak defences bombed the marshalling yards and Royal Arsenal accurately. Benghazi, the next night, was a very different proposition, however, strong defences and a violent storm, which forced three crews to turn back, making the operation the most hazardous to date.

More bad weather caused another operational hiatus until 5 December. But ironically it was during this quiet period that there occurred an event which was to alter circumstances radically: the German decision, on 30 November, to reinforce the *Luftwaffe* in the Mediterranean and neutralize Malta. To this end *Fleigerkorps* II was moved to Sicily, with its Headquarters at Messina. Its presence would be felt from the middle of December.

Having had a respite from operations, the ground crews were able to provide ten aircraft each night for raids on the Royal Arsenal, Naples, on 5 and 6 December. Both raids went well, but on the 5th, a clear moonlit night, two aircraft were intercepted by Fiat CR42 night fighters, and one (F/O Hutt) shot down after a long battle. Only Hutt and his second pilot (P/O I. E. Miller) survived.

On 9 December twelve crews bombed fuel stores near Tripoli, two of them (Sgt P. Barlow RCAF and P/O T. F. McCrorie) recently appropriated by AVM Lloyd. Then on the 11th, thirteen crews attacked docks and shipping at Patras, in Greece. This turned out to be more hazardous than expected, as Ivor Davies, Tony Armstrong's second pilot, recalls:

> The target—three fuel supply ships berthed at Patras—was hidden by 10/10th cloud at about 3000 feet, but by flying eastwards we were able to lose height and return to attack below cloud.

It was not only what Davies calls the 'claustrophobic proximity of the mountains in the Gulf of Corinth' which posed a problem. For over the target their aircraft was 'illuminated by a flare from another aircraft as we attacked the dock area and came under fairly hectic AA gunfire before escaping into cloud'.

On 13 December Benghazi was again the target, and Bruce Holloway recorded in his diary that

> our spirits dropped, especially when we found out it was a special job of minelaying in the harbour. This had never been attempted before and it was a dangerous job. The idea being for four machines to approach the harbour at 500 feet and drop their mines while another four flew low over the target and draw the searchlights and ack-ack fire.

In the event three runs over the target proved uneventful, but 'as we were coming away from Benghazi I could see them suddenly point all their guns out to sea and blaze away with everything they had, obviously one of our a/c just dropping his mines and I wondered who it could be'. It was in fact Sgt Easton's crew ('reckoned on being the best crew on the Squadron' Holloway noted next day) which failed to return, and this hit Tony Armstrong's crew hard, since he had been Gerald Easton's second pilot, and Norton Hardman, their former captain, had taken his place. The loss was the harder to take because the missing crew had occupied the next room. 'To see those empty beds,' Holloway wrote, 'gives me the creeps'.3

Attacks on oil storage tanks and warships at Taranto on the 15th and 16th, went smoothly in the face of ineffectual opposition, but on the 19th disaster struck when the first crews went out to their aircraft. John Tipton recalls:

> A bomb landed amongst us and we were thrown in various directions by the blast. I found myself lying under the port wingtip with a numb left leg. Looking back the fuselage was beginning to light up with flames and a body was lying outstretched underneath. It was Frank Sunley. I went back and pulled him away, and found one of the ground crew similarly dragging Sidney Shepherdson, who recognized me and said that his leg had gone. There was no sign of anyone else. They had been tossed away by the blast. But all survived.

Single-handedly, the intruder had destroyed three Wellingtons and put many more out of action with shrapnel damage. The effects were felt when, on 21 and 22 December, 40 could only muster three and five aircraft to attack Castel Benito aerodrome. Yet both raids went well, aircraft being destroyed and hangars set on fire. An attack on Tripoli harbour on Christmas Eve was equally effective, crews reporting hits on warehouses and docks.

Christmas Day was celebrated in traditional fashion, but Bruce Holloway, who served at the Airmen's Mess, later wrote bitterly of the comparison between what the airmen got—'a swell dinner, free beer and cigarettes'—and the meagre fare at the Poor House, where 'What there was of it wasn't too bad, but it was very little and half of the things shown on the menu we never had'.

An afternoon spent playing cards and searching unsuccessfully in Luqa village for food, was followed by a visit to the Officers' Mess for drinks. Afterwards most of the NCOs returned to the Poor House, but Ken Rees, Bob Munro and Peter Potter, an RCAF rear gunner, went, well-oiled, into Valetta and the infamous Gut. Ken writes:

> I only have vague recollections of the whole thing but it appears we were in some bar, somehow or other got entangled with the band, fell into it, bent a few instruments, put a foot through a drum and eventually finished off in the cells.

The fracas led to a court appearance next morning, where 'the Adjutant, who was a solicitor, represented us, explained what had happened, said we were young and innocent and fighting a war, etc. etc. and we got off'. Ironically, that afternoon Rees and Munro were before AVM Lloyd for successful commissioning interviews.

On Boxing Day it was business as usual, 40 despatching eight Wellingtons to Tripoli, and the *Luftwaffe* bombing Luqa. A raid while crews were carrying out their DIs did no significant damage, but a second, at lunch time, destroyed two Wellingtons. Then as crews were waiting to board their aircraft a third raid took place, while they were welcomed back from Tripoli by sirens and bombs bursting nearby.

The 27th of December brought almost continual raids, the first at dawn depriving everyone of breakfast, as the cook and waiters had disappeared into the shelters. By commandeering OADU [Overseas Air Delivery Unit] Wellingtons en route to the Middle or Far East, 40 was able to muster eleven aircraft for a raid on Tripoli, which was bombed, though probably not effectively, as cloud obscured the target.

Forty did not operate on 28 or 29 December, but the stand down was far from restful, amidst the heaviest bombing since the *Luftwaffe*'s return to Sicily. On the morning of the 28th one bomb load caused considerable blast damage to the Poor House, and there were further raids that night. A morning raid on the 29th did little damage, but in the afternoon Ju 88s and accompanying Me 109s destroyed nine Wellingtons, three of which belonged to 40 Squadron. Bruce Holloway spotted two 88s dropping their bombs, and

> dived to the ground alongside Martin [Sgt M. K. Johnson, WOp/AG] and waited for the bang, [which] seemed to lift us up and bash us down again and we were almost a mile away in the crew room. He had scored a direct hit on an a/c, one of ours already bombed up for tonight's operations. As the bombs and the petrol tanks exploded they caught the other machines alight and the whole dispersal area seemed to be ablaze. The fire had reached the bomb dump and we were all waiting for this explosion, it came alright and shook the whole of the island.

49. A familiar sight, December 1941. (A. E. Husk.)

In the expectation that other dumps would go up, everyone was evacuated, and Holloway wrote later: 'We were all down in the dumps and honestly I didn't expect to be alive the next day, nor did any of the other chaps.' Next morning crews made their way to Luqa to carry out DIs—if their aircraft had survived—and to inspect the damage. Bruce Holloway found that 'the bomb dump had . . . left a crater 30 feet deep and about 60 feet wide', while 'on either side of the road the place was littered with burnt out a/c'. 'For about one square mile', he continues, 'the place was absolutely littered with debris, engines, bits of propeller and other parts of the a/c strewn all over the place.'

After such destruction 40 and 104 could only put up seven aircraft between them for an attack on motor transport yards and petrol dumps at Misurata that night. One of these was U-Uncle, which scored a direct hit on what was believed to be the airmen's sleeping quarters, and then strafed vehicles on the Benghazi-Tripoli road. For Bruce Holloway, in the front turret,

> This was damn good fun, with a roar of the engines and all guns blazing we dived onto the road. We were at 200 feet as we swept along the road and I could see the transport stop and men running. We must have done quite a bit of damage there and I was sorry to leave it.

The year 1941 ended with a stand down, but a raid at lunch-time once again left aircrew without food as the Poor House staff took to the shelters,

50. Z1079 (Sgt Munro) at dispersal minutes before it was destroyed by strafing Me109s.
(J. D. Austin.)

and many went into Valetta for a meal and a film, the New Year being
ushered in to the sound of German bombers overhead.

January 1942 opened with a single aircraft (Sqn/Ldr Craigen) despatched
to Tripoli. Ground crew were working desperately hard to repair the
damaged Wellingtons, cannibalizing wrecks and achieving miracles of im-
provisation, and on the 2nd five aircraft were up on nuisance raids, two of
them Mk IIs from 104 Squadron, which was leaving for the Middle East.
Earlier, while Tony Armstrong's crew were doing their DI, Ju 88s arrived.
Martin Johnson, now the second diarist in the crew, wrote:

> Two sticks of bombs caught the neighbouring kite to U for Uncle on fire,
> and I shan't forget the feeling of helplessness when the dirt and cordite fumes
> had passed and the shrapnel began to fall.

The destruction continued the next day, when 88s and strafing 109s destroyed
two veterans, BL-F, which Bob Munro had brought from Alconbury in
October, and BL-U, whose destruction, Martin Johnson wrote, 'we took
as a personal loss'.

On 3 January the Luftwaffe hammered Luqa round the clock, and after
a broken night the NCO aircrew were not impressed to be summoned to
the airfield for a 9 am talk by AVM Lloyd. Bruce Holloway wrote:

> We expected to hear some good information about going back to UK as
> there had been rumours going round for weeks but no, he told us nothing

51. Castel Vetrano airfield, 5 January 1942. Circles indicate damaged aircraft, and the triangle dumped wreckage. (IWM CM2094.)

we didn't already know. He said we had to keep up a relentless bombing of Tripoli but he didn't say what with and how, so his little talk went into one ear and out of the other.

That night, however, the RAF hit Castel Vetrano airfield, in Sicily, where a large number of transport aircraft had been assembled because of the waterlogged condition of other airfields. A first blow, just before dusk, was struck by eleven Blenheims, which took the defences completely by surprise. They were followed by the five Wellingtons which were all that 40 could muster, four flying a second sortie. Twelve enemy aircraft were destroyed and forty-two damaged, 500 drums of aviation fuel lost, and vehicles and buildings damaged. Ivor Davies writes: 'We left in the first wave at about 1930, and had no difficulty in locating the airfield—the single runway stood out like a large white strip as we began to attack from 6000 ft'. 'We were greeted with very active anti-aircraft gunfire', he continues, 'but fires were soon started throughout the target area and were still visible when we were well into the return journey'.

Leading the first wave was Bill Craigen, who recalls:

I thought I'd cut back the engines and do a glide approach down the great column of black smoke there was from burning aircraft on the airfield. The flak stopped. There were no searchlights. What I'd forgotten was that as soon as I came out over this fire in the centre of the airfield I was lit up like daylight so then things began to get quite exciting. You could see people leaning out of the barrack block windows firing at us with their rifles and pistols.

All the first wave returned safely, but one of the second (Flt/Sgt J. F. Lewthwaite RNZAF) was shot down over the airfield. There were no survivors.

AVM Lloyd had stressed the need to keep hammering at the port facilities at Tripoli. But bad weather, and in particular high winds blowing across

Luqa's one runway, forced the cancellation during the next week of all but one small nuisance raid. On 11 January, however, despite atrocious weather, five crews attacked shipping at Tripoli, and on the 12th, again in foul weather, five more. Nuisance raids were flown over Tripoli on 14, 15 and 16 January, P/O McCrorie performing particularly well on the 15th, remaining over the target for two and a half hours despite 10/10ths cloud, electrical storms and sub-zero temperatures. On their return the crew was personally congratulated by AVM Lloyd.

On 10 January Holloway noted that 'the air raids don't seem so intense these days', but three days later he was less sanguine, since 'the air raids were still almost continuous and more than once we had to dive for shelter', while the entry for the 14th begins, 'Perfectly miserable morning and spent the whole time at the crew room just hanging about making an occasional dive for the shelter through the rain'. Often there was little warning of air attack since, as Jim Steel explains, 'To allow work to be maintained, critical military areas got their own local warning sirens to be sounded when it became obvious that that particular place was coming under attack'.

Forty had put almost all of its energies since the New Year into blocking the flow of supplies through Tripoli, but on 18 January attention shifted to Sicily, and Catania aerodrome. The aim was to disrupt an anticipated German bomber attack on a supply convoy from Alexandria by bombing continuously throughout the night. The first crews arrived over Catania soon after dusk, and the last not long before dawn, each making three bombing runs. Fires and explosions were caused by aircraft in the first wave, and there was further havoc when, near dawn, P/O McCrorie reached Catania just as lights were switched on to enable two Ju 88s to land. He followed them in, laying a stick of bombs along the runway, and the crew thought that one of the Ju 88s ran into the bomb explosions and other aircraft caught fire.

After the maximum effort against Catania, 40 returned to nuisance raids on 20 and 21 January and then, on the 22nd, sent eight crews to Tripoli. For most the trip was uneventful, but McCrorie had two encounters with night fighters. The first engaged the Wellington in searchlights over the target, but was evaded by a 300 mph dive, while the second followed him into the Luqa circuit, but was driven off by the anti-aircraft defences.

Attacks of this latter sort were not uncommon, Bill Craigen recalling an occasion when, on approach, his rear gunner (Flt/Lt R. Healey) warned him that they had a Ju 88 on their tail. They aborted the landing, and when things quietened down came in again:

Luqa put on the flarepath and as we came in Ron Healey called me up again, saying, 'The bugger's right behind you, coming in right behind you!' We were about 20 feet off the ground when they switched the flarepath off, leaving us to touch down in the dark. I swung off the runway just as the 88 dropped a stick of bombs right the way down the runway. The crew and I spent the next hour in a goat cave.

On 23 January a minelaying raid to Tripoli was postponed late in the day, information having been received from Ultra sources that a major convoy, T18, was en route to Tripoli. Escorted by an Italian force comprising a battleship, 3 cruisers and 14 destroyers, 4 freighters carrying tanks, trucks, and supplies had rendezvoused off Messina with the troopship *Vittoria*, carrying 1,300 panzer troops. These reinforcements, were they to reach Rommel, would enable the Afrika Korps to resume the offensive.

A plan was hurriedly devised whereby air and surface attacks would be made on the convoy. A force of cruisers and destroyers left Grand Harbour to intercept it south of Malta, and Fleet Air Arm and RAF units were briefed for a night attack. Led by Sqn/Ldr Steel as illuminator, 40 contributed eight Wellingtons, which were to bomb following an FAA torpedo attack.

The plan was promising, but failed. Disaster struck the naval force when it ran into a minefield, the cruiser HMS *Neptune* sinking almost at once, and the destroyer HMS *Kandahar* later, while the FAA crews failed to locate the convoy. It was therefore up to 40's Wellingtons. Jim Steel recalls:

> We carried out a pattern of flare dropping over the estimated position of the convoy. The flares were dropped from 8000 feet to give a maximum period of illumination for the bombing aircraft. By the time we reached the estimated target area the moon was setting in very hazy conditions. We got a brief glimpse of a ship but we had by then exhausted our flare supply and we had no bombs to attempt an attack.

None of the Wellingtons scored hits, but the failure of the operation could not be held against 40 Squadron, since it had been planned as a naval operation, and the use of aircraft was essentially an afterthought. The loss of the *Neptune* and *Kandahar* was the crucial factor.

Following the convoy attack 40 reverted to the usual nuisance raids on Tripoli, Catania and Comiso, before (on the 29th) attacking motor transport on the coastal road between Tripoli and Beurat. The relish with which this task was approached is evident from Bruce Holloway's diary entry:

> We were to bomb anything of importance that was on the road, mainly convoys and then go down and machine gun. This we did and as I was on the set tonight I went down and had a crack at the beam guns. We had quite good fun strafing that road and spent about an hour up and down it.

Ops on the next two nights were similar, with anti-shipping sweeps off the North African coast and attacks on motor transport near Tripoli. In fine weather with the moon providing near daylight conditions, crews relished their tasks, though as was now clear, ships at sea were a difficult target, rarely hit.

If things were going well in the air, they were less satisfactory on the ground. On 16 January those billetted there had been told that because the Poor House might be bombed, they were to move to the Naxxar Palace, forty-five minutes' drive from Luqa. Belongings were packed but the move did not eventuate until the 27th, when Bruce Holloway wrote in his diary:

> When we were shown the place where we were to sleep we couldn't believe it. It is quite a small room with 20 chaps in and the beds are so close together you can't stand between them. The whole room is filthy and nowhere to put your clothes except on the floor. The mess is a disgrace. There are 4 tables in the hall at the entrance to the Palace and this is where the Air Crew, Ground NCOs and ACs all eat. There are about 4 knives, 6 forks and a couple of spoons and about 6 mugs and about 100 people have to use these at the same time. The whole place is filthy and disgusting and is a disgrace to the Air Force, but no one in authority seems to mind. We are all living like a lot of pigs and are being treated as such and if things don't change in the near future there will be a lot of trouble.

Trouble there was the next day, which began badly when the food ran out at breakfast, and got worse when in the evening the NCOs were told 'that we were to sweep the room out, make the beds up and and make more room for more chaps to come in'. They refused until conditions were improved, and this led to a confrontation

> in which the Adjutant and Crimmins [F/O C. W. Crimmin, the Engineering Officer] were . . . surrounded by all of us and we told him [John Hutton, the Adjutant] all our moans and grievances, but all we could get from him was that the air crew of today is not half as good as it used to be.

The situation, Bruce Holloway noted, was exacerbated by a new requirement that 'we all parade at 9 o'clock every morning for inspection and after that go back and sweep our rooms and make up our beds'. 'This', he added, 'just about finishes it and there looks like being a mutiny'.

The resentment which Bruce Holloway and others felt was no doubt intensified by a comparison with conditions on the cruiser, HMS *Penelope*, which they visited on the invitation of three sailors they met in Valetta. Lunch was an eye-opener:

> soup with hot rolls and butter, then roast beef, roast potatoes and cabbage and for dessert a whole plate of peaches and jelly, on top of this another lot of rum. This was the best dinner I have had since I left England. Everything was so clean and well cooked and made us realise what we have to put up with.

By contrast, on 30 January, lunch at Naxxar consisted of '2 pieces of corned beef', and on 1 February, 'a very measly breakfast' was followed at lunch by 'a pretty awful snack'. Complaints about the food continued, especially about the 'awful M and V' [Maconachie's Meat and vegetable Stew, vividly recalled by all who served on Malta at this time], but in other respects conditions at Naxxar Palace improved somewhat.

During January 1942 more than fifty aircraft had been destroyed on the ground, and these heavy losses stimulated the construction of blast-proof dispersal pens. The building blocks were four-gallon petrol cans (of which there were vast numbers available) filled with limestone rubble, and for a Wellington it took 60,000 cases to build three 90ft walls, 14ft high. Some Maltese civilians were employed, but the bulk of the work was done by the Army. The pity was that such pens had not been built earlier.

On 2 February, (in poor weather) the Squadron put up six Wellingtons over Palermo and Naples, then sent seven crews to attack vehicles south of Tripoli on the 4th, and eight to a transport park north of the town the next night. Despite heavy flak, however, the greater dangers still lay at Luqa, Bruce Holloway noting: 'Continuously for about the last 6 weeks we get an average of 12 warnings a day and always we get bombs somewhere; there is not one safe place on the island'. The 5th of February certainly provided excitement, with Luqa strafed and bombed while crews were doing their DIs, and night intruders bombing the runway as they took off. Another hazard was a fierce cross wind, which nearly blew one aircraft into the CO's car, parked beside the runway. To complete an eventful night, a raid was in progress when the aircraft returned, and they had to wait off the coast until it was over.

On 6 February seven aircraft attacked the aerodrome at Sirte and the following night another seven went to Tripoli, which was visited again on the 11th and for a last time on the 12th, when six crews attacked the harbour and shipping. The defensive barrage was now noticeably heavier than when 40 first attacked the town in November, yet ironically the only crew lost in thirty-one raids was Sgt Colville's, shot down on the first, in October.

While concentrating on Tripoli in early February, 40 frequently sent crews on nuisance raids to aerodromes in Sicily. On 13 February Catania and Gerbini were each visited by three crews. The weather was poor, and some crews bombed almost blind—with startling results in the case of Tony Armstrong's crew, who 'dropped some incendiaries just to see what would happen' at Gerbini, then followed them with a few bombs when large fires were started, before moving to Catania to bomb visually. They were startled to learn later that another crew had reported burning aircraft where the incendiaries had fallen. 'This is damn good news', Bruce Holloway wrote, 'as we never expected to do any damage at all as we could hardly see a thing'.

Rumours about departure had been circulating ever since 104 Squadron left for Egypt at the beginning of January. On the 20th it was being confidently asserted that 40 was to fly out to the Middle East within a week.

These rumours proved unfounded, as did another, in early February, that the Squadron was about to be relieved by 115 Squadron. Then on 13 February Bruce Holloway noted a rumour that they were to be relieved by 37 Squadron, adding: 'This sounds too good to be true but quite a lot of chaps are positive about it. We are going to M.E., whether or not we are to operate.'

This time the rumours were well-founded. Personnel were told the next morning that they would be leaving Malta over the next few days, and that afternoon paraded in the garden of the Naxxar Palace for a talk by AVM Lloyd. Bruce Holloway wrote:

> He told us that our job in Malta was finished and that we were going to M.E. immediately. He thanked us all and told us to be proud of the work that we had done in Malta. He told us that we had dropped one third of the tonnage of bombs by 40 Squadron ever since the war broke out and had accomplished more than any other Squadron had ever done. He finally shook hands with us all and wished us the best of luck. To Tony and our crew he acknowledged the fact that we had done more flying than anyone else.

It was rumoured that when told 40 would be going to Egypt rather than returning to Alconbury, Wg/Cdr Stickley 'kicked strongly against it'. He certainly kicked strongly earlier against news that the Malta Echelon was to become 156 Squadron. With the active support of AVM Lloyd, he made strong and successful representations to London, as did 104's Wg/Cdr Beare, whose Malta Echelon, now in Egypt, was to be renumbered 158.

On 14 February the Squadron flew its last Malta operation, fifteen crews attacking Sicilian aerodromes in two waves. In the first wave 2 aircraft bombed Gerbini and 6 Catania, while in the second 7 were despatched to Comiso. Last off in the second wave (at 3.55 am) was Tony Armstrong, and as the crew waited at the aircraft for take off they twice had to run for shelter during an air raid. Two and a half hours later they landed at Luqa amid yet another raid. The experience typified what the Squadron personnel had, since mid-December, endured.

Another event which epitomized 40's experiences on Malta occurred at 6 pm on the 15th, when a bomb fell on the Regent Cinema in Valetta. Among the 150 people trapped under the rubble were the Gunnery and Signals Leaders, Flt/Lt J. S. Reeves and P/O E. G. Watson. Reeves was found after two and half hours, buried beneath a pile of stones, badly bruised, but with no bones broken. For Watson there seemed to be no hope, but nine hours later he was dug out of the rubble with nothing worse than a lacerated scalp. The luck which had enabled him to parachute to safety from his Blenheim over France in August 1940, and reach Gibraltar (for which he was awarded the Military Medal), had seen him through again. Nearly 130 others were not so lucky.

Though one aircraft, flown by Sqn/Ldr Craigen and the now P/O H. K. Rees, had left Malta earlier (27 January), the major exodus of 40 Squadron crews began on 15 February, when four aircraft got away. The next morning two OADU Wellingtons arrived from Gibraltar, and these were earmarked to fly out that night. Sadly, Sgt Jack Webb, who was running up the engines of one of them during an air raid alert, was killed when the Wellington sustained a direct hit. Again, an incident at the last typified what 40 had endured.

Bad weather prevented further departures until the 19th, while the last five, including the CO, Laurie Stickley, got away two nights later. It had been 120 days since the first crews arrived from Alconbury.

Despite the heroic efforts of the fighter pilots, outnumbered, and flying Hurricanes inferior to the Me 109Fs opposing them, the massive aerial assault which began in December 1941 brought up to twenty alerts on a busy day, with three to five major raids, as well as dive bombing and strafing. Conditions were hard for everyone, with sleep and work disrupted. But it was hardest on the ground personnel, who had no respite from the incessant attacks. Forty lost six crews on operations. But even so, most aircrew felt, from December on, that it was safer in the air than on the ground.4

One unfortunate aspect of operational flying on Malta was the very limited possibility of air testing machines. Ken Rees, for instance, flew thirteen ops during November, but no air tests, while Tony Armstrong air tested machines only twice in three months. Daily Inspections, of course, continued as usual, though a shortage of aircraft meant that at times half or more of the crews had no machine to inspect.

For ground crews, Malta was the severest of tests. Short-handed, without the sophisticated workshop facilities and backup available at bases in England, forced to cannibalize wrecked aircraft for parts, and constantly under air attack, they were the unsung heroes of the Malta Echelon. When, after a particularly punishing German raid, there were only a handful of Wellingtons airworthy, ground crews worked feverishly to get the numbers up. The raid in the early hours of 19 December left 40 with four machines capable of operating the following night, yet by Christmas Eve the Squadron was able to despatch ten. It was a remarkable achievement.

The intention was to fly all ground crew out to Egypt, and fitter Arthur Husk recalls that he and others were already aboard their aircraft when they were told that it had been decided to keep the remaining riggers and fitters in Malta in an attempt to repair the numerous unserviceable Wellingtons. This proved a vain hope, as most of the aircraft were destroyed in further raids, but it was not until June that these ground crew got away, just in time to join the reformed squadron at Shallufa.

Looking back on his time with 40 Squadron John Tipton comments:

It was in fact a feature of both Alconbury and Malta that there was very little squadron spirit as one experienced it elsewhere. Loyalty and friendship were mainly confined to one's crew and relationships from OTU. This was not a criticism of the CO. Wg/Cdr Stickley was respected by all, but in England Alconbury House provided sleeping quarters but no facilities for social cohesion, and the same situation existed in the Poor House at Malta.

Yet despite the hardships and the lack of squadron cohesion, 40 had performed with distinction during its first detachment to Malta, and survivors look back on those four months with pride, if with little pleasure.

# Notes

1. On all matters relating to air operations over Malta in 1941 see Christopher Shores et al., *Malta: the Hurricane Years 1940–41*. London: Grub Street Books, 1987.

2. These arrangements were changed when the German air raids made living on the airfield too dangerous, both the officers and ground crews being moved to the Naxxar Palace. Bill Craigen recalls:

   One morning—when I got back from a raid I slept quite heavily—I woke up with a window frame round my neck on the bed, and the place completely deserted. There was a hole in the ground outside the Mess you could have lost half a dozen London buses in. And the rest had looked in and seen me there with the window frame around my neck, and thought, 'Well, he's had it', so they'd left me there.

3. In fact Easton's crew survived, and the adventures which befell them are recounted by Norman MacMillan in *Tales of Two Air Wars* (London: Bell, 1963), pp. 189–98, on which this note draws. Despite severe flak damage which wounded the wireless operator (Sgt F. H. Cochrane) and left the Wellington without hydraulics, and the bomb doors, undercarriage and flaps hanging down, Easton managed to nurse the aircraft to Tobruk. From there the crew were flown to Cairo, where Cochrane's wounds were treated and the crew had a week's leave. On 22 December they boarded a Sunderland of 230 Squadron for the flight to Malta, but off Cyrenaica the flying boat was attacked by two Me 110s. In the fight which followed, Norton Hardman, Easton's second pilot, was killed by cannon fire, and the Sunderland's rear gunner seriously wounded. His place was taken by Sgt A. E. Boorman from the Wellington crew, who was himself slightly wounded as he and the other gunners shot down one of the German fighters. The Sunderland was crippled, however, and with both starboard engines out of action, and fuel tanks holed, the pilot, Flt/Lt S. W. R. Hughes, had no option but to come down on the sea. The wind drove the aircraft on to a reef near Benghazi, and the survivors, including the wounded gunner, reached the shore. There the survivors met up with Italian troops, who forced them to retreat west with them for two days, on the second of which the Sunderland rear gunner died. On the third day the RAF men, refusing to go further, were left to their own devices. They set out east, hoping to meet up with advancing Allied troops, and en route took willing prisoner groups of retreating Italians. On Christmas Eve they finally met up with a patrol from the 4th Indian Division, to whom they handed over their prisoners, now totalling over 150. The crew was tour-expired, since the Benghazi op was Gerald Easton's 40th.

4. See Christopher Shores et al., *Malta: the Spitfire Year 1942*. London: Grub Street Books, 1991.

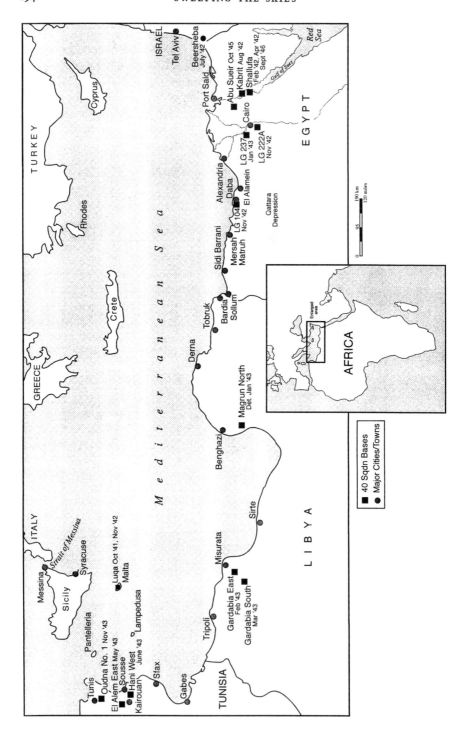

Map 4. North Africa, 1941–47.

15

# Disbandment and Re-formation:
## February–April 1942

THE evacuation of 40 Squadron from Malta to Egypt was completed on 22 February, when the last five aircraft arrived at Shallufa, the pilots including the CO, Laurie Stickley, and the B Flight Commander, Jim Steel. The flight from Malta to Egypt was not without its hazards, because of its length (upwards of seven and a half hours), the fact that most of it was over the sea, and that the weather was bad. Moreover each machine was heavily laden, carrying three or four passengers and kit, and take-offs were marginal under those conditions. During the evacuation two Wellingtons (Ivor Davies on 16 February, and Tony Armstrong on the 19th) had in fact suffered engine failure, forced-landing in the Western Desert.

After the rigours of Malta, rest and recuperation were required. Moreover, many aircrew were tour-expired, and postings-in few, so it was clearly going to take some time to rebuild the Squadron. Martin Johnson noted in his diary for 25 February:

This morning we were paraded at our new squadron offices where we listened to a talk from the Wingco. We were to be granted 7 days leave which we expected anyway. Also we were asked to keep up [the] 'reputation' of the Squadron in the event of our being asked to operate. Lastly, all people who had over 200 operational hours were to notify the Corporal [Mahler, Orderly Room clerk] and give their preference for future duties.

Jim Steel recalls 'pandemonium on arrival at Shallufa, but also what followed:

John Hutton, Bill Austin [Flt/Lt W. S. Austin RNZAF, Navigation Officer] and I headed for Cairo and stayed at the famous Shepheard's Hotel. My first action was to fill one of their large baths and soak in it—what a fantastic experience after four months of hand basins and showers, and not much hot water.

Leave over, personnel returned to a Shallufa rife with rumours. While those ground crew who had been evacuated worked on the aircraft, the aircrew waited for instructions. On 14 March an operation was scheduled, four crews joining 37 Squadron in an attack on airfields on the Italian island of Rhodes. The aim, to divert *Luftwaffe* resources from Sicily and ease

195

pressure on Malta, was not achieved, but Maritsa airfield was located and bombed, all aircraft returning safely.

Besides this one operation, the only flying involved air tests, and it was during one of these on 18 March that 40 suffered its only fatalities at Shallufa. Martin Johnson's diary entry reads:

> We were chatting in our hut when quite suddenly a high pitched whine developed similar to most American planes. We jumped to the windows just in time to see a white flash followed by the usual pall of black smoke. Bruce [Holloway] had been up a fraction of a second earlier and had recognized a Wimpy diving to earth. I collected my camera and raced off to the scene of the crash and never have I seen a Wimpy so spread about. It was in very small pieces spread over a very large area, and each piece was alight. It was impossible to recognize the type of kite and it appeared to have power-dived vertically into the ground.
>
> I took a photograph of the funeral pyre and we discovered that it was a 40 Sqdn. kite. Four people were killed, as two had not gone for an oil test. Garvin, the U.S.A. pilot, Jimmy Joss, Rhodesian W/Op., Robb, the rear gunner, and a W/O navigator—Johnson—who joined the Squadron here.

One lucky not to be aboard the Wimpy was George Reddy, who two days earlier had flown in the aircraft to an Advanced Landing Ground to check the facilities for bombing up and refuelling. There the Wellington was strafed by Messerschmitts, which damaged the flap mechanism. After temporary repairs they returned to Shallufa, where permanent repairs were effected. Having certified the Wellington as serviceable, Reddy was to have flown with Harry Garvin on the air test, but fell asleep, something he had never done before, and arrived at the Flight Office to see the Wellington taking off.

The cause of the accident was never established. The Court of Inquiry argued pilot error, but the CO disagreed, as did the AOC 205 Group. On squadron the belief was that Garvin, who had not been well, collapsed over the controls.

This crash apart, the days passed uneventfully. Ground crew occupied themselves with leisurely overhauls of the aircraft, but the aircrew were largely unemployed, killing time reading, writing letters, playing cards, taking in an ENSA concert or a film at the camp cinema, or (when transport was available) going into Suez. There was even a resumption of team sports not played since the Phoney War, Martin Johnson noting on 21 March that 40 Squadron had played 38 Squadron Signals Section, losing 3–2. 'It was a good match', he noted, 'with two professionals'. One of those in 40's team may have been pilot Ian Macpherson, who played for Glasgow Rangers before the war, and had a distinguished career with Arsenal after it.

There seems no record of the date of the disbanding of 40 Squadron, though 24 March seems likely, given Martin Johnson's diary entry:

> The days of 40 Sqdn are now over. Some crews going to India, some to remain, some going to 108 Squadron at Kabrit, others going home (I hope). Though I feel quite relieved at not having to operate, there seems to be a sort of sadness attached to this breaking up.

The crews going to India were to join 215 Squadron, then moving to Asansol, near Calcutta, as part of the RAF build-up in India after the fall of Singapore and the Japanese advance through Burma. Sqn/Ldr. Maurice Booth was posted to command the detachment of ten aircraft ('clapped out wrecks', George Reddy recalls) and Jim Steel, given the choice of returning to Britain a Squadron Leader, to instruct at an OTU, or going out to India as a Flight Lieutenant and Booth's deputy, chose the latter. Perhaps 40 ground crew accompanied the detachment.

While at Asansol the ex–40 Squadron crews, most of whom flew no operations, were billeted in a convent school, equipped with such comforts as a swimming pool. Even so, when early in May they were given the option of returning to Egypt to rejoin the re-formed 40 Squadron, most took it up. The first group away, including Jim Steel, left for Egypt on a BOAC flying boat on 11 May. Another group followed on the 13th and all were back in Egypt by the 16th. Curiously, the First Officer on the flying boat which carried the first group back from India was Gerry Easton, who had completed a tour with 40 at Alconbury and Luqa, and whose last op had had such an eventful outcome (see p. 193).

# 16

# Crisis and Recovery:
# May–December 1942

Forty Squadron was re-formed at Shallufa, in Egypt, on 30 April 1942, under Wg/Cdr R. E. Ridgway, then serving at RAF HQ, Cairo. Joining the RAF in 1937, Dick Ridgway had served in the Middle East since before the outbreak of war, first with 216 Squadron and then with 70, the first Wellington squadron in the Middle East.

The Squadron's role was night torpedo-bombing, then being pioneered by 38 Squadron, which had already converted one flight. The aircraft employed was the familiar Wellington Ic, but carrying two torpedoes mounted one above the other in the bomb-bay, and in some cases modified by the deletion of the front turret. The re-formed 40 Squadron had no aircraft, however, and the other Wellington squadrons in Egypt were required to assist. They responded as might have been expected, handing over their most worn-out aircraft. It was thus with a collection of six clapped-out hacks that 40 began its third existence.

One of Wg/Cdr Ridgway's first moves was to ask the AOC, Middle East, Air Marshal Tedder, for the return to Egypt of the 40 Squadron personnel who had been posted to India. Tedder agreed, and a message was sent to Asansol, offering former members of the Squadron the option of returning to serve with 40 in the Canal Zone. Most, air and ground crew alike, did so.

Though 40 had six aircraft, it did not, at first, have crews to fly them. Indeed, when Dick Ridgway flew

52. Wg/Cdr R. E. Ridgway.
(J. E. S. Morton.)

53. 40 Squadron Wellington dropping a practice torpedo, June 1942. (R. L. Spence.)

his first practice, on 11 June, with a Royal Navy lieutenant to 'show him the ropes', he was accompanied by one other aircraft, piloted by Sgt Blake Forrest RCAF: the two comprising the entire operational strength of the Squadron. Gradually numbers built up, perhaps five crews returning from India, including those captained by Sqn/Ldr Maurice Booth and Jim Steel (who reverted to squadron leader rank to command B Flight). Crews from the United Kingdom were also posted in, these including Australians, Canadians and New Zealanders, who formed a significant percentage of the Squadron strength over the next few months. Training over Suez Bay continued, aiming practice torpedoes at a yacht, the *Sagitta*.

In January 1942 General Erwin Rommel had swept the British 8th Army 250 miles back from the western border of Cyrenaica to Gazala, just west of Tobruk. There the front stabilized until, in May, Rommel struck again, victories at Gazala and then Sidi Rezegh (in June), followed on the 20th of that month by the fall of Tobruk, bringing the Axis forces to within seventy miles of Alexandria. These spectacular advances created a crisis of confidence in the capacity of the 8th Army (and particularly of its generals) to prevent Rommel from breaking through the last defence line at El Alamein to reach the Nile Delta. They also led to the redesignation of 40 as a bomber squadron.

When the decision was made, Dick Ridgway was in Beirut on weekend leave. On the way back to Egypt he landed at Lydda to refuel, to find a message instructing him to return with all possible speed. At Shallufa he found that seemingly out of nowhere, twenty new Wellingtons had been delivered, along with about thirty crews, some from 38 Squadron, but others tour-expired, taken off the ship in which they were embarked for repatriation and told that they were required to fly additional sorties. Another source of personnel was No. 5 Middle East Training School, which was closed on 23 June, 'personnel being attached', 238 Wing ORB notes, 'for operations to No. 40 Squadron'.

The ground personnel likewise came from a variety of sources. Many were from the United Kingdom, on their first squadron posting. But a substantial number were 40 Squadron veterans, either returned from India or evacuated from Malta, where about twenty had been left behind in February. Jack Wey recalls:

> When all our remaining serviceable aircraft were flown out to Egypt, the remaining five unserviceable aircraft and their crews were left with the intention that they flew out to rejoin the Squadron as soon as repairs were completed. Unfortunately, each night the damage became progressively greater, and eventually the remaining machines were destroyed.
>
> The crews (myself included) got involved in a variety of jobs with other Malta based units. Some did repair work on the Blenheims, Beauforts and other aircraft. Others fulfilled tasks with airfield control.
>
> Then on June 20th the survivors of the Malta debacle were flown out of Luqa in transit and replacement aircraft en route to the Middle East.

Through these men, and those returned from India, the 40 Squadron tradition was maintained unbroken.

By dint of enormous effort the first operational sorties were flown on the night of 22 June, when four Wellingtons joined thirty-five from four other 205 Group squadrons in attacking the German satellite aerodrome at Tmimi. No ORB seems to have been kept by 40 during June, but the Group ORB records that 'good fires' were started, aircraft straddled, and a 'large black fire' (presumably fuel) observed in a wadi. The following night four aircraft from 40 formed part of a thirty-nine strong force attacking landing grounds in the Gazala area.

On 24 June the target was shipping at Benghazi. For this operation which, the 205 Group ORB notes, 'heralded the commencement of our intensified effort', eighty-two Wellingtons were detailed, along with twelve USAAF B–24 Liberators of what was known as the Halverson Detachment. The attack was a success, with fires and explosions observed in the harbour, the moles and the town. Eight of 40's Wellingtons operated, and one (Sgt R. E. White) failed to return, crash landing in the desert twelve miles south of LG [Landing Ground] 117 after engine failure. The engines cut almost simultaneously, and though the altimeter was reading 600 feet, the Wellington flew into the ground at close to cruising speed, the undercarriage retracted. The observer, Eric Laithwaite, recalls:

> In no time she was one mass of flame. There were four of us out—the 2nd Pilot badly hurt and dazed, the Captain dazed with a black eye, the W/Op unhurt and cool, and myself bruised and dazed. The rear gunner could not get out, but the W/Op got him out shortly by using the butt of his revolver to widen the gap between turret and airframe. There was no sound from the front gunner, and no hope of getting to him.

Laithwaite and the wireless operator (Sgt Price) walked north and were spotted by SAAF personnel, who rescued the others.

Sgt A. J. Brogan, a Malta veteran, also had a difficult night. Hit by flak over the target area, his aircraft suffered hydraulic failure, and staggered back towards base at 100 mph, with the bomb doors, undercarriage and flaps down. Joe Brogan just made it to a Landing Ground, where the Wimpy was set down without further damage after what he terms 'an exhausting night's work'. Next day he was tour-expired.

Operations were flown nightly over the Battle Area at strengths of from eight to fifteen aircraft, 40 attacking enemy motor transport, landing grounds, railways and (on 27 June) Rommel's Headquarters. Only one aircraft (Sgt S. H. Gunn RNZAF) was lost, on 26 June. How successful 40's efforts were is impossible to determine, since the 205 Group ORB merely summarizes each operation, but the results on 28 June were particularly pleasing, with much damage inflicted on enemy transport at Charing Cross, a road junction near Mersa Matruh, and again on 30 June, when thirty-seven Wellingtons, including twelve from 40 Squadron, attacked landing grounds and transport, scoring direct hits on the railway line, and fires and explosions amongst transport and dispersed aircraft.

By the end of June the military situation was extremely threatening. Rommel had attacked at El Alamein, and there was no certainty that this last defensible position between him and the Nile Delta could be held. This feeling of uncertainty was heightened by the evacuation of the Royal Navy from Alexandria during the last days of June. The result, on Wednesday, I July, was what came to be known as 'The Flap', a panic which not only afflicted civilians but also (to some extent) the Military High Command. Over Cairo hung a pall of black smoke, out of which rained fragments of charred paper, evidence not only of the destruction of confidential files, but also of how little confidence HQ staff had that the Alamein line could be held. The panic was short-lived, but the effect of 'Ash Wednesday', as it was sardonically termed, was profound, and it took some time for life to return to normal.

The Royal Air Force responded more phlegmatically, but prudently planned bases in Palestine, to which units could withdraw should the Nile

54. An engine change at Beersheba. (A. E. Husk.)

Delta be overrun. For 40, this involved, on Ash Wednesday itself, establishing a tented encampment at Beersheba, where a small party of ground crew and administrative staff remained no more than two or three weeks, until it was evident that the Delta bases were secure. Perhaps it is just as well that Beersheba was not used, for Jack Wey recalls that 'it was appalling!'

The speed at which 40 became operational was remarkable, but not achieved easily, or without friction. Dick Ridgway writes:

> The air crew "were not going to put up their tents as they expected the airmen to do it for them", and when I told them to get on with it themselves, and they refused, I called in all their tents and told them to sleep on the sand under the stars—and they did. The next day they changed their minds!

This was the stick. The carrot was a squadron party:

> W/O Dick Carruthers, the Armament Officer, and I arranged a squadron party, held in the Airmen's Mess (the largest area under cover) when all messes gave what beer they could spare. What a party. All officers carried their rank badges in their pockets, and even John Hutton [the Adjutant] got a bucket of water over him!! So did I! It worked, and the Squadron never looked back.

By July 1942 an operational pattern had been established, involving attacks on Tobruk and the Battle Area around El Alamein. The latter took place on ten nights, with transport, tank depots and landing grounds the principal targets. Generally these attacks were made with other squadrons, but on 3 July 40 operated on its own, attacking a Tank Repair Shop at Mersa Matruh. By flares dropped by FAA Albacores, eleven aircraft located and attacked the Depot. Flak and searchlights were encountered, and one aircraft (Sgt W. L. Dwyer) was shot down in flames.

Of the Battle Area attacks the most successful were on 4 and 23 July. The first, on transport along the El Daba–Sidi Rahman road, brought spectacular results for Sgt P. R. Kingsford RNZAF, who reported 'a large explosion with an enormous orange flash and greyish smoke' which lifted the aircraft violently, even at 6,000 feet, damaging one of the propellers. An attack on LG 20 on 23 July, while less spectacular, was satisfying in that the nine crews reported that they had caused fires and explosions amongst dispersed Ju 88 and He 111 bombers.

Battle Area sorties occasionally encountered fierce opposition from Flak and searchlights, but often little or none, especially along the coast road. The seventeen raids on Tobruk in July, however, were another matter. For around Rommel's chief supply port powerful flak and searchlight defences had been assembled. Attacks were made, therefore, at a height of 8,000 feet or more (whereas in the Battle Area the Squadron frequently bombed from as low as 4,000 feet), and Blitz Times were introduced, to ensure that there would be a number of Wellingtons over Tobruk at any one time, instead of a single aircraft as the undivided object of attention.

If over Tobruk crews found strong flak and searchlight defences, to and from the target—a round trip in a Wellington Ic, cruising at 125–135 knots, took some eight and a half hours—they were able to relax more than their counterparts in Bomber Command, for whom flak and night fighters made operational flying hazardous throughout. In North Africa flak and searchlights were concentrated at key points, while the few night fighters lacked a sophisticated ground controlled radar system and were not a major hazard. Five crews reported attacks in July, but none were brought down by fighters then, or in August, unless the loss of Sgt L. P. Kerr RNZAF on 7 August was attributable to that cause.[1]

Two crews (Dwyer on the 3rd and Sgt V. Mitchell on the 27th) were lost to enemy action in July. But five other aircraft were destroyed, either through mechanical faults or pilot error, and in two cases lives were lost. On 22 July, after a difficult night, during which his aircraft was attacked three times by a fighter, Sgt R. King crashed while attempting an overshoot at Shallufa, the rear gunner (Sgt A. Macaskill) being killed. Three days earlier, the starboard engine of Sgt Kingsford's aircraft caught fire half an hour after take-off. After baling his crew out, Kingsford tried to crash-land the aircraft, but both he and the wireless-operator, Sgt R. J. Laing RAAF, who stayed with his captain, were trapped in the burning wreck, and died shortly after being rescued.

Another loss had a happier outcome. On 12 July compass failure prevented Sqn/Ldr Steel's crew finding their target and left them well off course on the return journey. Out of fuel, Jim Steel carried out a successful belly landing, 'gentle but accompanied by a hell of a scraping noise and lots of dust as the cockpit downward exit door burst open'. 'We were in a wide basin and on a hard surface', he writes. 'We could have landed with wheels down. It was about 5 a.m.'

The crew concluded that they were at the eastern end of the Qattara Depression, and Steel and his second pilot (P/O D. A. Adams RNZAF) decided to go for help, with the others remaining by the aircraft. After a day's walk Steel and Adams came across a small Arab encampment, and were given food and drink. With the assistance of one of the Arabs, who spoke some English, they made their way, over the next two days, to a larger encampment at El Magra, south of the Alamein line. There they were spotted by a 40 Squadron Wellington. John Mason, the second pilot, recalls:

> Sgt Vinall proposed that we should attempt to land and without hesitation all agreed to take the gamble. A mile or two distant Vinall spotted what appeared to be a suitable stretch to put down the plane, and we bumped down and careered across the rock strewn desert, throwing up a huge cloud of dust. The fact that we finally came to rest without apparent damage was a tribute to the sound design and construction of the Wimpy landing gear. During the bumps, thumps and jolting accompanied by shrieks and strains of the plane's structures, I for one thought we would be joining our stranded companions.

Steel and Adams were picked up, and the English-speaking Arab rewarded with all the money which they and Vinall's crew could muster—about £15 Egyptian. The rest of the crew had already been spotted by an RAF reconnaissance aircraft, and rescued.

July ended with four successive attacks on Tobruk, and the first nineteen nights in August were spent on the 'milk run'. During early July the Squadron occasionally put up as many as seventeen or eighteen aircraft, but as tour-expired crews were posted away this fell by mid-July to a still high average (given that Flights operated on alternate nights) of ten to eleven. Particularly effective raids were mounted on shipping during the first week of August, when Sgt R. N. Shard and P/O P. F. Greenway RCAF claimed hits on the 2nd, and Sgt F. Robinson on the 4th. Intense flak and searchlight activity frequently disrupted bombing, however, with crews reporting, for example, that they 'made an excellent run on a large vessel but got caught in searchlights and instead attacked several smaller vessels' (Flt/Lt H. Grant, 1 August), and that 'a/c made three attempts at attacking, finally diving out of flak

55. The rescue of Sqn/Ldr F. J. Steel and F/O D. A. Adams, 15 July 1942.
Jim Steel on the donkey: on his right, (?) Sgt R. Rogers. (R. Rogers.)

concentrations at 6,500'. Insufficient petrol decided captain to attack buildings 30 miles S.E. of Tobruk' (Sgt P. Le Brocq RCAF, 13 August). Night fighters orbiting just outside the flak zone were also a hazard, several crews reporting attacks. Perhaps the most alarming experience over Tobruk during this period, however, was Sgt Robinson's on 18 August. Caught in searchlights, he dived from 10,000 feet to 2,500 feet to escape, the aircraft shedding considerable amounts of fabric as it did so.

Engines cutting or failing, excessive oil temperatures, wireless or intercom failures and exploding IFF [Identification Friend or Foe] devices all hampered or aborted operational flights during July and August. In three weeks from 28 July onwards, six Wellingtons were lost, four because of engine failure. On 5 August P/O Wilf Young, the second pilot, was in the astrodome, looking out for fighters, when he heard his captain, Sgt Murray, say 'Port engine has packed up'. Despite the loss of the propeller, and jettisoning everything moveable, they gradually lost height, and after about twenty minutes it was decided to crash-land. Wilf Young writes:

> The crew went to crash positions and I checked Murray's harness. Just as I was moving back we hit the ground. We were about to lower our landing light, and I noticed that our height was 800 feet. Thus we landed on a plateau.

Murray and Young were injured, and the rest of the crew suffered varying degrees of shock. They tried to escape eastwards, but on the sixth day, handicapped by their injuries, were captured by Italian troops.

On 7 August two crews failed to return. Of the fate of Len Kerr's nothing is known, though the answer may lie in the fate of the other Wimpy lost. Having bombed, Flt/Lt Grant and his crew set course for base as the rear gunner, 'Ginger' Ware, recalls:

> We had been on our way back for about three quarters of an hour or so when Johnny [P/O A. E. Hull, the observer] asked me to take a drift for him. He threw out a marker and I got my gun sight on to it and took the drift for him—I'll always remember it read five degrees starboard. I looked up from reading it, to tell him the figure, when to my horror I saw another Wimpy right on top of us, coming from the port quarter! There was no time even to shout to the pilot before he hit us, there was a terrible crash, and I saw him go down in flames.

With the engines dead and the warning light in the turret flashing, Ware left his turret and kicked out the rear escape hatch. In the process of leaving the escape hatch when the Wellington hit the ground, he had one leg badly smashed. Grant gave him first aid, and in the morning they were joined by the second pilot (Sgt G. Whyte) and the W/Op (Sgt A. W. Dunn) who had both baled out, the latter with a broken leg and burns. They later found the body of Hull, whose parachute had not fully deployed, but no sign of the front gunner (Sgt C. E. Dauphin RCAF) who wandered for some time before being picked up by the Italians. With two crew members needing urgent medical attention, Grant and Whyte set out for the German lines, and were picked up twenty-four hours later, after walking through two minefields. German Red Cross aircraft found the two injured men, and flew them out to hospital, where Jim Ware's leg was amputated.

On 11 August Sgt C. E. Hickman and his crew also failed to return. Geoff Holt, his rear gunner, writes that an engine failed over the Gulf of Sollum on the return trip, and that they turned south to get over land, jettisoning everything moveable, but steadily losing height. At 2,000 feet they baled out:

> It was a clear moonlit night, and the front gunner and I could see each other quite clearly as we came down. By great fortune we landed almost on top of a camel caravan and about 30 camels which had bedded down for the night. These were in charge of three Senussi.

Heading east with the camel train, they met Hickman and the second pilot, and the next day the other two crew members, but all were eventually captured close to the Alamein line.

On 16 August yet another aircraft (Sgt J. Mason) was lost when near Tobruk flak set the port engine on fire, and the aircraft went temporarily out of control, losing a great deal of height. At 2,000 feet Mason gave the order to bale out, he and the co-pilot hoping then to maintain height and make for Allied lines, but this proved impossible, and they crash-landed, fortunately without injury. Though some at least of the crew were assisted by Arabs, all were eventually captured.

Besides the five crews killed or captured, two others made it back after baling out over Allied territory during August. Sgt G. Yates RCAF lost an engine returning from Tobruk on the 9th, but made it to Allied lines before baling his crew out, following himself some time later, when it became clear that he could not reach a landing ground.

Sgt R. Ceha had an equally eventful night on 22 August, when en route to Mersa Matruh the port engine seized. Though the propeller fell off, the aircraft lost height, and when the starboard engine began surging uncontrollably Ceha baled his crew out, following at 700 feet when the engine caught fire. Landing close to the burning Wellington, he remained by it, to be picked up next day, and flown to LG100, where he was reunited with his crew, who had just returned from a visit to the wreck, expecting to find and bury their skipper!

Shallufa was a permanent RAF station, well-equipped in every respect. Servicing could be carried out in the hangars, and personnel were accommodated in hutments, and looked after by cheerful Italian prisoners. On 20 August, however, 40 moved from Shallufa to a tented encampment at Kabrit, on the Great Bitter Lake. The move was initiated by Dick Ridgway,

56. The 40 Squadron encampment at Kabrit. (A. Hipperson.)

who anticipated that before long the Squadron would be on the move from the Delta bases, and needed to acclimatize itself to living rough. But the tents were only yards from the lake, and many recall the Kabrit lifestyle with pleasure. John Robertson, a ground wireless operator, writes:

> Three or four of us found an abandoned 12 foot yacht with a drop keel. We caulked it, and with the help of the riggers on the Squadron we made a sail. Many a happy time we had aboard, especially at nights.

Fitter Bill Greengrass likewise recalls that 'several ground crew including myself built (to our own peculiar designs) canoes made from scrap wood and doped aircraft fabric'.

Another fitter, Denis Ludman, recalls, however, a major drawback at Kabrit:

> I recall making my own bed there from old bits of packing cases and tent fabric. Later models that we made were quite ingenious. The scrap inner tubes from the aircraft were slit into rings and laced between two main lengths of wood. The snag with Kabrit and the wooden bed was the bugs. It was revolting, and I shudder now when I recall how we all felt that first morning we discovered them in our blankets. I painted my bed with dope to no avail but we all improved our lot by placing the bed legs in a tin filled with paraffin. To sweeten our beds and prevent bugs we used to sling the beds into the Great Bitter Lake which was about 5 or 6 yards away.

From Kabrit between 21 August and the end of the month 40 flew eight ops as part of round-the-clock bombing of Landing Grounds and Tobruk. The loads were principally made up of 250-lb GP [General Purpose] bombs, often of the rodded variety, designed to explode before burying themselves in the ground, but the mix depended on the target: for the attacks on LGs 20 and 104, for example, on 25 August, the 72 × 250-lb GP bombs (half delayed action) were supplemented by 18,000 caltrops, designed to burst the tyres of enemy aircraft, and render the Landing Grounds unusable.

The Battle of Alam Halfa began on the evening of 30 August, with panzer units seeking to wheel around the southern flank of the Eighth Army defences, and for the next four nights 40 bombed the battle area, making a particularly intensive effort on 2 September, when double sorties were flown. Ten aircraft flew the first sortie, starting good fires. The aircraft then refueled and rearmed at LG224, and returned to the battle area, starting further fires, and an explosion which threw fragments to 5,000 feet. As on the first sortie, there was no opposition, but the night ended badly when one aircraft (Sgt V. Baker) landing at LG237, blew up owing to a bomb hang-up. Baker and the rear gunner (Sgt J. Roach) both wounded, were the only survivors.

Defeat at Alam Halfa meant an end to the acute threat which Rommel had posed. For though his army was only seventy miles from Alexandria, the impetus which had brought him thus far was gone and, inadequately supplied with tanks and fuel, he could only remain where he was, hoping that his supply situation would improve and awaiting the inevitable counter-offensive.

The employment of 40 Squadron during September and October reflects these changed circumstances, its Wellingtons attacking Tobruk on twenty-five nights out of the twenty-eight on which it operated between 6 September and 20 October. In some respects the milk run was less hazardous in September and October than in July and August, certainly in respect to night fighters. Unless the loss of Sgt G. F. Langham RNZAF on 25 September is to be attributed to this cause, no crew was subjected to a fighter attack during this period. On the other hand there were now more heavy anti-aircraft guns and searchlights. Eric Laithwaite recalls a raid on 28 September, when he flew as observer with Sqn/Ldr Booth:

> Target coming nicely down the parallel wires of the bombsight. Then, just at release point, all the searchlights in Tobruk got us. And the flak. The smell of the cordite was strong. The bombs went—I did not think in the circumstances that I would get a medal for asking for a second run. Never had I experienced evasive action such as that performed by Sqn/Ldr Booth. The rudder bar was clanking behind my head as I tried to resecure the bombsight which came off the spigot, tried to operate the camera, tried to recover my parachute and harness, both of which came undone. All this in the blinding light of the searchlights and the exploding of the ack-ack shells. Thanks to the magnificent flying of Sqn/Ldr Booth we got away.

Stan Brew, a pilot who had flown a first tour with Bomber Command, agrees that 'the target was a bit of a sod. Anti-aircraft on the high ground, and as we were pin-pointing the harbour installations "straight and steady" was far from pleasant'. There were compensations, however:

> The Tobruk runs were about 8 and a half hours, the trip each way a little like the Arabian nights, moonlight, stars, the gleaming Med. We would listen to the BBC on the way home and often had a sing-song if the tunes were known—good spirits all round, and a super crew.

John Mason also recalls the journey home:

> We flew into the rising sun and it was not unusual to fly over a layer of cumulus cloud. It was fun to toboggan along the 'valleys' of cloud, and it caused an instinctive shock when we missed a turn and hit a 'hill' head on!

A diminishing hazard during this period was engine failure, only one crew (Flt/Sgt R. L. Spence RCAF on 7 October) being definitely lost to this cause, and two others returning on one engine.[2] The fewer engine failures were perhaps because of cooler autumn temperatures, since reports of over-heating are no longer found. On the other hand several crews had the unpleasant experience of seeing fabric tear away from the wings or fuselage, while others were frustrated by electrical (and particularly intercom) failures.

Of the few raids elsewhere than Tobruk, the most effective were on 24 September and 9 October, against Landing Grounds at Fuka and El Daba. The latter was an RAF response to news that the German airfields had been immobilized by flooding after heavy rain, medium bomber squadrons carrying out daylight raids, and Wellingtons following up at night. Crews were enthusiastic, Sgt T. Harrison's reporting that it had bombed about fourteen aircraft 'not well dispersed', and left several burning, while P/O R. T. Fleming RNZAF reported a large fire in the target area as they left, but the crew were unable to see where their own bomb load fell, as 'so many bombs were bursting'.

At 8.40 pm on 23 October, the Battle of El Alamein began with a barrage by 882 field and medium guns which lives in the memory of all who experienced it. On the ground the sound and the physical impact of the explosions were predominant. The 40 Squadron crews operating that night, however, remember the flash of the guns, lighting up the desert in a most remarkable fashion. Equally memorable was that night's briefing. Air Marshal Tedder was visiting the Squadron, and after talking informally to the officers and men, attended the briefing. When Dick Ridgway said, 'Well chaps, the push starts tonight', Eric Laithwaite recalls, 'the sigh which always followed the announcement of another Tobruk run [became] a gasp'.

Eight crews operated against artillery and what was thought to be the 21st Panzer Division. Of those attacking gun positions Sgt P. Denman achieved the best results, with two sticks of bombs dropped on gun positions which were firing at the time, one falling precisely on target. Those who attacked the Panzer formation found tanks and vehicles well dispersed, but two crews reported that their bombs burst on or among vehicles.

In planning the Battle of El Alamein, General Montgomery wrote that breaking through and 'crumbling' the German and Italian defences could be expected to take twelve days. He was right, for it was not until 4 November that enemy resistance broke, and Rommel began the withdrawal which was to take the Afrika Korps and its Italian ally back to Tunisia and surrender. During this period 40 operated on all but two nights, and twice flew double sorties. The targets were generally transport and armoured vehicles, with targets identified by flares dropped by FAA Albacores or by the Wellingtons themselves. Where the vehicles were well dispersed, hits were few, but when, as on the 26th, a concentration of motor transport was found, the result could be satisfying, Sgt M. W. Bishop and P/O J. Dickenson claiming direct hits, and Sgt Harrison dropping a stick of bombs across some tanks. Even when crews did not score hits, however, they were effective in unnerving their opponents with near misses or with parachute flares that lit up the ground like daylight, or just droning overhead, leaving the troops below wondering if bombs or flares were about to be dropped.

With the end of the Battle of El Alamein 205 Group concentrated on hampering the retreating Axis forces, 40's attacks on transport in the El Daba-Fuka area on the nights of 4 and 5 November resulting in direct hits, fires and explosions. Crews then operated further west, between the Halfaya Pass and Sollum on the 6th, Sollum itself on the 8th, and between Sollum and Capuzzo on the 9th, the most successful raid probably being the last, when nine aircraft scored direct hits on trucks.

Forty was now attacking enemy formations more than 250 miles west of Alamein, and in order to reduce the range, it was decided that the Squadron should move from Kabrit to LG222A, south-west of Cairo. Dick Ridgway protested, considering the Landing Ground unsuitable because of the loose sand covering the strip, and the fact that it lay in a slight depression, but Air/Cdre Ritchie refused to countenance a change in plans, and hence, perforce, 40 left Kabrit, the Advance Party moving up to LG222A on 5 November, and the Main Party two days later. For the first two nights, all went well, sorties against the retreating Axis army resulting in transport being attacked successfully at Sollum and Capuzzo. On 10 November, however, nine aircraft were briefed for the much longer trip to Tobruk, and Dick Ridgway, worried about the take-off performance of his Wellingtons under such conditions, reduced the bombload by 500 lb.

Despite this the outcome was as he feared. Two aircraft got away safely, but the third (Sgt R. G. Workman) crashed into the rising ground at the western end of the airstrip, killing everyone on board save the rear gunner, Sgt Quinn. Ridgway, horrified, refused to allow any further aircraft to take-off, and rang Ritchie to tell him so. A huge row ensued, ending (in the face of the CO's threat to approach Tedder) when Ritchie agreed to a move. It took place on 12 November, when the Squadron, having packed what it could into its aircraft, loaded up its convoy of trucks and began a twenty-three hour journey to LG104 near El Daba—a Landing Ground it had been bombing regularly a fortnight earlier! They left behind, Dick Ridgway recalls, seven trucks and the Coles Crane, all with defects of one kind or another. It was a fortnight before they arrived.

Not that this mattered particularly, since at El Daba the Squadron operated only once, eight aircraft attacking Kastelli Pediada aerodrome in Crete on 23 November. Two other operations were scheduled, but the worsening autumn weather forced their cancellation. For the remainder of the time the Squadron was on stand down, though unable to leave the base. Many

passed the time ferreting amongst the large quantity of material abandoned
by the Germans, searching for souvenirs, though conscious that particularly
tempting items might be booby-trapped.

Booby traps were not the only hazard associated with souvenir hunting.
Bill Burton, an RCAF gunner, writes:

> Searching an abandoned Italian dugout for whatever there might be, I felt
> itchy and discovered that my legs were absolutely alive with fleas. These were
> common, but not in these quantities. However, I got four or five months
> supply of Italian cigarettes along with the fleas. I also discovered, while in the
> desert, that to clean out fleas you took your gear flying with you every once
> in a while. I never did figure out whether it was the cold or the lack of
> oxygen that killed the little buggers but it worked.

Probably on 6 November (the records are vague), six aircraft of A
Flight had been detached, under Sqn/Ldr Booth, to operate from Luqa,
boosting Malta's offensive capacity in support of Operation Torch, the
sea-borne invasion of North Africa which took place on the 8th. The six
strong detachment concentrated on targets in Tunisia, through which the
Germans and Italians were now routeing most of their supplies, operating
on nine nights in a fortnight. The operational records from Malta are
scanty, but it seems that there were two losses. The more serious occurred
on 22 November, when after an attack on Bizerta, P/O Dickenson
forced-landed at Bone. After repairs the aircraft took off, but crashed,
killing two members of the crew—the second pilot (Flt/Sgt G. T.
Dawson) and the W/Op (Sgt. D. A. D. Golby). Earlier, on 10 November,
Sgt W. Setterfield had ditched fifteen miles north of Gozo. The starboard
motor seized, and (familiar story) despite jettisoning everything that could
be removed, they could not maintain height on the remaining engine.
The second pilot (Sgt R. E. C. Rainey RNZAF) wrote in his diary: 'We
did our drill—remove the astrohatch, pull the flotation (Bill didn't want
to be strapped in) remove chute harness and prepare for the worst! To
say the least we hit the drink with a smack (75 mph).' The ditching went
well, however, and Setterfield and his crew were rescued unharmed by
fishermen from Gozo.

At Luqa A Flight operated alongside A Flight, 104 Squadron, under
Wg/Cdr Saville, and subsequently the decision was taken to move the
remainder of 104, now at El Daba also, to Malta. On 20 November, Saville
arrived at El Daba in what Bob Ginn, 104 Squadron Engineer Officer and
historian, describes as 'an incredibly scruffy Wimpy Ic ex 40 Squadron', on
his way to Cairo, to convince HQ that the rest of 40 should join 104.[3]
Cairo agreed, and at midnight on 24 November nine Ics left, each carrying
four ground crew, together with two Mk. IIs of 104 Squadron, all arriving
safely at Luqa just after daybreak.

Old Malta hands knew what to expect, but new boys did not, and Denis Ludman recalls his first meal on the island, 'a plate of fatty bacon rind running in liquid and fat'. He continues:

> Everyone of us pushed it away and ate the small pieces of bread supplied with it. On the next table we noticed several lads who had been loitering, volunteer to eat it. These were regulars at Malta. On questioning them why, we were told in no uncertain terms that 'You bloody well will eat it in two or three days' time'. It was certainly true. The food was terrible. I've never been so hungry in my life.

In Egypt, the Rear Party left LG104 on 26 November, moving back to LG237 along with what was left of 104 Squadron. There, at what Bob Ginn describes as 'an expanse along the Cairo-Alexandria road—dusty, fly-infested, and in general worse than the true Desert landing grounds, but only 40 kilometres from Cairo',[3] they remained until the two squadrons returned from Malta late in January 1943, supplying replacement aircraft and crews for those arriving from Malta tour-expired. Four crews, indeed, arrived within days, Sqn/Ldr Booth's amongst them. His place as OC A Flight was taken by Sqn/Ldr D. S. Gladstone, who arrived at Luqa on 8 December.

From Luqa 40 began operating in strength on 27 November, when ten aircraft were detailed for double sorties on Bizerta docks. All completed the first sortie, but only six the second. This was a recurrent pattern during 40's stay on Malta, sometimes because of battle damage, but more often because of engine or equipment faults, or problems with the hydraulics or airframe. As in the desert, conditions were harsh and facilities primitive, and it is remarkable that so high a serviceability rate was maintained on the ageing Wellington Ics.

December started badly when on the 3rd a Wellington captained by P/O V. M. Todd blew up on landing, killing the wireless-operator (Sgt E. A. Aspell) and rear gunner, Sgt R. Semley. Dick Ridgway recalls:

> On returning from the op. I couldn't get permission to land. Eventually I got a "green" and landed to find Doc. Heard [the M.O., who had arrived in Malta the previous day] waiting for me. He was covered in blood from head to foot. One of the aircraft had had a hang-up, and on touching down the bomb had come down, hit the runway, bounced back into the aircraft and exploded.

Apart from visits to Sicily on 3 and 11 December, all targets that month were in Tunisia: Sfax, Sousse, Bizerta, Tunis itself and the harbour at La Goulette. Their object was, as ever, to deny the Axis forces in North Africa urgently needed supplies. The most successful attacks during the first three weeks of December were those on the 4th, 13th, 14th and 15th. On the 4th Sqn/Ldr J. S. Morton, who had replaced Jim Steel as OC B Flight, hit a ship in the harbour at La Goulette, setting it on fire, and on the 13th Sgt R. G.

Thackeray hit another in the canal leading to the inner basin, while Sgt M. R. Lovell reported a big fire after bombing a ship in the outer harbour. The next night 40's Wellingtons were over La Goulette again, P/Os Evans and R. W. Mathews claiming hits on ships, while on the 15th the marshalling yards at Tunis were severely damaged and a power house at La Goulette hit.

The Axis supply ports were as fiercely defended as Tobruk had been. The searchlights and flak rarely brought down an aircraft (the loss of P/O A. D. Bell on 7 December was perhaps due to that cause) but they made bombing difficult, and hampered the observation of results. Night fighters were not often encountered, though Sqn/Ldr Gladstone was attacked four times over Tunis on 10 December, evading by diving steeply.

A more serious hazard was the weather, which was often extremely violent. On 2 December, for instance, bad weather prevented any of the crews finding Sousse, while one aircraft (P/O Mathews) was struck by lightning on the outward journey, its wireless being rendered u/s, except to receive, and after jettisoning the bomb load the crew turned back, to have the trailing aerial blow up shortly afterwards in 'a sheet of flame'. Without direction-finding capacity, Mathews and his crew did remarkably well to reach base.

Mechanical failure also continued to be a hazard, and in December aircraft frequently returned with engines malfunctioning, and electrics or hydraulics unserviceable. This implies no criticism of the ground crews, working in very difficult circumstances, but rather reflects the age of the aircraft. The Wellington Ic had been superseded by the Mk. III in Bomber Command early in 1942, and the first squadrons in 205 Group were now re-equipping with it. In the coming months, keeping the elderly Ics flying would become a major problem.

Though Malta's air defences had been so strengthened that the *Luftwaffe* and *Regia Aeronautica* were unable to mount the devastating daylight attacks of a year earlier, night attacks were still frequent and disruptive, and could do considerable damage, as on 21 December, when the *Luftwaffe* arrived as Wellingtons were being refuelled and rearmed for a second sortie. Parked nearly wing tip to wing tip, they made a perfect target, and the Ju 88s destroyed seven and damaged three. Even more would have been lost had not a 148 Squadron fitter attached to 40 taken a hand, taxiing two aircraft to safety. For his actions, LAC E. J. Drury was awarded the George Medal.

The citation that Wg/Cdr Ridgway wrote for Drury was one of his last acts as CO. For on 20 December he handed over command to John Morton. Dick Ridgway recalls the circumstances:

> For several days I had been getting the 'shakes', but only in the air, and after a short while they went. I discussed it with Doc. Heard and told him I was sure it was 'flu. The next night he was awaiting my return from ops. I was

shaking like a leaf. We went to sick bay and he then told me that it wasn't 'flu, but that I was exhausted and that I was to see Sir Keith Park [AOC Malta] the next day. When I saw Sir Keith he told me he had been expecting me for several days.

Perhaps the most loved CO since Roderic Dallas, Dick Ridgway was a relaxed, good-humoured and sociable man, who gave a high priority to fostering squadron spirit. Bill Ball, an observer on the Squadron at its re-formation, comments:

> In my long career I never met such a kindly charming man, always approach-able. He had a smile for everyone, and in spite of adverse desert conditions he was always well turned-out, neat, trim, smart. He had a debonair, swash-buckling manner, and with his fair hair, blue eyes, and neat, fair moustache, he looked rather like Douglas Fairbanks Junr. He had time for everyone.

Ground crew felt the same, and Denis Ludman remembers 'the pep talks we had from Wing Commander Ridgway, whom I consider the best CO or boss I've ever had. He made everyone from cooks to pilots feel part of every raid and his regular briefs made everyone feel 10ft high.' Something of what made Dick Ridgway so popular with his men can be gauged from a story that he himself recalled:

> Alexandria was out of bounds, but to give the men a rest, I sent 3–4 trucks a week into Alex. Mostly airmen, a few NCOs and 2 officers. One Corporal driver, having offloaded the chaps, led the others to the Military Police Compound. This ruse worked every week, the MPs never queried why 40 Sqdn. wanted so much 'stores'. I was never let down, not a word was ever mentioned. One of the AOC's staff, Air Commodore Ritchie, asked me why my squadron was so happy, the others so morose.

To those who served under Dick Ridgway, the answer was obvious.

# Notes

1. It seems likely, in fact, that Kerr's aircraft crashed after an in-flight collision with that of Flt/Lt. Grant (see p. 206).

2. All six crew escaped from the aircraft safely, but the observer and second pilot were quickly captured. The other four—Spence, the wireless operator (Sgt J. K. Wood RAAF) and the gunners (Sgts A. W. Butteriss and E. A. Linforth)—set out for the British lines, some 300 miles to the east. They had, between them, four small compasses, three full water bottles, sixteen packets of hard biscuits, six tins of bully-beef, some chewing gum, chocolate, toffee, and milk tablets. On the first two days they were fortunate to find supplies of water and a two-gallon can in which they could carry additional water. On the sixth day Sgt Butteriss, who had exacerbated an ankle injury on landing, could go no further. Aware that this might happen, they had travelled close to the coast, and they were able to leave him sufficient food and water to get himself to the coast road, captivity and medical help.

57. Bob Spence, John Wood and their Arab guides, 4 November 1942. (R. L. Spence.)

The other three headed eastwards, and by the eighth night were south of Sidi Barrani. But Linforth, who had also injured his ankle on landing, could go no further, and he too was left with sufficient food and drink to reach the coast and safety.

Spence and Wood now had between them four tins of bully beef, three tins of chocolate, sixteen biscuits, and some milk tablets, along with three full water bottles and about a gallon and a half of water in the can. They had been eight days on the march, and estimated that another twelve should bring them to safety. In fact it was not until the 24th day that they encountered a British patrol north of El Maghra, and though they rationed their food strictly, and received generous assistance from groups of Bedouin whom they encountered, they ran out of food on the nineteenth night. Only two further encounters with Bedouin saved them.

Dick Ridgway recalls what followed:

> The Army gave them a meal and drink, but they refused to wash, change or do anything till they had reached the Squadron. They were flown to the Squadron, where I had them placed into sick quarters, not because they were ill, but to give them the pleasure of a proper bed and bath.
>
> After a few days of 'sick' treatment, I sent them on leave. They only wanted to go to Palestine, and as that was out of bounds, I gave them a 'To Whom it May Concern' open letter, giving details of their epic walk, lent them my Squadron light communication aircraft, a Magister, and sent them to Palestine. Everywhere they landed they got the VIP treatment.

3.  Robert Ginn, *Strike Hard! The Story of 104 (Bomber) Squadron, RAF*. Huddersfield: 104 Squadron Association, 1990. p. 106.

4. Ginn, p. 113.

5. Genial though he was, Dick Ridgway had a temper which could on occasion flare. Fitter Alex Hipperson remembers a rare church parade:

> We sat in blazing sun on the sand, a large packing case was plonked in front of us, covered with canvas, and a smaller case on top with two chairs. The parson and Ridgway sat down. The parson had made up his mind, it seemed, to give us a right doing, and hope to make up for all we had missed. He went on and on and on. Then we noticed Ridgway's fly swat was being flicked up and down. (To us this was an outward sign that you had better lose yourself until he had cooled down.) He asked the parson how much longer he intended to go on, as he was fed up, and could see that we all were. He stood up, down the ladder, and walked past us, and it was said that he was muttering something about '****** sky pilots'. I do not know why, but we were never bothered again.

# 17

# A Time of Transition:
# December 1942–March 1943

JOHN MORTON, who succeeded Dick Ridgway as CO of 40 Squadron on 21 December 1942, was a New Zealander serving in the RAF, and had flown his first tour of operations with 75 (NZ) Squadron, then instructed at No. 18 OTU, Bramcote, before joining 40 in August 1942, and succeeding Jim Steel as OC B Flight on 11 October. His appointment as CO was unwelcome in Cairo, where there were senior Squadron Leaders awaiting postings of this kind, because Dick Ridgway had worked through AVM Park, AOC Malta, to have the appointment approved—and

58. Wg/Cdr J. E. S. Morton.
(J. E. S. Morton.)

Park was directly responsible to London. But in arguing for Morton's appointment, Ridgway was seeking to ensure that whoever took over knew the conditions under which the Squadron was operating on Malta. Clearly, Park endorsed this view.

When John Morton took over, 40 had been on detachment at full strength since 26 November, operating intensively under difficult conditions. This continued into the New Year, 1943, the last sorties, by four aircraft against roads and dispersed transport in the Tripoli area, taking place on 19 January. In 30 days 40 operated on 20 nights over Tunis (8 times), Sousse (6), Sfax (2) and Tripoli (7). Winter weather often made target finding or iden-

tification difficult, and sometimes impossible, while conditions on Malta meant that the level of serviceability declined, despite the best efforts of the ground crews.

A typical raid illustrating these difficulties was that on Christmas night 1942, against Tunis and Sousse. Nine aircraft were detailed, but four did not operate, two because they became bogged and two others because they were unserviceable. Of those which did operate, only one (Flt/Sgt Spence) bombed a primary target. Three others returned with their bomb loads, two because of cloud over the target and one with an engine cutting, while the fifth (Flt/Lt L. McLachlan RNZAF) bombed the island of Pantelleria. To complete a night of woe McLachlan had to ditch off Malta, the crew being rescued by an RAF Air Sea Rescue launch.

The Christmas night raid was particularly unsuccessful; that on Tunis docks four days earlier, successful, for though two aircraft returned with their bombs, the other three did considerable damage. P/O B. A. Walker reported that his first stick burst on marshalling and repair yards, and his second started a fire in a fuel storage area, while Sgt Dobbie reported that his first stick set fire to a ship in the La Goulette canal. The greatest successes, however, were claimed by Flt/Lt M. Powell RAAF, with two certain hits on one ship and possible hits on another. Two large crimson explosions resulted, followed by a huge explosion, in which one ship appeared to disintegrate.

The raid on 21 December was little affected by flak or searchlights, but the defences could on occasions be highly effective. On the 28th, for instance, three aircraft attacking Tunis were subjected to 'intense and accurate' anti-aircraft fire. At Sousse there were no searchlights, but the few anti-aircraft batteries were well-directed, and Sgt C. Richardson's aircraft was hit in the port engine during its bombing run on 2 January. The engine failed, and rather than risk the 200 mile flight to Malta, Richardson set course for Bône, now in Allied hands. The Wellington steadily lost height, and at 4,000 feet, over rugged terrain, Richardson and his crew baled out.

During the first week in January, 1943, the targets were the Axis ports of Tunis, Sfax and Sousse. On 8 January, however, with the 8th Army approaching Tripoli, 205 Group shifted to tactical targets, with 40's a road junction near Tripoli itself. Seven aircraft located the junction (or others nearby) and bombed so accurately that a second sortie was unnecessary. A raid the following night was less successful, only five crews locating the junction. F/O R. C. Earl RNZAF had difficulty on the return flight, ditching not far short of Malta. The crew escaped without injury and were quickly rescued by an ASR launch.

After a brief switch back to Tunis and Sousse, 40 again attacked Tripoli 14–17 January, supporting the 8th Army's drive on the city. The targets were primarily supply installations and barracks, though on the 14th the railway station and native quarter were also bombed. All four raids were considered successes, with barracks and stores hit. The flak and searchlights were not particularly effective, especially on the third and fourth nights, when the ORB noted that 'Defences maintained a barrage over the harbour, and interfered little with the operation' (16th) and ' Heavy flak again in the form of barrage, and about 20 inaccurate searchlights' (17th).

Against such ineffective opposition, 40 operated without loss, but in declining numbers, from eight and seven on the first two nights to three and four on the last two. Four were, again, all that could be mustered for an attack on roads and transport near Tripoli on 19 January. The difficulties of operating from Malta—and particularly a shortage of parts, facilities, and replacement aircraft—were having their effect.

It was a relief, therefore, when on 17 January five aircraft left for LG237, carrying thirty-two aircrew and twenty ground personnel. The following day Wg/Cdr Morton transferred to L.G.237, and by 22 January all 40's aircraft were once more in Egypt. The return on the following day of the Adjutant (Flt/Lt J. J. Wilson), the MO (Flt/Lt R. G. P. Heard) and the Intelligence Officer (Flt/Lt S.E. Aubin-James), together with the Orderly Office staff and records, completed the move.

Not all 40 Squadron personnel, however, returned to Egypt. Because of a shortage of transport about sixty-five ground crew remained at Luqa, mainly servicing the ASV Wellingtons of 221 Squadron. To replace them forty-eight men from 221 Squadron, stranded in Egypt, arrived on 28 January, supplemented the next day by fifteen from 458 Squadron. This situation continued until the beginning of May, when the men from 221 and 458 Squadrons rejoined their units, and 40's ground crew on Malta were collected in squadron aircraft.

Though the threat from enemy action was less during 40's second Malta detachment living conditions were in many respects worse than a year earlier. Then the mess food had been monotonous, and often inadequate, but it was generally possible to supplement it with a sandwich from the NAAFI or, in Valetta, steak and chips. During the winter of 1942 food was so short, however, that eating out was no longer an option, while a strict mess rationing system was introduced. Bill Greengrass recalls:

> We were issued with a ration card marked with small squares for each day B D T S [Breakfast, Dinner, Tea, Supper] On entry to the mess a duty NCO would stamp out the respective letter with a special punch. Some of the desperately hungry among us would try to retrieve the stamped out piece and carefully glue it back into place for a second meal.

Denis Ludman adds: 'Honestly, the hunger was unbelievable and I can remember Johnnie Harvey and myself sitting in a bomb-hole crying our eyes out after looking at each other and our mess tins and both saying in unison, "I'm bloody hungry".'

'The Main meal' Denis recalls,

usually consisted of what we called Bully-duff—that was corned beef mixed
with army biscuits and with water and a cabbage leaf. And for sweet we had
what we called 'biscuit-duff' which was army biscuits and currants mixed with
water. We sometimes had a bar of emergency ration chocolate as a delicacy.

As Bill Greengrass observes, 'Whilst living in the Poor House it was certainly
a poor house menu'.

On 22 January the Squadron received instructions to re-equip and move
to the Benghazi area as part of 236 Wing. The move began on 4 February,
when an Advance Party left LG237 for Magrun North. Three days later the
Main Party, 208 personnel and 26 trucks, followed. But Magrun was merely
a staging post, since the ORB records, on 14 February, that the Squadron
Advance Party had arrived at a new Landing Ground at Gardabia East, and
that the Main Party had been instructed to move to the Misurata area. The
aircraft, meanwhile, remained at LG237, and it was not until 15 February,
with the Advance Party established at Gardabia East, that they were flown
up, the Main Party joining them on the 20th, and the Rear Party on 3
March.

During this period the Squadron had been non-operational, save for five
crews which, under the command of Sqn/Ldr Gladstone, had been posted
to Magrun on detachment to 70 Squadron, along with twenty-seven ground
crew. One of the aircraft (Sgt T. Patterson) was lost almost immediately,
going down in flames over Palermo on 29 January, but the others, David
Gladstone, F/Os J. D. Kitchin and R. G. MacInnes, and P/O D. C. Alderman
RAAF, operated against targets in Sicily, bombing Catania (29 and 31 January)
and Palermo (3 and 8 February) before rejoining the rest of the Squadron
at Gardabia East on 15 February.

At Magrun conditions had been good, Ces. Rainey writing that

We settled in comfortably—five of us in one tent with a plentiful supply of
food. The Arabs called each day to trade eggs: our best bargains were 15 for
a mug full of sugar which we had obtained from the cookhouse and 20 for
half a pound of tea bought in the NAAFI for six and a half piastres.

Gardabia he found far less hospitable, 'real desert again: nothing but sand
and rocks', while rear gunner George Henfrey recorded his first impression:

Beyond the scrub lined airstrip the scanty remains of a stone fort were visible,
and, still farther inland, a slight escarpment marked the limit of this coastal
plain. Stunted camelthorn was dotted over the landscape and under thousands
of stones scattered around lived armies of scorpions. Flies abounded, particularly
in the precincts of those artificial flowers, the 'Desert Lilies', which were
dotted about in suitably convenient spots.

59. Gilding a 'desert lily': Sqn/Ldrs M. Powell and D. S. Gladstone, and Wg/Cdr Morton. (R. G. McInnes.)

For Jack Liley, an RAAF observer who arrived at Gardabia, like George Henfrey, direct from OTU in England, 'at first sight it was a bit of a shock':

> All we could see was bare stony desert with about 20 Wimpies dispersed here and there, and at one end a tent encampment consisting of two or three large tents about half the size of a circus tent with smaller 12 feet by 10 feet army type tents and also scatterings of vehicles, mostly 3-tonne trucks, jeeps, etc., and including a van-like truck, used as a kind of control tower, beside which was a white arrow indicating the direction of the runway.

Liley and his crew were also 'surprised to find that Middle East Command Wimpies were flying with the old six-man structure of two pilots, front gunner, observer, wireless operator and rear gunner', abandoned in Bomber Command in May 1942. This caused disruption and resentment, since crews formed at OTU were split up, with the captain joining another crew as second pilot, and the others allocated to an experienced pilot or split up further.

The main party arrived at Gardabia East on 20 February, and that night the Squadron, boosted by six crews detached from 37 Squadron, put up ten Wellingtons to attack shipping in Palermo Harbour. The weather was bad, and a recall message was sent, but Flt/Sgt Thackeray and F/O MacInnes did not hear it, and finding the primary target obscured, bombed Trapani. Two nights later Palermo was again the target, eleven aircraft bombing

60. A typical desert crew, Winter 1942. (Rear (l to r) Sgts Bob Murray (Rhodesia), Len Cox (London) and Johnny Woods (Australia); Front: Sgt Ces Rainey (NZ), Flt/Sgt Bob Spence (Canada) and Sgt Stan Roberts (Australia). (R. E. C. Rainey.)

successfully, despite strong anti-aircraft defences and a smoke screen. One aircraft (W/O J. D. Massey RCAF, of 37 Squadron) did not return, and three made for Malta after bombing. Both David Gladstone and Ronald MacInnes had engine trouble, the latter's aircraft shedding a propeller over the target, while another (P/O Mathews) went into an uncontrollable dive immediately after bombing, dropping from 11,000 to 2,500 feet before he could regain control. Finding the aircraft would not climb, Mathews too made for Malta, where it was discovered that fabric had stripped from both wings.

Only two further operations were flown in February, each to Gabes, where the town and Landing Ground were attacked. One aircraft failed to return on 23 February, F/O A. B. Smith RNZAF ditching after engine failure. The crew spent eighty-two hours in their dinghy before reaching land and, with Arab help, Allied lines.

No further operations were flown in February, and during the first week of March only small numbers of aircraft operated, mostly flare-dropping. Why may be indicated by the fact that both aircraft detailed as illuminators on 1 March failed to carry out the task because of engine failure. Perhaps the loss of Flt/Lt McLachlan on 3 March was also due to engine failure: he failed to return from an attack on motor transport near Mareth. Certainly the upheaval of moving cannot explain the pause in operations, for though on 25 February the Squadron was ordered to move to a new landing ground at Gardabia West, the order was rescinded later that day. So while 104 and 462 Squadrons (the latter with Merlin-engined Halifaxes) moved to the new landing ground as 236 Wing, 40 remained at Gardabia East, under the direct administrative and operational control of 205 Group HQ. A move to Gardabia South, on 13 March, left the Squadron independent of Wing control, as it remained until late May.

On 9 March 40 despatched nine Wellingtons to Palermo. Two returned early with engine and wireless trouble, the others bombing successfully on flares dropped by F/O MacInnes. The operation was marred, however, by two crashes on the return journey. P/O K. F. D. Attwell crash-landed at Castel Benito, and he and two others were injured and admitted to hospital. Sgt J. Whale's trouble began when the aircraft went into a steep dive immediately after bombing, and, a report by his navigator (Sgt P. G. Hartley) states, 'the combined efforts of the two Pilots and the Bomb Aimer were necessary to pull the a/c out of the dive'. They flew north to gain height before turning south again to cross Sicily, and by the time the North African coast was reached, the aircraft was on its reserve nacelle tanks. Problems in locating beacons led to further delays, and shortly afterwards both engines failed, the aircraft crashing into a palm grove. Sgt Hartley continues:

> On making contact with the trees the A/C broke in two parts by the bomb inspection windows. The navigator was thrown clear. The front of the A/C concertina-ed against a palm tree; the Pilot was trapped beneath a pile of geodetic work. The rear gunner was found to be unconscious, lying half out of his crushed turret. The three remaining members of the crew were injured and shocked. Help was obtained at dawn, the Pilot was released. Attempts had been made (without success) to release the Rear Gunner, who died shortly before dawn. About 0630 hours members of an Army Unit came on the scene and gave valuable help. Shortly afterwards an Army M./O. arrived and despatched the pilot to Hospital, and tooks Sgts Turner, Rickard and Knight to Homs. The Navigator remained behind with the body of Sgt Sprattley, the rear gunner.

On 11 March 40 again sent flare-droppers to Palermo, four aircraft illuminating successfully. Then came a break in operations until the 18th, when six aircraft attacked enemy troops and transport in the Mareth-Ketana area. This coincided with an 8th Army assault on Rommel's Mareth Line, the breaching of which would open the way to a further advance on Tunis. Cloud hindered the observation of results, and the crews were unable to land at Gardabia South because heavy rain had rendered it unusable, diverting to Castel Benito and Gardabia West. Not until 23 March was the Landing Ground fit for use, 40 operating from Castel Benito in the interim.

The sorties on 18 March marked a reversion to the tactical bombing role for the first time since El Alamein. This continued during the rest of March, 40 operating on nine nights during the last fortnight, often bombing by flares dropped by FAA Albacores. The most successful attack was that on troops and transport on 29 March, when fifteen crews located the target and bombed successfully. Fires were started, buildings destroyed, and roads and bridges hit.

The raid on 29 March was notable in another respect, also. For on that night 40 Squadron operated the long-awaited Mk. III Wellingtons for the first time—five of them. The re-equipment of 205 Group squadrons with Hercules-powered aircraft had been under way for some months, and 40 was the last Ic equipped squadron to receive the new aircraft. Like 104, struggling on with its equally worn-out Mk. IIs, it was not to be fully re-equipped with the much superior Mk. IIIs and Xs for another three months.

On 31 March Wg/Cdr Morton relinquished command of 40 Squadron. His period as CO had been a difficult one, the period on Malta followed by lengthy spells when the Squadron was resting, re-equipping, or moving to new bases. In fact, apart from the detachment which operated with 70 Squadron, 40 operated on only 39 of the 101 nights during which John Morton was in command.

This must have been frustrating for one who was a fine and courageous pilot. Bill Burton, who flew as John Morton's rear gunner a number of times, writes:

He was a very good pilot, and a real cool type who could land a Wimpy without any need to brace with my hands on the turret roof to save my teeth. I felt very comfortable with him, and I recall that he never talked down to anyone in the crew, on the ground or in the air. He pushed team effort, not his rank.

Burton's comment about Morton's pushing team effort is echoed by Bill Emmett, another Canadian, who recalls that he 'addressed us all informally soon after I joined the Squadron. He emphasized the poor conditions of accommodation and problems with aircraft condition and maintenance, and stressed the need to "muck-in" in order to help each other in getting the job done'.

The 'problems with aircraft condition and maintenance' were indeed acute, and affected morale, as Bill Burton observes:

Our aircraft were worn out, and being Ics with Pegasus engines were under-powered at the best of times. We often carried rodded bombs, which had a

18 to 20 inch rod on the nose, the purpose being to detonate the bomb above the ground surface. These were very effective against thin-skinned vehicles and shipping. And they were also very effective . . . for blowing a chap to kingdom come if a belly landing occurred. They did little for one's peace of mind on take-off and landing with a set of sick engines.

Jack Liley particularly remembers the take-offs:

The strip was marked with goose neck flares fuelled by kerosene; these were dotted along the strip at intervals marking out the direction, and the end was marked by a red light beyond which was ordinary desert, which means that the larger stones had not been cleared from it. The first time at night, fully loaded, we roared down the strip, bumping up and down, and eventually passed the red light and still went on bumping before we came unstuck.

Strat. Judd, a New Zealand pilot, adds:

You were supposed to take off at about 85 mph, and you'd barely have 85 on the clock. All you could do was to get to the last flare, pull back on the stick and get the wheels up. Once you'd got your wheels up you cut your drag back and your speed would slowly build up but you'd need full power to 6000 feet. And half the Townend ring and the cylinder barrels would be red.

In such circumstances, it is hardly surprising that engine failures were frequent.

For the ground crews the situation was just as unhappy, since for all their dedication, serviceability levels dropped. Moreover, the conditions which ground crews endured in the desert were at times almost intolerable, Denis Ludman recalling that 'we used to take it in turns going up into the fuselage because you could stand about 60 to 80 seconds before you had to come out from the heat'. Yet despite this servicing routines had to be maintained, as Bill Greengrass recalls:

A typical day's work would involve inspecting the engines, and repairing damage or leaks; damage due to vibration or pipe chafing was quite common. The engines would be given a run for full power and cruise RPM boost check. Also a magneto drop test (switching off each magneto in turn), a large drop in RPM indicating faults on spark plugs or leads, which was fairly common. Then we would refuel the aircraft, both engine oil and fuel, which was 100 octane. The aircraft max fuel was 750 gallons, and this, supplied by a slow pumping bowser to overwing tanks, was always a tedious business. Such equipment as ladders and platforms for access to engines always seemed to be in short supply at N. African airfields, and I recall standing on a 50 gallon oil drum to reach the engine bay, then on the engine bearer tubes to get greater height. We used an ingenious tripod crane which was attached to points on the engine nacelle for engine and propeller hoisting. Two engine and two airframe mechanics were normally attached to each aircraft, with

61. Air and senior ground crew, 40 Squadron, late March 1943. The central group, seated, includes Flt/Lt E. M. Burdon, Sqn/Ldr Gladstone, John Morton, Sqn/Ldr P. A. F. Salmon (rubbing his eye), and Flt/Lt W. S. Austin (Nav. Ldr.). (K. Annable.)

attendant electricians, instrument men and armourers. Although it would not be admitted at the time, I am sure the riggers were the hardest working. They had the largest amount of machine to tend and spent so much of their time stitching and patching the large expanse of doped fabric with which the whole aircraft was covered, and subject to damage, both in flight and in the hot sun.

Living conditions were primitive for air and ground crews alike, with a shortage of water for washing and drinking so severe that clothes were washed in 100 octane fuel, and eventually became unfit to wear. Alec Hipperson recalls one of the rare visits by a stores team to issue new clothing. A large case was unloaded and an office tent erected:

> While the store types were getting the forms for signing out in the 'office', an engine type with his usual screw driver had levered off one side of this case. Hand inside and out came stockings. These were passed around. In no time someone was inside the case. Out came very smart herring bone pattern bush shirts. These were passed around. Soon the case was empty, and the side put back. Everyone disappeared. Out came he in charge; they gathered round the case, order of 'up' and it nearly flew over their heads! The new shirts were banned from issue; anyone wearing one would be in trouble. We carefully packed the shirts away and most buried them in the sand. We won. After a while they were issued, and we all suddenly appeared in smart new bush shirts.

One of John Morton's last acts as CO was to arrange for flight and squadron photographs—the latter one of only two taken during the war. The photographs show the NCO aircrew standing in informal poses in front of and on one of the Ics. The officers are seated, as expected, in the centre, but again informally. The photographs, like the decision to take them, express eloquently John Morton's style.

Eric Laithwaite, who served under both Dick Ridgway and John Morton, writes:

> My impression of John Morton is that he was considerate, but strong; stronger perhaps than Ridgway. I doubt though, that he ever tried to get to know all the crews, as Ridgway seemed to be able to do. One other difference in style was that Ridgway from time to time flew with the crews on operations, but always as a supernumerary. When Morton became CO he flew as captain.

His logbook shows that John Morton led by example, operating far more frequently than was expected of a CO. The difficulties which the Squadron experienced, especially after returning from Malta, and which limited its operational effectiveness, were not of his making.

# 18

# To Tunisia:
# April–December 1943

Wg/Cdr D. R. Bagnall DFC assumed command of 40 Squadron on the last day of March, 1943, and his first act was to order a Squadron Parade for noon the next day. The Parade marked the 25th Anniversary of the founding of the RAF, and his short address dealt with that event. Douglas Bagnall recalls:

> I thought that it would be an excellent opportunity to have a talk to the entire squadron, and at the same time give me an opportunity to see them and for them to see me. Although I am sure there was a good deal of muttering about the parade, and it was an unusual feature in those desert days, it served the purpose well.

In the contrast between John Morton's informal talk and Douglas Bagnall's parade we can see their differing views as to what constituted a team and teamwork. John Morton stressed the need to 'muck in together', and fostered a relaxed relationship between officers and other ranks. Douglas Bagnall found what he regarded as sloppiness and overfamiliarity, and there early appeared a notice drawing attention to the need to observe the appropriate relationship between ranks. By some this was resented, and a pilot, Sgt Frank

62. Wg/Cdr Bagnall addressing the Squadron, 1 April 1943. (C. H. Goodridge.)

Last, wrote a satire on the subject, 'To the Gentlemen of the Service', which read, in part:

> There's slaughter in the desert,
>     men are dying in the snows,
> And one by one before the storm
>     each old tradition goes.
> But 40's proud tradition
>     holds shield against the foe:
> That Officers and Sergeants mustn't mix.[1]

Interestingly, given their different approaches to running the Squadron, Douglas Bagnall was, like John Morton, a New Zealander. Entering the RAF in June 1938, he had, like Dick Ridgway, spent all his squadron service in the Middle East, latterly flying Wellingtons with 108 Squadron, where he was a flight commander. At the time of his appointment to command 40 he was on the staff of Middle East HQ.

63. Wg/Cdr Bagnall (as A Flight Commander, 108 Squadron, April 1942). Drawing by P/O A. B. Read. (D. R. Bagnall.)

The most pressing problem facing Douglas Bagnall was, as for his predecessor, the age and condition of the aircraft the Squadron was flying. A few Mk. IIIs had been delivered in late March, but conversion to the Hercules-engined marks then stalled, and for a time in May the majority of aircraft operating were Ics. For new arrivals during this period, flying the Ic operationally came as a shock indeed.

During April, alarmed by the condition of engines back from overhauls in Cairo, Douglas Bagnall persuaded a friend at a near-by Recovery Unit to take the head off one to seek a cause for the high oil consumption. About the same time Bob Ginn, the Engineer Officer of 104 Squadron, was similarly investigating the poor performance of their Merlin engines, suspecting sabotage. Douglas Bagnall's investigation did not reveal grounds for suspicion, but did show that the locally-made piston rings were unsatisfactory, and wearing far faster than they ought. The matter was referred to the AOC in Cairo.

After a four day break, 40 resumed operations on 4 April with the first of four raids designed to harass the retreating German and Italian forces, a highly successful attack on Sfax, when 16 Wellingtons hit the railway station and sidings as well as barracks. Two nights later 8 returned to Sfax to further disrupt the railway system, while 12 others attacked the retreating German and Italian forces on the Sfax-Mahares Road. One aircraft (Sgt R. A. Atterton) failed to return from the latter, while another (Sgt Rainey), crashed on landing, though without injury to the crew. A third raid, by 19 aircraft on the Sfax-Mahares road on 7 April, was again successful, crews reporting direct hits on the road and railway, dispersed motor transport and tented encampments.

The final raid, on 8 April, was a transition between the three which had preceded it and those which followed, since the target was both the road from El Djem to Sousse, and the Landing Ground at El Djem. No aircraft were found, and the first of seven further operations flown against enemy landing grounds over the next sixteen nights—to the Menzel Tmime Landing Ground on 10 April—was only marginally more successful. The following night, however, when twenty aircraft attacked St. Marie du Zit West Landing Ground, runways, dispersals and buildings were hit hard. Direct hits were scored on blast shelters containing aircraft, and twelve fires started. The excellent work of the illuminators, F/O J. G. Wynne and F/O H. E. Wilkinson, was at a cost, however. Jack Liley remembers:

> We saw some heavy and light flak open up in our vicinity and were horrified to see a Wimpy caught in it and then catch fire. The fire quickly spread from nose to tail and the aircraft crashed. When we got back to base I found it was F/O Wilkinson's crew, which included the members of my old crew: Peter Grace, Roly (Zeke) Milbourne and Peter Kipling.

Five further attacks on Landing Grounds took place between 12 and 24 April, two at least, Korba South (13th April) and St. Marie Du Zit (15th), producing good results. But they also brought heavy losses, two aircraft falling in flames over the target on 15 April and two more on the 19th. One of those came from 104 Squadron, but the others were from 40: Flt/Sgt J. G. Hibbert on the 15th, and Australians W/O G. A. Webb and Flt/Sgt A. St. C. Turner on the 19th. A combination of anti-aircraft fire and night fighters was suspected, for the latter were reported on at least three nights, while the flak was at times heavy and accurate, several aircraft returning damaged.

John Wright, F/O Wynne's front gunner, recalls the night of the 19th:

> This target was a nightmare come true. One second we were in pitch blackness and the next we were in the brilliant intersection of two searchlights. Straight onto us with no warning. This was our first encounter with radar controlled

searchlights. Down went the nose and we dived and weaved out of the light. While this was going on I was staring with breathstopping horror as other Wimpys were similarly caught. I saw one in flames and another go down in flames and hit the ground and explode. The scene from the front turret was laid out before me like some vast field. There was nothing I could miss. My view was unimpeded. My God, I couldn't believe my senses. Was this really happening?

Gordon Webb's crew was one of two flare droppers, and Jack Liley recalls that because of a shortage of flares designed to be dropped from 10,000 feet, the two were told to go in at 5,000 feet, assured that there would be little opposition. The Intelligence Officer could not have been more wrong, however, for the flak was intense and accurate, and crippled Webb's aircraft on its bombing run. Only two members of the crew, Liley and the wireless operator (Sgt A. S. Quick), escaped before the aircraft crashed.

An interesting feature of these raids was the presence of a Wellington from 162 Squadron. Flown by Flt/Lt Van Der Linden, and carrying a crew of eight, the aircraft was described in the 40 Squadron ORB as being on 'Special Operations'. In fact 162 Squadron was an electronic surveillance and counter-measures unit, and it seems that night fighter activity was being monitored, since the 'Special operations' were carried out only during attacks on Landing Grounds.

Between 25 April and 3 May no operations were flown, and cloud hampered efforts on 4 May, when eight aircraft bombed roads and motor transport in the small area of Tunisia still held by the enemy. Four more raids followed, the last on 10 May being the final night bombing attack of the North African Campaign, the Axis force of more than 150,000 officers and men surrendering on the 13th. During this period three aircraft failed to return to base, but only one crew (Sgt J. R. Hough) was lost, crashing in the target area on 6 May. Two others (Sgt W. Dench on 4 May, and F/O Wynne on the 8th) baled out, but returned to their units.

The Axis surrender brought a pause in air operations, only two—against Messina on the 21st and 23rd—being flown during the rest of May. Both attacks were directed against the Ferry Terminal, presumably in an attempt to hinder the build up of German forces in Sicily, where at the time of the Axis surrender in Tunisia, there were scarcely 5,000 German troops to bolster the large but demoralized Italian defence force. Both raids were successful, the flak proving inaccurate, and night fighters, though encountered, being evaded. No aircraft were lost. Sadly, however, Sgt W. A. Stewart was killed on 22 May, when the Ic he was air testing inexplicably crashed.

A happier event was the return of the ground crews who had been retained on Malta when the Squadron returned to Egypt in January. On 2 May six Wellingtons flew to Malta to collect the sixty-four men, ferrying over in their place sixty-three from 221 and 458 Squadrons. Their return was timely, because on 4 May an Advance Party left Gardabia South for a new Landing Ground near Kairouan. The journey was completed on 11 May, when Wg/Cdr Bagnall flew in to inspect the new base. Ten days later, however, the Advance Party moved to Alem East, and it was for there that the Main Air and Road Parties left on 26 May. The Road Party, comprising thirty-six vehicles and 200 personnel, arrived on 30 May, and the whole squadron, except for a Rear Party clearing up at Gardabia, was reported on 1 June as 'just about settled down' with all sections functioning normally, though no operations were flown until 3 June.

For sergeant pilot Harry Bartlett, 'Everyday life on the Squadron at Gardabia was quite simply tedious. An occasional open air film gave some respite from gambling and cheap gin.' RCAF rear gunner Red Norbury adds:

> Nights when we weren't on ops were spent supping wine in the mess tent along with just about everyone else who wasn't flying. If you stayed in your tent having a bull session with someone or went visiting the noise from the mess was incredible. Great choruses of 'Cats on the roof tops' and 'O'Reilly's daughter' roared out in the desert night.

The Squadron stores had some cricket gear, and occasional games took place, using matting wickets, while wireless operator Reg Curtis recalls that 'we played football when the dust storms abated'. Another sport with a distinctly local flavour was played indoors. Red Norbury explains:

> One pastime was catching sand spiders and arranging fights between yours and someone else's. At least we called them sand spiders, but I now know that they were really Solifugids, a relative of spiders. They were very large. Some of them were about two inches long with legs spanning over three inches. They had tremendous double jaws, and will attack anything. When you caught one you placed it in a cut down paraffin tin or similar container, and let it be known that you were ready to accept all challenges.
>
> Soon someone would arrive with their hairy champion, bets were placed, the combatants placed in the arena (one of the tins) and the battle began.
>
> It was fast, brutal, and to the death. The trick, then, if your spider was the winner, was to get it away from the corpse of the loser, which it would be busily devouring. If you let it finish its meal it became very sluggish and ended up on the menu after the next engagement.
>
> I had one called Blue (which I had marked with a small drop of ink for identification) which won many fights and a goodly number of francs for me.

Another successful owner was the M.O., Flt/Lt Heard, whose spider won so frequently that it was rumoured that it was drugged it.

Other forms of recreation were more dangerous, and frowned upon. One, pilot Bill Armstrong recalls, was the habit of throwing 'found' Italian hand grenades around and letting off .38 revolvers out of sheer boredom. Boredom may also have led some to cultivate eccentricities, though the general view of such as the veteran officer pilot who, Bill writes, 'behaved totally as if he had an (imaginary) snake companion wherever he was' was that they were 'sand happy': i.e., had been in the desert too long. No doubt some had. Fortunately, other members of the Squadron seem to have been remarkably tolerant of eccentricity.

With North Africa secured, the next step was the invasion of Sicily, but first it was necessary to eliminate the Italian garrisons on Pantelleria and Lampedusa, which denied an invasion fleet the possibility of surprise. A decision was taken to attempt the reduction of Pantelleria by bombardment, which began on 18 May. The Squadron's first visit to the island was on 3 June, when fifteen aircraft attacked the docks and town. The demoralized garrison offered little opposition then or subsequently, and crews were able to concentrate on bombing accurately, the most spectacular results going to Flt/Sgt D. C. Challis, who started a large fire (3 June), F/O Horry, who scored a direct hit on a burning ship lying at a jetty (7 June) and Flt/Lt C. P. Towsey RNZAF, whose bombs caused 'a large red explosion' (9 June).

The last raid on Pantelleria was on 10 June, when eighteen Wellingtons were detailed to attack. On take-off the thirteenth (W/O N. Kennedy RCAF) crashed, and four members of the crew were killed, only the rear gunner (Sgt Powell) surviving. It was a sad conclusion to a successful series of raids, made under optimal conditions, and in which, the ORB noted, 40 Squadron 'had the distinction of dropping the last night bombs on Pantelleria before its surrender'.

After Pantelleria 205 Group turned its attention to Lampedusa, 40 sending five aircraft to attack the town and aerodrome on 11 June, the island surrendering the next day. Sicily now became the primary target, though to keep the enemy guessing as to where the next invasion would take place, the air attacks included targets in Sardinia and mainland Italy, while those on Sicily itself could easily be construed as supporting an assault on Sardinia.

The first five operations flown by 40 Squadron after the fall of Pantelleria and Lampedusa reflected this need to disguise Allied intentions. For after two attacks on Sicilian targets—airfields at Sciacca and Trapani, and the Ferry Terminal and Marshalling Yards at Messina—the Squadron attacked the marshalling yards at Naples and then (twice) Olbia, in Sardinia, before returning to mainland Italy once more, with an attack on ships and mar-shalling yards at San Giovanni, on the Straits of Messina. Two further attacks on Messina (28 and 29 June) were then followed, on the 30th, by a return to Sardinia, with seven Wellingtons attacking the barracks and railway station at Cagliari.

Of these raids, the majority achieved but mediocre results. Only one of the three on Messina (28 June) produced clear evidence of accurate bombing, darkness and haze making the others inconclusive, while the attack on Cagliari was similarly handicapped, though a 4,000-lb 'cookie' dropped by Sgt A. V. Rippengal near the railway station started a large fire. The most successful raids, in fact, were the two on Olbia (22 and 24 June), which resulted in accurate and destructive bombing.

The raid on San Giovanni, on 27 June, was in most respects unsatisfactory. It was well illuminated by Flt/Sgt J. C. Fraser RAAF and Sqn/Ldr Gladstone, but only eight aircraft out of sixteen bombed the harbour and marshalling yards, and without spectacular results. Yet though disappointing, it was significant as 40's last raid employing Wellington Ic aircraft.

Douglas Bagnall had pressed since taking command for 40's complete re-equipment with the Mk. III or (preferably) the Mk. X. It was not until 19 June, however, when the Group Equipment Officer visited the Squadron, that an assurance was received that priority would be given to fully rearming 40 with Hercules-engined variants, and to re-equipping the Squadron with Hercules spares and tools. This proceeded rapidly, with one Mk. III and fourteen Mk. Xs delivered within a week.

The 1,500 hp. Hercules XI engines of the Wellington III conferred 50% more power than the Pegasus engines of the Ic, raising the maximum speed from 235 to 255 mph, and the service ceiling from 18,000 to 19,000 feet. With the Mk. X, powered by 1,675 hp Hercules XVI engines, performance was further enhanced, the service ceiling rising to 22,000 feet. In both the propellers were fully feathering, and this and the increased power made maintaining height on one engine feasible. There were gains in armament, too, both defensively, with the four gun rear turret, and offensively, since all Mk. IIIs and Xs could carry the 4,000-lb 'cookie'.

The value of the cookie was amply demonstrated in the first of the ten raids carried out in July prior to the invasion of Sicily, one dropped by F/O R. Dolden RAAF bursting in the centre of the main railway sidings at Messina, Allan Brodie, the bomb aimer, recalling that 'complete railway engines and trucks were thrown bodily into the air'.[2] This success was followed by two more, on Trapani, when the marshalling yards and military installations were hit on successive nights. After an unsuccessful visit to Villacidro Landing Ground, in Sardinia, there followed attacks on Landing Grounds in Sicily on 5 July (Gerbini), 7th (Catania and Gerbini) and 8th (Catania, Gerbini and Comiso). None of these was particularly successful, and three aircraft were lost, one (Sgt W. Dench) being seen to crash north of Gerbini on 5 July, and two (F/O J. K. Piry and Sgt S. H. N. Hart) failing to return on the 8th—half of the small force sent to Catania aerodrome that night.

64. Flt/Lt A. Brodie (Bombing Leader) and 'Duce', astride a 4,000 lbs 'cookie', Kairouan.
(J. E. Oram.)

The invasion of Sicily began shortly after 2200 hours on 9 July 1943, with the arrival off Cape Passero of glider-borne units of the British 1st Airborne Division. Their mission was to take the strategically important Ponte Grande bridge over the River Anapo, near Syracuse. A combination of circumstances, including inadequate training, a head wind and anti-aircraft fire, led to many gliders being released early, and nearly half came down in the sea. 252 men drowned, while many others, including Maj-Gen. G. F. Hopkinson, their CO, spent hours in the water before being rescued. The bridge was captured by the small part of the force which landed as planned, but in many respects the operation was disastrous.

Forty's role that night was a difficult and dangerous one: to prepare the way for the 1st Airborne Division's advance into Syracuse by bombing the seaplane base and nearby roads. This was carried out most efficiently, as the ORB indicates:

3 crews undertook the difficult task of destroying the seaplane base at SYRACUSE. Aircraft 'P' (Sgt BERVEN) went in first, its bombs falling across the target, closely followed by 'K' (F/O DOLDEN), 8 of whose bombs fell close to the hangar, causing a large cloud of smoke. A few moments later, 'S' (Sgt BARTLETT) scored 2 direct hits on the hangar.

6 other a/c attacked the narrow area S.E. of the harbour at SYRACUSE which had been allotted to them as the target for the remainder of this

diversionary attack. Small though this area was, bombing was well concentrated within it, causing clouds of dust which at times obscured the target.

The ORB entry, which goes on to quote a message from Maj-Gen. Hopkinson, thanking 40 Squadron for a task 'magnificently done and extremely accurate', gives only a bald outline of what was involved. The bombing had to be done without flares, to avoid illuminating airborne operations, and at low level, to achieve the necessary accuracy. It also had to be carried out continuously over a period of three hours. So dangerous did the operation seem that Gp/Cpt MacNair, OC 236 Wing, suggested it was a case for volunteers. Douglas Bagnall recalls, however, that when he outlined the operation to the aircrew 'there was no hesitation in response'.

In the event the operation went without a hitch and amazingly (given that it was a brightly moonlit night and that each of the nuisance crews was over the target area for half an hour, dropping 18 × 250-lb bombs in five sticks) without loss. Douglas Bagnall attributes this to the fact that 'the heavy flak could not get at us properly at the height we were flying, and the light flak would probably have to have been brought from elsewhere to concentrate over the small area'. 'However', he adds, 'it was quite hairy enough'.

In the next week 40 flew six ops, attacking Naples and Reggio di Calabria, as supply points for Sicily, as well as targets on the island itself. Undoubtedly the most successful raid was on 12 July, when many fires were started amongst buildings and at dispersals on Monte Corvino Ravella airfield. Sgt R. Allan scored the most spectacular success with a direct hit on a large hangar which burned fiercely, and then blew up. By the end of the raid black smoke covered the airfield, and photo reconnaissance revealed more than forty aircraft destroyed.

Prior to the invasion of Sicily, 40 had on many raids dropped leaflets directed at both the military and civilian populations. Designed to exploit distrust between the Italians and their German allies, pamphlets such as *Foglio Volante*, *Quale Germania Combattera* and *Soldati Italiani* sought to convince the Italians that they were being used, and that ridding itself of Mussolini as a prelude to an early cessation of hostilities was in Italy's best interests. As the invasion of Sicily progressed, this leaflet campaign was extended to include Rome and Naples, as well as Palermo and Marsala. On the night after the Italian government did in fact force Mussolini's resignation 40 also targeted German forces near Catania, dropping 600,000 copies of *Italien Steht*.

The Squadron spent the remainder of August attacking docks, railway yards and airfields, mostly on the Italian mainland. The most successful night was 19 July, when eleven Wellingtons were part of a force which attacked the airfield at Aquino, in central Italy. In good weather, and without opposition, the bombing was accurate, and the airfield severely damaged. Buildings were a mass of flames, and twenty-one aircraft were set on fire.

Thick black smoke enveloped the airfield, and rose to a height of more than 5,000 feet, while the fires could be seen burning for sixty miles.

August began with attacks on the transportation system at Naples and at Catanzaro Marina, in Calabria. The first attack on Naples, on 1 August was not a great success, the target being obscured by thick haze. Wg/Cdr Bagnall, flying with Sgt C. S. Field, brought back a photograph plotted directly over the marshalling yards, but for their pains they were caught in searchlights and, as the ORB puts it, 'chased out to sea'. On return it was found that the aircraft had holes in the wings and tail plane, while a shell nose cap was embedded in the bomb doors.

The next night, however, excellent illumination by P/O F. C. Derry RCAF and the newly commissioned P/O Challis provided an opportunity for effective bombing. 'A large number of Wellingtons took part in the raid,' the ORB states, 'and our crews were lyrical in their descriptions of the scene'. The marshalling yards and the surrounding industrial area were a mass of flames, and one crew was reminded of the fireworks displays at 'the Crystal Palace in its best days'.

On 4 August the docks and railway yards at Messina were successfully attacked, but since the Axis forces were beginning an evacuation of Sicily, 205 Group switched the following night to the beaches along the Straits of Messina. Fourteen aircraft operated, searching from Messina to Cap Peloro for targets, and in particular small boats. One was set on fire by the first of six sticks of bombs which Wg/Cdr Bagnall dropped, while the beaches were machine gunned by F/O R. Cheek. Two crews (P/O Challis and Sgt W. L. Boundy) did not return, and before the attacks on the beaches ended, on 15 August, four more were lost: W/O H. S. Shepherd RNZAF and Flt/Sgt H. Bartlett on the 11th, Flt/Sgt W. R. Walters RAAF the following night, and Sgt K. C. Bamford on the 14th.

How Challis, Boundy and Walters were brought down is not known, but Bamford's aircraft caught fire, crashing behind San Giovanni, on the Calabrian side of the Strait. Two of the crew, Bamford and the wireless operator (Sgt A. G. Payne) survived, evading capture, but did not return to the Squadron.

We can be more certain about the losses on 11 August. Harry Bartlett writes:

> We had been over the target area some time and dropped half our bomb load when I saw up ahead what I thought might be one of the high level flares the Germans were supposed to be using. It closed very quickly and within seconds appeared as a Wellington going the other way and completely in flames—wings, fuselage, everything. This was of course W/O Shepherd, although I didn't know it then.

Shortly afterwards, Bartlett's Wimpy was hit by flak, and the starboard engine caught fire. Bartlett continues:

> We were then flying inland at 6000 feet towards mountains which rose to about 4000 feet. I started the procedure to put out the fire—shut down engine, feather, press extinguisher button. The bomb-aimer said, 'Shall I feather?' I shouted, 'No, Leave it alone'. But it was too late. He feathered the port engine. Six thousand feet, hills at four thousand feet, one engine stopped, the other throttled back and in flames. Air space was needed, so I turned back over the Straits to sort things out. We were losing height quickly when the rear gunner reported a fighter attacking. Steep turns on one engine cost yet more height, and at 1,500 feet, under fire from the ground, we seemed to be running out of options.

Bartlett gave the order to bale out, and then, unable to reach his parachute, ditched the Wellington just off shore. The ditching went well, 'the impact confused and wet, but not at all violent', and the only contretemps was when he discovered the $CO_2$ bottle on his life jacket didn't work. 'It turned out not to be my jacket', he adds, 'Someone must have popped theirs back at base, and swapped it with mine to avoid confessing to the storekeeper. I paddled ashore where two German soldiers were waiting.'

Bartlett and his W/Op and rear gunner (Sgts R. Curtis and A. Ash) spent the rest of the war as POWs, while the navigator (F/O W. Lester) either drowned or died when his chute failed to open. But the finger-happy bomb aimer (Sgt L. Atkins), who was taken prisoner by the Italians, returned to his unit. He reported that he was neither interrogated nor searched, and that when it was obvious the end of Axis resistance in Sicily was near, the Italian CO gave his men, and Atkins, the choice of getting out, or remaining. Many chose to remain, as did Atkins, who met up with US troops on 18 August.

The six crews lost in nine days represented the heaviest losses since 40 was re-formed in May 1942, and it is little wonder that survivors recall the attacks on the beaches as particularly dangerous. Yet even if the Squadron did not, as some firmly believe, lose crews every night, the loss rate of 6% for this period was very high. Harry Bartlett reflects the tension that these losses engendered:

> Gambling became more and more important as time went on. During the last days of the Sicily campaign it became almost frantic. On one evening just before I was shot down I gambled away every penny I had. First poker, then pontoon, ending with just cutting for high card. I lost not only all I had with me but all the money lying undrawn in my pay account, which I drew and settled next morning. NCOs and officers were in the mess every night, playing poker for what seemed to us enormous stakes. It didn't seem real. Ops were the only reality.

It would be satisfying to record that results compensated for the Squadron's losses. Sadly, they did not. For the Italians evacuated 59,000 troops, 3,000 sailors, and 227 vehicles without loss, and the Germans nearly 54,000 troops and casualties, 9,789 vehicles, 51 tanks and 163 guns, as well as fuel, ammunition and equipment, losing only one German soldier killed. This was not the fault of 205 Group, which did all that was asked of it. Rather it was a failure on the part of the Chiefs of Staff, who neither devised in advance a strategy for preventing an Axis withdrawal, nor acted sufficiently vigorously to prevent it when it began.[3]

Sicily taken, attacks resumed on bridges and marshalling yards on the Italian mainland, with particularly successful raids on yards at Bagnoli and Torre Annunziata (26 and 29 August). One crew was lost to flak (Sgt Field on 19 August), crashing in flames. A second crew (Flt/Sgt F. A. Noonan RAAF) failed to return from an attack on the marshalling yards at Bagnoli on the 26th, but reached Borizzo, in Sicily, on one engine. The next day, however, a Beaufighter of 255 Squadron, in which he was flying as a passenger, was mistaken for a Ju 88 by two American Spitfires, and shot up. Both Noonan and the Beaufighter pilot were killed.

Noonan's was the last death in a grim month for the Squadron. Seven crews had failed to return—a rate twice as high as the next in 205 Group (104, with four losses) and constituting 40% of the Group's total losses of seventeen aircraft. Fortunately, September and October were to prove happier.

September opened with attacks on airfields and marshalling yards. Those on airfields were not particularly successful, Viterbo proving as hard to locate on 9 September as on 16 August. Marshalling yards proved easier to hit, however, an effective attack on Villa Literno, near Naples, on 5 September, being made possible by successful illumination by F/Os D. J. Lemon and W. J. A. Armstrong.

These raids were part of the preparations for the landings at Salerno, which took place on the night of 8 September. From then until the 19th, 40 operated almost nightly in an effort to disrupt the land and air routes by which enemy forces might be brought in to counter the landings, and then to bomb troop concentrations and roads just behind the battle area. On the 12th, eleven aircraft attacked Castelnuovo, destroying a crucial road junction and its approaches. Attacks on the next three nights were also successful, with roads and bridges near Pompeii badly damaged. On 13 September F/O Cheek followed up with machine-gun attacks at 1,500 feet, and the following night, after bombing the Battipaglia-Eboli road, three other crews followed suit. Cheek's attack was not the first his crew had undertaken. Indeed, by now they had a reputation for strafing, which they had begun over the Messina beaches.

On 16 September 205 Group resumed its attacks on airfields, and 40 arrived over Cisterna Littoria to find fires already burning. With the target thus illuminated the ten crews were able to bomb accurately, W/O S. F. Judd RNZAF claiming a direct hit on the central hangar. The attack on Cerveteri the following night went less well; with flares scattered and illumination hampered by smoke, most of the bombing was concentrated north of the target. To complete a night of misfortune, one of the illuminators, (W/O B. M. Berven RCAF) caught fire shortly after leaving the target area, and crashed off shore. The 205 Group report on the raid speculates that this might have been caused by a hung-up flare.

On 21 September, with the Salerno bridgehead secure, 205 Group turned its attention to Corsica, targeting Bastia, the chief evacuation point for German troops on the island. Crews reported good results in the face of modest opposition, and no losses were incurred. Three nights later 40 attacked the other end of the evacuation route, the Italian port of Leghorn.

First bombed on 30 September, Formia was also a target three times early in October. Little opposition was encountered, and no aircraft lost to enemy activity, but two crashed. On 8 October Flt/Sgt R. Rickard and crew found themselves over base with both hydraulics and the electrical system faulty, the bomb doors open and only one wheel down. It was also suspected that a bomb had hung up, so that a belly landing was out of the question. The crew therefore baled out, their Wellington crashing in 231 Wing dispersals. A week earlier Sgt S. Costin's crew were unable to locate base owing to dense cloud, and forced-landed at Djeida. The aircraft hit a pylon and telegraph pole and the undercarriage collapsed, but only the navigator was slightly injured. Costin again had problems on 30 October, when during an attack on Perugia airfield his Wellington was hit by flak. With the hydraulics out, and the bomb aimer (Sgt J. Bruxby) wounded, Costin landed at El Aouina without flaps or brakes, overshot, hit tents and a jeep, and further damaged the aircraft, though not, fortunately, the crew.

Bad weather hindered operations in the last week of September, and October proved equally inclement, with stand downs on eleven nights. When the Squadron did operate, it was mostly against road and rail communications close to the battle area south of Rome, or airfields used in support of the retreating German forces. Of the airfield attacks the most successful were undoubtedly those on Rome/Marcigliani (15 October) and Guidonia (23rd) when crews reported good conditions and accurate bombing. At Marcigliani four crews also strafed the airfield at low level, with the most spectacular results reported by Dick Cheek, whose crew claimed six aircraft on fire, of which three exploded. The following night they were again prominent, as one of only three crews which managed to locate the airfield at Rome/Casale. After bombing in two sticks, the second of which caused a large fire and explosions, Cheek and his crew made two circuits of the airfield at 500 feet, firing into trees which were believed to be sheltering dispersed aircraft. During the second circuit the Wellington was hit repeatedly by small arms fire.

Opportunities for strafing were less frequent when the Squadron attacked bridges or marshalling yards, but occasionally crews descended to low level after bombing, in order to shoot up targets of opportunity. On 14 October, for instance, after attacking a railway bridge at Orbetello, two crews made low level attacks on the nearby seaplane base, one of them (Sgt D. H. Ricketts) being hit by flak which put the rear turret out of action. Four days earlier, F/O Cheek dropped flares along the Appian Way and then dived to 500 feet, enabling the rear gunner (F/O L. R. Newton) to machine-gun vehicles. A DSO, announced on 31 October, was fitting recognition of the work that Cheek and his crew were doing.

In November bad weather again restricted flying, only thirteen operations being flown, mainly against marshalling yards and railway bridges, several of them in Southern France and Northern Italy. At extreme range, these necessitated the use of overload tanks, with aircraft carrying 4,000-lb bombs using landing grounds in Sardinia for refuelling. The first such operation was on 10 November, when twelve aircraft attacked the railway viaduct at Recco, east of Genoa. Wg/Cdr Bagnall, carrying a 4,000-lb General Purpose bomb with an eleven second delay fuse, refuelled at Decimomannu. He recalls:

> When I arrived it was deserted and looked in very poor shape. However, I landed and was met by an army officer who had no idea what I was doing there. After much hard bargaining I managed to obtain fuel but no flare path. I also managed to prevail upon him to park two Jeeps at the end of the runway pointing towards me with their headlights on, but having seen the size of the bomb we were carrying he said did I mind if he did not wait with the Jeeps during the take-off.
>
> The take-off in the dark over the shocking runway surface seemed endless. Thoughts of a burst tyre, and the 4000 pounder underneath rather naturally came to mind. The second pilot [Flt/Lt R. Dolden RAAF], who was the normal captain of this really excellent crew, swears that he heard me let my breath out some time after we were airborne.

Bombing was equally heart-stopping, the railway disappearing into a tunnel in an almost sheer cliff immediately beyond the viaduct, and Douglas Bagnall remembers that

> just as we reached the viaduct on a dummy run with a few hundred yards to go to the cliff the flare above us went out. We had already frightened the wits out of ourselves and we had not yet started the bombing run. The latter did not seem quite so bad, however; perhaps we were too numb to feel

anything. But in the break away after bomb release, this time in the light of flares, the rear gunner said he could see the trees on the cliff flashing past his turret. He added that he preferred the darkness so that he could not see how close they were.

Bombing was made more difficult by the failure of almost all the flares dropped by Flt/Lt Lemon, but Allan Brodie, the bomb aimer, writes:

> We circled back and saw that a huge section of the viaduct had been completely destroyed and that a train emerging from the tunnel on the north side had been caught up by the blast.[4]

The other ten aircraft then bombed, reporting bursts on and near the target, which was rapidly obscured by dust.

On 12 November two aircraft were detailed to make a similar attack on a rail bridge at Cecina, with Sgt Rippengal as flare dropper and F/O Cheek bombing. The 4,000-lb bomb was successfully dropped, and Cheek's crew saw a hole in the bridge and river bed, but no explosion occurred until three aircraft, probably from 104 Squadron, attacked the bridge and, 205 Group concluded, set off the 4,000-pounder. Aerial reconnaissance later showed that 'a large portion of the bridge—two thirds of its width—[was] missing on the seaward side near the centre'.

Cheek and his crew had also distinguished themselves the previous night, when after a successful attack on marshalling yards at Prato, they made two visits to the airfield and marshalling yards at Pistoia, which they had strafed on 24 October. At the yards they attacked a line of trucks with incendiaries, starting fires, while at the airfield some 30 aircraft were seen, and hits were scored on about 12 of these, as well as a vehicle and a gun emplacement. The attacks on the airfield were made at very low level, and the undercarriage was lowered to prevent damage to the propellers, the wheels touching the ground at one point.

Successful attacks on railway bridges and viaducts in Northern Italy led 205 Group to plan a more ambitious raid, on the Villar Perosa ball bearing factory, in Turin, on 24 November. Forty contributed 15 aircraft to the 83 strong force, 76 of which set off for Turin. Amongst those which did not get away were 6 aircraft (including 2 from 40) which, carrying 4,000-lb 'cookies', had been despatched to Elmas, Sardinia, for refuelling. Facilities there proved hopelessly inadequate, and as the 205 Group report on the raid observes: 'in the light of later events, this was, perhaps, a fortunate miscalculation'.

The raid was a disaster comparable to the Nüremberg raid by Bomber Command in March 1944. Only 9 out of 76 aircraft reached Turin, of which 3 did not bomb. The cost was 17 Wellingtons and 14 crews. The cause was a severe and unexpected front encountered in the Gulf of Genoa, crews reporting 10/10ths low cloud north of Corsica, and over Turin. An unexpectedly strong westerly wind also hampered navigation.

A report by the Group Navigation Officer on the raid stated that the problems encountered by the crews depended on

> the decision of the captain in the early part of the flight: (a) Those who climbed above the weather and stayed above, navigating by D.R., and (b) those who flew 2,000 feet or under and endeavoured to maintain contact flying until they reached the Italian coast.'

'The crews in the first category', it concluded,

> seem to have experienced little difficulty beyond icing in the cloud tops. Drifts were obtained up to 11,000 feet through gaps and so reasonable tracks were maintained. Apart from those who decided to return early, the majority carried on to D.R. target area.

On the return journey, similarly, 'these crews obtained accurate loops in view of their height and were able to correct any tendency to drift to the east'.

It was crews in the second category, the report declared,

> which experienced the greatest difficulties. Conditions were extremely bumpy under the cloud layer and navigators were doubtful of trusting the drifts obtained. Many of them realized that the westerly wind had increased in strength when they found themselves approaching Elba, and by large corrections arrived over Cape Corse.

The report continues:

> However, stronger winds still were experienced north of Cape Corse in the Gulf of Genoa, and in spite of substantial allowances, the majority of landfalls were to the east of Portofino in the region of Spezia, several crews finding themselves over hilly coastline when they thought they were still over the sea.
>
> Unable to penetrate the weather here, the captains decided to return as they realized they would be too late for blitz time even if they climbed over the cloud layer.
>
> The return journey at low height was still difficult as pinpoints were few and loops only accurate as the range became shorter. The majority reached base satisfactorily.

'In spite of the extremely bad weather', the 205 Group Navigation summary for November concluded, 'and the distance involved (approximately 620 miles), the standard of navigation was remarkably good and there was only one case of a complete navigational failure.' To which must be added that there was only one *known* case of navigational failure. Amongst the thirteen crews who perished there were presumably others.

Equally, the report understates the icing problems crews experienced in attempting to climb over the bad weather. Red Norbury, rear gunner in a highly experienced crew, comments:

> Everything went well until we approached the enemy coast. Then we were met by a towering mass of clouds. We entered it at 7000 feet and immediately encountered severe icing. Ed. [Sgt E. Beetz RCAF] got us turned around and we flew back out of the cloud. Then we climbed as high as Wellington LN513 would go and tried again. Same result. Ice and more ice.
>
> So, back out over the Med. and down to try to sneak in under it. More icing. So we had a conference which ended with Ed. deciding to abandon ops and return to base.

While some crews crashed into high ground in northern Italy, others ditched, and intensive searches were carried out by sea and air from Bizerta and Corsica. No trace of the missing crews was found, however, the ASR launches reporting that 'sea conditions were such that there was little hope that aircraft dinghies could survive them'. Of the three 40 Squadron crews lost, two (Flt/Sgt N. Carter and Sgt F. H. Haegi) crashed in northern Italy A radio message from the third (Sgt T. J. Gosling) stated that they were baling out over Sardinia, but they landed in the sea, and none survived.

After Turin 40 flew only three further operations from North Africa. On 26 November fourteen aircraft attacked a railway bridge over the River Ombrone, near Grossetto, Flt/Lt M. Blyth claiming a hit on the north end. The second raid was on 28 November, when nine aircraft bombed the Rome/Ciampino airfield in the face of slight but accurate opposition. Then on 1 December nine aircraft operated against the marshalling yards at Pontassieve. Three dropped flares, providing excellent illumination, and with no opposition crews bombed accurately, one 4,000-lb bomb bursting on the western end of the yards.

The Pontassieve raid was the last by 205 Group from North Africa. It had been evident for some time that as the Italian front moved northwards, and longer flights were involved, a move to Italy would be necessary, but only with the capture of the Foggia plain, with its airfield complex, was it possible to contemplate moving to the mainland.

For 40 the move to Italy came after a lengthy period in the Kairouan area. The Squadron had moved from Gardabia South to Alem East at the end of May. A local move to Hani West on 25 June followed, the shift being completed the same day, and further adjustments were made on 14 October, when a shift of landing ground to the newly-constructed LG14 occasioned no change to 40's domestic site, and on 18 November, when the Squadron moved to Oudna No. 1.

Red Norbury remembers the move to Oudna principally for the presence of the local Arabs, who 'were already in attendance before we had our tents

65. Target photo: Pontassieve Marshalling Yards, 1/2 December 1943. (F. Rooke.)

down'. 'It soon became apparent', he goes on, 'that anything not closely guarded was fair game for our neighbours. They were all around the camp and every now and then one would stray innocently over to some gear left momentarily unguarded'. Suddenly two Arabs were spotted fossicking through the contents of the dismantled hospital tent, which had been left briefly unattended. Red continues:

We all yelled and started over to chase them off when a little Austin staff car appeared. It was the CO and he was going full out.

The Arabs immediately hicked up their sheets, as their nightshirt-like clothing was called, and went tearing away with the Austin right on their heels. The closer it got to them the faster they ran, and the higher they hoisted their sheets. Since they wore nothing under them, once they got to waist level the scene became a real comedy.

Just when it seemed that the Austin was going to win the race they jumped down into a wadi and escaped. That ended the performance and before long

TO TUNISIA247

our gharry arrived, we loaded our kit, and tent aboard, and at 10.30 we took off for Oudna.

Pilfering had in fact been endemic at Kairouan, thefts from tents at night leading at one point to the (unsuccessful) boobytrapping of a tent with hand grenades. But the faults had not been all on one side. For there was sometimes cheating during barter deals, as by passing off the appalling 'Victory' cigarettes as a more palatable brand, or a bag of sand as sugar. There were also numerous examples of thoughtlessness, such as low flying to panic a camel train, loosing off pistol shots to 'hurry up' a donkey and its rider, or (as Red Norbury recalls) undertaking gunnery practice in the desert without checking to see that the area was clear:

> Out in the desert, all hell was loose, with yells and shouts and clouds of dust and flocks of sheep and goats scattering in all directions. I don't think any of us had seen them. They were a good distance away, but still within range.
>
> We stopped firing and were standing around having a smoke when an Arab came riding along on a donkey in a great hurry. Dismounting, he went up to Flt/Lt Irwin [Gunnery Leader], dug a package of American cigarettes out of his sheets and offering him one, saying in a rather pleading tone, 'No boom-boom sheep'.
>
> I don't know whether we had boom-boomed any of his sheep or not, but certainly I could have done so quite accidentally, or even have boom-boomed some of his friends and relations.

At Kairouan the Squadron had better facilities than at any time since Kabrit in November 1942. On 29 June the ORB noted that 'For the first time since the Squadron left the Delta area, an Army Mobile Bath visited the Unit', and the following night a Mobile Cinema, which showed *Star Spangled Rhythm* to a 'large and appreciative audience'. On 18 July a Squadron Concert Party was formed, and 'The Forty Thieves', as they called themselves, put on what the ORB described as 'a show of music, comedy and drama' at the Ecole Koranique, Kairouan, on 12 October.

Even if the facilities were superior to those at earlier desert landing grounds, they were still primitive. Red Norbury's crew arrived at Kairouan West in mid August, direct from the United Kingdom:

> There were no frills. You carried 'your' irons, enamel mug, tin plate, knife, fork, and spoon, to the mess tent three times a day for your meals and you washed them yourself afterwards and carried them back to your tent. Then in the evening you carried your mug back to the mess tent and got it filled with whatever kind of booze was on tap, and so ended the day.
>
> During our seven day respite before starting ops we managed to get ourselves oriented and fairly well equipped. We acquired a chatty, or clay water jug, which was supposed to keep water cool, dug a small ditch around our tent as we were advised to, and generally got settled in. I bought a two burner

66. Dhobi Day: Flt/ Sgt Brian Jeffares
scrubbing a shirt, Kairouan, Summer 1943.
(G. P. B. Henfrey.)

primus stove from someone who was leaving, so we could have hot water for shaving and washing and laundry. It turned out to be a great investment.

The first autumn storm demonstrated the need to keep the ditch in good repair, for Red woke to find the tent awash, and the crew spent the rest of the night clearing the ditch, retying broken ropes, driving pegs deeper into the sand and holding down the tent poles. Not all the tents had fared so well, for Red recalls:

Down to flight parade the next morning to find that the flight tent has disappeared 'Into the blue'. Said Sqn/Ldr Bodman, 'My tent has gone to the same place as the flight tent. We hope to get your records back together sometime'.

From Kairouan, a swimming gharry (lorry) drove each day to the beach at Sousse, and Red Norbury comments that 'we occasionally took advantage of this, but it was a long way to ride in the back of a truck for a swim. There was nothing else to do in Sousse.' George Henfrey recalls, however, another form of recreation:

During the enemy's retreat in Tunisia, much of his transport had been left behind in a hurry, and some of it was captured almost intact, so much in fact that a great deal of joyriding began to take place in and around camp, at all hours. Fiat Trucks and BMW motorcycles were seen to be buzzing round all over the place.

Douglas Bagnall also recalls the vehicles, commenting:

For a while we were magnificently mobile, even to the extent of a German half-track, which proved most useful. But I knew that it was too good to last, and eventually all units were required to give up their captured enemy vehicles. This did not go down well, particularly as a good deal of effort had gone into rendering them serviceable.

As the Axis retreated through Tunisia, attractive coastal resorts became available as rest camps, and Cyril Moore, the navigator (and only officer) in New Zealander Flt/Sgt Brian Jeffares' crew, recalls a leave spent with his friend P/O R. W. Holdsworth, the navigator and only officer in Sgt Boundy's crew:

> Luckily they got leave at the same time as ours. His crew went with mine to the sergeants' 'Holiday Camp' on the seafront at Hammamet. The crews found room for us, and we joined them there. As we spent most of the time in bathing trunks, swimming, drinking, and playing cards, badges of rank were not in evidence. Bob and I stayed at Hammamet for three days and then went to Tunis, where we did some sightseeing, had some good meals in restaurants, and went to a concert of solo piano music: the pianist being, if I recall correctly, Solomon.

The move to Italy was a major logistical exercise, which began on 2 December, when kit and equipment was partially packed. The Main party, under the command of F/O Newton, left on the morning of 5 December by road for Bizerta, the port of embarkation. There the vehicles were parked in the marshalling area, cooking facilities being provided by the local military authorities. The ORB notes that 'a cinema, operated by Americans, provided welcome relief from the tedious business of awaiting embarkation orders'.

Tedious it was, for the Main party did not embark until 1300 hours on 8 December, but a pleasant surprise awaited personnel aboard the LST:

> The presence of bunks, hot and cold water, and dining saloons, were a pleasant surprise to all personnel, who had expected conditions far less favourable aboard a vessel built primarily for tank and M.T. transporting.

67. En route to Italy, December 1943. (C. H. Goodridge.)

The ORB entry continues:

> Our vessel, in company with about a dozen other similar craft, escorted by
> two ships of the corvette type, sailed at 0900 hrs from Bizerta harbour. The
> next few days were spent, quite uneventfully, making the slow trip to ITALY,
> with everyone looking forward, eagerly, to their return to Europe.

It was not only 40 Squadron personnel who derived pleasure from the
crossing, for when disembarkation took place at Taranto, at noon on 12
December, the Captain of the LST complimented F/O Newton on the
behaviour of the men under his command, adding, so the ORB proudly
records: 'The cleanest body of men I've yet transported'. For 40, after so
many months living rough, and with water in short supply, this was an
accolade indeed.

## Notes

1. Wg/Cdr Bagnall was briefed, on appointment, by Air/Cdre O. R. Gayford, AOC 205
   Group, who told him that the general standard of the Squadron was unacceptable, and
   that he [Douglas Bagnall] had a free hand to effect whatever changes were needed in
   order to improve serviceability and operational results.

2. Allan Brodie, *Adventure in My Veins*. London: Jarrolds, 1968 (repr. Farnham:, Triple A
   Publishing, 1989), p. 57.

3. See Carlo D'Este, *Bitter Victory* (London: Collins, 1988), especially Chapter 30, 'The
   Great Escape'.

4. *Adventure in My Veins*, p. 60.

19

# A Hard Year:
# December 1943–December 1944

Forty Squadron disembarked at Taranto on 12 December 1943, and that night camped north of the city. The next morning they set off for Cerignola, on the Foggia plain, spending two nights camped by the roadside outside the city before moving, on 15 December, to Cerignola Landing Ground No. 2. Douglas Bagnall recalls:

> The ground was flattened, muddy and there was obviously an awful lot of water retained in that area. They cleared a lot of olive groves away to lay this strip out and moved in a good deal of earth, from which the runway itself was raised. The first takeoff was a hairy experience. The excess water was actually forced up through this runway as you went over it. It squirted up in little water spouts which was really most frightening.

The tented encampment was equally wet, and after two days it was moved to a drier site where, bomb aimer Ron Black writes,

> We were based in an olive orchard, a nice change from the sand at Oudna. We spent a couple of weeks seeing the local area and each night drinking the local wines and singing the Squadron songs in the mess.

Meanwhile the officers, after camping briefly in a school, appropriated a large house in Cerignola, opposite the Cathedral, the ORB noting with satisfaction that the mansion was owned 'by a notoriously pro-Fascist Baron'.

Between 19 and 24 December, the ORB states, 'much time was spent "digging in" and creating all possible comfort under existing conditions'. Ovens were built, and put to excellent use when 'in spite of the fact that the Squadron had been such a short time in the country, an excellent Christmas dinner was provided, and Christmas was celebrated in the time honoured way, including the traditional custom of officers and senior NCOs serving dinner in the Airmen's Mess'.

With the Landing Ground virtually unusable, the decision was taken to shift the Squadron, which on 30 December moved to Foggia Main aerodrome—accompanied by the Squadron Rear party, under Flt/Lt Brodie, which had reached Cerignola the previous day. The New Year was thus seen in at the base which 40 would occupy for the rest of the war.

Map 5. Italy: Bases and Targets, 1941–45.

68. Greetings Card, Christmas 1943. (W. G. Norbury.)

A former *Regia Aeronautica* base, Foggia Main offered in some respects little improvement over Cerignola. For the unsealed runway showed the effects of repeated bombing, not least in the myriad metal fragments which worked their way to the surface and wrought havoc on the treadless tyres of the Wellingtons. Moreover, the area set aside for the Squadron's tents was a ploughed field, and during a severe storm on the first night many blew down. Douglas Bagnall writes:

> In the middle of the night all the troops in the area went mad. They were firing guns in the air and anything that had a pyrotechnic ability was let loose. This woke me up. I found my tent had gone and I was sleeping on a camp bed in a puddle of water. I was so exhausted that I hadn't even woken up, but I leapt into action and charged round the place to find that everybody else was mooching around and rubbing their eyes to find their tents had gone as well.

Next day the CO sought accommodation in Foggia, and through the good offices of General Doolittle, the USAAF commander in Italy, obtained the use of a partly-bombed school, where officers and NCO aircrew were housed. Conditions were spartan in the extreme, as wireless operator Bernard Burdsall found on arrival in early March:

No facilities, no windows, a cold water tap and buckets for toilets. 'Take that section of floor, fellows', said the Mess Sergeant. This was for us Sgts; Doug Dovey [F/O navigator] went some place else, just as bad. Well, there were about 30 bodies in this place. Some had rough beds or had pinched furniture from the empty houses in Foggia. The heating was a 45 gallon drum with a pipe going out of the window, the others being boarded up. We burnt wood and had lots of fun pulling down window blinds and breaking up fittings for firewood.

Without a roof over their heads, ground personnel were in some respects less fortunate, the conditions they endured being reflected in the CO's January Summary, which notes that 'the tented Airmen's Mess, after having been blown down twice, was re-erected, every effort being made to ensure its safety and permanence'. The Summary also notes that 'School desks, salvaged from destroyed schoolhouses, have been installed, and provide seating arrangements for meals etc'.

Despite the protection from the weather, however, aircrew were happy at the end of March to shift to the airfield and tented acommodation. 'The town was getting full of Italians and Americans', Bernard Burdsall comments, adding that when they moved to Foggia Main,

We took a school desk, wooden doors, tins, rolls of telephone wire; sounds like in a POW camp, but they were needed. The tent held four men, one in each corner. As there were no beds or sheets issued we made a wooden frame and wrapped it around with telephone wire to make springs, and used a stuffed flying suit as a mattress. The results weren't bad.

The doors were used as a raised platform down the centre of the tent to keep our things off the ground, which was often wet from the sudden heavy thunderstorms. The school desk was used to sit at while shaving and a tin helmet was used as a wash basin.

Water was in short supply at the airfield, navigator Bill Goodbrand recalls:

Running water was provided from a bowser—one jerry can per day for washing, shaving, etc. However in downtown Foggia a large ablution block provided showers for all service personnel, including Americans, which led to a little friction at times. For some reason the Yanks didn't like one of our songs sung to the tune 'John Brown's Body' and which started, "We fly our Flying Fortresses at 40,000 ft", and in which every verse ended in "But we've only got a teeny weeny bomb." This being a reference to the fact that a twin-engine Wellington carried a bigger bomb load than the four-engined Forts.

The first operation from Foggia Main was flown on 7 January, when 236 Wing (40 and 104 Squadrons), bombed the Reggiane Aircraft Factory at Reggio Emelia. The operation was an unqualified success, flares dropped by Flt/Sgt P. W. North, Flt/Sgt H. T. Bell and F/O W. K. Dunn enabling accurate bombing. Photos taken during the raid and the next day by the

69. Reggio Emelia aircraft factory, 10 January 1944: a reconnaissance photo. (F. Rooke.)

leading aircraft of a B–17 formation of the 15th Air Force, which had come
to complete its destruction, showed the severe damage which the factory had
suffered, rendering it useless, in the opinion of experts. A copy of the USAAF
photograph was supplied to the captain of each Wellington that took part.

This outstanding raid was followed by two more. The first, an attack on
the German fighter base at Villaorba, left aircraft burning and the airfield
unusable for some days. The second, on 10 January, was a raid on Sofia, in
Bulgaria, a squadron 'first'. Twelve aircraft were detailed, but one (Flt/Sgt
Allen) crashed on take-off, as the navigator, Ian Matley, recalls:

> A tyre burst on take-off and we ran off the runway and ended up with the
> tail broken off and a 4,000-lb bomb trying to come up through the floor.
> The bomb finally was pushed out through the side of the aircraft and lay

between the fuselage and one of the engines. The most sinister aspect of the whole experience was the sound of petrol gushing out of the tank after we came to a stop. There were many sparks from the breaking wires of the electrical circuits, but luckily they had ceased before the petrol tanks leaked.

The remaining aircraft attacked to good effect, and the 205 Group summary for the month noted that this raid and one the previous day by the 15th Air Force, had brought the 'disordered and wholesale evacuation of over 300,000 people [and] undoubtedly led to considerable chaos in Sofia in particular, and Bulgaria in general'.

An interesting feature of the raid was the reaction of aircrew to the announcement at briefing that the aiming point was the city centre; i.e. that this was an area bombing raid. Navigator Fred Rooke writes:

> On the one occasion when we were briefed to hit the centre of a city (Sofia) on 10/1/44 as a morale raid to influence the Bulgarian people, there was quite a commotion amongst the crews, who objected. This was silenced by the CO, who said, 'Those are orders and must be obeyed'.

An attack on Piraeus Harbour, near Athens, on the 11th, also went well, despite haze and intense flak, and searchlights. The event of the night, however, was an outstanding feat of airmanship by Flt/Sgt S. J. St. Clair RAAF, whose aircraft was involved in a collision with a 104 Squadron Wellington shortly after take-off. Two blades broke off the port airscrew, and the engine caught fire. Despite this, and the failure of the intercom system, St. Clair made a successful landing with bombs on board.

After Piraeus it was not until the 17th, when nine aircraft bombed the marshalling yards at Pisa, that crews were again satisfied with their night's work. Less successful raids on the Italian railway system followed, but on the 21st there was a signal success when the Squadron attacked the naval factory and docks at Fiume. Fires from burning oil storage tanks were visible 100 miles distant, and later reports indicated that the torpedo factory, oil refinery, shipyard machine shop and a timber factory were set on fire, and two U-boats sunk.

Of the remaining raids in January, only that on Arezzo marshalling yards, on the 27th, was an unqualified success, haze hampering the identification of the other three targets—one of them a 'first' in Yugoslavia, the Maribor aircraft factory. Arezzo brought success of another kind, too, when Flt/Sgt Bell's rear gunner (Flt/Sgt C. Watkins) shot down a twin-engined aircraft which had approached them in a hostile manner. The aircraft crashed into the sea.

Two aircraft were lost in January. Returning from Sofia on the 10th Flt/Sgt J. D. Coape-Smith RAAF and his crew baled out when they ran out of fuel. All landed safely, returning to base the following day. But P/O L. T. Puddephat and his crew died when, after an abortive search for the

railway between Fano and Ancona on 8 January, they crashed in the hills
north of San Marco. Their bodies, found several days later, were buried
with military honours in the British Military Cemetery at Foggia on 22
January. Their loss was keenly felt, since the crew was on the last operation
of its tour.

February began with three unsuccessful operations, against the Maribor
aircraft factory and marshalling yards at Padua and Rimini, before switching
to tactical bombing in support of the Allied forces at Anzio, where the
beachhead, established on 22 January, was under severe pressure. On four
of these seven ops double sorties were flown. Bombing was frequently
hampered by haze, but during the second sortie on 14 February clearer skies
and moonlight helped crews concentrate their bombing, German transport
being hit. A successful attack was also made, on 16 February, on the harbour
at Porto San Stephano, used by enemy craft supplying the battle areas at
Anzio and Cassino.

Little opposition was encountered during these ops, and no aircraft were
lost to enemy action, though two to accidents. On 16 February Flt/Sgt A. F.
Mason RAAF and crew were killed when their aircraft crashed in the hills
near Murhe Sarachelle, their bodies being found by villagers the following
day. Then that evening a Wellington piloted by F/O K. W. Lyon, another
Australian, crashed shortly after take-off. Only the rear gunner (Sgt F. Jones
RAAF) survived the crash and subsequent fire, which also killed a soldier
and several civilians. Miraculously, only three bombs exploded, the remainder
being defused by the Armaments Officer, F/O Carruthers.

On 18 February the Squadron narrowly escaped a third loss when aircraft
returning from Genzano encountered 10/10ths cloud over Foggia and one
(Flt/Sgt T. R. Bradshaw RCAF) iced up and became uncontrollable. Bradshaw baled his crew out, but then found his parachute out of reach. By a
fine piece of airmanship he regained control of the Wellington at 500 feet,
and made a successful landing. His crew, meanwhile, spent a cold night in
the countryside.

On 19 February Wg/Cdr J. D. Kirwan DFC succeeded Douglas Bagnall
as CO. His had been, at eleven and a half months, the longest period of
command in wartime since Leonard Tilney in 1916–17, and one marked
by considerable operational success. Appointed CO at a difficult time,
Douglas Bagnall had from the first stamped his personality and style on the
Squadron. Not all had appreciated this, his greater formality grating with
those who liked his predecessor's approach. But many came, like Harry
Bartlett, to recognize what the new CO achieved:

> I remember him as being easy to talk to, very much in charge and, on
> operations, setting a standard that we all felt impelled to emulate. The 40
> Sqdn I left was a very different body from the one I joined. It was more

70. 'The two Binders': Flt/Lt A. P. Fincher (bomb aimer) and F/O R. Carruthers
(Armaments Officer), Foggia. (J. E. Oram.)

tightly knit—a unit. Everything felt more positive and efficient. Wg/Cdr
Bagnall must surely have had a lot to do with this, although his influence
was not made aggressively obvious.

The impression many got of Douglas Bagnall was of a man tough, and
impervious to fear. They also knew him—many at first hand—as a fine
pilot, dedicated to achieving the highest possible quality results, whatever
the circumstances. What many never realized was how 'Bags' or 'Doc'
(derived from his initials, D. R.) felt about 40 Squadron. His pride in its
achievements was matched by his dedication to its interests, and Red
Norbury, who writes that he was 'a legendary figure as far as I was concerned',
recalls that there were tears in Douglas Bagnall's eyes when he announced
at briefing that he was leaving.

John Kirwan, Douglas Bagnall's successor, was, Alan Brodie recalls, 'a
very large and jovial Australian'. CO of 150 Squadron when it transferred

to North Africa in January 1943, he had been injured on 19 January when he and his crew baled out of their crippled Wellington, and in mid-February, not fully recovered, relinquished command. Now, fit once more, he was to command a squadron with a substantial Australian presence.[1]

The Squadron's first operation under John Kirwan's command, a raid on the Daimler-Puch factory at Steyr in Austria on 24 February, was a thorough-going failure, bad weather, poor illumination, and snow combining to mislead most crews into bombing Vocklabruck, some thirty-five miles from the target. It was not a propitious start.

March brought further bad weather, 40 operating on only eleven nights. The first two raids, on 1 and 2 March, were in support of the troops at Anzio, but only the second of these, on Porto San Stephano, was a success, eight aircraft attacking by good illumination. A target in Jugoslavia was set for 3 March, but heavy cloud obscured the primary target, and the six aircraft attacked Zara or Belgrade.

Forty did not operate again until 18 March, when 12 Wellingtons bombed the marshalling yards at Plovdiv, in Bulgaria. The previous night 205 Group had sent 67 aircraft to Sofia, and in very bad weather lost 12. The weather was less violent on the 18th, but cloud and thick haze meant that the most crews could report was that they reached the Sofia-Plovdiv area. Further attacks on the Bulgarian capital followed on 24 and 29 March. The latter was successful, all 9 aircraft locating the target, and bombs bursting amongst buildings and railway facilities. But on 24 March 10 aircraft bombed the estimated position of Sofia with unobserved results. Three aircraft were lost, though two crews were recovered. F/O D. B. Young ditched in the Adriatic, the crew being rescued by High Speed Launch, while Sgt G. S. Waddell crash landed near Manfredonia after one engine failed and the other began to malfunction. Lt F. F. Williamson and his crew were less fortunate, being taken prisoner after baling out, Williamson the Squadron's first SAAF casualty.

While 40 was directing its main effort against Sofia on 29 March, two aircraft, accompanied by three illuminators, were attacking a railway bridge at Fano. The two crews (Wg/Cdr Kirwan and W/O Bradshaw) carried 4,000-lb GP bombs of the type used earlier against bridges and viaducts. The illuminators did an excellent job, and though Kirwan's 4,000 pounder fell 100 yards short of the bridge, Tom Bradshaw's bomb-aimer (Flt/Sgt I. B. H. McKenna) was on target, the bomb exploding on the third span from the north end of the bridge.

Of five other operations during March against Italian targets, two, to the Marshalling Yards at Padua (19 March) and the port of Monfalcone (22nd) were highly successful. At the latter, the most active shipbuilding centre on the Adriatic coast, reconnaissance confirmed damage to workshops in the shipyard, the CANT aircraft factory, and a chemical works.

April brought further attacks on targets in Italy, mainly against shipping and ports like Genoa, Leghorn, Piombino, La Spezia and San Stephano. Many of these were of the harassing type, as to San Stephano on 2 and 10 April, and Leghorn on the 23rd and 29th, with aircraft arriving in waves, prolonging the period of bombing, and causing maximum disruption. Opposition was generally slight, and no losses were incurred.

Besides these raids on Italian targets, 40 also visited Hungary, Yugoslavia, Romania and Bulgaria. Of these raids the most unusual was a daylight attack on the Yugoslav town of Nicsic. Requested by Marshal Tito, Commander of the Yugoslav National Army, the attack, under Spitfire escort, included one aircraft (F/O Dunn) from 40 Squadron carrying a 4,000-lb GP bomb with an eleven second delay. Ken Dunn writes:

> The aiming point was a long barracks. We were quite low and approaching just at the right angle and although no other aircraft were in sight I decided we would bomb straightaway as we were sure of the target and we had a good run in. We stayed low and the rear gunner reported that the bomb had gone off just in front of the building. We then climbed up and circled over the village and by this time other aircraft were making their approach. As they bombed we photographed the explosions and craters —most within the target area and one bomb landing directly on the building. I suppose we stayed for 5–10 minutes—there was some light flak but nothing serious and no sign of any fighters.

Ken Dunn adds what he describes as 'a rather sad note':

> when the photos were enlarged a speck on the road as we approached the target turned out to be a donkey and cart and after our bomb had exploded this had disappeared. We hoped this was the only civilian casualty.

Forty raided Budapest twice in the first half of April, the targets being the Manfred Weiss factory on the 3rd, and the Ferencvaros marshalling yards on the 12th. One aircraft failed to return from the first of these, Flt/Sgt L. J. Redden RAAF losing an engine over the target, and eventually ditching in the Adriatic. Leo Redden writes:

> The plane only floated about 30 seconds and I had broken my arm and cut my head, making me dizzy. The escape hatch over my head was open and water came in as the plane sank. This woke me up and I realized I was going down with it, as my helmet was still on and connected to the oxygen. I released my chin strap and the helmet went down with the plane but my right flying boot caught in the aerial and took me down again, so I kicked the boot off and that too went down with the plane and I popped up and got into the rubber dinghy where I found the rest of the crew, thank goodness.

The crew were rescued by an ASR Walrus and returned to Foggia, where Redden was admitted to hospital.

A ditching also followed the second visit to Budapest. Sixteen aircraft—a maximum effort—were briefed, and twelve bombed successfully by illumination provided by W/O Bradshaw and Flt/Sgt St. Clair. Night fighters were reported, but no combats, and the ditching of the Wellington piloted by the recently arrived Flight Commander, Sqn/Ldr C. E. Mervyn-Jones, was caused by a holed petrol tank. Cameron Mervyn-Jones writes:

> The aircraft bounced once then dug its nose into the water. The dinghy in the starboard wing opened automatically. Except myself in front and the rear gunner in the tail, the rest of the crew climbed along the wing into the dinghy. I swam round from the nose which was sinking and then we paddled to the tail to pick up the rear gunner, P/O Tester. He was high and dry on the tail plane, and being rather cheerful, but he stepped off and missed the dinghy so we had to drag him out of the water. However he kept up his high spirits and did wonders for our morale during the rest of the venture.
> By this time the aircraft was lit up from inside by all the incendiaries going off—then it quickly slid under the surface with a cloud of smoke and flame. It seemed only a minute of so—then we were sitting quietly on our own in a rubber dinghy in the misty moonlight.

On 15 April 40 sent fifteen aircraft to the marshalling yards at Turnul Severin, the highest point on the Danube accessible to sea-going vessels. Two aircraft (P/O J. R. Perkins RAAF and W/O Bradshaw) provided what the ORB describes as 'perfect illumination' and twelve aircraft bombed in very close concentration. Photographs taken the following day by the 15th Air Force showed heavy damage to the yards, docks, grain silos and industrial buildings. Success, though, came at a cost, 40 losing one aircraft (Sgt J. C. J. Bailey) to flak.

The last non-Italian target for April was Plovdiv in Bulgaria on the 17th. Only three Wellingtons detailed got away, however, for the fourth (F/O E. P. Payne) burst a tyre on take-off, crashed and caught fire. Ground crew and ambulance men got the crew out before the bombs exploded, but only the rear gunner (Sgt A. Knight) escaped injury, all the others sustaining burns, from which the bomb-aimer (F/O J. E. Emery) later died. As this crash demonstrated, despite the strenuous efforts that were made to cope with the problem, including an inspection of tyres prior to the take-off run, there could be no guarantee of safety. The problem was principally the metal fragments left by Allied bombing the previous year. The Group Engineering Officer designed and built a powerful magnet which was towed behind a truck, but though it proved effective, fresh fragments were constantly working their way to the surface.

Tyre damage caused a very high wastage rate, and the Engineering Report appended to the April 205 Group ORB drew attention to a shortage of Wellington tyres, and to a request that that only heavy treaded tyres be

71. Post mortem: JA509, 18 April 1944. (l to r) Flt/Sgt Paddy Montgomery,
Flt/Sgt C. H. Goodridge, Sgt A. G. Reddy. (C. H. Goodridge.)

supplied for use by the Group. The problem was not solved, however, until
the Wellingtons were replaced by Liberators in March 1945.

During the first four months of 1944 the number of nights on which
operational flying took place was disappointingly low: 15 in January, 11 each
in February and March, and 18 in April. May brought better weather, 205
Group squadrons operating on 27 out of 31 nights, and 40 Squadron on 22
of these. But the increased tempo was accompanied by increased losses, 40
losing eight crews during the month.

Save for a successful attack on La Spezia on the 1st, the only raid on an
Italian target during the first ten days of May was by three aircraft on Genoa
on the 9th. Seven attacks, however, were mounted on targets in Hungary,
Romania and Southern France. The first of these, against Bucharest on 3
May, was foiled by strong cross winds which prevented all but the flare-
droppers (W/O Bradshaw and P/O Perkins) taking off. On the next two
nights, however, 40 was involved in highly successful attacks. On 4 May
twelve crews attacked the Rakos marshalling yards, Budapest, bombing
accurately. Night fighters were active, one Wellington (W/O T. J. Wasson
RAAF) being attacked by an Me 410. The fighter opened fire at 400 yards,
damaging the Wellington's hydraulics, but was driven off by the rear gunner
(Sgt D. Heathcote). Wasson bombed successfully, then made a good landing
at Foggia without flaps.

Night fighters were also active on the 5th, when eleven Wellingtons
attacked Campina marshalling yards and oil refinery, north of Ploesti. Many
direct hits were scored on the marshalling yards, oil storage tanks and refinery

buildings. Two crews reported fighter attacks, the rear gunner driving off the fighter in each case, but a third (Flt/Sgt D. H. Royle) went down in flames over the target.

On 6 May the targets were again Romanian, eight aircraft being sent to Bucharest, and one (F/O Dunn) carrying out a low level precision attack on a bridge at Pitesti. The latter proved a difficult target, and neither Dunn nor a crew from 330 Wing hit it, though Dunn's 4,000 pounder landed only about twenty-five yards away. He brought his Wellington back to Foggia unscathed, but two of those raiding Bucharest were not so lucky. One aircraft (Flt/Sgt K. C. J. Martin RAAF) was hit by flak over the Yugoslav coast, and first one and then the other engine failed. Keith Martin recalled that after the rest of the crew had baled out,

> I made my way to the hatch and then remembered that I had not destroyed the I. F. F. and so went back to the cockpit and did so and finally jumped. I have no recollection of the descent. My next memory is some 45 minutes later when I found myself walking along with my parachute trailing behind me. I had no idea where I was or where I had come from, but knew that I had to hide my parachute.

Martin and his crew were captured by the Bulgarians and spent four months in conditions even more wretched than those in the Romanian camp where fellow Australian John Coape-Smith and three of his crew found themselves. After bombing, Coape-Smith's Wellington was lit up by flares which had ignited above the aircraft, rather than, as was supposed to happen, well below. A night fighter took advantage of this, killing the rear gunner (Flt/Sgt R. G. Sauerwald RAAF) on the first pass and wounding the wireless operator (Sgt R. D. Kilroy RAAF) on the second. George Dealtry, the bomb aimer, recalls:

> Before we had gone very far fire broke out in the centre section seemingly in the bomb bay, presumably started by a flare damaged in the attack. Unable to get to the seat of the fire it soon swept through the plane and Johnny gave orders to all of us to bale out quick smart. Dick, the wireless operator, was the first to go after the hatch had been opened. His chute was clipped on, he grabbed the ripcord handle and we pushed him out. He was still conscious despite the leg wounds. Jed [Flt/Sgt G. Cormie] the navigator was next, followed by me, after I had passed a parachute to Johnny from the stowage rack much to his surprise and no doubt heart-felt relief as only seconds earlier we had discovered one chute partially destroyed by fire; leaving us one short, we thought.

A feature of the Bucharest raid of 6 May was the first use of the Halifaxes of 614 Squadron in the Pathfinding role for which they had been training.[2] Beginning with a raid by on Plovdiv marshalling yards on 19 April, they had operated on their own throughout that month, developing the H2S radar techniques which were to be employed in target finding and marking for all 205 Group squadrons. Despite its designation 614 was scarcely an elite unit at this time, for the 205 Group summary for April comments:

> Training of No. 614 Squadron continued and 'Nursery targets' were attacked using 'Newhaven method'. Results were very varied and the poor quality of crews supplied by the UK was apparent at every stage. Improvement, however, was sustained, and towards the end of the month the Squadron was beginning to attain a reasonable standard.

John Coape-Smith and his crew no doubt thought that 614 still had something to learn.

Having sent eight crews to Bucharest and one to a bridge on 5 May, 40 repeated the process the following night. The bridge, at Filiasi, had been attacked without success on the 5th by three Wellingtons, one flown by the CO of 104 Squadron, Wg/Cdr H. E. Turner. The next night Turner went back to Filiasi again, accompanied this time by W/O Tom Bradshaw and his highly experienced crew.

Turner bombed from 600 feet, again without success, and Bradshaw's crew, after a dummy run, came in at 200 feet. Knowing that at this height the Mk XIV bombsight was useless, Bradshaw and his bomb aimer (P/O McKenna) had devised a method of sighting whereby the guns in the nose turret were trained at a previously calculated angle of depression. When the aiming point passed the muzzles of the guns, the bomb aimer, in the turret, released the bomb.

On the run in Bradshaw's Wellington was engaged by light flak, and McKenna called out that he was hit, but could still aim the bomb. He called 'Bomb gone', but when the W/Op (Sgt W. Taylor) went forward to help, he found McKenna dead. Meanwhile the Wellington was in trouble, with the starboard fuel tanks holed and the port engine over-revving dangerously. The crew therefore baled out, the four survivors meeting up with Chetnik partisans, and returning to Foggia fourteen weeks later.

While Bradshaw's crew were attacking the Filiasi bridge, eight others were following up the previous night's bombing of Bucharest. Seven located and bombed the target; the eighth, (Flt/Lt G. W. Williams) was shot down in flames, only the rear gunner (F/O H. D. Calvert) escaping by parachute.

Forty had now lost five crews in three nights, and the bad luck continued on 9 May, when one of six Wellingtons attacking a glider bomb factory at Portes-les-Valences, France, failed to return. The Wellingtons, operating at extreme range, refuelled at Ajaccio, Corsica, and the plan called for the breaching of a wall surrounding the factory, enabling the Maquis to seize key components for transmission to Britain for examination. Ken Dunn recalls that four crews were to 'come down over the factory at 500 feet to drop our 4,000-lb medium case bombs against the factory wall', while as a diversion other crews would attack a secondary target near by. 'The success of the operation', Dunn continues, 'depended on pinpoint bombing, which in turn depended on clear visibility.' Unfortunately, despite a promising forecast, thick cloud obscured the target. Attempting to get below the cloud, one aircraft (F/O J. Huggler) crashed in the hills near Valence. It was the crew's last operation of their tour, Huggler's second with the Squadron.

Two crews were also lost attacking Italian targets in May. On the 11th 40 carried out the first of three harassing attacks on Porto Ferrajo, Elba. Little opposition was encountered, and the loss of P/O D. M. Cleeve was possibly due to the weather. The same cause was suspected when Sgt F. J. Broad failed to return from Valmontone on 24 May, other crews reporting severe electrical storms and icing. Valmontone was attacked because it lay on the route between Rome and Cassino, where an Allied offensive had been launched, and attacks on Viterbo and Subicco were also in support of the new offensive. Targets in the battle area were hard to locate, however, and the results often uncertain.

Two further raids during May deserve mention. The first, on the 28th, was another individual attack, W/O Wasson's crew targeting the railway through the Brenner Pass. The brief, an imaginative one, was to drop a 4,000-lb bomb on the mountainside in the hope of starting an avalanche, blocking the line. Wasson's crew located the target, bombed, and obtained a good photo. There was little snow, however, and it was thought unlikely that an avalanche resulted.

The other raid of note, on 31 May, was a first for 40, though 205 Group had despatched Liberators and Wellingtons to lay mines in the Danube on three occasions since 12 April. Requiring moonlight to locate the river and the 'bed' allocated to each aircraft, and carried out at low level (no more than 300 feet) and at 100 mph, the mining operations could be 'dicey' if there were flak barges on the river, or emplacements on the banks. The raid of 31 May was without loss, but one of 40's eleven Wellingtons was hit by flak en route to the target. With the trimmers unserviceable, Flt/Sgt A. T. Boswell and his crew went on to drop their mines and strafe barges.

May had been a hard month for 40, with eight crews lost, a quarter of the nine-squadron Group total of 32 aircraft. Moreover Foggia Main continued to be much the most hazardous 205 Group base for take-offs and landings, the Group engineering report for May noting that 'an average of only 3 operational take-offs and landings was maintained [for each tyre] throughout the month . . . [where] the other wings averaged from 7 to 9 operational take-offs and landings per main wheel tyre.' No 40 Squadron aircraft had crashed on take off or landing since Peter Payne's on 17 April, but the anxiety level remained high, and with reason.

June 1944 brought a continued mix of Italian and other targets, the former mostly in support of ground operations. On 3 June, with the Americans approaching Rome, 205 Group carried out a particularly successful attack on a bridge over the Tiber between Rome and Ostia. Seven aircraft operated as part of a fifty strong force which in good weather, and without opposition, bombed accurately, badly damaging the bridge approaches. Later in the month, Italian oil installations were singled out, with a particularly successful raid on the Aquila Oil Refinery at Trieste (26 June). Opposition was slight, and no aircraft were hit, but one (Flt/Lt D. B. Rodd RCAF), having had one tyre burst on take-off, burst the other on landing. The crew escaped injury, but the runway was blocked, and other aircraft were diverted to Tortorella and Amendola.

Forty attacked targets outside Italy on eleven nights in June, hitting oil refineries, marshalling yards, and aerodromes in Hungary, Romania, Bulgaria, Austria and Southern Germany. The hottest target was undoubtedly Munich, on 13 June. Four 205 Group aircraft failed to return including one (P/O M. R. Denson RAAF) from 40 Squadron. The Wellington was coned near Munich, and the wireless operator, Phil Kirby, recalls that the aircraft 'did a complete slow roll with the help of flak bursting under one wing before the old lady gave up'. Denson and his crew, including a wireless operator on a 'look and see' trip (Sgt A. W. Belverstone) were lucky to get out before the aircraft exploded.

The Munich raid was a failure, crews being unable to identify the Railway Station aiming point. There were few other failures during the month, however, and some notable successes, including attacks on oil refineries at Brod (Yugoslavia), Budapest, and Almasfuzito (Hungary), and Giurgiu (Romania), which was hit particularly hard on 2 June at the cost of one aircraft (Flt/Sgt F. R. Hughes RAAF), which crashed near Pirot, in Yugoslavia. Only the navigator (Flt/Sgt K. Shaw) survived.

While 205 Group attacked by night, the USAAF's 15th Air Force bombed by day, and during June 205 Group attempted to assist the Americans by hitting enemy fighter bases. A raid on Karlovo aerodrome, in Bulgaria, on 24 June, was cancelled because of bad weather, and an earlier one on the 11th also posed weather problems, with 10/10ths cloud, electrical storms and icing en route. Even so five crews identified the aerodrome, and bombed from 7,000 feet, causing a great deal of damage; 205 Group received a Message of Commendation for this raid, in which many fighters were destroyed or damaged. After bombing P/O J. Bellock RAAF decided to go down and strafe:

> I put Bob Clegg [bomb aimer] in the front turret and of course Roly Bowering stayed in the rear turret. We swooped over the main runway at a very low

level. Both Bob and Roly were very excited and claimed that they had set on fire a very large hangar as well as some German fighter planes.

At debriefing, Jack Bellock recalls, it was pointed out that the hangar the crew claimed to have set on fire could not be seen in the photos taken before the raid. He adds:

> I remember worrying that my crew and I might be branded as "bull-artists". It was quite a relief when 24 hours later pictures taken by a photo reconnaissance plane showed clearly the burned-out hangar that we'd claimed, as well as many aircraft destroyed.

After May's heavy losses June brought a respite, with 2 crews lost out of a Group total of 34. But July was to see 40 again suffer heavily, this time losing 10 aircraft, the most in a single month during the entire war. Moreover 6 of those crews were to be lost in the first week.

The month opened with a Danube minelaying operation. 205 Group rated the operation a success, but it was dearly bought for 236 Wing, which lost four aircraft. Intense and accurate light flak and searchlights were encountered over 40's beds, east of Belgrade, and as the Wellingtons dropped their mines two were shot down and three others damaged, one of these (Sgt E. E. R. Paterson) returning with the rear gunner (Sgt T. Horwood) dead in his turret. The only member of Sgt Waddell's crew to survive was the rear gunner (Sgt K. Withnall), who was blown clear in his turret, which (miraculously) had its landing cushioned by trees. Close behind Waddell's aircraft when it exploded was Sgt W. Booth's. Bill Goodbrand, the navigator, writes:

> We followed and, as the banks of the Danube at that point were higher than our 200 feet, the flak and machine-guns were actually firing down at us. Just after dropping our mines we were hit quite badly, and although Wally Booth, our skipper, managed to get us back up to 800 feet, it was obvious we were not going any further. We headed south and then baled out. I was second last out and was, I think, still in the air when I heard our aircraft crash.

Booth's crew were fortunate enough to fall in with a Chetnik band, and in August were flown out to Italy, together with members of two other 40 Squadron crews.

On 2 July five aircraft bombed Prahova Oil Refinery, Bucharest, on Target Indicators laid accurately by 614 Squadron. Night fighters were active, downing a SAAF Liberator and two 40 Squadron Wellingtons. Both fell on the return journey to night fighters which raked them from below, killing the rear gunners. One (F/O L. F. Tichbourne RAAF), crashed in Romania, the four remaining crew baling out safely. The other (Flt/Sgt R. D. Sutcliffe RCAF) was brought down over eastern Yugoslavia when, after three attacks the Wellington became uncontrollable and Dick Sutcliffe ordered the crew out. Sgts. J. E. Turnbull and J. D. Yole, the bomb aimer and navigator, were first to go, Turnbull meeting a Chetnik band and returning to the Squadron with Boswell's crew. Yole, however, was shot either as he parachuted down, or after he landed. Sutcliffe himself was fortunate to escape through the hatch over the pilot's head, sucked out by his already opened parachute, while the W/Op (Sgt E. H. Turner) who had been lying stunned on the floor of the aircraft, and taken for dead, came to in time to bale out himself. Both Sutcliffe and Turner were taken prisoner by the occupying Bulgarian army.

On 29 June, 6 of 40's Wellingtons were part of a force of 74 which bombed Feuersbrunn Aerodrome, west of Vienna. All claimed to have bombed the target, starting fires, and scoring hits on aircraft in the dispersal areas. Only light AA fire was encountered, and just two 205 Group aircraft failed to return. On a return visit on 6 July, however, the Luftwaffe were waiting, and in clear moonlight 13 out of 61 aircraft were lost, a loss rate of 21%. Forty lost 2 crews, captained by RAAF P/Os R. T. Collins and E. Hall, and returning crews reported seeing as many as 3 aircraft falling at once in flames in the target area and to the south of it. Many crews also sighted night fighters, and one (P/O Bellock) had a successful encounter, the rear gunner (Flt/Sgt R. Bowering RAAF) shooting down a Ju 88.

Forty had now lost six crews in a week, and two more (Sgt N. Walters and P/O C. Charalambous) failed to return from raids on the Lambrate marshalling yards, Milan, on 10 and 13 July. The raids, however, were highly successful, rolling stock trapped in the yards when the exits were destroyed during the first raid being destroyed in the second. It seems that a night fighter accounted for the second loss, but that of Sgt Walters was probably due to flak.

After the visit to Milan on 13 July, only one further attack that month was made on an Italian target, thirteen Wellingtons bombing the Ronsa Oil Refinery, Fiume, on the 19th. Oil targets were also prominent in the places attacked outside Italy, Brod and Smederevo in Yugoslavia, Pardubice in Czechoslovakia, and Prahova and Ploesti in Romania. Of these raids the least successful were probably those on Prahova, on 23 and 27 July, neither of which did much damage, while that on Ploesti on the 26th was foiled by a very effective smoke screen, crews bombing on the estimated position of the target.

The attack on the oil refinery at Pardubice also began badly, with two aircraft returning early and a third (Sgt R. W. F. Bodley) turning back near the Yugoslav coast with fuel problems, the crew abandoning their aircraft over the Italian coast. The remaining nine crews bombed on TIs and flares, starting a fire with thick black smoke which blanketed the target, but it was subsequently found that this was a factory some distance from the aiming-point.

72. Tour completed: P/O Jack Hall RAAF and crew, July 1944.
(l to r) Flt/Sgt T. Briggs (AG), Flt/Sgt A. Bridge (AB), P/O J. Hall (Pilot),
F/O D. Dovey (Nav) and Flt/Sgt B. H. Burdsall (W/Op). (B. H. Burdsall.)

The three raids on Yugoslav targets all went well, the most satisifying being the first on oil storage tanks at Brod, where fires were visible for nearly 100 miles. A second attack, on 14 July, was also successful, though the smoke from fires made observation of bomb bursts difficult, while that on the refinery at Smederevo on 16 July resulted in a large fire, one crew (Flt/Sgt J. A. Hall RAAF) reporting that its 4,000-lb bomb exploded amidst the TIs. There were reports of night fighters, and one aircraft went down in flames over the target. This was probably captained by Sgt A. W. Radley, whose crew was the ninth lost in July.

The final operation for the month, on 30 July, was to mine Danube beds in Hungary, Yugoslavia and Romania. Forty's beds were in Romania, near Moldova Veche, where the Danube flowed between steep cliffs. These made low flying hazardous, and eight light flak positions on the river banks added to the risks. Nonetheless, the five Wellingtons completed the drop successfully and without loss, Flt/Lt Rodd's gunners strafing a motor patrol boat, and 7,000 rounds being fired at barges from the front and rear turrets of W/O A. L. Mayers' aircraft.

July was a bad month for 205 Group, which lost 44 aircraft, and for 40 Squadron, which lost 10 aircraft and 9 crews. The Group had now lost 110 aircraft in three months, 20 of them from 40 Squadron. With a loss rate comparable with that in Bomber Command, yet crews required to fly forty ops for a tour, the effect on morale was considerable, and it was fortunate that the July loss rate did not continue.

August 1944 opened with eight days respite, but when 40 did get airborne, on the 9th, the target was a tough one: the Romana-Americana oil refinery at Ploesti. Five Wellingtons operated that night, (others were grounded by contaminated oil, which restricted 104 Squadron to 4 aircraft) part of an 81 strong force of which 11 failed to return—a loss rate of 12.5%. The target was defended by up to 100 searchlights and sixty heavy guns, and the Pathfinder Halifaxes were repeatedly coned, hence the Target Indicators were less than certainly placed, while the Ploesti smokescreen obscured ground features. Crews bombed on the TIs, but photo-analysis revealed that their bombs were scattered to the north of the target.

Flt/Sgt Ian Arrowsmith RAAF was flying a 'second dickie' trip with W/O Mayers that night, prior to taking his crew on their first operation together. It was, he recalls, 'a rather frightening experience for a young fellow':

> By the time we arrived it was just a continual sea of blacky-grey smoke and the target markers that had been put down by the pathfinders became lost in the smoke.
>
> I was very impressed with Mayers' crew. They were very, very competent and alert. Sitting in the cockpit with Mayers, as we turned on our last leg and went towards Ploesti, we could see there in front of us, the most frightening display of pyrotechnics, . . . dozens and dozens of guns firing up the radar operated searchlight beams.
>
> The guns were blasting away in a continual sheet of explosions above the refineries and it was amazing that aircraft managed to fit through them. Our height was about 10,000 feet. Mayers opened up his engines, put his nose slightly down and charged through, straight as a die, hard as he could to get up to speed, wandering up to about 220–230 knots (which was very fast for a Wellington) really pushing it along. We bombed in the middle of the target markers as we were supposed to do and then, when he turned away, he immediately started diving for the ground. He told me that this was the practice and it was quite possible in these areas; it enabled them to dodge the night-fighters. Mayers then flew low over the Danubian fields. When we reached the Yugoslav mountains we put on power and climbed up over them.

Mayers escaped unscathed. Jack Bellock's aircraft was coned, and though he tried everything he knew, including diving from 9,000 feet to 6,000 feet, it was of no avail. He recalls:

> Suddenly, something hit my plane. The port engine was completely covered with smoke. I lost control of the plane, the controls actually jerked loose from my hands and the plane started going down in a crazy dive. I tried to level

it off but couldn't and in desperation told my crew to stand by to bale out. Roly Bowering, our tail gunner, saved us. In a very calm voice he said, "Come on skipper, you can get us home."

Though they were diving at 325 mph, Bellock managed, by 'straightening out the control stick then putting my two feet on the panel in front of me and yanking the control column with all the strength I had, to get the aircraft out of its dive at 600 ft., and clear of Ploesti.' 'I recall very vividly', he continues,

> returning back to Foggia without our radio or our hydraulic system. We didn't know if we could put our starboard wheel down. We were not sure if it was going to hold or not. I remember landing, not knowing if I was going to make it. But again we were lucky and the wheel held. I remember taxiing it off the runway, getting it into the dispersal, calling up the control tower and announcing that we'd landed, taxied back and completed our tour of operational flying, and saying what a relief it was. Then I remember getting out of our faithful Wimpy, our faithful N for Nuts, hugging the crew, hugging our ground crew, watching Harry McClure [W/Op] kissing the ground.

The 9 August raid was the penultimate attack on Ploesti before the Romanians capitulated. The last was on 17 August, when eleven Wellingtons were put up. Two returned early, while two others were lost en route to the target. Nothing was heard of Sgt D. J. Francis after take-off, but his may have been the aircraft which crashed into a hillside north of Lake Scutari, and burst into flames. The other aircraft lost (Sgt Paterson) crashed, killing all aboard, near Pitesti. Reports suggest that his Wellington may have been crippled by a night fighter, then brought down by flak. The results of the bombing were not considered particularly successful, and it was subsequently established that little damage was done to the Xenia refinery.

Besides the two visits to Romania, and four to Italian targets, 40 also attacked targets in Hungary and Yugoslavia during August. The Yugoslav target, the Kraljevo marshalling yards, was hit hard on 10 August, but the raid on the Hungarian air base at Hadju Boszormeny, two days later, was less satisfactory, the TIs being placed south-east of the aerodrome, and photo-analysis showing that only Flt/Sgt R. S. Trigg had bombed the hangars and dispersal area. Two further Hungarian targets, the oil refinery at Komarom and marshalling yards at Miscolc, were attacked on 21 and 22 August, with accurate bombing on well-placed TIs. There was substantial ground and air opposition on both occasions, with aircraft shot down south of the target on the Komarom raid. One of these may have been that captained by F/O J. Barnett, which failed to return.

In support of the Allied landings, 40 also attacked two targets in Southern France during August. The first, on the 14th, on the port of Marseilles, went well, the six Wellingtons concentrating their bombing on well-placed

TIs. By contrast, at the La Tresonie aerodrome, near Valence, the next night, the TIs were well off target. Neither raid met much opposition, but the Hermann Goering Works at St. Valentin, Austria, on 20 August, was a different proposition, with 70–100 searchlights operating in belts and cones in the Steyr-Linz region, supported by accurate heavy flak. One aircraft (W/O R. J. A. Church) was coned, and suffered considerable damage, the fabric inboard of the nacelle being stripped from the upper surface of the port wing. In retaliation Church's rear gunner (Sgt E. Knott) shot out a master searchlight, which caused about eight or nine others to go out. Despite the damage, Church landed safely at Foggia.

The six raids on Italian targets during August were almost all in support of Allied ground forces. On the 25th the target was the already damaged marshalling yards at Bologna. Photo reconnaissance showed additional damage to the Station (40's target) and nearby buildings, though the tracks remained serviceable. The next night it was Ravenna's turn, a successful raid resulting in heavy damage to tracks and wagons in the marshalling yard, and to quayside and canal basin facilities. Eight aircraft operated, one, captained by the A Flight Commander Sqn/Ldr S. D. Angus RAAF, and including the Bombing Leader (Flt/Lt C. F. Mohs RCAF) being detailed to attack a gun position to the north of the town. Having circled for a few minutes, however, waiting for the gun to fire, they joined the bomber stream.

August ended with a three day 'mail run' to Pesaro, anchor on the Adriatic coast for the German Gothic Line. The principal target was a German division reported in the town, and on 26 August harassing tactics were employed, the six Wellingtons bombing by their own flares. The next two nights, however, 614 Squadron dropped TIs. The bombing was well concentrated and opposition light, which was probably just as well for a Liberator which 'provided a diversion for some of [40's] crews' in leaving the target with its navigation lights on.

The weather in August was often bad, but September proved kinder, with 40 up on eighteen nights, to targets in Italy, Greece, Yugoslavia and Hungary. Nine of the twelve raids on Italian targets involved marshalling yards, Ferrara, Ravenna, Rimini, Milan, Brescia and Bologna being hit, the last three times. Two of these ops, on 1 and 12 September went well, but the raid on the 6th failed, with 10/10ths cloud over the target. Two crews jettisoned their bombs in the sea, while the remainder bombed the estimated target area, or a glow and flak seen through the cloud. Ground opposition was light, and fighters were not encountered, so the loss of F/O G. P. Roberts' crew, on their first operation, was mysterious. They may have come down in the Adriatic, since several crews saw flashes which seemed to be a signal of some kind, perhaps from a dinghy.

The results of the other attacks varied from failure (Milan, 10 September) through partial success (bombs well grouped on inaccurately placed target markers, Ferrara, 2nd) to highly successful (Brescia, 17th). No further losses occurred, though night fighters were occasionally encountered, forcing one aircraft (Sgt D. Hanson) to jettison its bombs and turn back on the 2nd.

The attacks on marshalling yards were an indirect method of supporting Allied ground forces. More directly, on 18 September ten Wellingtons bombed a German troop concentration near Rimini, reporting good illumination and accurate bombing, while four nights later the Squadron bombed a pontoon bridge and nearby troops and transport at San Benedetto. Crews bombed the TIs accurately, but photographs revealed that they had were wide of the target.

Six targets outside Italy were scheduled in September. Three were in Greece, where the German forces were beginning their withdrawal, the first two, on 13 and 14 September, with Tatoi aerodrome, Athens, as the target. Scattered flares and ground haze hampered the first attack, while on the second only three crews claimed to have bombed Tatoi, others believing they hit Kalamaki or Eleusis aerodromes. At the latter Flt/Lt G. A. McGaw reported three large fires as he left.

The third Greek target was Salonika on 21 September, when nine aircraft bombed port facilities used by German divisions withdrawing from the Aegean islands. The bombing was scattered, with the main weight of bombs falling on the marshalling yards a short distance inland. The flak was heavy, and one aircraft (Sgt R. Regan) returned to base with its flaps ripped away and hydraulic system damaged.

Two attacks on Hungarian marshalling yards were made in September, Szekesfehervar being attacked on the 19th, and Hegyeshalom the following night. Misplaced TIs meant that the town suffered more than the marshalling yards in the first raid, but the second was accurate and destructive, one fire being visible for eighty miles on the return journey. The flak was light and inaccurate on both nights, but on the second fighters were encountered, with several aircraft shot down. Flt/Sgt C. C. Westwood RAAF and his crew came down in Yugoslavia, but were aided by partisans and returned to the Squadron on 23 October.

The last non-Italian target for September, Barovnica railway viaduct, was bombed unopposed. One span had been blown up by partisans in 1941, and it was the replacement, a steel lattice structure, which was the main objective. The TIs were well-placed, with one group so close to the viaduct that it was illuminated by them, and the excellence of the bombing was confirmed by photo reconnaissance.

Minelaying could only be carried out at full moon, or nearly so, in order to identify the Danube 'beds'. On 5 September, six Wellingtons were

73. A-Able safely away, Foggia Main, Autumn 1944. (O. W. G. Chant.)

allocated two beds in the Yugoslav section of the river. Five dropped as designated, but the sixth (F/O A. V. Rippengal, on his second tour with the Squadron) missed its bed, and dropped its mines in a bend of the Danube above Paks, where there were many barges, the rear gunner silencing flak positions which opened up on the aircraft. On 4th October a further mining operation was mounted, with nine Wellingtons detailed for beds between Medve and Bratislava. Flak was encountered, and one aircraft was lost and another badly damaged. Sgt Regan, laying mines near Dobrohost, encountered accurate light flak, which shot off the Wellington's port elevator, but returned safely. W/O Mayers, close behind, was less lucky, for his aircraft was hit, caught fire and exploded.

The mining op of 4 October was the last flown by 205 Group, and Mayers' aircraft the last shot down. Forty had lost three aircraft in four raids, with others seriously damaged. These figures fall far short of the claims of many who took part in the minelaying that heavy losses occcurred on every raid. But their memories convey the dread which Danube mining aroused. 'Running the gauntlet' is a phrase frequently used, and accurately. Yet the mining campaign was effective, intelligence reports indicating that river shipping in August was 70% below the figure in April, when mining began. For cost-effectiveness, the mining of the Danube must rate as one of 205 Group's greatest achievements.

Bad weather prevented 40 operating again until 9 October, when eight Wellingtons carried out harassing attacks on airfields around Athens being used by Ju52s evacuating German troops from southern Greece, seven bringing back photos which clearly showed the various airfields. At Eleusis F/O Rippengal had the satisfaction of seeing bombs hit hangars, causing explosions.

On the next four nights 40 was active against marshalling yards. On the 10th and 11th, the target was Verona, a crucial point in the German supply system using the railway through the Brenner Pass. On the 10th the bombing was inaccurate. The next night, however, 40 did better, the bombing being concentrated, and good photos obtained. Verona was well defended, however, and on the 11th two aircraft (Flt/Sgt Bodley and P/O F. Wood) failed to return. These may have been the Wellingtons coned and shot down over the target.

With A and B Flights operating alternately, the Squadron customarily put up six to eight aircraft a night. On 8 October, however, following the disbanding of 330 Wing, 11 crews were posted in from 142 and 150 Squadrons, and operating at a strength not seen since June and July 1942, the Squadron put up 12–15 crews nightly, and occasionally 16 or 17, until by attrition the numbers fell to normal again. In December this would happen again, with the posting in of six 37 Squadron crews which, near to completing tours, did not wish to convert to Liberators.

On 12 October, the Squadron bombed the yards at Bronzolo. Patchy cloud made target identification difficult, and the markers were late, though accurate. Four crews thought they had bombed the yards, but reconnaissance showed negligible damage. By contrast, an attack on the Szekesfehervar yards the next night was most successful, all ten aircraft bombing accurately. Large fires were started, and it took German and Hungarian repair teams several days to recommission the yards. The flak and searchlight defences were described as moderate to intense, and fighters were active. Of four bombers lost one (Sgt G. W. Moore) was from 40 Squadron. There were no survivors. Australian Flt/Lt Ted Marriott was captain of one of the crews up that night, and he recalls:

> This was only our fourth op. and we were still pretty green. We had been admiring the pretty colours of mysterious lights seen here and there until at debriefing we heard of all our planes which had been shot down.

Three successful attacks on marshalling yards followed, Opicina (Trieste) and Zagreb and Vincovci being visited on 15, 16 and 17 October, and the Yugoslav yards completely blocked. The pontoon bridge at San Benedetto, to which 40 returned on 20 October, was a tougher proposition, however. It had been attacked twice previously, and unsuccessfully, on 22 September and 4 October. The third attack which involved only 40 Squadron, was in three waves, and designed to destroy the bridge if possible, but at least to disrupt its use. Each wave consisted of two flare droppers and three bombers, the latter reporting that the bridge was well illuminated. Even so, the most that crews could claim was that approach roads had been hit.

On 20 October Soviet forces and Tito's Yugoslav National Army liberated Belgrade. With large areas of the countryside now in YNA hands, and German garrisons on the defensive, support for Tito was stepped up, and on the 29th there was a 'first' for 40 Squadron, with the dropping of supplies by day to the YNA north-east of the German-held port of Kotor. Sixteen aircraft operated, but only one located the ground marker, a Y in white stones, the remainder dropping the supply canisters on dead reckoning or Gee fixes. It was later found that though an incorrect fix had been signalled, the containers fell in partisan-held territory, and most were recovered. Two days later a second supply drop took place further inland, near Tuzla. Two crews saw the ground marker, but others identified the town, while sky markers appeared well-placed.

The supply drops on 29 and 31 October were followed by many more in November, generally to Tito's forces, but occasionally to Italian partisans. The majority of these drops were made by day, reflecting the total dominance of the skies by the Allied air forces. Typical of such operations were drops to the Yugoslav forces on 5 November, and Italian partisans on the 10th. The first of these was a daylight operation and all crews identified the drop zone near Karlovac, the containers falling close to the marker. Townsfolk were seen waiting for the canisters to be dropped, and later arrivals saw a pile of containers in a lane awaiting transportation. Only scattered and ineffectual flak was encountered.

The Italian drop was in the Chiapovano area, east of Udine, where small groups of partisans were harrying the German supply route to Ljubljana. Eleven aircraft operated, but in very bad weather, with electrical storms and a low cloud base, one (Flt/Sgt J. P. Baker) crashed into a hillside near San Severo soon after take-off, killing all aboard. The bad weather also forced Flt/Sgt Arrowsmith to turn back after a severe shaking had rendered the Artificial Horizon and Turn and Bank Indicators inoperative. The remaining nine aircraft found, however, that the weather improved as they flew north, and the H ground marker and D flashed as ID were easily discerned. A successful drop followed.

Interspersed with the supply drops were bombing operations, all but two on Yugoslav targets. Communications were invariably the target, whether marshalling yards, roads or motor transport. Typical raids were those on the marshalling yards at Sarajevo (7 November) and on roads near Novi Pazar (18th). In the latter attack eight aircraft were detailed to search out motor transport. Small groups of trucks were located and bombed, and F/O

74. Wg/Cdr John Kirwan congratulates LACs R. E. Williams and W. J. Clarke, awarded
the George Medal for their part in the rescue of P/O Payne and crew, April 1944.
(J. E. Oram.)

H. Smart unloaded on a convoy which became enveloped in smoke. When
this cleared four or five trucks were missing.

Outside of Italy and Jugoslavia 40's only target in November was the
marshalling yards at Szombathely, in Hungary. It was undoubtedly the most
difficult that month, and also the greatest failure. Pathfinder Halifaxes operated, but no markers were seen *en route*, or over the target. Flares were
observed on time, but only three crews judged them to be in the target
area, and bombed, as they did not illuminate satisfactorily. One other crew
claimed to have found and bombed Target Indicators, while another bombed
a railway one mile south-east of the estimated position of the town, with
the remainder jettisoning their bombs over the sea.

There was negligible flak, but the night fighters were very active. F/O
W. L. Priestly RAAF was attacked over the target, but evaded by cork-
screwing, the bombs being jettisoned. Air to air firing was noted near by,

75. Target photo: Ballinclay drop zone, 4 December 1944. (C. F. Mohs.)

and this may have been the exchange between Sgt H. A. C. Butler's rear gunner (Sgt J. A. Skerritt) and a Ju 88. The latter's fire was inaccurate, Skerritt's was not, and the 88 caught fire and crashed. Two other fighters were then sighted, one of which attacked, but was driven off. Sgt J. Dunling's rear gunner (Sgt L. Burnett) was also in action, firing 1,000 rounds at a pursuing fighter. No results were observed, and though a flash was seen on the ground immediately afterwards, the crew refrained from claiming success. One Wellington (Flt/Sgt A. J. M. Starr) was lost.

Supply drops to partisans continued with eight drops in December. No aerial opposition was encountered, and flak only occasionally, the chief problems being weather, locating the drop zones and the embarrassingly frequent failure of parachutes to open. A typical night drop was that on 3 December, when six crews were detailed to supply partisans near Berane. 10/10ths cloud covered the drop zone, and aircraft dropped on Gee co-ordinates, as briefed. All the containers were dropped, but at least eight parachutes either failed to open, or opened only partially. The next night clear visibility enabled the twelve crews to drop containers accurately, but again there was a high percentage of faulty parachutes: 10 out of 70. No opposition was encountered, but Sgt J. V. Claney landed on the NYA-held island of Vis after the port engine failed. Repairs effected, Vic Claney and his crew returned to Foggia, the pilot (inevitably) 'Vis' Claney thereafter.

While 6 crews were supply dropping on the night of 3 December, 15 others were resting after a daylight bombing attack on retreating German forces near Podgorica in Montenegro, the first of 8 during the month. Cloud obscured the target, only 9 aircraft identifying it visually. These aimed for roads and concentrations of motor transport, sticks falling across tightly packed vehicles. The remaining crews bombed through cloud on Gee, crews who obtained a visual fix reporting that this bombing dropped on or near the roads. Accurate light and medium flak was reported.

The other seven attacks were made on successive days beginning on 15 December, when the first arrivals found sufficient light to identify many vehicles heading north, and F/O H. B. Elliott and Sgt Hanson started fires with their 'cookies'. Later arrivals, unable to distinguish transport, bombed fires which were eventually visible for ninety miles. Early arrivals encountered intense and accurate light flak, but later this diminished. Another successful attack took place on the 18th, when transport and troop concentrations were attacked between Bioce and Kolasin. Convoys of vehicles were found in close order, especially at bridges near Bioce and Opasanica, and at the end of the attack the valley was filled with smoke rising to 7,000 feet, with twenty to thirty fires burning.

Late in the month 40 also returned three times to targets in Italy, attempting to destroy railway bridges over the Piave and Tagliamento rivers. An attack on the Susegana bridge over the Piave on 27 December was particularly successful, five crew claiming hits, and reconnaissance showing that one span had collapsed.

On 13 December 40 was involved in another 'first', transporting troops and equipment to Greece, where the communist partisans, ELAS, were in armed conflict with the interim government. Fourteen Wellingtons, stripped of bomb sights and other equipment, and carrying only a pilot, navigator and wireless operator, airlifted 122 men with their kit, PIAT anti-tank weapons and mortars from Grottaglie to Kalamaki aerodrome (now renamed Hassani). The weather was very bad, and one aircraft (P/O J. Burnett RAAF) returned to Grottaglie after trying unsuccessfully for forty-five minutes to fly through a storm, while several others had to fly at 150 feet to avoid icing. Conditions were equally unpleasant in Athens, where crews spent a cold night in empty billets, without blankets, amidst gunfire, navigator George Jones recalling that 'some of the Squadron planes were parked near one end of the runway at Kalamaki and some at the opposite end—at one stage some aircraft were in rebel territory, but were re-possessed as the rebels were overcome'.

The Squadron hoped for Christmas Day off, but was required to fly a daylight YNA supply drop to Crnomelj. Eight of the nine crews successfully dropped their canisters on markers which they described as well-placed. The one aircraft which failed to locate the supply area, because of Gee failure, and hence had to return with its cargo, was John Kirwan's.

Meanwhile Christmas was being celebrated at Foggia, the ORB reporting that

> An excellent bill-of-fare was provided by the cooking staff and meals were served in the time-honoured style by officers and NCOs. An intended 'few words' by the Commanding Officer, Wing Commander J. D. KIRWAN (DFC) were not spoken because he was busy dropping supplies to Jugo-slav partisans. The Adjutant expressed everyone's regret over the C.O.'s absence at dinner.

After dinner, George Jones recalls, 'most of the Squadron gathered round the only piano in the Airman's Mess singing raucous, bawdy, rugby type songs. One innocent song was always sung to the tune of Lili Marlene':

> Wing Commander Kirwan leads us on our way
> He leads us when we're flying, he leads us when we play,
> He'll shoot a line when he gets back—
> How he has bombed despite the flak,
> It's dicey flying Wimpeys around Italian skies!

Forty carried out further supply drops near Zagreb on Boxing Day and Fiume on the 28th. Both drops were carried out without loss, as were the attacks on bridges mentioned earlier. December thus ended loss-free, the only month in 1944. Beginning with light losses (5 crews in four months) 40 had suffered severely in May, June, and July, when 20 crews failed to return, with a further 10 between August and November. The 35 crews lost made 1944 the Squadron's worst, only 1941 (with 33) running it close. It was indeed 'dicey flying Wimpeys around Italian skies'.

If 1944 had been a hard year in the air, so had it been on the ground, for conditions at Foggia Main remained primitive. In August, following what the CO's Survey called 'appalling thunderstorms', the Squadron HQ was moved from 'a collection of tents and hutments to a farm building, where it became possible to set up a proper H. Q. organization'. In October gales likewise demonstrated that the tented messes, erected when aircrew moved to Foggia at the end of March, were inadequate, and needed to be replaced by sturdier accommodation.[3] Steps were then taken to requisition farmhouses, and to erect hutments where by the end of November the Officers' and both of the Sergeants' Messes were accommodated.

Yet despite these improvements, the year ended with all personnel (save the CO, in his trailer) still under canvas. As it became obvious that the Squadron was likely to be at Foggia for a lengthy period, however, and perhaps for the rest of the war, much effort had been put into making tents more liveable. Denis Ludman recalls:

> We all modified our tents by increasing the height of the tent poles, which enabled us to build up the sides of the tent with ammo boxes etc. thus giving us more room.

In time the modifications became more elaborate, packing cases being used for walls, and one 'tent' being rebuilt in half-timbered style. Even more elaborate was the building in the autumn of the 'Casa Grande'. Cecil Mohs writes:

> Hardy [Flt/Lt. J. Hardy, the Signals Officer], Arnott [P/O. G. E. Arnott RCAF] and myself didn't like living in tents so we built our casa from stone. We used Lightning aircraft tanks for water, got a basin from the bombed out buildings and fixed it so we had running water. We used another tank from a Lightning and rigged it up outside for a mixture of oil and petrol. Fuel pipe was then run from the tank to the fireplace inside with a valve which allowed a drip on the stones in the fireplace. When this was lit it was quite warm and comfortable during the wet and cold days.

During the severe winter of 1944–45 most tent dwellers also installed drip feed heating of one form or another. Denis Ludman comments:

> Once the drip fires were established as a source of heat the problem of obtaining used oil became the next problem. Each crew obviously had access to its own used oil but the appetite of the heaters outstripped the supply and it was the case of needs must and everyone was scrounging and pilfering where they could.

Not surprisingly, these burners, made from 5-gallon oil drums, were a fire risk, and a number of tents were burnt down.[4]

Another improvement was brought about by the installation of an electric lighting system. Eric Baddeley, the Squadron Engineering Officer, recalls:

> A major contribution to the quality of life was what we used to call "Campey's Green Box". Norman Campey [the Wing Engineering Officer] had somehow wheeled out of the Italian authorities an old transformer unit—believe it or not, a horse-drawn affair, wood encased, painted bright green with a skull and crossbones and "Pericolo de Morte" painted on the side. With this he'd tapped the local grid and ran cables all over the domestic site for lighting. The junction boxes were old parachute containers and whenever it rained these got very wet and all the lights went out. A disconsolate Campey would then have to splash from box to box drying out the contacts, since nobody else dared touch them.

76. Refuelling the central heating system, Foggia, Winter 1944. (A. Hipperson.)

Local ingenuity was also responsible for another amenity: radio. Denis Ludman writes that his tent mate Bill Greengrass 'sent home for some crystals and, obtaining four earphones, rigged up a crystal set each'. 'It was quite remarkable', Denis adds, 'what good reception we got from the AFN [American Forces Network] in Foggia. We heard all the programmes from the States—Jack Benny, Perry Como, Bing Crosby—in fact all the great names of the radio at that time.' Capping this success, Bill Greengrass then provided short-wave reception with a radio 'appropriated' from a crashed aircraft, rigging up an old motor bike to charge the batteries. 'The noise that came from that radio was tremendous', Denis adds. 'We received programmes from around the world at a touch.'

Bill Greengrass himself recalls live entertainment:

We were getting regular ENSA shows. They were put on in a bombed-out theatre in Foggia. It wasn't too badly damaged—it had a roof which was covered over with a tarpaulin. I can remember nothing about the shows but recall vividly the little Italian conductor-pianist. Oh how seriously he took it all. And he was so enthusiastic. His signature tune was the highlight for everyone at the show.

77. The shanty town, Foggia. (A. F. Jewell.)

Perhaps it was under this conductor that, Ken Dunn recalls, 'one local Italian group began Schubert's Unfinished with only half the orchestra, and the rest joined in as they arrived singly or in groups during the first and second movements'.

Another form of recreation, George Arnott remembers, was a trip to the beach:

> We were only about an hour's drive from the Manfredonia coast, with nice beaches and good swimming, and we would take a truck load of us over for an hour or two.

For ground personnel such breaks were the most that could be routinely expected, but as Ken Dunn notes,

> Operational crews had 6 days leave every 6 weeks and on 40 Squadron we enjoyed a series of holidays—at Roch, north of Manfredonia, swimming in the Adriatic, in Sicily at Taormina and in the Hotel Alberto on Mt. Etna attempting to ski, and 2 leaves at Sorrento lazing on the beach or visiting Naples and Pompei. All this a far cry from the blackouts and rationing and bombing in UK.

As in North Africa so at Foggia the meals that could be derived from RAF rations were adequate but uninteresting. In an attempt to widen and

vary the diet, therefore, the CO gave permission for the Messing Officer
to forage for additional rations, buying at the Foggia market or in the
countryside. George Arnott, Messing Officer during the latter part of 1944,
recalls: 'At least once a week I used to get a truck and take off with the
driver into the hills with soap and cigarettes and barter for vegetables from
the different farms we stopped at'.

Similar efforts were made to enhance the alcohol supply, as Cecil 'Eski'
Mohs recalls:

> I was the Bar Officer for the Squadron and one of my duties was to purchase
> the wine and liquor for the Officers' Mess. At first this was a real chore. We
> went to a place called Barletta to purchase what we wanted. They had
> enormous vats and the owner would have me sample the wines, cognacs, and
> vermouths before buying. This was too much for me. After the second trip
> I took along a few airmen and let them do the sampling. They really enjoyed
> that.

Ironically, regulations prohibited the serving of anything but beer in the
Airman's Mess, and Mohs raised with John Kirwan the possibility of providing
wine, and he and the deservedly popular OC 236 Wing (Gp/Capt Paul
Harris) obtained permission for this. 'That', Mohs comments, 'helped to
raise the morale on the Squadron considerably'.

It seems, in fact, that from October onwards there was a need to raise
morale. Navigator George Jones, whose crew arrived at Foggia Main on 22
October, writes:

> The reception was hardly one of welcome, for although the Adjutant had
> said there were plenty of billets in the aircrew sergeants' lines, none appeared
> willing to offer space, and the sergeants eventually extracted a bell tent from
> the stores. Two things were very clear within the first few hours on the
> Squadron: morale was at a low ebb, and the interest in flying was minimal.
> That the tent pole broke in the early hours of the morning was the major
> excitement on joining the Squadron.

In part the problem that George Jones noted may have been due to the
influx of crews from 142 and 150 Squadrons, which must have diluted the
Squadron identity for a time. But without doubt a significant factor was the
increasing reclusiveness of the CO. John Kirwan had been seriously ill earlier
in the year, spending eight weeks in hospital, and though he returned to
duty in August, he was but a shadow of his former self. After the heavy
losses which the Squadron had earlier experienced, forceful leadership was
needed. This, it seems, he was latterly unable to provide; 1944 had been a
hard year.

# Notes

1. In March 1944, of perhaps 85 aircrew 39 were RAAF, 13 RCAF, 2 RNZAF, and 2 SAAF. Like all 205 Group RAF squadrons, 40 retained a strong Dominion flavour until the war's end.

2. In January 1944 an Australian Halifax squadron, No 462, was told that it was to retrain as a pathfinding unit for 205 Group, and several crews returned to the United Kingdom to learn new techniques, returning with Halifaxes equipped with H2S ground scanning radar, the Gee navigational aid (introduced in 205 Group in March or April) and the Mk XIV bombsight. On 3 March 462 was renumbered No 614 Squadron.

3. The Airmen's Mess had been rehoused in early March.

4. On at least one occasion the conflagration was deliberate, Bernard Burdsall recalling that a 'voodoo tent', to which five crews had failed to return, was burnt down.

# 20

# To VE Day:
# January–May 1945

THE New Year, 1945, brought no operational flying until 3 January, when four aircraft dropped supplies to Italian partisans, while eight bombed bridges over the Isonzo. On the 4th and 5th further bridges were attacked, on the Latisana and Bosna rivers, the latter, in daylight, proving no easy target. The railway bridge was on the escape route being taken by the German forces which had broken out of the Podgorica pocket. The bombing was effective, the approaches to the bridge being wrecked, but the flak defences were vigorous, and one aircraft (F/O C. F. Wellman) was holed in each wing, while a second (F/O J. N. Hickey) sustained a direct hit on the starboard side during its second run over the target. The Wellington was out of control for a few seconds, during which the bomb aimer (Sgt. K. V. Dennis) jettisoned the remaining bombs. The pilot brought the aircraft back to base despite severe damage to the wing, fuselage, and tailplane.

After the bridge attacks, 40 carried out only one further bombing raid during January, to the marshalling yards at Udine on the 20th. Though snow made it difficult to distinguish ground detail, the bombing appeared well concentrated, and five crews claimed hits on the locomotive shed, while a satisfyingly large explosion occurred late in the attack.

Six supply drops were flown during January: all but one to Tito's YNA, and all but one of those in a drop zone designated 'Crayon', near Chirchina village, north of Idria. Seven Wellingtons undertook the first drop, a daylight operation on 8 January. The weather was poor, but the supplies were urgently needed, and crews took considerable risks in trying to get under the cloud base, though without success. A second attempt on the 15th was also foiled by heavy cloud cover, and of the fourteen aircraft only one (W/O A. V. Tennant RAAF) was able to spot the V marker, and to drop its containers. Better luck attended a third attempt three days later, eight of the nine aircraft locating the marker. Rear gunner Ron Turner has a vivid recollection of this drop:

> We had dropped our containers and noticed a small medieval town nearby and John Dunling, our skipper, decided to go down and have a look. In my mind's eye now I see a small river with buildings on either side (we must

only have been at 100 ft) and a stone bridge over this river with a horse and cart about to cross, the horse bucking and the driver trying to control it. Opposite the bridge a small boy gave a quick look up and then scampered up a tiny alley. I think it's amazing that I can remember this scene which can only have lasted about 3–5 seconds.

A further drop on the 19th was cancelled at the last moment, but on the 21st seven of thirteen Wellingtons located the marker, and dropped their loads successfully. The last drop for the month, to Tuzla, was equally successful, eight of the nine crews locating the marker. The only opposition was four heavy flak units at Zenica, but these operated effectively, one aircraft (F/O A. E. Fitzsimons RNZAF) having fabric strip from the starboard wing after a flak fragment hit it, while crews reported a Wellington from another squadron falling in flames.

A four day stand down because of bad weather completed a month during which weather frequently disrupted operational flying. Snowstorms had created what the CO's January summary described as 'impossible conditions overhead and on the ground', and even when the Squadron operated, icing made flying hazardous, and heavy cloud often prevented crews identifying targets, particularly on supply drops. That only 239 of 467 containers were dropped highlights the problems that the Squadron had faced.

The fierce snowstorms also severely tested the Squadron's shanty town accommodation. Despite the near ubiquitous drip-feed oil heating system, the 'tents' were often intensely cold, and Australian pilot John Perry remembers 'a number of the colder nights going to bed in my complete flying uniform with flying boots, under the eiderdown'.

On 31 January John Kirwan handed over command of 40 Squadron to Wg/Cdr P. N. Smith, DFC, a flight commander with 104 Squadron. It was the last of a series of personnel changes which had occurred since 31 December, when the B Flight Commander, Sqn/Ldr

78. Wg/Cdr P. N. Smith.
(R. D. Thirsk.)

J. E. Oram, was posted. His replacement was Sqn/Ldr E. J. Fisher, while Sqn/Ldr Angus, who left on the same date as John Kirwan, was replaced by Sqn/Ldr R. D. Thirsk.[1]

John Kirwan came to 40 Squadron with a distinguished record, and having been a popular and successful CO of 150 Squadron. That posting had, however, been terminated by illness, and at Foggia he was again taken ill, spending eight weeks in hospital with a serious chest infection. Though he returned to duty in August, it is clear that thereafter John Kirwan was not his former self. In the early months of his command he had been a genial and convivial figure, as Fred Rooke recalls:

> We had a party on 29th February [1944] to celebrate Ferdie Maycock's departing for his rest. Kirwan had such a good time with us all (officers and sergeants) that he became gloriously drunk—he was very friendly and sympathetic to all, and we liked him a lot.

By the time he completed his tour, however, John Kirwan seems to have been exhausted, and his reclusiveness in the final months certainly had an effect on morale. With the benefit of hindsight, it can be seen that the decision to allow him to return to the Squadron after his illness, however keen he was to do so, was a mistake.

205 Group had begun to convert its four remaining Wellington squadrons to the American Consolidated Liberator B.VI in the autumn of 1944, and in December six crews had been posted in from 37 Squadron to complete their tours on Wellingtons. January, by contrast, saw the departure of five 40 Squadron crews as a preliminary to a 236 Wing Liberator conversion programme, and eight pilots and navigators volunteering for conversion to PFF duties with 614 Squadron, then converting from the Halifax to the Mosquito.

During the first month under Peter Smith's leadership, the mix of partisan supply drops and bombing continued as in January, though with a marked difference in the ratio between the two. In January 6 of the 10 operations flown were partisan drops. In February this fell to 6 out of 19, the bombing of ports and marshalling yards in Northern Italy taking precedence.

Of the six supply drops, four were during the first week, when urgency attached to the supply of Tito's forces in northern Yugoslavia. Three drops in the 'Flotsam' area went well, with markers clearly identified and the drops well concentrated. An attempt on 4 February to supply partisans in the 'Crayon' area, however, was a disaster. The weather was bad at Foggia, with 10/10ths cloud with a 2–3,000 ft. base, and rain showers. Since the forecast was for clearing weather over the Adriatic, however, and the supplies were urgently needed, the operation was attempted. With such a low cloud base, and the mountainous Gargano Peninsula a source of concern, crews were instructed to keep under the cloud and make out to sea through the San

Severo Gap. Two crews did not make it, hitting the hills around San Severo. All of F/O Hickey's crew were killed, and all but the rear gunner (Sgt Lambert) in F/O Wellman's. On the return journey a third aircraft crashed in the San Severo area, only the rear gunner (Sgt R. Coles) surviving, seriously injured, from Flt/Sgt C. Sunderland's crew. Thirteen men died, and for nothing, since the drop zone was cloud covered, and all containers were brought back to base.

Two further supply drops were carried out during February, of which that on the 14th was particularly significant, in that the nine Wellingtons detailed were accompanied by a single Liberator, captained by the CO. This, however, was a one-off, as no further Liberator sorties were flown until the departure of the Wellingtons in mid-March.

The targets bombed during February were all marshalling yards and naval and port facilities in that part of northern Italy still under German control, save for a raid on the marshalling yards at Graz, in Austria, on 13 February. This was a most successful operation, with bombing concentrated on well-placed TIs, with over forty hits scored by 205 Group on the heavily loaded yards, and 120 units of rolling stock damaged or destroyed. Another successful raid was that on 15 February, when the primary target, the Pola naval yard, was obscured by cloud, and 40's Wellingtons bombed Fiume. Their target, the oil refinery, was not heavily damaged, but the nearby marshalling yards were. Attacks on Fiume and Trieste on the next two nights were equally successful, while at least two of the four raids on the Verona marshalling yards were adjudged successful also. Ground opposition was rarely effective, save at Verona, where the German forces had concentrated their flak defences. Night fighters were occasionally seen, but only one inconclusive exchange of fire took place.

A successful supply drop to Tito's partisans on 25 February was 40 Squadron's last, its operations thereafter being restricted solely to bombing. In March the targets were overwhelmingly marshalling yards, only two of sixteen (coal wharves at Arsa and the naval yards at Pola) falling outside this category. Of these two the first, on 1 March, was unsuccessful, cloud preventing bombing, while the second, two nights later, went well, though the TIs went out prematurely, forcing 40's second wave to bomb more or less blind.

Mixed results were achieved in the attacks on marshalling yards, the least successful being on 7 March, when bad weather prevented all but two aircraft bombing the yards at Gemona, and nearly caused the loss of Sgt G. Hewitt's crew, their Wellington icing up, and falling out of control from 8,000 feet, Hewitt regaining control only when the aircraft emerged from cloud at 1,000 feet, and completing recovery less than 100 feet above the sea. The attack on Casarso on the 4th was most successful, however, with the bombing concentrated and accurate, while the last three raids carried

79. Target photo: Fiume Shipyards, 16 February 1945. (E. G. Jones.)

out with the Wellington, to Verona, Padua and Treviso on the 11th, 12th and 13th, all went well, and that on Padua particularly so.

With the conversion of 104 Squadron to the Liberator at the beginning of March, 40 became the last squadron in the RAF using the Wellington in the bomber role for which it was designed, hence the last Wimpy operation, scheduled for 14 March, assumed considerable significance, with crews vying to fly it. Ironically, however, fog forced its cancellation at the last moment, so that the honour of undertaking the last Wellington night bombing sorties went to the six crews who on the 13th bombed the marshalling yards at Treviso. The aircraft and crew captains on this historic occasion were: LP 331 (Flt/Sgt. W. Brookfield), LP 362 (Flt/Sgt M. G. Lihou), LP 646 (W/O J. Webb), LP 658 (P/O J. Burnett, RAAF), LP 718 (Sgt. D. Argile), and LP 720 (Sgt. J. Whitter).

Forty had been operating Wellingtons since November 1940, and their departure was an event of considerable sadness for many. Most were flown

80. Flt/Sgt J. P. Perry RAAF and crew, Foggia, 1945. (J. P. Perry.)

to Blida, in Algeria, to be handed over to the French, and Trevor News-holme, who took part in a delivery flight as wireless operator in F/O A. Williams' crew, comments:

> The trip to Blida was in daylight, and was a rather sad and uneventful journey with our beloved Wimpys. It felt like taking a faithful horse to the knacker's yard.

The aircraft supplanting the Wellington, the Liberator B.VI, represented as great an advance over its predecessor as had the Wellington over the Blenheim. The equivalent of the B24H and J in USAAF service, the Mk. VI Liberator was the culmination of a development programme which brought the original Consolidated Model 32 of 1939, promising but opera-tionally inadequate, to a point where it was selected as the standard RAF heavy bomber in the Mediterranean and Far Eastern Theatres of War.

Powered by four 1,200 hp Pratt and Whitney Twin Wasp engines, the Liberator VI was capable of a maximum speed of 270 mph at 20,000 feet. With a bomb load of 12,000 lbs, the range was 990 miles, but with a reduced bomb load the maximum range was 2,290 miles. The defensive armament was formidable, with eight .5 Browning machine-guns in nose, dorsal and tail turrets, and in the waist positions. On some aircraft the nose turrets were replaced by a solid fairing, but even those not so modified carried no front gunner: as on the Wellington, the bomb aimer occupied the turret when needed.

Even without a front gunner, however, the Liberator required a crew of eight as against the Wellington's five, and to enlarge crews that were converting numbers of gunners were posted in. This was only one consequence of the conversion programme, however, the March CO's summary noting 'large scale reorganization of aircrews, many personnel being put up for disposal to make way for an intake of trained crews from other directions'. Thus five crews were posted out on 22 March, to be converted to Liberators by 37, 70 and 178 Squadrons, while the following day five Liberator crews were posted in. Not until April did the situation stabilize, the CO noting that 'for the first time for about three months . . . the spate of postings died down'.

Despite the upheaval, conversion to the Liberator took place expeditiously, the Squadron being non-operational only four days. The conversion on squadron followed a pattern not unlike that when 40 converted to Wellingtons, in that Wg/Cdr Smith and F/O Elliott were converted to the type, and then converted others.

Ron Thirsk, who joined 40 as A Flight Commander on 10 March, comments:

> Liberators were a little bit daunting at first. One thing that I didn't like was that the various switches, which were probably about four or five times the number you would find in a Wellington, were all exactly the same sort and grouped in neat rows, and this, to my mind, didn't make for easy identification.

He continues:

> I might say that the Liberator had its compensations. I thought it flew like a cow, but one didn't really have to fly it by hand very much because it had a magnificent 'George', an auto pilot, the like of which I never dreamt, which not only flew it very accurately, but also took all the muscular strain out of flying.

Vic Tennant, however, recalls that there was a trick to getting the best out of the Liberator:

> Consider the Liberator being flown by two different pilots. They are both to fly an operation at—say—20,000 ft. The first pilot has not yet got the hang of it and he climbs to 20,000 ft. He trims the aircraft to climb and on reaching the required height trims again for level flying and throttles back. This would be fine for most aircraft, but our pilot finds the aircraft still has a slight 'nose-up' attitude and is not flying at either the airspeed or ground speed expected. Pilot number two has experienced the same thing, but has realized that if he goes an extra 1000 ft or so, then puts the nose slightly down to the required height, throttles back and when at the correct height trims for level flight his aircraft will be holding height, although it is flying slightly 'nose down' and is flying faster; it does not have an attitude of squashing and wallowing like our first pilot experiences. Coming back

81. Liberator VI KK311. (G. Wootton.)

from operations at a certain distance from home (and this was all experience and skill), if the pilot put the nose down slightly for a long slow descent, using engine revs as per level flying, it was amazing how quickly the old Liberator would cover the ground.

The first operation with Liberators (apart from the Partisan supply sortie flown in February) was by three aircraft to Bruck marshalling yards, in Austria, on 19 March. The raid was not a success, but the following night, when four crews were up, an attack on the yards at Pragerako went well, with the bombing accurate and concentrated. Five more operations, with up to six crews operating, followed on successive nights, the targets including Novska on 21 March, and Villach the following night.

The raid on Villach did not go well, crews bombing (as the Master Bomber instructed) on TIs, but subsequent reconnaissance showed that they were well off target, while the few railway lines cut were rapidly repaired. The attack on Novska, on the other hand, was most successful, with all through lines cut, and rolling stock and track badly damaged. Spectacular explosions followed a hit on an ammunition train, and it later emerged that 180 German troops had been killed.

After operating seven nights in a row, 40 had five days rest before operating again, nine aircraft attacking the marshalling yards at Graz on the 31st. The results were not memorable, for though crews bombed as instructed by the Master Bomber, reconnaissance confirmed only slight damage to the yards.

Ron Thirsk remembers the operation, however, both for the great height at which they flew, and because

> it was realised that some the gunners, especially, might get very cold, and I had to radio back on the return journey whether I thought a rum issue might be warranted.

'The message', Ron adds, 'was really written, I think, before we went.'

On 1 April six aircraft successfully attacked the canal wharf at Arsa, and a return to the Monfalcone shipyards on the 5th also went well, none of 40's aircraft being troubled by the lively flak defences, though other 205 Group aircraft were hit. Then followed three attacks on marshalling yards. The raids on Novska (3 April) and Brescia (4th) were both successful, the first despite nothing being heard from the Master Bomber, but Trento (2 April) was a failure, cloud and a target marking failure resulting in scattered and ineffectual bombing, though severe damage was done to the roof of Trento Cathedral. A second attack on Trento on the 8th went somewhat better, but again there was less than satisfactory concentration.

No aircraft were lost during these raids, but one, captained by Sqn/Ldr Thirsk, crashed on return from Novska, fortunately without injury to the crew. Ron recalls that earlier the machine which crashed had been flown by one of the best pilots on squadron, and that he had said that on approach 'he had felt he hadn't proper control of the aircraft'. Ron himself found that

> as soon as I partially closed the throttle and put on a few degrees of flap prior to lowering the undercarriage the aircraft started to misbehave, with the chief symptom lack of control from the ailerons. I was having to move them in an exaggerated fashion to keep the aircraft steady.

On the landing run things got worse, and 'a few yards after I had come over the boundary the aircraft, so to speak, dropped out of my hand, just fell on the deck'. The aircraft bounced some fifty to sixty feet, fell heavily to the ground, and smashed the undercarriage.

A Court of Enquiry was convened, and just as a verdict of pilot error or inexperience was expected,

> to my aid came a communication that a certain number of, I think, Liberator VIIIs had come into the group, and they were not to be flown until the handling notes for them had been received and read. When these were obtained they made the point that the instrumentation was different and that the position error on the airspeed indicator was much higher than in the ordinary Liberators, and they should be brought in about 20 knots faster.

'This rogue aircraft', Ron recalls, 'was a Ford-made Liberator from Willow Run, and we saw no more of them in 205 Group. We remained solely equipped with Consolidated-built aircraft.'

Since early January, 40 had been employed predominantly in a strategic role, principally hampering German rail traffic. On 9 April, however, the Squadron returned to a tactical role, twelve Liberators bombing just ahead of the rapidly advancing 8th Army. The adjacent target areas (identified as 'Pig' and 'Whistle'), were to be marked by ground-fired TIs, but 'Whistle', 40's target, was not marked during the attack, and nine crews bombed 'Pig'. The ground attack next day demonstrated the effectiveness of the bombing, since the forces met little opposition at 'Pig', but made virtually no progress at 'Whistle'.

After an effective raid on marshalling yards at Innsbruck on 10 April, 40 returned to the tactical role, with three operations in support of the 8th Army in the Argenta gap. All were successful, the first (on the area around the crossroads at Bastia on 11 April) proving a copybook raid, with the TIs well-placed, the Master Bomber's instructions clear, and the bombing concentrated. More tactical bombing followed in the period up to 19 April, a particularly effective attack on Porto Maggiore on 13 April leaving part of the town devastated, and roads cratered and blocked. On the 16th, likewise, ten Liberators participated in an attack on a bridge and troop concentrations at Casalecchio. Though the bridge remained open to one-way traffic, the approaches were devastated, and nearby buildings gutted.

On this, as on most raids during March and April, little opposition was encountered. Only slight flak damage was caused, and though fighters were occasionally sighted, only inconclusive exchanges of fire took place. Other squadrons were not always so lucky, however, and the Operational Record Book several times notes sightings of aircraft going down in flames.

On 15 April the Squadron, casualty-free since 4 February, was lucky to maintain its record when, returning from an abortive raid on Villach, the Liberator piloted by Flt/Sgt Millett crashed on landing. Bomb aimer John Wray recalls:

> the aircraft ran along the runway a short distance, then the nose rose, the Liberator went into the air, stalled, turned, hit the runway, spinning and turning. As it did so, bombs broke loose, smashing the bomb doors as they went through.
>
> Eventually it came to rest, the undercarriage smashed, the nose wheel bent 90 degrees, a wing broken, an engine nearly out of its housing, and beginning to burn.
>
> Some of the crew got out through the emergency hatch, others from the beam openings, and ran as fast as they could from the aircraft, expecting it to explode. Fortunately it didn't.

On the 16th, however, W/O V. W. Greensmith and his crew were less fortunate when their Liberator, also returning with bombs aboard, crashed on approach to Foggia.[2] The aircraft was wrecked, and all the crew injured,

Greensmith himself, on his second tour with 40 Squadron, dying of his injuries. As with the crash on 15 April, the cause was never established.

After Casalecchio, the Squadron operated only five times more before the German capitulation. Two of these operations (on 17 and 19 April) were against tactical targets at Porto Maggiore and Malabergo. Both went well, with the bombing concentrated and effective. Of the three strategic attacks, two were on a target that 40 had attacked frequently in the past—the Verona-Parona railway bridge over the Adige. Though neither succeeded in destroying the bridge, they severely damaged the approaches, rendering it unusable for a time.

On 15 April ten Liberators bombed the marshalling yards at Villach. The raid was a complete failure, with 10/10ths cloud obscuring the target. But on the 25th an attack on the marshalling yards at Freilassing went entirely to plan. Twelve aircraft bombed with so high a degree of concentration that individual sticks were often impossible to distinguish. Reconnaissance subsequently established that this, the Squadron's last operation of World War Two, had been an outstanding success, with the target area devastated, 300 units of rolling stock destroyed, and nearby houses and factories gutted.

Freilassing had been targeted because it lay at the heart of what was rumoured to be a Nazi 'Southern redoubt'. In fact the redoubt never existed, and the German collapse continued, articles of surrender by the German and Italian fascist forces in Italy being signed by *Feldmarschall* Vietinghoff on 29 April, and taking effect on 2 May, two days before the signing of surrender documents on Lüneberg Heath which ended German resistance in North-west Europe, and six days before the War in Europe came to an end officially at midnight on 8 May 1945. For 40 Squadron the war was over.

Several weeks later Ron Thirsk entered, on impulse, the Nissen hut which had been used as the briefing room. He writes:

> After V.E. Day we did not use the Ops Room for the ferrying of freight and passengers that kept us so busy, and I do not know why I pushed open the door of this big hut and went in. It had not been touched since the last briefing, papers were scattered around, and the route was taped on the wall map. In all my time I do not remember ever feeling grief or shedding a tear for lost comrades—what had befallen them might befall us. But not so now. I started to weep, initially I think for the death of the Squadron. Illogical, what a mercy that we need fight no more. But when I turned to go I realised for the first time the significance of that door through which we all went out to face whatever might befall. In those days Houseman was my comforter, and two things sprang to mind—*Last Poems* VII " . . . Walk the resounding way to the still dwelling'—and *A Shropshire Lad* XIII "They carry back bright to the coiner the mintage of man, / The Lads that will die in their glory and never be old."

# Notes

1. John Oram, who had flown his first tour as an observer with 37 Squadron in North Africa, had the distinction of being the first and only 40 Squadron flight commander who was not a pilot. Ronald Thirsk had flown a first tour with 104 Squadron.

2. The raid, on a bridge at Casalecchio, had in fact gone well; so well that after only half the force had bombed, the TIs were obscured by smoke, and the Master bomber ordered the remaining crews not to bomb.

# Epilogue

During nearly six years of war, 40 Squadron suffered the following casualties:

| Killed or died of wounds: | 538 |
|---|---|
| Prisoner of War | 126 |
| Wounded | 20 |
| Injured | 42 |

Tabulated by year, these figures break down as follows:

| Year | Killed | POW | Wounded | Injured |
|---|---|---|---|---|
| 1939 | Nil | Nil | Nil | Nil |
| 1940 | 51 | 23 | 8 | 4 |
| 1941 | 156 | 36 | 10 | 5 |
| 1942 | 69 | 32 | 1 | 9 |
| 1943 | 115 | 6 | 1 | 9 |
| 1944 | 133 | 29 | Nil | 7 |
| 1945 | 14 | Nil | Nil | 8 |

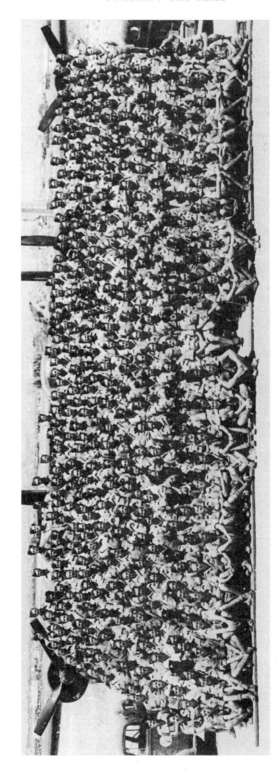

82. 40 Squadron, Foggia Main, 1945.
Centre, Wg/Cdr P. N. Smith and his flight commanders, Sqn/Ldrs R. D. Thirsk (l) and E. J. Fisher (r).
(H. Scholar.)

21

# Post-war:
# May 1945–April 1947

WHEN the war ended 40 Squadron had been operationally inactive since 25 April, hence the cessation of hostilities brought little immediate change in routine. But on 7 May the Squadron began the transport flights which were to occupy it throughout much of the month, eleven Liberators carrying petrol and rations to 8th Army units in Northern Italy. The first two missions were to Rivolto, where the Liberators put down in a large field, to be met by a welcoming party of Partisans. Subsequent trips were made either to Lavariano or Aviano, however, where aerodrome facilities were available. In all 40 was active in ferrying supplies on sixteen days in May, the operation being completed on the 27th.

By then, however, a much more ambitious ferrying operation had commenced, repatriating ex-POWs. A series of dummy runs for familiarization purposes began on 12 May, and the ferry flights began on the 21st, towards the end of the month two aircraft a day being thus employed. Typically, the ex-POWs were picked up at Pomigliano, while in England the usual point of destination was Holmesley South. George Jones recalls that 'Pete Smith pulled off a master stroke with a UK brewery, and most aircraft returning brought back to Italy one 36-gallon barrel of beer', but adds:

> Occasionally when the weather was foul an aircraft would have to climb high over the worst of it. Beer barrels are not designed for such treatment, and pilots who burst barrels were not very popular!

Though the Liberator had a capacious fuselage, and could carry up to twenty-four men on the long haul to the UK, the accommodation was primitive, most passengers being seated on makeshift wooden benches in the bomb bay—the coldest place in the aircraft. To alleviate the monotony—and discomfort—crews allowed passengers to visit the flight deck and bomb aimer's compartment. Whether seated in the bomb bay or moving around the aircraft, however, they were a potential risk, and so on boarding they were given an information sheet which set out 'A few points to remember', including

> iii) The aircraft is not a regular transport, and switches, cocks, control cables and wiring are exposed and within your reach. In almost every case, tampering

with them would be serious; remember what curiosity did to the cat: even if you feel sure that a certain tap might deliver a pint of beer, TOUCH NOTHING and don't let anyone else do so either.

and

(vii) Toilet arrangements are very makeshift and bear a striking resemblance to some old oil drums. As movement of passengers around the aircraft must be kept to a minimum, please do your best before getting aboard.

On 4 June, the Squadron also began repatriating French ex-POWs and deportees from Yugoslavia, using Istres as the French base, and frequently returning with Italians also being repatriated. The last of these flights took place on 13 June. Five days later the first transport flights to Egypt took place, when three Liberators carried 15,000 lbs of freight from Foggia to Cairo West and Heliopolis. During July, however, personnel constituted the usual cargo, many planeloads being transported to Egypt for repatriation to South Africa. On the way back from the Middle East, calls were frequently made at Hassani, in Greece, to pick up British troops for transport to Italy. These, presumably, were some of those transported to Greece in December the previous year to assist the Government in defeating the communists.

Ferrying to the UK involved rapid round trips, making leave impossible. There was great rejoicing, therefore, when it became known, in mid-July, that a leave scheme was to be implemented. The first personnel were ferried to the United Kingdom on 1 August, when twelve airmen left Foggia for Glatton, and by the end of the month eighty-eight had enjoyed leave, more than a third of those on squadron at the time. The scheme continued throughout September, ending only with the Squadron's move to Egypt.

In chapter 20 it was noted that after large-scale personnel movements, in April 'the aircrew personnel became stabilized and the spate of postings died down'. May was likewise quiet, but further changes came in June, with the departure of the last four RAAF officers (P/Os C. L Dun, J. J. Sykes, A. V. Tennant and J. P. Perry) for Australia. With RCAF, RNZAF and SAAF aircrew already gone, 40 was once more an RAF squadron in the strict sense of the word.

Though an average of 700–800 hours flying was done each month during the summer, ferrying personnel and freight to Egypt and the United Kingdom, and carrying out local flying and bullseye exercises, there was a great deal of spare time, and efforts were made to keep everyone busy not only with sport (the universal stand by) but a comprehensive Educational and Vocational Training scheme. John Wray recalls:

From the end of June to mid September a series of compulsory EVT meetings were arranged at which discussion took place on pre-selected topics (eg. tax, town and country planning, resettlement, international problems of the post-war world, duties of 205 Group). A selected member of aircrew was instructed and briefed to lead the discussion. A motor engineering course was arranged and took place in a room in a building housing Number 4 General Hospital, Foggia.

Under the same scheme educational flights were made to Florence, Venice, Rome and Pisa.

On 5 July polling was held for the General Election in the United Kingdom. The ORB notes that there were 'a considerable number of votes recorded on the Squadron, but there were quite a large number of complaints over the non-arrival of ballot papers for personnel whose applications had gone astray'. The inability of some members of the Squadron to vote would not, however, have made any difference to the outcome of the election, a Labour landslide.

The CO's summary for September states:

Preparation for the re-deployment of the Squadron to the MIDDLE EAST was the predominant thought in our minds. After having been 18 months on FOGGIA MAIN the move will not be so easy as previous moves.

The redeployment, which involved both 40 and 104 Squadrons, began on 21 October, when two Liberators ferried passengers and equipment from Foggia to Abu Sueir, 236 Wing's new base. The transfer continued during early November, being completed on the 9th, when Wg/Cdr Smith flew out the last aircraft. He recalls that 'We burned everything before we left, leaving the camp site in immaculate order', but that 'as we moved down the runway the local people were already moving in'. Sgt Frank Jewell led the clear-up party which also left that day, and he recalls the rumpus which broke out as they boarded their aircraft. The Military Police were preventing local farmers removing galvanized iron sheets from the Nissen huts, and 'as we taxied out the locals were pointing at us: it looked a real ding-dong'. He asked his squad if they knew what was going on, to be told that they had 'sold the hut for three jerry cans of vino'. 'It went down well on the flight to Egypt', he adds.

Foggia Main had, for all the improvements carried out during the last months of the war, remained very much an improvised base, with much in common with a shanty town. Abu Sueir, on the other hand, was a pre-war RAF base, with permanent accommodation and facilities which included, John Wray recalls,

water closets, hot and cold showers, a swimming pool, cinema, NAAFI, YMCA, church, bookshop, sports shop, jeweller's shop, tennis courts.

With the Japanese capitulation on 14 August, it became clear not only that the Squadron would not be required to transfer to the Far East, but also that for some demobilization was a not too distant prospect. A scheme, promulgated later that month, provided for a phased release programme, with personnel within each trade categorized according to priority. On 22 September the groups to be released in November and December were announced. In most trades two groups were to be released, but the ORB notes that 'there were a number of trades lagging well behind'. Two months later, on 22 November, the ORB records that

> There was great speculation amongst several personnel, tour-expired on a 4 years basis, up to June '46, as to whether or not they were likely to be beside their firesides by X'Mas. Some little disappointment was experienced today on receipt of a signal which laid down that a large number would not in fact arrive home until February 1946.

Amongst those who left the Squadron at this time were several long-serving SNCOs, and Wg/Cdr Smith marked their going by posting a notice which recognized the departure of 'the last of the original personnel who came overseas with the Unit'. 'Those now posted 'overseas tour expired', the notice continued,

> some of whom were with 40 Squadron in France before Dunkerque, and who have all been through the entire campaign in North Africa, Malta and Italy, are:-
>
> F/S. R. G. Sanders
> Sgt. M. C. Ferguson.
> Sgt. D. E. Eggilton.
> Sgt. A. G. Reddy.
> Sgt. J. H. Wey.
> Sgt. T. Stockley.

and, nearly all the time:

> Sgt. K. A. Longman.[1]

In mid-December 91 men were posted for repatriation to the UK, and by the end of the month, the CO's summary noted, nearly 100 had gone, so that the unit was now 'down to rock bottom in ACHs, Cooks, and MT personnel'. Nor could the position be expected to improve, since on Christmas Day advance notice was received concerning personnel scheduled for repatriation in February and March.

In September 1944 Wg/Cdr Kirwan had posted a notice drawing attention to the fact that 'when hostilities cease', 'emphasis will once again be laid on the externals of what we know as discipline'. It stated, *inter alia*:

> 4. Orders have been issued, and will continue to be issued, with a view to tightening things up in this direction. These orders are directed simply at two main things—to bring home to all ranks the fact that they are part of a force

which wears a recognised and honourable uniform, and to insist on that simple mark of respect as between ranks which comes from saluting.

With the war's end the process of formalizing quickened, and George Jones recalls that during the summer he found himself in charge of a major kit inspection for all ground staff. 'The Adjutant', he writes,

> took the view that any items they were short of was due to negligence, and should be paid for by the airman, or NCO, and proceeded to have lots of 664B's written out. As the officer deputed to conduct the kit inspection I was supposed to agree, but when you work with groundstaff of the calibre of Chiefie Sword and George Reddy you know that negligence is not one of their characteristics. I wrote on all the 664B's 'Certified no negligence', and signed my name. The adjutant nearly went beserk, but Pete Smith agreed with my interpretation.

The increased formality at Foggia, however, was nothing to what was met at Abu Sueir. Frank Jewell recalls both the view from the air on approach, with gleaming runways and sand which it turned out was rolled daily, and the immaculately clad Group Captain and his staff, waiting to greet the last arrivals. 'We got out' Frank continues,

> and I knew what was coming. We were scruffy like refugees, wearing half Yank and South African uniforms. The Groupy turned to the Adjutant and spluttered, 'Get them out of my sight. Get them re-kitted as soon as possible', and stalked off.

'Next day', he continues, 'we were paraded, and when the Adjutant said "Fall in" it was chaos, so we were drilled up and down. It was ties at all times'.

The return to strict peacetime standards in dress eventually brought a near-mutiny, John Wray recalling that in December there was serious unrest over an order that after 5 pm airmen must wear 'best blue'. On the 19th a group went to the cinema not dressed according to the order and were refused admission. John continues:

> A crowd of them gathered and created a commotion. They then went down to the officers mess and asked to see the CO. He was not available and after a while the Adjutant (Flt/Lt L. F. Wolsey) came out and remonstrated with them for about three-quarters of an hour. Apparently they argued that the order was an example of 'bull', they had joined a wartime force, not a peacetime one. They threatened to do no work the following day until they had seen the CO. The adjutant left them to cool down. Next day no work was started. They saw the CO and after due consideration he in his wisdom amended the order.

The run-down in ground personnel mentioned earlier was difficult enough in itself, but there were added problems in that the postings coincided with the conversion of the Squadron from Liberator to Lancaster aircraft. Supplied

83. The first Lancaster, BL-A. (W. F. Greengrass.)

under the Lend-Lease scheme, the Liberators were to be flown back to the United States for disposal, and in their place all 205 Group squadrons were to re-equip with the Lancaster. News of this came in September, when the CO noted that 'aircrew personnel have their time fully occupied with lectures and demonstrations on the ground, keeping their technical knowledge up to date, and preparing them for conversion to Lancasters'.

The first 40 Squadron Lancasters arrived at Abu Sueir during the latter half of November, and a conversion programme was begun. Then on 10 December the first Lancaster crew (F/O P. Cullen) arrived from the UK. Three more followed by the end of the month, assisting in the conversion programme, and the Squadron was declared fully crewed at the end of January 1946. Surplus Liberator crews had been posted out, and by the middle of January none remained.

The Lancaster B.VII, with which the Squadron was now re-equipped, was a development of the Mk. I used in Bomber Command from 1942 onwards, and differed from the latter primarily in the fitting (and location further forward) of a Martin dorsal turret in place of the Nash and Thompson turret of the Mk. I. The Mk. VII was also fitted with the Rose-Rice tail turret, armed with 2 × 0.5-in machine-guns, in place of the standard Mk. I armament, a Nash and Thompson turret with 4 x 0.303s.

Equipped with four Merlin 24 engines of 1,640 hp., conferring a service ceiling of more than 24,000 feet, a maximum speed of 287 mph at 11,500 feet, a cruising speed of 210 mph, and a range of 1,660 miles with 14,000 lb. of bombs, the Lancaster VII had a performance in many ways comparable with the Liberator VI that it was replacing. The Liberator had a superior service ceiling (32,000 feet), and on only three-quarters of the power, a maximum speed (270 mph) not much less than the Lancaster. Yet these figures are misleading, since in most respects crews found the Lancaster a much livelier and higher performing aircraft. George Jones writes:

> We had supreme faith in our new toy. The Liberators by comparison were lumbering giants, and those who had converted would fly alongside those still flying Libs, cut one motor, then two. By this stage the Lib. having tried to do the same would be beginning to fall out of the sky. But then came the coup de grace, one more motor was cut on the Lanc and it still continued to fly straight and level.

Ted Green, a member of one of the incoming Lancaster crews, writes:

> We arrived from England with our brand new magnificent Mark VII black and white Lancaster at Abu Sueir and reported with that inevitable 'Bomber Command swagger' to the navigation section. We were immediately presented with charts of the Persian/Russian border and were informed by the Nav. Leader that we would be patrolling this region in the forthcoming weeks. I can assure you that this took the smile and the smirk off our faces, and we returned to the normal aircrew slouch of cheesed-off, conned ex-op. types.

Ted adds: 'We had volunteered because we were offered the opportunity of bringing troops back from the Far East, and therefore obtaining Southern Hemisphere Navigation experience, essential for getting into civil flying. Needless to say I never did cross the Equator'.

The Squadron's first peacetime Christmas was celebrated in style, with many of the usual service features, including the officers serving at the Airmen's Mess. George Jones recalls:

> Bert [Smart] and I found a donkey from somewhere and did a ceremonial tour of the messes, which put everyone in a good humour. For some reason Pete Smith and Groupie [G/Capt A. H. Smythe] were late to lunch, probably involved in pre-drinking elsewhere. As the donkey and a camel were still available Bert and I repeated our ceremonial tour of the Officers Mess by donkey, and Jerry Higson bravely mounted the camel and joined us. Pete Smith and Groupie continued with their late lunch, behaving as if it were quite normal for donkeys and camels to circle them with officers riding bare back.

For much of the seven months since the end of hostilities in Europe, 40 had been engaged in trooping. By the end of 1945 most of this traffic had ceased, however, and though the Squadron carried out ferry runs from time to time, generally to Bari (Italy), Aqir (Palestine), and Hassani (Greece), but later further afield, to Nairobi, Mogadishu, Shaibah and Habbaniyah, and frequent duty runs to other bases in the Canal Zone, flying was otherwise confined almost entirely to day and night cross-country exercises. Mid January 1946 brought proposals for a new flying training policy, however, consisting of cross-country flights, fighter affiliation exercises, practice bombing, and formation flying. These proposals aroused a 'somewhat noticeable reaction', the Adjutant, Flt/Lt. Wolsey, noted in the ORB on 17 January, adding that while it was realized 'that cross country flights proved of great value in maintaining high standards, enthusiasm [was] far from keen on suggested Practice Bombing, Fighter Affiliation, and Formation Flying'. The evident lack of enthusiasm for the proposed programme may have had some effect, at least, for though practice bombing (and later air to ground firing) became a regular feature of the flying programme, formation flying and fighter affiliation exercises were carried out only rarely.

February 1946 saw the departure of Wg/Cdr Smith, who had been CO since 1 February the previous year. Assuming command of a weary squadron, he had made a first-class job of restoring vigour and enthusiasm, and by the war's end 40 was the equal of any unit in 205 Group. Though Peter Norton-Smith himself credits the smooth running of the Squadron to his adjutant, Flt/Lt A. R. Fasham, 'a gem of a man', there can be no doubt of what George Jones calls the CO's 'quiet efficiency', or his willingness to lead from the front.

Peter Smith's successor as CO was Wg/Cdr G. A. Mills, who arrived on 6 February 1946, and assumed command on the 18th. For Geoffrey Mills this was a special occasion, since he had served with 40 Squadron thirteen years earlier, when newly graduated from Cranwell. With Gp/Capt Smythe, another junior member of 40 Squadron in the early thirties, as Station Commander at Abu Sueir, there was now a strong connection between the pre- and post-war squadrons.

The new CO found an extraordinary mix of similarities and differences in situation between 1933 and 1946. While the daily routine of service life had much in common with that pre-war, both for air and ground crews, there was much also that was different. For one thing, there was, in place of a welcoming Oxfordshire community, an Egyptian populace increasingly hostile to the British presence in the Canal Zone, and given to showing this by rioting. These riots were particularly widespread and fierce in the latter part of February, and on the 24th all towns were placed out of bounds to squadron personnel on this account. Even though this ban was later lifted, antagonism to British service personnel continued.

Yet another difference between the pre- and post-war situations lay in manning. Pre-war, there was no difficulty in maintaining personnel levels

84. 40 Squadron aircrew, Abu Sueir, 1946.
Centre Wg/Cdr Mills and Sqn/Ldrs Melrose (l) and Townsend (r).
(G. A. Mills.)

even during a period of expansion. In 1946, however, there was a shortage of both air and ground crew, with the position regarding the latter made worse by a change to a three year tour of overseas duty. Thus the ORB notes, on 12 April, that instruction had been received concerning the posting to 21 PTC, for return to the United Kingdom, of personnel who had been posted overseas in November and December 1942. Two days later nineteen men left, tour-expired. With the Squadron already well below establishment, these were losses that could ill be afforded, and though some ground personnel had been posted in from the disbanded 231 Wing, and others arrived from the United Kingdom, the CO's summary for April noted that 'the Unit is still approximately 15% under establishment'.

In the same summary Geoffrey Mills also noted that 'the response of aircrew and groundcrew personnel to re-engage or extend their service has so far been very poor, and a talk was given by Air Chief Marshal Slessor at RAF Station Fayid on this subject'. Since the May summary noted that the rate of re-engagement or extension continued to be very poor, it seems that neither ACM Slessor's talk, nor one by Gp/Capt Smythe to ground crew on 25 April, had much effect.

In June the consequences of this shortage of personnel were seen in the reduction of the Squadron to cadre strength, six crews ferrying surplus Lancasters to the United Kingdom, leaving just six aircraft and crews at Abu Sueir. These continued a regular regime air tests, local duty flights, practice bombing, air to sea firing, bullseye cross-country and bombing exercises, and occasional fighter affiliation. Formation flying, it seems, had been abandoned, while ferrying and freight flights were reduced in frequency.

With all its Lancaster squadrons at cadre strength, 205 Group rationalized its dispositions during July and August. First to move to Shallufa, where 37 and 70 Squadrons were already based, was 104 Squadron, the other component of 236 Wing, which took with it 'sufficient domestic personnel to be self supporting', as the 40 Squadron ORB put it. By the end of August 236 Wing had also moved, leaving 40 at Abu Sueir as a satellite unit. On 12 September, however, a 40 Squadron advance party flew to Shallufa, and the relocation was complete by 17 September, with the Squadron once more at the base it had occupied during the spring and summer of 1942.

In his CO's summary at the end of August 1945 Wg/Cdr Smith had commented:

> for the fourth month in succession the Squadron got through without a single accident. 'Representing 3,100 hours flying, 40 Squadron's record will be difficult to better' were the remarks of the A.O.C. 205 Group. With such a record the Squadron remains well on top of the 205 Group ladder.

At the end of August 1946 the Squadron had completed sixteen months accident-free, a remarkable record which ended tragically when on 19 September news was received that Lancaster NX690 had crashed near Homs, Tripolitania, after an early morning take-off from Castel Benito. In the crash died F/O D. R. Faber and his crew of five, along with nineteen RAF passengers. On hearing the news, the new CO, Sqn/Ldr J. D. Melrose DFC, took off for Castel Benito to investigate, but returned under orders from the Station Commander at Shallufa.[2] The following day, however, Sqn/Ldr Melrose flew to Castel Benito to attend the funerals of the crash victims, who were buried at Tripoli Military Cemetery on the 21st.

Later in September the Squadron underwent further diminution, the CO's summary noting:

> Further reductions in strength were effected towards the end of the month, being finally stabilised at four aircraft and five aircrews with an established ground strength of 58 airmen of all trades.

At such a low manning level the Squadron had difficulties, at times, in maintaining its flying training programme, Sqn/Ldr Melrose noting at the end of October that 'the Squadron had two crews away in the U. K. for three weeks during the month, severely restricting the use of aircraft'. The situation was made even more difficult during November, when a number of aircrew were tour-expired, but stabilized during December, Sqn/Ldr. Melrose noting that 'several aircrew have extended their service by various amounts, and with the help of regulars there should be no difficulty in keeping the Squadron going for at least six months'.

The process of attrition continued in the first months of 1947, the CO noting that February had seen 'the Squadron strength again depleted by Class A Release and Overseas Tour Expiry'. The shortage of ground crew was countered by the pooling of the maintenance personnel of 40 and 104 Squadrons and 236 Wing. The shortfall in aircrew was more difficult to resolve, but early in March two almost complete crews joined the Squadron from the United Kingdom, bringing the Squadron almost up to strength. Prospects seemed good, but late in the month it was learnt that 40 was to be disbanded, and aircrew and ground personnel posted to the remaining units in Middle East Command. For Doug. Melrose, who was not at Shallufa when the decision was taken, the news came as a bitter and, he felt, undeserved blow, since the situation with regard to ground crew, a critical factor, was better on 40 Squadron than 104. Nonetheless, on 1 April the Squadron was disbanded for a third time.

# Notes

1. Another SNCO of equally long and distinguished service, Flt/Sgt Charles Goodridge, had left in the Spring of 1945. Wg/Cdr Smith's acknowledgement of the crucial part these men had played in the Squadron's achievements may stand, more generally, as an acknowledgement of the work of the ground crews generally. They figure little in these pages, yet without their dedicated and unremitting efforts, the operational achievements which form a major feature of this history would not have been possible.

2. Doug. Melrose, previously a flight commander, succeeded Geoffrey Mills on 5 September 1946.

# 22

# Load Carrying:
# December 1947–March 1950

I N late 1947 RAF Transport Command was reorganized and expanded in response to growing Cold War tensions. As part of that process two Abingdon-based squadrons equipped with Douglas Dakotas were moved to Oakington, to be replaced by squadrons there equipped with the Avro York. This move involved 242 Squadron, part of which, on arrival at Abingdon, became 40 Squadron, which was officially re-formed on 1 December under Sqn/Ldr W. Beringer. He would remain with the Squadron only until March 1948, however, his place being taken by Sqn/Ldr B. G. Meharg, AFC, CO until the Squadron disbanded in March 1950.

The re-formation of 40 at Abingdon was fitting, given the Squadron's pre-war affiliation as 'Abingdon's Own'. This link was to be fostered by the borough and the Squadron during the three years of its third existence, as was that with its history and traditions. A first step in that direction was taken on 13 January 1948, when Flt/Lt Harris flew to Wyton to collect the Squadron silver, stored there since February 1942.

The Avro York C1, with which the Squadron was to be equipped, was a four-engined long range transport aircraft which was essentially a marriage of a capacious new fuselage with Lancaster wings, engines, tail unit and

85. 40 Squadron aircrew, Abingdon, January 1948. Centre Sqn/Ldr W. Beringer.
(R. H. Philips.)

undercarriage. The York was flown in 1942, but did not go into full production until after V.E. Day.

As might be expected of an aircraft derived from the Lancaster, the York had a good performance. With four 1,280 hp Merlin XX engines, it could carry a crew of five and twenty-four passengers or an equivalent amount of freight up to 2,700 miles at a cruising speed of 233 mph. It also proved reliable, 40 suffering no accidents during three years of operation, much of it under heavy operational pressure.

Despite its bulk the York was pleasant to fly, as Danny Smith, captain of one of the crews transferred from 242 Squadron, recalls:

> When correctly trimmed it would fly "hands on" for long distances (hands on, rather than auto-pilot), with little effort. But it suffered a typical RAF fault—a fixed high pilot's seat, designed with a long legged, long armed pilot in mind. The engine controls were in the roof, so for a short pilot, it was a case of left arm at full stretch on the control column, right arm at full stretch on the throttles, up in the roof, and legs at full stretch on the rudders, keeping the aircraft straight on take off. (That's why I always carried around two folded blankets to put behind my back on the pilot's seat.)

The process of hiving off 40 Squadron from 242 took some time to complete, for on 22 January 1948 the Abingdon ORB notes that '242 Squadron is now divided into 40 and 242 Squadrons'. It is hard to see why this took so long, however, since there was not full unit separation. For the Yorks of the four squadrons were held in a Station pool, and serviced by personnel on Station postings. The flying complement of each squadron consisted of one Squadron Leader (Flying) and sixteen crews (comprising co-pilot, navigator, signaller and engineer) under Flight Lieutenant captains.

The principal task of the Abingdon squadrons was to maintain passenger and freight services to the Middle and Far East. Lyneham was the point of departure, with the Yorks flown there the previous night, and crews accommodated at nearby Clyffe Pypard. The routes were designated UM and UMF (to Luqa, Malta, or Castel Benito and then Fayid in the Canal Zone), UDY and UDYF, continuing to Habbaniya (Iraq) and Mauripur (Pakistan), and UCS and UCSF flying the further stages to Negombo (Ceylon) and Tengah, Singapore. The suffix F indicated a freight-only flight.

The first 40 Squadron crew to fly one of these routes was that of Flt/Lt L. Dale, which took off from Lyneham on UCS 947 on 2 December, twenty-four hours after the Squadron had been reformed. The following day a second crew (Flt/Lt J. J. Teare) left for Mauripur, flying UDY 073, and on the 8th an aircraft (Flt/Lt C. Glossop) left for Fayid on UMF 079. By the end of the month nine round trips had been completed.

Some statistics are of interest here. Dale's crew was away 11 days, returning to Abingdon on 13 December, after 80 hours flying time, having brought

86. A 40 Squadron York takes off from Abingdon. (B. A. Crespin.)

back from Singapore 14 passengers, 32 lbs of mail and 1,424 lbs of freight. Teare and his crew were absent 11 days also, but amassed only 47 hrs 45 mins. flying time. They brought back 24 passengers, but no mail or freight. Glossop's crew were only away 4 days, however, their flight to the Canal Zone and back having taken just over 28 hours flying time. This was a freight only flight, 8,383 lbs being brought back to Lyneham.

The basis on which the Squadrons operated is explained in the Abingdon ORB, which notes on 1 January 1948 that 'the four squadrons had started working route flying on a weekly basis. Each squadron doing a week's scheduled services at a time'. It continues:

> The week before a Squadron operates the route Scheduled Services it takes over all Wing Duties and Station Duties for one week, supplying all Duty Executive Officers, Orderly Officers, Flight Planning, Airfield Controllers and any other Station Duty that crops up. There is a laid down leave policy for crews operating the Route. Crews operating on the Singapore run get 5 days leave on returning to base and [on] the shorter Karachi and Fayid runs, the crews get 48 hrs or they do a Karachi and Fayid trip successive, and get 5 days.

When not route flying crews underwent ground and air training, the Abingdon ORB noting:

> The Wing also has a Ground Training School where a few crews are detailed to attend for 3 weeks instruction. After this they have their Categorization

examinations and if successful they are then fit for the route again. The standard laid down for these exams is quite high: 80% being needed to attain a B category.

The training requirement included 100 hours of flying a month. In December all four squadrons met this target despite bad weather.

Weather was but one obstacle to a sufficient number of flying hours, however. Frequent references in the Abingdon ORB to a 'shortage of aircraft' or to the 'unserviceability of aircraft' point up one of the drawbacks to pooling, economical though it was. Route flying took priority, and at times there were insufficient Yorks to maintain the required training.

Nor were shortages of aircraft the only causes of complaint. On 14 February a Station Commander's Parade was held at 0830 hrs. The station ORB records the outcome:

> The parade was not very successful owing to the small number of personnel who turned up. Wg. Cdr. Sellick, DSO DFC, [Wing Commander Flying] decided that in future all officers, aircrew and ground personnel should go on parade. The duty squadron will provide 100% personnel and the other three squadrons will provide 50% of the personnel.

The casual attitude towards such parades reflects the changes wrought within the RAF by the Second World War, of which many of the aircrew were veterans. These men took less than kindly to a Station Commander's Parade on a bleak February morning. Sqn/Ldr Beringer shared their views:

> 'Shrub' Sellick decided to turn the clock back to pre-war days and poor old 40 Squadron aircrew and ground crew paraded every day before work! What a waste of time. Unbelievable, but true.

The pattern of squadron life, with route flying alternating with local flying and ground training, was now well-established. Danny Smith recalls that the passengers were a mixture of service personnel and fare-paying passengers, engaged mainly in the oil, rubber and tin industries, and that Yorks provided the only landplane service to Singapore apart from KLM Skymasters.

> Servicing was carried out by personnel of the RAF manned Staging Posts. Accommodation was satisfactory, likewise the food. Cigarettes and drink were cheap, and the odd delay allowed a drink. At Negombo spirits were 10% the price of beer! (Scandinavian lager). Flying rations from Negombo were always most interesting and tasty!
>
> Take off from there was often just pre-dawn and was accompanied by a warning to watchout for elephants on the runway (they were used for timber operations in the jungle and the mahoots sometimes took short-cuts). Arrival at Negombo on a Monday involved an extra night stop as Changi closed on Tuesday (after the homeward bound York had taken off).
>
> Ceylon is of course famous for its tea—and the tea growers lost no time in

advertising it. All on landing were directed to the "tea hut" (a typical "jungle hut"). The tea was made with unboiled luke-warm water with floating tea leaves, lashings of sugar and Carnation milk! We always brought a pound back but made it the right way at home.

As for social life—it was fairly restricted with "living out of a suitcase". We would normally meet one or two of the other crews at the various stops—but not always of one's own squadron. Sometimes one needed to think of the names of one's own squadron crews. However, we were all doing the same task and doing it well, with a first class safety record.

This comfortable pattern of activity (Flight Engineer Doug. Adamson recalls that 'we flew between 8–12000 feet at 156 knots cruising speed and so had plenty of time to "view" the world') was broken on 29 June, when RAF Abingdon was told that the York squadrons were to participate in the air supply of Berlin, Operation Carter-Paterson—later known as Operation Plain Fare. All route and training flights ceased immediately in preparation for this, and five aircraft with eight crews from Abingdon left for Wunsdorf in the British Zone of Germany on 1 July. By the 6th twenty-one aircraft and thirty-five crews had been provided.[1]

The origins of the emergency airlift in which 40 now found itself involved dated to the end of World War Two, and the establishment of four zones of occupation in Germany—British, French, American and Russian. The four powers also agreed that Berlin should (though within the Russian zone) be itself divided into four zones, and run by the Allied Control Commission.

The euphoria of victory over, difficulties began to emerge over the management of Germany, and particularly of Berlin. By the autumn of 1946 East-West relations were poor, and Anglo-American plans for German recovery, including the establishment of a German administration and the fusion of their Berlin zones, led to a further deterioration. The Soviets walked out of the Allied Control Commission and systematic obstruction of land access to Berlin began. A crucial bridge over the Elbe was closed 'for repairs', road traffic was turned back at Soviet checkpoints and trains were ordered not to stop at stations in the British sector. The Soviets also prevented canal barges from reaching Berlin.

Ignoring a Soviet ban, on 22 June the Western powers introduced the new West German Deutschmark to their zones in Berlin. On the 24th the Russians responded by stopping all rail traffic from reaching the Western zones and cut the supply of electricity to the Western sectors. The blockade had begun.

In response the Western Allies began to supply Berlin by air. By 29 June the RAF was averaging 75 tons daily, using Dakotas, and it was envisaged that with Yorks that would rise to 400 tons. The USAAF likewise anticipated that when its C47s were replaced by C–54 Skymasters 1,000 tons a day could be delivered. Before long these figures would be well exceeded.

Supplying Berlin by air was not just a matter of aircraft numbers and capacity, but also of logistics. When the Yorks and C–54s arrived they did not immediately increase the tonnage of supplies carried because the loading and refuelling capacities of the airfields were inadequate. There were also problems with the weather, as Eric Brown recalls:

> Gatow was simply not equipped for the task, nor for that matter was Wunsdorf! Fighter squadrons had been hastily moved out of Wunsdorf to make way for the Yorks. The Officers' and Sergeants' Messes were bursting at the seams with aircrews. The Yorks, which had to park on grass, soon churned the dispersal area onto mud and major work was required of the Royal Engineers using German labour to lay down large areas of pierced steel planking (PSP) to allow us to operate. Later these were further upgraded to tarmac in anticipation of a prolonged siege. Similarly at Gatow an extra parallel runway had to be laid with PSP to be used for take-off after unloading.

By the second week of July some of the handling problems were resolved, and tonnage figures began to rise. In June 1,404 tons were flown in, but on July 8 alone 1,117 tons were carried, while on July 11 the total was 1,264 tons and on the 15th 1,480. The western powers also began bringing in coal to supply the power stations in West Berlin. Industrial goods were flown out and a backlog of mail was cleared.

As a shuttle service was established, it became clear that it was possible to resume training at Abingdon, and on 12 July it recommenced, the ORB noting that the 'main task was directed towards training crews to Green Card instrument rating standards, and to provide replacement crews for Operation PF'.

At this point crews involved in Plain Fare were rostered individually, spending 19 days at Wünsdorf, followed by five days' leave in the United Kingdom. A typical twenty-four day cycle for one crew and its aircraft during the airlift was as follows:

1. Abingdon—Wünsdorf.
2. stand by.
3–7 one or two trips to Gatow each morning.
36 hours rest
9–13 one or two trips to Gatow each night.
36 hours rest.
15–19 one or two trips to Gatow each afternoon.
20 Wünsdorf—Abingdon
20–24 leave in UK.

This system worked well, but did little to foster squadron identity, and after two months steps were taken to address this, a September entry in the 40

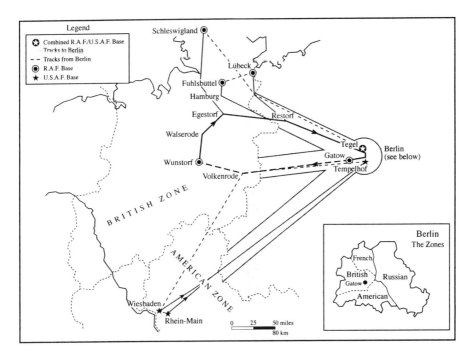

Map 6. Operation Plain Fare, June 1948–July 1949.

Squadron ORB noting the introduction of a new system whereby 'the whole squadron will return to base together, and spend 7 days per month in the UK.'

During October, therefore, individual comings and goings were replaced by a squadron roster, so that thirteen crews returned from Wünsdorf between the 4th and 16th, and left again between the 20th and 23rd. In November, settling fully into this new pattern, the crews all returned to Abingdon between the 7th and 10th, leaving for Wünsdorf again between the 17th and 20th. Doug. Adamson recalls this new arrangement with pleasure as

> the only time the Squadron all came together under one roof as it were. It meant that one could meet other members of one's own squadron for the first time; very pleasant indeed as one tended to live very isolated lives "on the routes" and not really feel part of an organisation at all.

The intensity of Operation Plain Fare required adherence to a strict pattern of flying. Eric Brown writes:

> The route into Berlin was down the corridor to a beacon in West Berlin, north of Gatow with a right handed pattern turning south and then west from a direct landing on the main runway. If the wind was easterly, a left hand

circuit applied for landing, with departures from Gatow right to avoid the incoming flow. If a landing was not made on the first approach the standard drill was to overshoot and return loaded to base, unless Air Traffic were able to give special permission for a circuit if a clear gap existed between the waves of aircraft. Intervals between aircraft were 3 minutes, which, in the 'state of the art' for control in those days, was pretty intensive! Sortie time was about 2 hours total; about 1:10 for the pattern into Berlin and about 50 minutes directly homebound, the latter being flown at the lower level of 1500 feet to achieve vertical separation from inbound traffic.

Despite the precise rules there were many hazards. Danny Smith was involved in a near-miss:

> On many days the route was enveloped in thick stratus cloud, but was absolutely smooth so that there was the sensation of being almost stationary in cotton wool. Taking off one such day on a mixed flight (civil Tudors and RAF Yorks) I was behind a Tudor of, I think, a one aircraft firm. Flying the corridor at 3,000 feet, in smooth cloud at 3 minute intervals, on nearing Fronhau I felt a tremor pass through the aircraft, followed by another stronger one. This could only be the slipstream of an aircraft dead ahead, so I shot up 50 feet. I was about to report my action to Fronhau when the massive fin and rudder of a Tudor appeared below my nose. I was on my first flight of the shift, and on landing, that, as far as I was concerned, was the end of the matter—calamity avoided. However, the crew were quite shaken and on return to Wünsdorf were told to skip the second flight.

Eric Brown was also involved in a hazardous situation when, on take off from Gatow one night, the fire warning light for the No. 3 engine came on. He continues:

> To abort would have meant a crash overshoot into the rough ground and pine trees at the end of the runway (and probably with extensive fire in the process); the only decision was to press on and get airborne, even with a fire.

Lightly laden for the return trip, the York climbed easily with one engine feathered, and the fire extinguisher operated swiftly and efficiently. At Wünsdorf it was found that a con-rod had broken, and smashed through the engine casing, hitting a fire warning switch in the process. Hence the fire had been extinguished as it began.

As autumn came on, and then winter, fog was a frequent hazard, though an experienced crew could sometimes overcome it, as Eric Brown notes:

> On one very clear night we returned in early daylight to Wunsdorf, calling at around 15 miles for direct approach and landing as was routine with a Westerly wind or still air conditions. We were told that the airfield was in fog and we would probably have to divert. Permission was given to make an approach, subject to usual limits, and we continued on BABS [Beam Approach Beacon System] towards the runway. Yellow sodium lights showed

clearly as we approached in the clear air above the fog. I flew over the approach lights towards the runway and landed between the sodium lights on either side of the runway, seeing the ground only at the last minute during the round-out to touch down. The fog was no more than 50 to 100 feet thick and the landing was really no problem with the bright sodiums to guide us; taxying to dispersal required great care. Ground crews were suitably impressed.

The strict schedule was maintained on the ground as in the air, as Danny Smith recalls:

Each aircraft was met by a team of Germans and trucks and the aircraft unloaded in record time. German women gave the aircraft a sweep out on completion, and also enhanced their rations (the lift provided German civilians with about 1000 calories per day) by separating the sweepings into their multi-pocketed overalls. There was normally a small return load—a few manufactured steel objects—light girders, etc or castings or young children evacuees. They sat on the floor along one side, with a rope stretched in front of them and anchored at each end.

Loads at Wunsdorf were the responsibility of the Army and comprised an assortment of standard loads. Typical loads were (all in pounds):

16,000 coal (the most unpopular load, the Yorks increased in weight throughout the lift due to coal dust under the floor boards)
16,000 clothing
16,000 butter
10,400 paper and 6,000 flour
7,500 flour, 3,000 milk (dried) and 4,500 vitamin tabs
12,000 flour and 4,500 potatoes (all veges were dried)
As these were all in 50kg sacks with leaks, the aircraft sweepers often got a bonus, and I've no doubt spent the evening sorting out their pickings!

Return loads, apart from manufactured goods and children, were mail—almost always 2,000 lb of it on each aircraft.

That the Yorks returned loaded was due, perhaps, to the fact that they flew better in ballast than empty.

Though the RAF and USAF had supplied the basic needs of West Berliners during the summer and autumn, it was doubtful whether they could do so during winter. By dint of superb organization—ground controllers were landing one aircraft every five minutes—and aided by better than usual weather a crisis was avoided, and as spring came it was evident that the attempt to influence Western policies over Germany had failed, and in early July the Soviet authorities began to ease their grip on the city.

During June 1949, the last full month of the blockade, 40's Yorks flew 474 hours on Operation Plain Fare, and 91 in training seven new crews. With the easing of the blockade, however, the position changed radically. The only Plain Fare flight in July seems to have been on the 1st, by Flt/Lt

87. Sqn/Ldr B. G. Meharg and crew during their Scandinavian tour, August 1949.
(l to r) Flt/Lt Arthur Brown (Nav), Flt/Lt Bill Richards (Sig), Sqn/Ldr Meharg, Flt/Lt
Doug Adamson (Fl Eng) and seated, Flt/Lt Ken Bettles (2nd Pilot). (A. C. Brown.)

S. Mackay, and thereafter, with crews back at their home base, almost the
entire squadron was given twenty-eight days leave.

When members of the Squadron returned from leave, however, it was
not to Abingdon, for on 15 June 40 had moved to Bassingbourn, in
Cambridgeshire. Marking the event, the Mayor and council had two days
earlier entertained Sqn/Ldr Meharg and some of the officers at a cocktail
party in the council chambers. Only the previous month the CO had
attended a dinner given in Abingdon by the Mayor, during the course of
which he had 'presented the Mayor with an engraved trophy to commemo-
rate the asociation of the Squadron with Abingdon.' Earlier still, in March,
so the ORB records, the Adjutant had visited the Air Historical Branch in
London 'to collect past squadron history'.

At Bassingbourn 40 resumed its old patterns of activity, and August saw
it return to its combination of long-haul route flying and ground and air
training, though with three exceptions, as when Flt/Lt Mackay flew to
Ellenikon (Athens) and back (2–5 August) and Flt/Lt Ware took thirty
American and Canadian ATC cadets for a day tour of the Ruhr.

The third out-of-the-usual flight was that which took Sqn/Ldr Meharg
to Scandinavia as support for a goodwill tour by 66 and 92 Squadrons. The
CO and his crew left Bassingbourn on 16 August, joining the two fighter
squadrons at Duxford, and did not return until the 31st. Their itinerary took

them to a series of Swedish and Norwegian bases. and the flavour of the tour can be gauged from Sqn/Ldr Meharg's ORB summary:

> An extremely warm welcome was extended by the Royal Swedish Air Force and the Royal Norwegian Air Force during the tour and the crew were kept fully occupied by Official functions and sight seeing tours. The only complaint the crew could possibly have was that the programme was too full.

On 22 September Flt/Lt Harris took off on a route proving flight from Lyneham to Nairobi. The route, which became UNF, was part of the British government's response to the Mau Mau insurgency in Kenya, now assuming serious proportions. It would continue to be flown until disbandment.

September 1949 was a difficult month, with massive postings in, and many crews requiring training to bring them up to route flying standard. Training at Bassingbourn was severely curtailed during the month, however, because runways were under repair, and because the ferrying of Yorks ex-Operation Plain Fare to Maintenance Units for overhaul or disposal took priority. The repairs were so disruptive that in October eight crews under training were detached to Upper Heyford, not returning until 9 November.

During October things settled down again, with scheduled runs to Nairobi, Tengah, and Mauripur, and special flights to Germany, Egypt, and, beginning on the 23rd, the longest yet, to New Zealand. This flight, by Flt/Lt L. A. P. Tapp, did not conclude until 15 November.

November and December saw the usual mix of scheduled and training flights, but the hours flown declined (281 hours route flying in December compared to 430 in October), and 40 was now flying only five scheduled services per month. In January and February 1950 this was reduced to four, though special flights continued, one being made in January (to Fayid), and two in February (to Copenhagen and Sydney: the latter from 19 February to 16 March).

By the time this flight had returned from Sydney, however, 40 Squadron had been disbanded. The decision had been announced on 6 March, and postings out were completed on the 14th, the ORB noting that six crews had been posted to 115 Squadron to 'form part of the nucleus of a B29 Squadron, while the remainder have been distributed amongst the various Bomber Command squadrons'. Disbandment occurred formally on 15 March 1950.

To mark the event a Guest Night was held in the Officers' Mess at Bassingbourn on 10 March, the guests including, inter alia, Wg/Cdrs R. E. Ridgway and D. E. Cattell, the latter a junior officer with 40 in 1935–6. The evening began with the guests taking cocktails with the CO, and those dining assembled in the anteroom at 1930 hrs. Among those making after-dinner speeches were Sqn/Ldr Meharg and Wg/Cdr Ridgway. On behalf of the Squadron P/O Flinn presented the CO with two engraved tankards, and the 'extremely enjoyable evening wound up', so the ORB records, 'at 0500 hours the following morning'.

The AOC Transport Command marked the Squadron's disbandment with the following signal:

> It is with infinite regret that I find myself sending you this signal of farewell to you and your squadron on being disbanded with your magnificent record throughout the years of hostilities and your great contribution to the Berlin air lift. I can only say "Adieu" until some future time you rise again out of the ashes of economy.
>
> I am certain that wherever you go you will take with you some of the traditions and quality of No. 40 Squadron. Good luck to you all.

## Note

1. On all aspects of the Berlin Blockade see Ann and John Tusa, *The Berlin Blockade* (London: Hodder & Stoughton, 1988), to which this chapter is indebted at various points.

# 23

# Bombers Again:
# October 1953–December 1956

F ORTY SQUADRON arose, phoenix-like, out of 'the ashes of economy' when
Cold War tensions dictated an enlargement of Bomber Command. It
was re-formed on 28 October 1953 at Coningsby, Lincolnshire, under the
command of Sqn/Ldr K. B. Rogers, DFC, AFC, joining four other Canberra
squadrons there.

A medium bomber squadron and part of the Main Force, Bomber
Command, 40 was equipped with the new and (in performance) revolutionary English Electric Canberra B. Mk. 2. The RAF's first jet bomber, it
had entered service in May 1951. With two Rolls Royce Avon jet engines
each delivering 6,500 lb of thrust, the B2 was capable of a maximum speed
of 570 mph at 40,000 feet. Bomb load was 6,000 lb, and the aircraft had a
range of 2,660 miles.

At the end of October 40 Squadron was skeletal, with only Sqn/Ldr
Rogers and his two Flight Commanders, Flt/Lts G. S. Wilkes and W. G.
Bennett, and four navigators. A month later, however, it was at full strength,
with eight pilots, besides the CO and Flight Commanders, and nine navigators in addition to the Navigation and Bombing Leaders.

88. 40 Squadron Canberra B2, W1727. (via Andy Thomas.)

Where aircraft were concerned, however, the situation was less satisfactory. For 40 was still three short of its establishment of ten Canberras, and those it had had major deficiencies, as Keith Rogers noted in his CO's summary for November:

> The Squadron's aircraft are not equipped with bomb sights and computer boxes. Four aircraft have two Light Series Bomb Carriers fitted per aircraft, and full Gee-H Blind Bombing Gear. The remaining equipment is on demand. It is hoped to have one aircraft equipped for visual bombing early next month.

Given this situation, it is hardly surprising that only one aircraft was able to take part in a station exercise on 12 November, and one in a radar calibration operation on the 26th. Most of the flying during November was, in fact, given over to training and the checking out of crews by the CO and flight commanders.

In November Keith Rogers expressed the hope that in December 40 would be sufficiently supplied with aircraft and personnel to be divided into flights. This happened, though most of the Canberras were still being fitted with bombing equipment, and five were provided for exercises during the month. No station exercises were flown, though, because 'political pressure . . . closed the bombing ranges during the month. The conditions imposed at present,' the CO's summary continues, 'are such that worthwhile exercises are impossible'.

At re-formation, 40's Canberras were crewed by a pilot and navigator, but December saw the addition of a plotter, or safety observer. To fill this third role five officers and one sergeant were posted in during January. Trevor Wilson, who served successively as a navigator and observer, comments:

> Initially we flew as 2 men crews, being selected and brought together at No 231 OCU, Bassingbourn. My skipper was F/O D. H. (Don) Clelland. [But] the accuracy of navigation demanded was such that the task needed the full time attention of one navigator, leaving the second man (observer) to handle blind and visual bombing as well as the many other tasks, such as fuel graphs, map reading, looking out as were applicable on a particular flight. Often it was the case that there was far too much work for one man but not enough for two.

The safety observers remained with the Squadron until June, when seven fully trained navigators were posted in as their replacements.

On 1 December a cocktail party in the Officers' Mess marked the Squadron's re-formation, and traditional celebrations began on the 10th with an Airmans' Christmas Dance in the NAAFI, with an Informal Christmas Dance in the Officers' Mess on the 17th, and children's parties on the 19th.

Personnel returned from leave on 6 January, but bad weather prevented flying until the 9th, and less than a fortnight later 40 moved to a new base. The advance party had left for Wittering on the 22nd, the aircraft and aircrew following two days later. Seven aircraft lined up on the runway and took off at ten second intervals, but a farewell run over the aerodrome was, the CO's summary notes, 'made rather ragged by poor visibility'. On the 25th the main party moved to Wittering, and the Squadron resumed operational flying the following day.

Like Abingdon a Lutyens design, Wittering offered pre-war spaciousness, with junior officers 'two to a room, with coal fire and civilian batman', but also, as Trevor Wilson recalls, an earlier austerity in that 'the ablutions as they were called were down the corridor, and unheated, not exactly the lap of luxury'. 'But we ate and drank well', he adds.

What was the composition of the aircrew who were, now that servicing was on a station basis, the bulk of 40 Squadron? All but one safety observer, Sgt. G. White, were officers, and most were on short service commissions, of either four or eight years, and some on two years National Service. There were few career officers, though some extended their short service commisions to twelve years or more.

That some did this was not surprising for, as Trevor Wilson notes,

Life was very relaxed in the RAF of that era. The war was over, there were no risks from enemy activity, only your own stupidity, the threat from Communism had not reached the proportions it finally did, and 40 Squadron flew during the week and went home for the weekends.

'It was an idyllic life', he adds:

no real responsibilities for us batchelors, looked after from dawn to dusk, plenty of sporting facilities, village pubs, summer balls, winter balls, the occasional bit of work, at which we all excelled, and naturally a continuous shortage of cash.

February 1954 saw 40 settled into a full flying and ground training programme; 127 sorties were flown, with a total of 304 hours, 128 by night. Over the next few months the sorties reached a high of 172 in June, though usually averaging 140 or so. Typically, 40 took part in two or perhaps three exercises a month, examples being, in April, 'Re-arm' and 'Kingpin'. The first of these, which took place on the 7th and 8th, saw 40 supplying aircraft for four waves, the last a maximum effort, for a simulated bombing run on Kristiansand, Norway. 'Kingpin', on 24 and 25 April, was designed to achieve concentration over the target, a point near Heligoland, and for this purpose, the CO noted,

89. 40 Squadron aircrew, Wittering, April 1954.
Rear (l to r): F/O R. A. Jackson, P/O Henry, P/O D. C. Elmy, F/O T. Wilson,
F/O D. E. Tuthill, F/O P. G. Squirrel, F/O M. J. Sechiari, P/O G. F. Burroughs,
Sgt G. White, F/O J. McRoberts, F/O C. S. Glidle, F/O I. S. Headley,
F/O B. A. Turner, F/O E. A. Pike.
Front: P/O J. Hendry, P/O G. G. Ness, P/O M. A. Pringle, F/O D. H. Clelland,
P/O E. D. Lucas, Flt/Lt W. G. Bennett, Sqn/Ldr K. B. Rogers, Flt/Lt E. A. Brown,
Flt/Lt G. S. Wilkes, F/O F. J. W. Stevens, F/O J. A. Ledger, F/O L. J. B. Conway,
P/O D. L. Waltham. (T. Wilson.)

the aircraft were flown in pairs, with one minute between each pair. The exercise was in two waves, with six squadron aircraft in the first wave, and five in the second. It concluded with a simulated Gee-H bombing run at Folkestone and a Gee letdown for each aircraft at base.

During May a ground exercise provided a challenge of a different sort. 'Park Flit' was a four day escape and evasion exercise for personnel from Wittering, covering Leicestershire and Rutland, and designed to give aircrew experience in 'the arts of escape, evasion and survival'. The police and defence forces acted as the enemy, but caught only 20 of the 70 'evaders'.

During the late spring and early summer of 1954 cloud and rain frequently curtailed flying. Exercise Demolition, on 30 June, had to be cancelled, and though three small scale exercises in early July were completed, Dividend, which began on 16 July, was disrupted to some extent. It was also weather which was responsible for a fatal crash on the 24th—the only one 40 was to suffer while operating Canberras. Two crews were on a planned diversion to Marham at the conclusion of Dividend sorties, and one (Flt/Lt Wilkes) crashed on final approach. All three crew members, Wilkes, F/O D. Nelson and Sgt White, were killed.

For navigation, the Squadron relied on Gee, and with a view to lessening that reliance and preparing for flights beyond Gee range, an effort was made in July to test other navigational aids. The ORB comments:

> Many cross-countries with limited aids have been flown, using Astro and Pinpoints in place of the usual Gee. Astro has been found reasonably accurate when shot in front of the aircraft, but not so accurate to the sides.

Trevor Wilson explains that 'it turned out that the aircraft had a slow, unappreciated Dutch Roll which rendered star shots on the beam useless, although fore and aft shots were reasonable. This using a hand held sextant!' With astronavigation impracticable, navigation beyond Gee range depended, Frank Stevens writes, 'on VHF radios when we were with range of ground stations that could have given us bearings', but otherwise was 'principally based on DR navigation and what map reading could be achieved'.

August brought innovation with the first two 'Lone Ranger' exercises undertaken by 40 Squadron. On the first, leaving on 5 August, F/Os F. J. W. Stevens and P/Os M. I. S. Anderson, and C. S. Glidle, with SAC Graham as passenger, flew to Wünsdorf and then to Idris, in Libya. The second, begun on the 26th, also concluded at Idris, but F/Os L. J. B. Conway, T. B. Patterson, and B. A. Turner, with Cpl Goldsworthy as passenger, were routed via Gibraltar. Frank Stevens recalls:

> In August we flew a Lone Ranger Exercise. This will have been a reward for gaining our combat category on 13th July and these overseas flights were a great bonus to the routine of visual, GH, Cross-countries and the normal squadron life, and to go down to Tripoli, Idris and Wünsdorf was a very pleasant trip.

Sadly, budget constraints were to strictly limit the number of these exercises, as the October ORB notes:

> The Lone Ranger exercises have been shortened considerably, and P/O Pringle's Lone Ranger on October 1st was to Gibraltar and back, staying there less than 36 hours. F/O Clelland's Lone Ranger later in the month was cancelled because the quota had been exceeded.

October was a quiet month, noteworthy principally for a liaison visit paid to G-H stations on the continent. Frank Stevens recalls:

> We had a trip to Gutesloh and Fasberg in Germany. This was made at the request of the O.C. of a radar station in Germany. The radar station's task was to provide one or some of the signals we used for GH bombing. The

unit operated was mobile, operated from a little convoy of truck and trailers. It was a very tedious job, I suppose, for the airmen who had little idea of what they were doing or the importance of it, so we were sent over as a crew to visit them and to explain what we did, how an exercise was laid on, the war-time type briefing, the takeoff in radio silence without lights to progress through time gates, to attack our targets using their signals.

Stevens and his crew, F/O Glidle and P/O Anderson, were chosen for the liaison visit because they were closest to achieving the coveted Select category rating. Frank Stevens writes:

> As our experience and ability increased, we were cleared up the bombing ladder from progressively great heights, and I see about October we were bombing from 40,000 feet, including nominated bombs which would have been intended to qualify us for our next category which was Select Category.

Operating at such great heights brought its problems, as Trevor Wilson recalls:

> We could and did find flying conditions somewhat hairy in clear air turbulence or the tops of nimbus clouds. Remember we were operating at new levels up to 52,000 ft, and learning all the time. To enhance safety when we started operating the Canberra we kept a running fuel graph so that we knew to the minute the aircraft's endurance.

In November both Stevens' crew and F/O E. D. Lucas's (F/O's G. Hasel and D. E. Tuthill) achieved Select rating, and on the 18th the CO received a message from 3 Group HQ congratulating the Squadron on being the first Canberra unit in 3 Group to achieve Select classifications, and remarking upon the 'relative juniority of the crews'.

The next day Lucas's crew left with F/O D. H. Clelland's on Lone Ranger exercises. Both flew to Gibraltar via a refuelling stop at Idris, where Clelland's Canberra burst a tyre on landing. His return to Wittering, on 29 November, was equally eventful, since on landing the nosewheel of WJ990 collapsed. The crew were unhurt, but the aircraft sustained damage to the underside of the nose and the nosewheel bay.

On 23 January 1955 Stevens and Lucas left Lyneham for Khartoum on their Select Lone Ranger exercises. For Flt/Lt J. O. Thomas, however, there was a less pleasant experience that day when both engines failed while he was on a bombing run at 38,000 feet over Chesil Bank. Fortunately he managed to re-light both engines and returned to base, where one jetpipe was found to be buckled.

Though 40's establishment was ten Canberras, it had never had more than eight on charge. In February 1955, however, two further B.Mk.2s were received, along with a dual-control T.4, perhaps shared with the other Canberra units.

Navigating by Gee, crews were dependent on the stations and the accuracy of their signals. Yet difficulties were often experienced, and March was exceptional in this respect. On the 10th Exercise Bombex included a Gee-H run at Nordhorn, but 'no bombs were dropped because the aircraft were unable to contact the range', while another Bombex on the 17th was also disrupted by a malfunction at Nordhorn. Earlier, on the 11th, three aircraft had taken part in Exercise Midstogen, involving visual bombing runs on towns in Norway. The new Central German Gee chain was crucial to the exercise, but its signals were found to be inaccurate, and considerable navigation difficulties followed.

In April F/Os Conway and Pringle flew Lone Rangers on the route Khartoum-Aden-Amman-Fayid. No further Lone Rangers were flown until June, however, when four crews flew to Idris, one (F/O M. A. Pringle) going on to Shaibah, another (F/O Lucas) to Khartoum and Aden, and a third (F/O Stevens) to Nairobi. This was an exceptional month, however, and compensated for in July when no Lone Rangers were flown. A more usual quota was one a month, as in August, when F/O M. J. Blofeld flew to Idris.

During August Exercise Blue Trident Two had 40 Squadron deployed to Malta as a strike force operating against the United States Sixth Fleet in the Ionian Sea. This was a delightful change of venue and activity and also a resounding success. Thirty sorties were flown, and twenty-eight successful visual bombing attacks made on ships of the Sixth Fleet. On the first two days (1st and 2nd August) 'raids were planned at 5 minute intervals between aircraft, flying between 41000 and 48000 at speeds of 0.76 MACH direct to target and 0.79 MACH on return direct to base'. On 3 August, however, tactics were changed:

> The Squadron aircraft were split into 3 waves. Two waves were at height between 41000 and 48000 feet and were routed to attack on reciprocal tracks with 4000 feet separation between waves. The 3rd wave was routed direct to the Fleet position at 40000 feet with a maximum Rate Descent allowing about 8 minutes for a low level run and attack at maximum speed, returning to base at low level.

For the US Navy, though, the exercises must have been a galling experience, to judge by the section of the RAF report headed 'FIGHTER TACTICS':

> Fighter attacks were expected throughout the exercise from either COUGAR or BANSHEE aircraft of the United States 6th Fleet. No fighter opposition was seen on the 1st and 3rd days of the exercise. On the 2nd day Fighter aircraft were observed by the majority of crews but at much lower heights, the nearest being reported at 10000 feet below the Canberra force. All sightings were made in the target area only. No interceptions were made.

Immunity to fighter attack was nothing new for 40 Squadron, however, as Trevor Wilson recalls:

> Large scale service wide and inter-service exercises were held regularly, and our Canberra aircraft, who were the attackers, were always restricted in both speed and altitude as the contemporary fighters, DH110s and Hunters, could not match our performance. Even restricted we still felt superior as we watched the contrails of the poor fighters struggling to reach us. Only once were we well and truly bounced, and that was on a night attack against Heathrow, when the new 'Javelin' aircraft caught us.

September saw a resumption of the series of exercises which continued uninterrupted over the next seven months, one of the most interesting being 'Phoenix', in late September, which involved reconnaissance and bombing attacks on the Home Fleet. Two 'Polar Bear' exercises over Norway were also flown, in November 1955 and January 1956, together with two liaison flights to bases in Northern Germany. Lone Rangers continued to be flown at an average of three a month, until on 3 April 40's Canberras were grounded.

The problem that grounded all Canberra B2s (but had not, fortunately, occurred on any of 40's aircraft) is explained by Peter Landon, later CO of 50/40 Squadron:

> The moveable tailplane was used for fore and aft trimming and was actuated by a very powerful electrically driven "screw jack" ostensibly only controlled by a switch on the control column. However the electrics could short circuit causing fully up or down trim which had some fatal results (not ours fortunately) and was surprising at 400 knots.

With only the T4 available, crews had a great deal of spare time, and various ground training programmes were instituted, including a Combat Training Course for all officers, additional sport and PT, lectures and outside visits. The first of these, on 11 April, was to the Air Traffic Control Centre at Watnall, but during May, June and July visits were made to major industrial plants in the Midlands: Tollemache's Brewery in Cambridge, Player's in Nottingham, the Ketton Cement Works, and the Rolls-Royce factory in Derby.

Two officers, Flt/Lt M. P. F. Daniels and F/O M. A. Innes-Smith also took part in Army exercises. Joining the King's Regiment in camp at Bury St. Edmunds they were attached to two companies which took part in an exercise designed to get an imaginary bullion wagon through an ambush set by a third. Seeking to assist the companies to which his officers were attached, Keith Rogers borrowed a DH Chipmunk from St. Andrews University Air Squadron, in summer camp at Wittering, and spotted for them, using a walky-talky set fitted behind the cockpit. He located the ambush, but the

Army CO decided to ignore this information rather than get the bullion through the area without a battle.

Keith Rogers' intervention in the army exercise says a good deal about the man, and explains something of his popularity. 'A New Zealander, keen rugby man, and a good bloke to work for', as one man put it, Rogers had built up a strong *ésprit de corps*, setting and demanding high standards, but maintaining a relaxed and accessible leadership style. There was considerable regret, therefore, when he was posted out, command passing on 5 May to Sqn/Ldr E. L. Wallane.

Despite all the additional activities laid on during the grounding of the Canberras, it was a relief when flying resumed on 21 July, several aircraft having been modified by the fitting of an extra switch in the tailplane actuator circuit. Three of these took part in a flypast in honour of a visit by the Queen to RAF Marham on the 23rd. Two days earlier Flt/Lt Daniels carried out a Lone Ranger exercise to Amman, the first to any destination since 24 March, while on the 24th Flt/Lt Thomas flew to Nicosia on a not very diplomatically named Turkish Delight Exercise. On the same day there was excitement at Wittering when F/O Blofeld found that the undercarriage of his Canberra could not be lowered, and was forced to make a belly landing. Though the underside of the fuselage was damaged, the crew were uninjured.

In August 40 was involved in Exercise Accumulate. Part of the British preparations for the Anglo-French reaction to Colonel Nasser's nationalization of the Suez Canal, Accumulate saw 40's Canberras making a total of twenty-three sorties to Malta within a week, each aircraft carrying six 1,000-lb bombs. It was to be the Squadron's only contribution to the ill-fated invasion, which began with air attacks on 31 October.

Four exercises were held at the beginning of September, in preparation for the main summer exercises, Stronghold and Whipsaw, which aimed to test the United Kingdom fighter defences. Prior to the exercises there had been a race against time to bring the five Unclassified crews to Combat status, the task made all the harder by the unserviceability of Gee-H ranges, and the fact, as the ORB puts it, 'that the Squadron had no priority anywhere at the times aircraft became serviceable'. Nonetheless, four of the five crews reached Combat category grading by the time the autumn exercises began on the 19th.

The major exercise in October was Ratchet, testing a new naval radar installation at Portsdown. Forty made four 'raids', four or five aircraft participating each time. Each sortie was of nearly four hours duration, aircraft attacking from points over France at heights between 35,000 and 45,000 feet, at speeds of 0.72 to 0.76 Mach. The Squadron ORB notes that 'interceptions were made by RAF and Naval fighters over the channel in many cases' and also that 'weather interfered with the exercise to a great extent, morning take-offs being hampered by fog, while high cross winds caused one raid to be diverted to Lyneham'. The exercise was discontinued on 31 October because of the situation in the Middle East.

Another reaction to the growing crisis was the acceleration of 40's move from Wittering, where it was now the sole remaining Main Force Canberra squadron, to Upwood, where it was due to join four others. The move had been signalled for sometime, but was only confirmed a few days before the move, on the last day of October.

The departure from Wittering was marked by a squadron dining out at a Station Guest Night on 24 October, and an all ranks party at the King's Head, Oakham. The occasion was also marked by a visit, on 26 October, from the AOC 3 Group, AVM Cross, who addressed the Squadron before lunching with the officers.

At Upwood, 40 resumed its usual pattern of activity, 135 sorties being flown during November. Three Lone Ranger exercises were flown, two to Wünsdorf and one to Gibraltar, while two crews flew to Nicosia on reinforcement flights. December began similarly, but the Squadron was operating under a shadow, since it had become known that under a re-organization of Bomber Command units, whereby pairs of squadrons were amalgamated to form single units with an establishment of sixteen aircraft, 40 would be amalgamating with 50 Squadron.

Throughout 1954 the original aircrew complement remained largely unchanged. From early 1955, however, personnel were replaced at a faster rate, some because they had completed their short service commissions, others because of postings. Six at least left in that year, and a further four in the first two months of 1956, and by May, when Keith Rogers was posted, there were only three 'originals' left: Flt/Lt L. B. J. Conway, and F/Os I. S. Headley and B. G. Turner. They were still with 40 at its disbandment.

For administrative purposes, 40 Squadron was disbanded on 1 February 1957, but operationally the change took place with effect from 15 December 1956, when 50/40 Squadron was formed under the command of Wg/Cdr E. P. Landon, DFC, Sqn/Ldr Wallane becoming OC B Flight. As the final entry in the 40 Squadron ORB noted, 'With effect from 15 December, 1956, all 40 Squadron operational and other occurrences will be recorded in the Form 540 of No. 50 Squadron under the heading of B Flight.'

At disbandment the Squadron silver was taken into custody by the President of the Officers' Mess, RAF Upwood. A list included Pewter and EPNS tankards presented by officers over the years. Amongst them were tankards given by the first CO of the re-formed 40 (B) Squadron, Sqn/Ldr M. L. Taylor and two other officers in the early thirties, D. G. Morris and

H. V. L'Amy. Another was a survivor of the pair presented to the Squadron on 24 April 1941 by Sqn/Ldr Hugh Lynch-Blosse's father, Captain Lynch-Blosse. Others again were presented by recent members of the Squadron, including Keith Rogers. The silver items included the Gordon Bombing Trophy (a silver Fairey Gordon mounted on a plinth), an Inter-Flight Bombing Trophy (silver Fairey Battle), and an Inter Flight Gunnery Trophy (a silver Panther engine).

If most, at least, of the Squadron's silver had survived, other items of value seem not to have. The final entry in the ORB notes:

> The signed Squadron Crest, the board of Commanding Officers and Honours and Awards, have not been seen since the Squadron disbanded at Royal Air Force BASSINGBOURN on the 10th March, 1950. A great deal of correspondence has taken place in attempts to locate these, particularly the signed crest by H. M. King George VI on 20th April, 1937. The Air Historical Branch, previous Stations, Maintenance Units and individuals have been asked for information but nothing has come to light.

# A Postscript

THE unsuccessful search for missing items of historical significance is a sad note for the 40 Squadron ORB to end on, but not inappropriate. For the disappearance of these items, as of the World War One memorabilia not seen since February 1942, symbolizes, in a way, the fate of 40 Squadron itself, and the writing of its history. In the nearly eighty years since its formation at Gosport, much of the history of 40 Squadron has vanished, either with the death of those who served with it, or in the loss of documents, public and private, and photographs. A good deal of what has been preserved, either in memory or more tangibly, has also been inaccessible to me, largely because I have been unable to trace more than perhaps 20% of former members of the Squadron still living. I hope more will come forward as a result of the publication of *Sweeping the Skies*. I'd like to hear from them.

If in one respect I was thwarted, however, I was successful beyond my expectations in another. For having begun the history when I failed to find those who had known my father and his crew, I discovered, paradoxically, that in researching the book I found those I had earlier sought unsuccessfully. To Margaret and the late Bill Johnson (brother of Robbie Johnson, the rear gunner), Anna Close (cousin of the navigator, Vallance McCall), and Betty Richmond (sister of the bomb aimer, Harry Hesketh), my thanks for wholehearted support and encouragement. My thanks also to Dick Sutcliffe (close friend of the pilot, Les Mayers), and to his wireless operator, Eric Turner, who was a friend of my father's, serving with him both at No 1 AOS, Millom, in 1941–2, and again at Foggia Main.

I should like also to express my thanks to Charles Hamshire, bomb aimer in my father's crew, who completed his second tour a fortnight before their deaths, and who was in Naples awaiting repatriation to the United Kingdom when he heard of their loss. For his memories of the crew and their operational flying I am most grateful. In him and Pat Fincher, who flew two ops with the crew after Charles was tour-expired, and in Ian Arrowsmith, who flew as a second dicky to Ploesti on 9/10 August 1944, I have crew member eye-witnesses to every op Les Mayers' crew flew except the last.

And even there I have been lucky, for from Stuart Sigley, who was rear gunner in the aircraft just ahead of Les Mayers' on the mining run, and from Ian Arrowsmith, who had just completed his drop, I got vivid accounts of what happened. Nor did my good fortune end there, since, when in May 1992, I made a long-planned visit to Czechoslovakia, and to my father's grave in the Commonwealth War Graves Commission cemetery at Olsany, Prague, I travelled also to Dobrohost, near Bratislava, where A-Able was shot down. And there, by the Danube, I met Vincent Szelle, who on the night of 4/5 October 1944 was walking with his wife in the moonlight, and not only witnessed the shooting down of MF 458 by a German light flak unit, but found my father's body on the river bank, alongside one wing of the aircraft.

At Dobrohost, listening to Vincent's vivid account of what happened that night, I completed a search which had, in ways it took many years to recognize, preoccupied me since childhood. An alloy panel from A-Able, souvenired by Vincent before he reported his find to the Germans, and given to me, reminds me of the completion of that search as now, a little over fifty years since 205 Group's last Danube mining op, and the death which provided its initial impetus, *Sweeping the Skies* also comes to completion.

David Gunby
Christchurch,
New Zealand.
31 October 1994

# Bibliography

## 1. Books and articles with specific reference to 40 Squadron and its personnel

[Archer, Wesley D.]. *Death in the Air*. London: Heinemann, 1933 (repr. London: Greenhill Books, 1985).

Balfour, H. H. *An Airman Marches*. London: Hutchinson, 1933. (repr. London: Greenhill Books, 1985).

[Bond, Aimée Constance.] *An Airman's Wife*. London: Herbert Jenkins, 1918.

Brodie, Allan. *Adventure in my Veins*. London: Jarrolds, 1969. (repr. Farnham: Triple Cat Publishing, 1989).

Burdsall, B. H. 'Memories of 40 Squadron, 1944'. *The Canadian Amateur Radio Magazine*: Part 1, 02/88 (1988), 30–2, Part 2, 05/88 (1988), 21–3.

Campbell, George Frederick. *A Soldier of the Sky*. Chicago: Davis Printing Works, 1918.

Collis, Bob. 'The Saga of "H for Harry"'. *Flypast* (Nov. 1985), 28–31.

de Vere Robertson, F. A. 'No. 40 (Bomber) Squadron'. *Flight*, 13 May 1932, 411–16.

Dudgeon, James M. *'Mick': The Story of Major Edward Mannock*. London: Robert Hale, 1981.

Franks, Norman. 'Dallas'. *Cross and Cockade (Great Britain)*, Vol 3, no 4 (1972), 147–54.

Franks, Norman, & Chaz. Bowyer. 'Forty Squadron 1916–1919'. *Cross and Cockade (Great Britain)*: Part I, Vol 4, no 4 (1973), 176–85, Part II, Vol 5, no 1 (1974), 1–12.

Gilbert, F. T. 'McElroy of "Forty"'. *Popular Flying* ( June 1936), 132–3, 160.

Gilbert, F. T. 'Memories of 40 Squadron'. *Popular Flying* (Apr. 1935), 24–7, 33.

Grosz, Peter M. & Karl S. Schneide. 'In Search of Mrs. Cockburn-Lange', *Cross and Cockade (Great Britain)*, Vol 16, no 4 (1985), 145–67.

Hudson, James J. 'Interview with Reed Landis'. *Over the Front*, Vol 5, no 1 (Spring 1990), 4–26.

Jones, Ira. *King of Air Fighters*. London: Nicholson & Watson, 1934.

Keeling, E. H. 'An Escape from Turkey in Asia'. *Blackwoods Magazine*, Vol CCIII, no MCCXXXI (May 1918), 561–92.

Lewis, Gwilym H. *Wings over the Somme 1916–1918*. London: William Kimber, 1976. (Re-published, enlarged, 1994 by Bridge Books, Wrexham.)

Lihou, Maurice G. *It's Dicey Flying Wimpeys Around Italian Skies*. New Malden: Air Research Publications, 1992.

Loraine, Winifrid. *Robert Loraine: Actor, Soldier, Airman*. London: Collins, 1938.

Lynch-Blosse, Hugh. *Wings—and other things*. Worcester: Square One Publications, 1990.

MacMillan, Norman. *Tales of Two Air Wars*. London: Bell, 1963.

Mallahan, Patrick. 'Shot with Luck!: The Story of Robert Alexander Anderson'. *Over the Front*, Vol 5, no 2 (Summer 1990), 154–65.

'McScotch' [W. A. MacLanachan]. *Fighter Pilot*. London: Routledge & Kegan Paul, 1936 (repr. London: Greenhill Books, 1985).

Oughton, Frederick (ed.). *The Personal Diary of Major Edward 'Mick' Mannock*. London: Neville Spearman, 1966.

'Passmore, Richard' [Roger Peacock]. *Blenheim Boy*. London: Thomas Harmsworth, 1981.

Penwarn, Robert E. 'Ages of an Airman'. *Flypast* (Dec. 1988), 46–7.

Reid, P. R. *Colditz: The Full Story*. London: Macmillan, 1984.

Rofe, Cyril. *Against the Wind*. London: Hodder & Stoughton, 1956.

Strange, L. A. *An Airman Remembers*. London: John Hamilton, 1933.

Tappin, David. 'Chidlaw'. *Cross and Cockade (Great Britain)*, Vol 20, no 2 (1989), 57–67.

Whetton, Douglass. 'Flying with Forty: Recollections of Lt. Lionel B. Blaxland MA, 40 Squadron, RFC'. *Cross and Cockade (Great Britain)*, Vol 1, no 4 (1970), 78–81.

Whetton, Douglass. 'Roderick Stanley Dallas, Forgotten Ace'. *Cross and Cockade (Great Britain)*, Vol 2, no 1. (1971), 1–10.

Also at many points, *Flight* and *The Aeroplane*.


## 2. Other works consulted

Allison, Les, *They Shall Grow Not Old*. Brandon, Man: Commonwealth Air Training Plan Museum, 1991.

Allison, Les, *Canadians in the Royal Air Force*. 2nd ed. Privately published, Roland, Man, 1993.

Andrews, C. F. *Vickers Aircraft since 1908*. London: Putnam, 1988.

Bowyer, Chaz. *Wellington at War*. Shepperton: Ian Allan, 1982.

Bowyer, Chaz. *Bristol Blenheim*. Shepperton: Ian Allan, 1984.

Bruce, J. M. *Aeroplanes of the RFC (Military Wing)*. London: Putnam, 1982.

Chappell, F. R. *Wellington Wings*. London: William Kimber, 1980.

Cole, Christopher. *Royal Air Force 1918*. London: T. Donovan, 1990.

Cole, Christopher. *Royal Flying Corps 1915–1916*. London: T. Donovan, 1990.

D'Este, Carlo. *Bitter Victory*. London: Collins, 1988.

Franks, Norman. *Valiant Wings*. London: William Kimber, 1988.

Ginn, Robert. *Strike Hard! The Story of 104 (Bomber) Squadron*. Huddersfield: 104 Squadron Association, 1990.

Gray, Peter, & Owen Thetford. *German Aircraft of the First World War*. London: Putnam, 1970.

Hare, Paul R. *The Royal Aircraft Factory*. London: Putnam, 1990.

James, John. *The Paladins*. London: Macdonald, 1990.

Jones, H. A. *The War in the Air*. 6 vols. Oxford: Oxford University Press, 1928.

Macdonald, Patrick. *Through Darkness to Light*. Haddington: Pentland Press, 1990.

Middlebrook, Martin, & Chris. Everitt. *The Bomber Command War Diaries*. Harmondsworth: Viking, 1985.

Morris, Alan. *Bloody April*. London: Jarrolds, 1967.

Shores, Christopher, & Brian Cull (with Nicola Malizia). *Malta: The Hurricane Years 1940–41*. London: Grub Street Books, 1987.

Shores, Christopher, & Norman Franks and Russell Guest. *Above the Trenches*. London: Grub Street Books, 1990.

Shores, Christopher & Brian Cull (with Nicola Malizia). *Malta: The Spitfire Year 1942*. London: Grub Street Books, 1991.

Taylor, H. A. *Fairey Aircraft since 1915*. London: Putnam, 1988.

Thetford, Owen. *Aircraft of the Royal Air Force 1918–57*. London: Putnam, 1957.

Tusa, Ann & John. *The Berlin Blockade*. London: Hodder & Stoughton, 1988.

Wadsworth, Michael P. *They Led the Way; The Story of Pathfinder Squadron 156*. Beverley: Highgate Publications, 1992.

## 3. Primary Sources at the Public Record Office, Kew

Royal Flying Corps:
  Communiqués 1915–18 AIR 1/2116/207/57.
40 Squadron, 1916–19:
  Combat reports AIR 1/1222/204/5/2634, & 1/1411/204/28/42 & 48.
  Squadron Record Books AIR 1/1405/204/28/1–10, 31–35 & 44–47.
  Daily Routine Orders AIR 1/1405/204/28/11–12.
  Recommendations for promotion, honours, and awards AIR 1/1411/204/28/40
40 Squadron, 1933–47:
  Operational Record Books and appendices, AIR 27/412–5.
40 Squadron, 1947–50:
  Operational Record Book AIR 27/2413
40 Squadron, 1953–56:
  Operational Record Book AIR 27/2698
205 Group:
  Operational Record Books and appendices AIR 25/816–34
RAF Station records:
  Abingdon: AIR 28/8 & 28/769
  Kabrit: AIR 28/402
  Luqa: AIR 28/502–6
  Shallufa: AIR 28/702
  Upper Heyford: AIR 28/806

# Appendix A
## Operational Losses

Including (a) aircraft struck off charge as a result of operational flying, whether or not death or injury resulted; and (b) aircraft returned with dead, wounded or injured aboard.

## World War One

Note: those with no known graves are commemorated on the Arras Memorial.

**5 August 1916**
FE8 7595                         **Offensive Patrol**
2/Lt H.C Davis          Killed  A/c crashed accidentally, 8.10pm. 2/Lt Davis is
                                buried in Aire Communal Cemetery.

**26 August 1916**
FE8 6394                         **Patrol**
2/Lt P.H. Smith                  Crashed on landing

**27 August 1916**
FE8 6396                         **Patrol**
Lt L.R. Briggs                   Machine wrecked on landing.
FE8 6388
2/Lt H.C. Todd                   Machine wrecked on landing.

**25 September 1916**
FE8                              **Escort**
2/Lt R. Gregory                  Propeller shot away, and aircraft wrecked in
                                 force-landing.

**26 September 1916**
FE8 6407                         **Patrol**
2/Lt. L.V. Drake        Injured  Crashed on landing.

**9 November 1916**
FE.8 7624                        **Offensive Patrol**
Capt T.G. Mapplebeck    POW      Attacked by two LVGs after destroying a balloon at
                                 Hulluch. Fuel line cut; forced-landed.

339

FE.8 6409                                      **Offensive Patrol**
2/Lt H.F. Evans              POW    Forced to land after engine shot up in a clash with
                                    enemy scouts.

**15 November 1916**
FE8 7614                                       **Escort**
2/Lt K.S. Henderson          Injured Crashed at Auchel.

**22 November 1916**
FE8 6458                                       **Hostile aircraft patrol**
Lt J.A. Barton                      Crashed. A/c wrecked.

**23 January 1917**
FE8 6388                                       **Line Patrol and photographic escort**
2/Lt J. Hay                  Killed  Shot down in flames near Lens by Manfred von
                                    Richthofen. 2/Lt Hay is buried in Aire Communal
                                    Cemetery.

**6 February 1917**
FE8                                            **Patrol**
Lt C.G. Gilbert                     Forced-landed at Hesdin, wrecking machine.

**16 February 1917**
FE8 7825                                       **Line Patrol**
2/Lt L.B. Blaxland                  A/c damaged by AA fire and spun from 9000ft to
                                    1000ft. Pilot landed OK but machine was shelled by
                                    the enemy.

**9 March 1917**
FE8 A4874                                      **Offensive Patrol**
2/Lt G.F. Haseler            POW    Shot down between Estevelles and Pont à Vendin.

FE8 6397
2/Lt W.B. Hills              POW    Shot down by Ltn. Karl-Emil Schaeffer.

FE8 6456
2/Lt T. Shepard              POW    Shot down by Ltn. Wolff near Annay.

FE8 6399
2/Lt R.E. Neve               Wounded Shot up by Ltn. K. Allmenroeder. A/c burst into
                                    flames on crashlanding in the British trenches.

**21 March 1917**
Nieuport 17 A6734                              **Escort and Patrol**
Lt E.L. Benbow               Wounded Hit in the back by AA fire, Lt Benbow landed near
                                    Ablain St. Nazaire.

**22 March 1917**
Nieuport 17 A6679                              **Line Patrol**
2/Lt S.J. Stocks             Wounded Shot in the stomach and forced-landed NW of Hersin.

**30 March 1917**
Nieuport 17 A6780 | **Line Patrol**
Lt D.M.F. Sinclair | Killed | Shot down near Vimy; buried in Orchard Dump Cemetery, Arleux-en-Gohelle.

Nieuport 23 A6786
2/Lt A.S. Talbot | Injured | Stalled taking off in a cross wind.

**3 April 1917**
Nieuport 17/23 A6674 | **Escort**
2/Lt S.A. Sharpe | POW | Shot down by Ltn. Gustav Nernst of Jasta 30.

**6 April 1917**
Nieuport 17/23 A6667 | **Special Mission**
2/Lt H.S. Pell | Killed | Brought down by ground fire while attacking Sallaumines balloon; buried in Orchard Dump Cemetery, Arleux-en-Gohelle.

**29 April 1917**
Nieuport 17/23 A6739 | **Offensive Patrol**
Lt J.A.G. Brewis | Killed | Left 6.45 am with 2/Lt Bond; commemorated on the Arras Memorial.

Nieuport 17/23 A6745 | **Offensive Patrol**
Capt F.L. Barwell | Killed | Shot down after a 30 minute solo fight and buried in Beaumont Communal Cemetery.

**6 May 1917**
Nieuport 17/23 B1519 | **Offensive Patrol**
Lt H.E.O. Ellis | Injured | Crashed on landing at Mazingarbe. Concussed.

**7 May 1917**
Nieuport 17/23 B1631 | **Special Mission**
Capt W.E. Nixon | Killed | Shot down in solo combat with numerous enemy a/c; buried in Masny Churchyard.

**13 May 1917**
Nieuport 17/23 B1640 | **Offensive Patrol**
Lt A.B. Raymond | POW | Shot down by Lt Ermecke of Jasta 33.

**24 May 1917**
Nieuport 17/23 B1642 | **Offensive Patrol**
Lt L.L. Morgan | Injured | A/c hit by allied shell which blew away part of the engine and front fuselage.

**1 June 1917**
Nieuport 17/23 A6784 | **Offensive Patrol**
Lt W.E. Bassett | Wounded | Hit by AA fire.

**5 June 1917**
Nieuport 17/23 B1548                          **Offensive Patrol**
Capt W.T.L. Allcock            Killed    Shot down near Lambres by Vzfw. Reiss of Jasta 3;
                                          commemorated on the Arras Memorial.

**7 June 1917**
Nieuport 17/23 B3674                          **Offensive Patrol**
Lt J.W. Shaw                   POW      Shot down by Hptm. Stenzel of Jasta 8 near
                                          Gheluvelt.

**24 June 1917**
Nieuport 17/23 B1693                          **Offensive Patrol**
2/Lt W.A. MacLanachan    Injured    Crashed on landing; concussed.

**14 July 1917**
Nieuport 17/23 A6783                          **Offensive Patrol**
2/Lt G. Davis                  POW      Shot down by Lt Erwin Boehme of Jasta 29 near
                                          Bersee.

**21 July 1917**
Nieuport 17/23 B1694                          **Offensive Patrol**
2/Lt F.W. Rook                 Killed    Shot down by Oblt. von Tutschek and crashed near
                                          Boursies; commemorated on the Arras Memorial.

**22 July 1917**
Nieuport 17/23 B1688                          **Offensive Patrol**
Capt W.A. Bond, MC                       Direct hit by an AA shell over Sallaumines;
& Bar                          Killed    commemorated on the Arras Memorial.

**12 August 1917**
Nieuport 17/23 A6771                          **Offensive Patrol**
Lt W.D. Cullen                 POW      Shot down by Cpl Heiligers of Jasta 30.

**14 August 1917**
Nieuport 17/23 B1684                          **Offensive Patrol**
2/Lt A.E. Godfrey            Injured    Crashed near Mao-Maroueuil during a thunderstorm.

**15 August 1917**
Nieuport 17/23 B1682                          **Offensive Patrol**
Capt W.G. Pender               Killed    Shot down by Oblt Hans Bethge of Jasta 30;
                                          commemorated on the Arras Memorial.

**22 August 1917**
Nieuport 17/23 B3473                          **Offensive Patrol**
Lt H.A. Kennedy                Killed    Shot down by L/Cpl Funk of Jasta 30; buried in
                                          Cabaret Rouge British Cemetery, Souchez.

**21 September 1917**
Nieuport 24 B3606                             **Offensive Patrol**
2/Lt P.W. Smith              Injured    Engine failure. Forced landing near Houdain, pilot
                                          stalled and crashed.

**22 September 1917**
Nieuport 17/23 A6669          **Patrol**
2/Lt P.D. Learoyd          Injured

**23 September 1917**
Nieuport 17/23 B1670          **Offensive Patrol**
2/Lt J.L. Barlow, m.i.d.          Killed   Aircraft collapsed in the air, perhaps while stunting; buried in Bruay Communal Cemetery.

**28 December 1917**
SE5a B570          **Special Patrol**
2/Lt J.W. Wallwork          Injured   Crashed on forced-landing near Division after engine problems and Lewis gun falling on his head.

**3 January 1918**
SE5a B665          **Line Patrol**
2/Lt W.L. Harrison          Crashed into lorry on landing.

**9 January 1918**
SE5a B57          **Patrol**
2/Lt F.P. Chaplin          Crashed on landing.

**22 January 1918**
SE5a          **Offensive Patrol**
2/Lt W.E. Warden          Engine cut at 100 ft. A/c wrecked.

SE5a B73          **Reconnaissance**
2/Lt H.S. Wolff          Lost his way and crashed when forced landing.

**26 January 1918**
SE5a B24          **Offensive Patrol**
2/Lt J.H.F. Hambly          Injured   Ran out of fuel in bad weather, stalled and crashed.

**29 January 1918**
SE5a B20          **Offensive Patrol**
Capt. A. Hepburn          Injured   Forced landing with engine trouble near drome. A/c wrecked.

**18 February 1918**
SE5a B42          **Offensive Patrol**
Lt C.O. Rusden          Engine cut on take-off. A/c wrecked.

**24 February 1918**
SE5a C9534          **Offensive Patrol**
2/Lt L.A. Herbert          Wounded   Landed at Naval Eight, St. Pol.

**26 February 1918**
SE5a C5336          **Offensive Patrol**
2/Lt R.C. Wade          Killed   Probably shot down by Vfw. Redel of Jasta 12. Buried in Cabaret Rouge British Cemetery, Souchez.

**9 March 1918**

SE5a C9538                                        **Offensive Patrol**
Maj. L.A. Tilney, MC        Killed    Last seen diving on E/A during a large-scale
                                      engagement with Jasta 52. Believed to have broken
                                      up in the air, but claimed by Lt. Paul Billik. Buried
                                      in Cabaret Rouge British Cemetery, Souchez

SE5a C5348
Lt P.La T. Foster           POW

SE5a B587
Capt R.J. Tipton            Wounded   Forced-landed near Hersin. Died 12.3.18 and buried
                                      in Barlin Communal Cemetery.

**21 March 1918**

SE5a B587                                         **Offensive Patrol**
2/Lt W.H. Smith                       Crashed just after take-off in bad weather.

**27 March 1918**

SE5a D3507                                        **Bombing**
2/Lt F.C.B. Wedgewood       POW

**6 April 1918**

SE5a C5438                                        **Offensive Patrol**
Capt G.H. Lewis                       Crashed when engine cut at low level.

**9 April 1918**

SE5a D3534                                        **Bombing**
Lt R.E. Bion                Killed    Commemorated on the Arras Memorial.

**10 April 1918**

SE5a B191                                         **Bombing**
Lt A.H. Carnegie            Wounded   Landed at Choques.

**14 April 1918**

SE5a B4879                                        **Special Reconnaissance**
Maj R.S Dallas, DSO,                  Hit in the foot by ground fire.
  DSC & Bar                 Wounded

**15 May 1918**

SE5a D3509                                        **Offensive Patrol**
2/Lt W.L. Andrew            POW       Missing after his flight attacked a DFW CV.

**17 May 1918**

SE5a D3555                                        **Offensive Patrol**
Lt L.J. Seymour             POW       Shot down in combat with 8 e/a near Bois de Biez.

**20 May 1918**

SE5a D3938                                        **Offensive Patrol**
2/Lt G. Watson              Killed    Shot down in combat with three Pfalz Scouts near
                                      Hinges; commemorated on the Arras Memorial.

**1 June 1918**
SE5a D3530                          **Offensive Patrol**
Maj. R.S. Dallas, DSO,              Brought down and killed by Ltn Werner of Jasta 14
   DSC & Bar            Killed     while on solo patrol; buried in Pernes British
                                    Cemetery.

**6 July 1918**
SE5a D8445                          **Offensive Patrol**
Lt H.W. Clarke          Wounded

**22 July 1918**
SE5a B180                           **Offensive Patrol**
Lt I.L. Roy, DFC        Killed     Shot down in flames near Carvin in combat with
                                    Fokker DVIIs; buried in Estevelles Communal
                                    Cemetery.

**31 July 1918**
SE5a E1310                          **Offensive Patrol**
Capt G.E.H. McElroy, MC            Brought down by ground fire near Laventie; buried
& two Bars, DFC & Bar   Killed     in Laventie Military Cemetery, La Gorgue.

**7 August 1918**
SE5a E1284                          **Offensive Patrol**
1/Lt D.S. Poler USAS               Forced landing with engine failure. A/c wrecked.

**9 August 1918**
SE5a D3527                          **Offensive Patrol**
1/Lt P.V. Burwell USAS             Forced landing with engine failure. A/c wrecked.

**12 August 1918**
SE5a E3984                          **Offensive Patrol**
Capt I.F. Hind          Killed     Shot down in flames near Brie; buried in Peronne
                                    Communal Cemetery.

SE5a D6193
Lt H.H. Wood            POW        Last seen near Brie.

**13 August 1918**
SE5a B875                           **Offensive Patrol**
Lt D.F. Murman          Injured    Fuel problems. Landed in cornfield, and crashed
                                    trying to avoid workers and machinery.

SE5a C5358                          **Offensive Patrol**
2/Lt W.V Trubshawe                 Forced-landed after engine failure. A/c swung and
                                    crashed.

**17 August 1918**
SE5a 3183                           **Offensive Patrol**
2/Lt F.H. Knobel                   Forced-landed after engine seized. A/c shelled.

**19 August 1918**

SE5a E1304                  **Offensive Patrol**

2/Lt W.V. Trubshawe            Engine failure; forced-landed in trench system. A/c wrecked.

**24 August 1918**

SE5a E3947                  **Offensive Patrol**

Lt L.B. Bennett           Killed    Brought down by AA fire while attacking a balloon at Wavrin. Jumped from burning machine at 25 ft. but died of injuries shortly afterwards. Buried at Wavrin.

**27 August 1918**

SE5a C8882                  **Offensive Patrol**

Lt R.A. Anderson USAS    POW    Forced down in combat with Fokker DVIIs.
                                  Wounded

**2 September 1918**

SE5a D8445                  **Offensive Patrol**

2/Lt H.W. Clarke         Killed    Was seen engaged with about 12 enemy a/c and going down with steam coming from radiator; he is buried in Dury Mill British Cemetery.

**16 September 1918**

SE5a E3979                  **Offensive Patrol**

Capt G.C. Dixon        Wounded    Crashed after engine failure. A/c wrecked.

**17 September 1918**

SE5a E4053                  **Offensive Patrol**

2/Lt F.W. King           POW    Last seen S of Cambrai.

**18 September 1918**

SE5a C5357                  **Bombing** Patrol

2/Lt L.C. Band         Wounded    'Pilot . . . was not aware of attack by e/a'.

**24 September 1918**

SE5a E4054                  **Offensive Patrol**

Capt G.J. Strange       Killed    Shot down in flames during combat with Fokker DVIIs; commemorated on the Arras Memorial.

**27 September 1918**

SE5a C9135                  **Bombing**

2/Lt P.B. Myers         Killed    All three were last seen between Cambrai and Douai about 8.20 am. 2/Lt Myers is commemorated on the Arras Memorial.

SE5a E1350
2/Lt G.M.J. Morton  Killed  2/Lt Morton is buried in Chapel Corner Cemetery, Sauchy-Lestree.

SE5a B8442
Lt N.D. Willis  POW
  Wounded

SE5a E1345
1/Lt R. Mooney USAS  Wounded  Forced-landed.

**8 October 1918**
SE5a D3992  **Bombing**
Lt W.V. Trubshawe  Wounded  Landed in no man's land N of Cambrai and burned his machine.

**9 October 1918**
SE5a E4037  **Bombing**
2/Lt W.L. Field  Injured  Forced-landed under enemy fire at Escadoeuvres after engine cut.

**10 October 1918**
SE5a B8445  **Bombing**
Lt W.H. Jordan  Forced-landed when radiator was hit by ground fire. Pilot abandoned a/c a short distance from enemy machine guns.

**11 October 1918**
SE5a E4089  **Bombing**
Lt W.D. Archer  Wounded  Forced to land when machine gun fire hit the engine and radiator.

**28 October 1918**
SE5a F5536  **Bombing**
Lt T.H. Turnbull  Killed  Last seen by other pilots on Valenciennes front at 13.30; buried in Curgies Communal Cemetery.

**30 October 1918**
SE5a D8443  **Offensive Patrol**
Lt W.H. Jordan  Forced-landed with engine trouble at 206 Squadron. A/c turned over and was wrecked.

**3 November 1918**
SE5a E5739  **Offensive Patrol**
Lt P.G. Greenwood  POW  Engaged by Fokkers and was last seen at 15.45 going N.W. with E.A. on tail but at a long range.

**7 November 1918**
SE5a
Lt L.A. Brais  Wounded

# World War Two

Note: those with no known graves are commemorated on the Runnymede, Malta and El Alamein Memorials.

**10 May 1940**

Blenheim IV L8776

|  |  | **Reconnaissance: Dutch-German border** |
|---|---|---|
| F/O R.M. Burns | POW | Damaged by flak and crash-landed in a field beside |
|  | Wounded | the Rhine at Wesel. |
| Sgt J.R. Brooker | POW |  |
|  | Wounded |  |
| Cpl G. Hurford | POW |  |
|  | Wounded |  |

Blenheim IV L8828

|  |  | **Ypenburg aerodrome, Holland** |
|---|---|---|
| F/O P.J.H. Rowan | Killed | Shot down by ME 110s. Crashed into the sea off |
| Sgt G. Beardwood | Killed | Rotterdam. F/O Rowan, Sgt Beardwood and Cpl |
| Cpl T.F.S. Clark | Killed | Clark are buried in Rozenberg General Cemetery, |
|  |  | Gravenzande General Cemetery, and Rockanje |
|  |  | (Zeeweg) General Cemetery respectively. |

Blenheim IV P6901

| Sgt A.J. Robertson | Killed | Crashed in flames near Voorburg, on the SE |
|---|---|---|
| Sgt F. Checkley | Killed | outskirts of The Hague. Sgts Robertson and |
| AC1 J.A. Webster | POW | Checkley are buried in Voorburg Eastern General |
|  | Wounded | Cemetery. |

Blenheim IV L8831

| Sgt I.L. Thomas | Killed | Crashed on the outskirts of The Hague. All are |
|---|---|---|
| Sgt V. Spurr | Killed | buried in The Hague (Westduin) General Cemetery. |
| LAC H. Bridson | Killed |  |

Blenheim IV L8827

| F/Lt H.L. Smeddle | Wounded | Attacked by Me110s. Compass and wireless smashed. |
|---|---|---|
| Sgt B.C. Wooldridge | Wounded |  |
| LAC G.D.P. Quinn |  |  |

**15 May 1940**

Blenheim IV N6817

|  |  | **Roads, Dinant** |
|---|---|---|
| Wg/Cdr E.C. Barlow | Killed | Both aircraft were shot down by Me 109s near |
| Sgt E. Clark | Killed | Ecaussinnes d'Enghien, 18 km NE of Mons. The |
| LAC A.E. Millard | Killed | crews are buried in Ecaussines D'Enghein |
|  |  | Communal Cemetery. |

Blenheim IV P4913
F/O J.E. Edwards          Killed
Sgt C.T. White            Killed
LAC S.J. Johnson          Killed

**21 May 1940**
Blenheim IV L8757                    **Troop Concentration, Abbeville**
F/Lt. R.H. Batt                      P/O Ewels was wounded by ground fire.
Sgt. B.L. Harris
P/O L.H. Ewels            Wounded

**23 May 1940**
Blenheim IV P4909                    **Enemy columns, Arras**
Wg/Cdr J.G. Llewellyn     Killed     Hit by flak and crashed between Beuvry and
Sgt J.A.D. Beattie                   Sailly-Labourse, ESE of Béthune. Sgt Beattie landed
P/O W.G. Edwards          Killed     in French held territory and returned to the
                                     Squadron. Wg/Cdr Llewellyn is buried in Beuvry
                                     Communal Cemetery; P/O Edwards in
                                     Sailly-Labourse Communal Cemetery.

Blenheim IV L8834
F/O R.H. Jacoby           POW        Shot down at Miraumont, 13 km NNE of Albert,
Sgt P.A.M. Burrell        Killed     France. Sgt Burrell and LAC Whittle are buried in
LAC P.R. Whittle          Killed     Miraumont Communal Cemetery.

**25 May 1940**
Blenheim IV L4920                    **Enemy columns, Rety-Fiennes-Guines**
Sgt S.I. Tonks            POW        Shot down near Rety, 5 km ESE of Marquise,
Sgt J.L. Alexander        Killed     France. Sgt Alexander and LAC Goffe are buried in
LAC D. Goffe              Killed     Rety Communal Cemetery.

**6 June 1940**
Blenheim IV P4927                    **Troop concentrations, St. Valery**
Sgt D.J. Rice             POW
Sgt R.C. Moffat           POW
Sgt D.E. Peters           POW

Blenheim IV L8827
Sqn/Ldr B. Paddon         POW        Shot down by Me 109s.
Sgt V.C. Salvage          POW
Sgt T.A. Foreman          POW

Blenheim IV L9410
P/O B.B. James            Killed     Lost without trace. All are commemorated on the
Sgt J.E. Garcka           Killed     Runnymede Memorial.
Sgt W. Furby              Killed

Blenheim IV P4917

| P/O P.F.T. Wakeford | Wounded | Crippled by flak and forced-landed. Baker, in a |
| Sgt A.F. Wallace | Wounded | French hospital, was briefly taken POW, escaped |
| Sgt B.G. Baker | POW | and made his way back to the UK via Brittany. |
| | Wounded | |

Blenheim IV R3692

| P/O V.G.W. Engstom | Wounded | Forced-landed in the battle area. P/O Engstrom |
| Sgt M.R. Chouler | POW | went for help, but the others were captured. |
| Sgt D. Liddle | POW | |
| | Wounded | |

## 12 June 1940
Blenheim IV R3893                    **St. Valery**

| Sgt C.D.W. Bartlam | POW | Shot down by flak at Eletot, 7 km NE of Fécamp. |
| Sgt D.L. Dorris | Killed | Sgt Dorris is commemorated on the Runnymede |
| Sgt E. Rodgers | POW | Memorial. |

## 14 June 1940
Blenheim IV N3592                    **Battle area**

| Sqn/Ldr G.W.C. Gleed | Killed | Attacked targets near Ereteuil. Crashed at Fresney, |
| Sgt R.W. Burge | Killed | 13 km SE of Evreux. All are buried in Fresney |
| Sgt A.F.W. Sammells | Killed | Churchyard. |

Blenheim IV R3693

| P/O W.M. Lewis | | Shot down by flak. Crashed at |
| Sgt R. Currie | | Garancières-en-Drouais, 8 km SW of Dreux. Sgt |
| Sgt S.W. Johnson | Killed | Johnson is buried in Garancieres Communal |
| | | Cemetery. |

## 27 June 1940
Blenheim IV R3778                    **Photo-reconnaissance, Boulogne area**

| Sgt J.L. Morton | Killed | Shot down into the Channel by Me 109s. All are |
| Sgt A.D. Kelso | Killed | commemorated on the Runnymede Memorial. |
| Sgt J.C. Winston | Killed | |

Blenheim IV R3811

| F/O C.W. Bromley | | |
| Sgt F. Little | | Damaged in the same fighter attack. Crash-landed at |
| Sgt J.A. Gamble | Wounded | Hawkinge. |

## 9 July 1940
Blenheim IV L8836                    **Reconnaissance, Lisieux area**

| S/L R.H. Batt, DFC | Killed | Shot down over the Channel. The bodies of S/L |
| Sgt A. Spencer, DFM | Killed | Batt and Sgt Johnson were recovered and identified |
| Sgt P.E. Johnson | Killed | by HMS *Brilliant*, then buried at sea. All are |
| | | commemorated on the Runnymede Memorial. |

**25/26 July 1940**

Blenheim IV R3763                    **Eelde Aerodrome**

Sgt P.H. Steele          POW    Brought down by flak while attacking the airfield at
Sgt J. Moore             POW    Eelde, 14 km N of Assen, Holland.
Sgt R. Peacock           POW

**14/15 August 1940**

Blenheim IV P4908 'R'                **Chartres aerodrome**

Sgt K. Newton            POW    Crippled by flak and ditched in the Channel off
                     Wounded    Cherbourg
Sgt F.M. Hotchkiss       POW
Sgt G.A. McCreary        POW
                     Wounded


Blenheim IV R3609 'X'

P/O G. Parker            POW    Sgts Easton and Watson evaded capture and reached
Sgt G.H. Easton          Evaded  Gibraltar. Watson was awarded the Military Medal
Sgt E.G. Watson          Evaded  for the information he gathered en route.

**25/26 August 1940**

Blenheim IV R3811 'G'                **Maupertus aerodrome**

Sqn/Ldr F.G.R. Thomas    Killed  Lost without trace. All are commemorated on the
P/O G.L. Bayliss         Killed  Runnymede Memorial.
Sgt G.M. Dickson         Killed


Blenheim IV T1927 'F'                **Querqueville aerodrome**

Sgt C.P. Riley           Killed  Lost without trace. Also commemorated on the
Sgt F.H. Newson          Killed  Runnymede Memorial.
Sgt J.S. Smith           Killed

**30/31 August 1940**

Blenheim IV R3745 'H'                **Emden**

P/O W.R. Evans           Killed  Crashed shortly after take-off and burst into flames.
Sgt F. Little            Killed  P/O Evans is buried in Southwick; Sgt Little in
Sgt J.A. Watt            Killed  Spondon; Sgt Watt in Edinburgh (Liberton) Cemetery.

**1/2 September 1940**

Blenheim IV L8796 'C'                **Nordenham**

P/O R.V. Whitehead       Injured  Stalled after overshooting on landing at West
Sgt A.R. Coburn          Killed  Raynham. Sgt Coburn is buried in Belfast City
Sgt J.E. Robbins                 Cemetery.

**2/3 September 1940**

Blenheim IV L8757 'T'                **Schlebusch**

Flt/Sgt R.B. Broadhurst  Killed  Crashed in the North Sea. Flt/Sgt Broadhurst is
Sgt A. Marsden           Killed  buried in Texel (den Burg) General Cemetery. Sgts
Sgt A.J. Burns           Killed  Marsden and Burns are commemorated on the
                                 Runnymede Memorial.

## 8/9 September 1940

| Blenheim IV R3612 'V' | | **Ostend docks and shipping** |
|---|---|---|
| Sgt L.F.S. Patrick | Killed | Lost without trace. All are commemorated on the |
| Sgt T.G.S. Jarman | Killed | Runnymede Memorial. |
| Sgt V.W. Pegler | Killed | |

## 16/17 January 1941

| Wellington Ic T2912 'S' | | **Wilhelmshaven** |
|---|---|---|
| Sgt A.E. Jones | Killed | 'Task completed' signal sent. Lost without trace and |
| Sgt E.G. Robertson | Killed | commemorated on the Runnymede Memorial. |
| Sgt J.H. Lee | Killed | |
| Sgt H.F. Lander | Killed | |
| Sgt D.R.C. Cannell | Killed | |
| Sgt E.F. Todd | Killed | |

## 12/13 March 1941

| Wellington Ic T2515 'U' | | **Boulogne** |
|---|---|---|
| Sgt D.W. Gough RNZAF | Killed | A/c crashed in flames at Wimille, 5km N. of |
| Sgt T.G. Webb RNZAF | Killed | Boulogne. The crew is buried in Wimille |
| Sgt T.H. Rose RCAF | Killed | Communal Cemetery. |
| Sgt F. Stones | Killed | |
| Sgt H. Jones | Killed | |
| Sgt W.J. Morgan | Killed | |

| Wellington Ic R1013 'B' | | **Berlin** |
|---|---|---|
| S/L E.H. Lynch-Blosse | POW | Hit by flak over the target and the crew baled out |
| P/O H. Heaton | POW | when one engine failed and the other gave trouble. |
| Sgt D.R. Clay | POW | |
| Sgt W. Hammond | POW | |
| Sgt H. Caldicot | POW | |
| F/O S. Palmer | POW | |

## 23/24 March 1941

| Wellington Ic R1166 'M' | | **Berlin** |
|---|---|---|
| P/O P. Billyeald | | Hydraulics damaged by flak. Crashed while making |
| Sgt D.F. Youldon | Injured | a second attempt to land. Overran the runway and |
| P/O C.S. Gill | Injured | collided with a wooden hut and nearby trailer. |
| Sgt Williams | | |
| Sgt A.E. Varnsverry | Injured | |
| Sgt J.W. Crook | Injured | |

## 7/8 April 1941

| Wellington Ic R1007 'L' | | **Kiel** |
|---|---|---|
| Sgt T. Gamble | Killed | Crashed in the target area. All are buried in Kiel |
| Sgt L.E.E. Bundock | Killed | War Cemetery. |
| Sgt J. Sharkey | Killed | |
| Sgt N. Benfield | Killed | |
| Sgt F. Sherratt | Killed | |
| Sgt J.S. Crane | Killed | |

## 10/11 April 1941

| Wellington Ic R1493 'P' | | **Merignac aerodrome** |
|---|---|---|
| F/Lt F.A. Bowler | POW | A/c ran out of fuel and ditched in the English |
| P/O A.B. Trench | POW | Channel, but searches failed to locate it. P/O |
| P/O L.S. Dunley RNZAF | POW | Branson is commemorated on the Runnymede |
| Sgt E.A. Jewson | POW | Memorial. |
| Sgt E. Spencer | POW | |
| P/O J.P.L. Branson | Killed | |

## 18/19 April 1941

| Wellington Ic R1331 'R' | | **Berlin** |
|---|---|---|
| Sgt K. Jenner RNZAF | | Navigational difficulties on the return journey. A/c |
| Sgt H.T. Bagnall RNZAF | | crash-landed on a hillside near Combe Martin, |
| Sgt C.D. Noble RCAF | | Devon. Sgt Griffin baled out but his parachute did |
| Sgt Jordan | | not deploy fully. He is buried in Ayr Cemetery. |
| Sgt A. MacAskill | | |
| Sgt J. Griffin | Killed | |

## 11/12 May 1941

| Wellington Ic R1461 'Z' | | **Hamburg** |
|---|---|---|
| Sgt F.T. Luscombe | Killed | Shot down into the North Sea. Sgt Chappell is |
| Sgt D. Chappell | Killed | buried in Sage War Cemetery, Oldenburg; Sgt |
| Flt/Sgt E.M. Mulligan | Killed | Hodges in Becklingen War Cemetery, Soltau; and |
| Sgt J.E. Hodges | Killed | Flt/Sgt Mulligan in Hamburg Cemetery, Ohlsdorf. |
| Sgt J.A. Harris | Killed | The others are commemorated on the Runnymede |
| Sgt J.D.C. Long RNZAF | Killed | Memorial |

| Wellington Ic R1330 'H' | | |
|---|---|---|
| Sgt R.E. Finlayson RNZAF | Killed | All the dead are buried in Kiel War Cemetery. |
| Sgt J.B. Murray | Killed | |
| Sgt D. Fletcher | Killed | |
| Sgt H.C. Tuckwell | Killed | |
| Flt/Sgt J. Shaw | POW | |
| | Wounded | |
| Sgt P.N. Beckett | Killed | |

Wellington Ic T2911 'A'

| | | |
|---|---|---|
| P/O R.M. Smith | | Attacked eight times by Me 110 and badly |
| Sgt R.D. Hesketh | | damaged. Sgt Martin is buried at Marham. |
| Sgt Bowers | | |
| Sgt J.E. Robbins | Wounded | |
| Sgt Ison | | |
| Sgt K.B. Martin | Killed | |

## 15/16 May 1941

Wellington Ic R1167 'N'        **Hanover**

| | | |
|---|---|---|
| Sgt W.E. Moore | Killed | All are buried in Reichswald Forest War Cemetery. |
| P/O D.F.R. Whyte | Killed | |
| Sgt D.J. Kennard | Killed | |
| Sgt R. Meech | Killed | |
| Sgt I.J. Adey | Killed | |
| Sgt P. Addison | POW | |

## 2/3 June 1941

Wellington Ic R1436 'U'        **Dusseldorf**

| | | |
|---|---|---|
| Flt/Sgt P.D. Sargent | Killed | Stalled after overshooting at Alconbury in poor |
| Sgt E.A.B. Beadman | Killed | visibility. Flt/Sgt Sargent is buried in St. Albans |
| Sgt A.F. Hicks RCAF | Killed | Cemetery; Sgt. Beadman in Cheshunt New Burial |
| Sgt R.W. Body | Killed | Ground; Sgts Hicks and Dougherty at Wyton; and |
| Sgt L.D. Dougherty RCAF | Killed | Sgt Body at Norwich |
| Sgt R.C. Hillebrandt | Injured | |

## 11/12 June 1941

Wellington Ic R1461 'L'        **Dusseldorf**

| | | |
|---|---|---|
| P/O R.F. Payne | Killed | Shot down by a night-fighter (Lt Gerhard Loos, |
| Sgt M.S. Soames | Killed | I/NJG1) and crashed at Meerlo, Holland. All are |
| P/O L.J. Moore | Killed | buried in Jonkerbos War Cemetery, Nijmegen. |
| Sgt N.S. Wilson | Killed | |
| Sgt G.L. Tompson | Killed | |
| Sgt E.W. Tyler | Killed | |

Wellington Ic R1312 'J'

| | | |
|---|---|---|
| Sqn/Ldr M.E. Redgrave | POW | Damaged by flak, and taking evasive action at low |
| Sgt A.F. Potter RNZAF | POW | level, crashed on a sand bank in the Scheldt estuary |
| | Injured | off Hellevoetsluis, Holland. |
| Sgt C. Rofe | POW | |
| | Injured | |
| Sgt P. Rockingham | POW | |
| Sgt R. Alldrick RCAF | POW | |
| | Injured | |
| Sgt J.A.S. Abernethy | POW | |
| | Injured | |

## 12/13 June 1941

| | | |
|---|---|---|
| Wellington Ic R1647 'M' | | **Rotterdam** |
| Sgt M. Evans RNZAF | | Attacked by Me110. Hydraulics damaged, and |
| Sgt A.C. Shilletto | Wounded | undercarriage collapsed on landing. |
| Sgt S.G. Kybird | | |
| Sgt F. Lowrey | | |
| Sgt C. Turl | Wounded | |
| Sgt J. Hoban | | |

## 26/27 June 1941

| | | |
|---|---|---|
| Wellington Ic R1406 'C' | | **Köln** |
| P/O D.W. Horrocks | Killed | Crashed at St. Laureis, 7 km NW of Eeklo, |
| P/O K.F. Glock | Killed | Belgium. P/Os Glock and Green, and Sgt Morris |
| P/O W.G. Green | Killed | are buried in Adegem Canadian War Cemetery. |
| Sgt L.C. Page | Killed | The remainder are commemorated on the |
| Sgt J.S. Clover | Killed | Runnymede Memorial. |
| Sgt T. Morris | Killed | |

## 29/30 June 1941

| | | |
|---|---|---|
| Wellington II W5456 'P' | | **Hamburg** |
| F/Lt A.B. Baird RNZAF | Killed | Lost without trace and commemorated on the |
| P/O J.H. Walls | Killed | Runnymede Memorial. |
| Flt/Sgt J.N. Lister | Killed | |
| Sgt A.S. Rowan | Killed | |
| Sgt S.E. Bird | Killed | |

## 6/7 July 1941

| | | |
|---|---|---|
| Wellington Ic N2843 'L' | | |
| P/O J.E.MacK. Steeds | | **Munster** |
|   RNZAF | Killed | Shot down by a night fighter and crashed in the sea |
| Sgt F.C. Pocock | Killed | off Texel. Sgts Varnsverry and Oliver are buried in |
| Sgt D.M. Evans | Killed | Vlieland General Cemetery and the remainder |
| Sgt A. MacAskill | POW | commemorated on the Runnymede Memorial |
| | Wounded | |
| Sgt A.E. Varnsverry | Killed | |
| Sgt A.G. Oliver | Killed | |

## 9/10 July 1941

| | | |
|---|---|---|
| Wellington Ic R1770 'C' | | **Osnabruck** |
| F/O G.C. Conran | POW | Believed shot down by Oblt. Lent, 4/NJG1 P/O |
| P/O P.B.G. Edwards | Killed | Edwards is buried in Hanover War Cemetery and |
| Sgt B. Kay | POW | Sgt Davies in Reichswald Forest War Cemetery. |
| Sgt S.D. Swindells | POW | |
| Sgt J.A. Tracey | POW | |
| Sgt G.E. Davies | Killed | |

## 16/17 July 1941

| Wellington Ic X9630 'J' | | **Hamburg** |
|---|---|---|
| Sgt A.W.P. Bird RNZAF | Killed | Crashed in the sea off the Dutch coast. Sgts Bird, |
| Sgt B.F.T. Johnson | Killed | Harrison and Hassall are buried in Texel (den Burg) |
| P/O J.R. Jamieson RCAF | POW | General Cemetery, while Sgts Johnson and Platt are |
| Sgt L.J. Harrison | Killed | commemorated on the Runnymede Memorial. |
| Sgt B. Hassall | Killed | |
| Sgt O.J. Platt RCAF | Killed | |

| Wellington Ic X3320 'H' | | |
|---|---|---|
| Sqn/Ldr R.G. Weighill | Killed | Blinded by searchlights and dived into the ground |
| Sgt R.D. Hesketh | Killed | near Great Yarmouth. Sqn/Ldr Weighill and Sgt |
| Sgt W.E. Gibb RCAF | Killed | Gibb are buried at Scottow, Norfolk, Sgt Hesketh |
| Sgt V.H. Leng | Killed | in Manchester Southern Cemetery, Sgt Leng at |
| P/O A.W. Wilkinson | Killed | Mortlake Crematorium, and Sgt Price in |
| Sgt D.A. Price | Killed | Portsmouth (Milton) Cemetery. P/O Wilkinson is |
| | | commemorated on the Runnymede Memorial. |

## 24 July 1941

| Wellington Ic T2986 'A' | | **Brest: Scharnhorst and Prinz Eugen** |
|---|---|---|
| Sgt M. Evans, DFM, | | Hit by flak on the bombing run and fell in flames. |
| RNZAF | Killed | All are buried in Brest (Kerfautras) Cemetery, |
| Sgt H.T. Ellis | Killed | Lambézellec. |
| Sgt S.G. Kybird | Killed | |
| Sgt F. Lowrey | Killed | |
| Flt/Sgt C.S. Beresford | Killed | |
| Sgt J. Hoban | Killed | |

| Wellington Ic X9662 'U' | | |
|---|---|---|
| P/O A.D. Greer RNZAF | | A/c attacked repeatedly by Me109 after bombing. |
| Sgt M.S. Holliday RAAF | Killed | Rear turret rendered u/s, and w/op and rear gunner |
| Sgt G. Watson | | wounded. Hydraulics damaged and a/c returned |
| Sgt J. Hobbs | Wounded | with wheels, flaps and bomb doors down. |
| Sgt Davey | | Sgt Holliday is buried at St. Eval. |
| Sgt T. Gould | Wounded | |

## 12/13 August 1941

| Wellington Ic R1168 'B' | | **Hanover** |
|---|---|---|
| P/O A.R. Fitch | | Attacked three times by Ju88 over Nijmegen. Pilot |
| P/O D.F. Hutt | Wounded | escaped by diving into cloud. |
| P/O A. Kinniburgh | | |
| Sgt T. Robertson | | |
| Sgt J.C. Beauchamp | Wounded | |
| Sgt W.P. Hudson | Wounded | |

## 25/26 August 1941

Wellington Ic T2514 'D'  **Karlsruhe**

| | | |
|---|---|---|
| Sgt D.F. Youldon | Killed | All are buried in Rheinsberg War Cemetery. |
| Sgt W.H. Cole | Killed | |
| Sgt T. Appleby | Killed | |
| Sgt J.D. Duthie | Killed | |
| Sgt W. Fisher | Killed | |
| Sgt E.C. Shea | Killed | |

Wellington Ic X9749 'J'

| | | |
|---|---|---|
| Sqn/Ldr A.C. Martin | Killed | Crashed near Handzame, 10 km ESE of Diksmuide, |
| P/O T.R. Fyles | Killed | Belgium. All are buried in Handzame Communal |
| P/O R.R. Reynolds | Killed | Cemetery. |
| Sgt R.J.F. Perras RCAF | Killed | |
| Sgt. G. Knight | Killed | |
| F/O W. Wright | Killed | |

## 28/29 August 1941

Wellington Ic Z8839 'L'  **Duisberg**

| | | |
|---|---|---|
| P/O J.E. King | Killed | Crashed at Mülheim. The three who died are |
| Sgt J.C. Bredin RCAF | POW | buried in Reichswald Forest War Cemetery. |
| Sgt B.T. Kearsley | Killed | |
| Sgt A.A. Cormack | Killed | |
| Sgt A.C.T. Barter | POW | |
| Sgt T. Arnold | POW | |

Wellington Ic T2701 'S'

| | | |
|---|---|---|
| P/O A.R. Fitch | | Crashed with full bomb load at Wyton 15 minutes |
| Sgt T. Stabler | | after take-off. |
| P/O A. Kinniburgh | | |
| Sgt T. Robertson | | |
| Sgt A.C.S. Delgado | | |
| Sgt W.V. Parslow | | |

## 2/3 September 1941

Wellington Ic R1030 'R'  **Frankfurt**

| | | |
|---|---|---|
| P/O A.R. Fitch | Killed | Ditched in the North Sea after engine failure. Four |
| Sgt T. Stabler | | crew were rescued by a trawler. P/O Fitch is buried |
| P/O A. Kinniburgh | Injured | in Middelkerke Communal Cemetery and Sgt |
| Sgt T. Robertson | Killed | Robertson in Cupar New Cemetery, Fife. |
| Sgt A.C.S. Delgado | | |
| Sgt W.V. Parslow | | |

Wellington Ic X9669 'F'
P/O M. Baker RAAF
Sgt Robins
Sgt Holtby
Sgt A. Simpson
Sgt E. Crook
Sgt MacLachlan

Returned early, and crashed while trying to land in poor visibility. A/c caught fire, and AC Riden was instrumental in helping rescue the crew. Through his devotion to duty serious injury was averted.

## 12/13 September 1941

Wellington Ic R1328 'T'

**Frankfurt**

| | | |
|---|---|---|
| Sqn/Ldr J.C. Atkins | Killed | Sent a message to base saying port engine had failed. |
| Sgt R.C. Thompson | POW | A sweep over the North Sea revealed no trace of |
| P/O R.M. Ryder RAAF | Killed | the a/c. Sqn/Ldr Atkins and P/O Ryder are buried |
| Sgt A.E. Hough | POW | in Rheinberg War Cemetery |
| Sgt B.T. Banner | POW | |
| Sgt D.F. Darlow | POW | |

## 12/13 October 1941

Wellington Ic X9822 'T'

**Bremen**

| | | |
|---|---|---|
| Sgt G.F. Bateman | Killed | Shot down by a night-fighter (Oblt. Lent, 4/NJG1) |
| Sgt P.A. Milton | Killed | and crashed 7 km SE of Dokkum, Holland. All are |
| Sgt F. Jenkins | Killed | buried in Kollumerland (Westergeest) Protestant |
| Sgt E.B.B. McGrath | Killed | Cemetery. |
| Sgt H.F. Eyre | Killed | |
| Sgt H.R. Legg | Killed | |

Wellington Ic X9619 'M'

**Nuremburg**

| | | |
|---|---|---|
| P/O I.M.V. Field RNZAF | Killed | Crashed near Dinant, Belgium. All are buried in |
| Sgt P.F. Collis | Killed | Dinant (Citadelle) Military Cemetery. |
| P/O E.J. Sugg RAAF | Killed | |
| Sgt R.A. Dundon | Killed | |
| Flt/Sgt T.I. Duxbury RCAF | Killed | |
| Sgt H.R.D. Chapman | Killed | |

## 14/15 October 1941

Wellington Ic Z8782 'H'

**Nuremburg**

| | | |
|---|---|---|
| Sgt K.G. Edis | Killed | Exploded in mid-air near Karlsruhe. All are buried |
| Sgt J.E. Hawkins | Killed | in Durnbach War Cemetery. |
| Sgt R.E. Bates | Killed | |
| Flt/Sgt R.M. McIntyre RCAF | Killed | |
| Flt/Sgt J.E. Weir RCAF | Killed | |
| Flt/Sgt I.J. McDonald | Killed | |

Wellington Ic X9926 'T'
| | | |
|---|---|---|
| P/O G.B. Buse | Killed | Also buried in Durnbach War Cemetery |
| Sgt R.C. Tyrrell | Killed | |
| Sgt F.E. Ridler | Killed | |
| Sgt J. Chapman | Killed | |
| Sgt R.H.G. Collins | Killed | |
| Sgt S.C. Hodge | Killed | |

Wellington Ic X9882 'W'
| | | |
|---|---|---|
| Sgt J.R. Hiscock | Killed | Lost without trace. All are commemorated on the |
| Sgt D.A. Scott | Killed | Runnymede Memorial. |
| Sgt J.P.B. Cambray | Killed | |
| Sgt B.C. Dymott | Killed | |
| Sgt A.J. Thomas | Killed | |
| Sgt J.H. White | Killed | |

## 16/17 October 1941

Wellington Ic Z8862 'B'                **Duisberg**
| | | |
|---|---|---|
| Sqn/Ldr T.G. Kirby-Green | POW | The five dead are buried in Reichswald Forest War |
| Sgt J.A. Lamb | Killed | Cemetery. Sqn/Ldr Kirby-Green was shot by the |
| Sgt J.A. Jacques RCAF | Killed | Gestapo (29.9.44) after the Great Escape from Stalag |
| Flt/Sgt P.L. Hennigan, | | Luft III, and is buried in Poznan Old Garrison |
| DFM | Killed | Cemetery. F/O Campbell-Martin was attached from |
| Sgt A.H. Harman | Killed | 264 Sqdn. |
| F/O P.C. Campbell-Martin, | | |
| MC | Killed | |

## 23/24 October 1941

Wellington Ic X9912                **Alconbury – Luqa, Malta**
| | | |
|---|---|---|
| Sgt J.D. Paine | Killed | Ditched out of fuel north of Sicily. Sgt Hewitt is |
| Sgt W.D. Stuart RNZAF | Killed | buried in Catania War Cemetery, Sicily, and the |
| Sgt R. Jackson | Killed | remainder are commemorated on the Runnymede |
| Sgt C.R. Eastman | Killed | Memorial. |
| Sgt B.W. Nicholls | Killed | |
| Sgt E.W. Hewitt | Killed | |
| Passengers | | |
| Sgt E.W. Sherwood | Killed | |
| Cpl J.B. Robinson | Killed | |
| AC1 W.A. Hodges | Killed | |

## 26 October 1941

Wellington Ic X9974

| | |
|---|---|
| P/O C.G.R. Saunders RCAF | Killed |
| Sgt H.L. Steadman RCAF | Killed |
| P/O A. Lodge | Killed |
| Sgt A.N. Irving RCAF | Killed |
| Sgt D.Y.N. Crosby RCAF | Killed |
| Sgt V.J. Hale | Killed |
| Passengers | |
| Flt/Sgt H. Higginson | Killed |
| Sgt E. Beard | Killed |
| Cpl G.I.F. Davies | Killed |
| LAC C. Robson | Killed |

**Hampstead Norris - Gibraltar**

A/c clipped boundary fence on take-off and lost pitot tube. Pilot attempted a circuit preparatory to landing, but stalled and crashed. P/Os Saunders and Lodge, Sgts Beard, Crosby, Irving and Steadman are buried at Wyton; Sgt Hale at Crowthorne; Flt/Sgt Higginson at Leicester (Gilroes) Cemetery; Cpl Davies at Thatcham; and LAC Robson in Warley Congregational Cemetery, Halifax.

## 2/3 November 1941

Wellington Ic X9763 'U'

| | |
|---|---|
| Sgt G.D. Colville | Killed |
| Sgt I.R. McCalman RAAF | Killed |
| Sgt H.M. Forth | Killed |
| Sgt E.D. Spry | Killed |
| Sgt T.W. Robson | Killed |
| Sgt J.T. Ackroyd | Killed |

**Tripoli**

Sgts Colville and Robson are buried in Tripoli War Cemetery, and the remainder commemorated on the Malta Memorial.

## 11/12 November 1941

Wellington Ic X9765 'A'

| | |
|---|---|
| Sqn/Ldr A.D. Greer RNZAF | POW |
| Sgt D. Moorey RAAF | POW |
| Sgt C.P. Greenhill | Killed |
| Sgt J.I. Henderson RCAF | Killed |
| Sgt F.G.S Fox RCAF | POW |
| P/O J.H.S Bebington | Killed |

**Naples**

Ditched after engine failure. P/O Bebington drowned at that time; Sgts Greenhill and Henderson when the dinghy overturned in a storm. All three are commemorated on the Malta Memorial.

## 24/25 November 1941

Wellington Ic Z1046

| | |
|---|---|
| Sgt T.W. Parker | POW |
| Sgt E.I. Cooper | POW |
| Flt/Sgt M.R. Chabot RCAF | Killed |
| Sgt D.R. Kelly | Killed |
| Sgt G.S. Stephens | Killed |
| Sgt H. Whitaker | Killed |

**Benghazi**

Ditched out of fuel after navigation difficulties caused by radio failure. The survivors spent 5 days in a dinghy. The four dead are commemorated on the Malta Memorial.

## 5/6 December 1941
Wellington Ic R1066 'K'  **Naples**

| | | |
|---|---|---|
| F/O D.F. Hutt | POW | Shot down by a Italian CR42 night fighter (Mar. V. |
| P/O I.E. Miller | POW | Patriarcha). The four dead are buried in the Salerno |
| P/O A.J. Pyle | Killed | War Cemetery. |
| Sgt W.H. Poole | Killed | |
| Flt/Sgt T.J. Arsenault RCAF | Killed | |
| Sgt L.J. Abbott RAAF | Killed | |

## 13/14 December 1941
Wellington Ic X9993  **Minelaying, Benghazi harbour**

| | | |
|---|---|---|
| Sgt G.H. Easton RNZAF | | Hydraulics hit by flak, and with flaps, undercarriage |
| Sgt C.N. Hardman | | and bomb doors down flew to Tobruk, where it |
| Sgt G.A. Little RCAF | | crash-landed. Crew was returning to Luqa by |
| Sgt F.H. Cochrane | Wounded | Sunderland on 22 December when it was attacked |
| Sgt K.R. Blackhurst | | and crippled by Me110s. Sgt Hardman was killed, |
| Sgt A.E. Boorman | | and Sgt Boorman slightly wounded. Hardman is |
| | | commemorated on the El Alamein Memorial. |

## 4/5 January 1942
Wellington Ic Z9036  **Castel Vetrano Aerodrome**

| | | |
|---|---|---|
| Flt/Sgt J.F. Lewthwaite RNZAF | Killed | Brought down by flak during a low level attack. All buried in the Catania War Cemetery. |
| Sgt P.F. Lill | Killed | |
| Flt/Sgt W.R. Pick RCAF | Killed | |
| Sgt W. Chalmers | Killed | |
| Sgt M. Bryan | Killed | |
| Sgt S.H. James | Killed | |

## 10/11 January 1942
Wellington Ic X9837  **Wilhelmshaven**

| | | |
|---|---|---|
| P/O P.S. Sanders | POW | Ditched in the North Sea. The dead are |
| Sgt F. Pearson | Killed | commemorated on the Runnymede Memorial. |
| Sgt L.J. Benson | POW | |
| Sgt G.W. Tode | POW | |
| Sgt A.D.E.St.C Smithe | Killed | |
| Sgt E.W. Wainwright. | POW | |

## 14/15 January 1942
Wellington Ic X9842  **Hamburg**

| | | |
|---|---|---|
| P/O E.G. Broad RAAF | Killed | Lost without trace. All are commemorated on the |
| Sgt J.R. Fenwick | Killed | Runnymede Memorial |
| Sgt C.D. Russell | Killed | |
| Sgt J. Priestley | Killed | |
| Sgt P.J. Timmons | Killed | |
| Sgt T.H. Thomas | Killed | |

**11/12 February 1942**

| | | |
|---|---|---|
| Wellington II Z8904 | | **Mannheim** |
| P/O L.J. Ackland | | One engine cut and the other malfunctioned soon |
| Sgt P.L. Hall | Injured | after take-off. 4000 lb bomb dropped in the sea off |
| P/O R.F. Davies | | Clacton. With radio u/s and the remaining engine |
| Flt/Sgt C.T.T. Brady | | failing the crew baled out over Essex. |
| Sgt H. Gallaher | | |
| P/O R.M. Grieg | | |

**12 February 1942**

| | | |
|---|---|---|
| Wellington Ic DV507 | | **Search for Scharnhorst and Gneisenau** |
| F/O Barr | | Crossing the English coast near Lowestoft was fired |
| Sgt Deacock | | on by AA batteries. Landed at Lakenheath. |
| P/O Hellyer | | |
| Sgt Thompson | | |
| Sgt C.A. Robson RCAF | | |
| P/O W.A. Leavett | Wounded | |

**24/25 June 1942**

| | | |
|---|---|---|
| Wellington Ic DV652 'E' | | **Benghazi** |
| Sgt R.E. White | Injured | Crashed after the engines cut, out of fuel, and |
| Sgt L.W.H. Chappell | Injured | caught fire. Sgt Rees is commemorated on the El |
| P/O E.H. Laithwaite | Injured | Alamein Memorial. |
| Sgt Price | | |
| Sgt P.D. Rees | Killed | |
| Sgt Wheetley | | |

**26/27 June 1942**

| | | |
|---|---|---|
| Wellington Ic 'V' | | **Battle Area: El Alamein** |
| Sgt S.H. Gunn RNZAF | Killed | Crashed near Halfaya railway station. All are buried |
| Sgt P.T. Halstead | Killed | in the Halfaya Sollum War Cemetery. |
| Flt/Sgt H.F. Thompson RCAF | Killed | |
| Flt/Sgt O.M. Kileen RCAF | Killed | |
| Flt/Sgt S. Gregory RCAF | Killed | |
| Sgt H.J. Morgan | Killed | |

**3/4 July 1942**

| | | |
|---|---|---|
| Wellington Ic HF914 'G' | | **Tank Repair Depot, Mersa Matruh** |
| Sgt W.E. Dwyer | Killed | Hit by flak on the bombing run and went down in |
| Sgt S.R. Burford | Killed | flames. All are commemorated on the El Alamein |
| Sgt W.F. Lefevre | Killed | Memorial. |
| Sgt A.L. Potts | Killed | |
| Sgt W.T. Balchin | Killed | |
| Sgt J.A.P. Goss | Killed | |

**10 July 1942**

Wellington Ic HX374 'F'
P/O K. Liversidge
Sgt C. Mortimer
Flt/Sgt J. Reddell RNZAF
Sgt H.G. Horton RNZAF
Sgt R. Beatson RNZAF
Sgt J. Hammond

**Tobruk**

Engine trouble shortly after take-off, so a/c returned. Caught fire on landing and burnt out. Bombs exploded.

**12/13 July 1942**

Wellington Ic HX373 'N'
Sqn/Ldr F.J. Steel RNZAF
P/O D.A. Adams RNZAF
P/O R. Sharp
Sgt A. Aldersey
Sgt G. Herford
P/O E. Proctor

**Tobruk**

Target not located because the compass was u/s. A/c off course on return journey for the same reason. Fuel ran out and a/c crash-landed.

**19 July 1942**

Wellington Ic HX399 'S'
Flt/Sgt P.R. Kingsford
  RNZAF   Killed
Sgt J.A. Tovey RNZAF
Sgt J. Clark
Sgt R.J. Laing RAAF   Killed
Sgt L. McTaggart
Sgt I. Goss

**Tobruk**

Starboard engine caught fire and the a/c crashed near Wadi Natrun. Kingsford and Laing stayed with the a/c, and were trapped in the ensuing fire. Both are commemorated on the El Alamein Memorial.

**22 July 1942**

Wellington Ic HX440 'U'
Sgt R. King
Sgt N. Housden
Sgt L. Greenwood
Sgt T.R.A. Merry
Sgt J. Smart
Sgt A. Macaskill   Killed

**Motor transport near El Alamein**

Survived three attacks by night fighters, but crashed on attempting to overshoot at Base. Sgt Mackaskill is buried in the Suez War Memorial Cemetery.

**27/28 July 1942**

Wellington Ic HX370 'Y'
Sgt W.H. Mitchell   Killed
Sgt H.G. Graham RCAF   Killed
Sgt R.H. Lowe   Killed
Sgt G.McK. Duff   Killed
Sgt C.E. Tipper   Killed
Flt/Sgt J.J. Thompson
  RCAF   Killed

**Landing ground 20**

Believed crashed in flames near target. All are commemorated on the El Alamein Memorial.

## 5/6 August 1942

Wellington Ic HF898 'B'　　　　　　**Tobruk**

| | | |
|---|---|---|
| Sgt V. Murray | POW | After losing port propeller a/c lost height and crew |
| P/O W.H.Young | POW | baled out. |
| Sgt J.S. Cameron RAAF | POW | |
| Sgt A.R. Tonkin RAAF | POW | |
| Sgt W.R. Thompson RAAF | POW | |
| Sgt P.W. Northway RAAF | POW | |

## 7/8 August 1942

Wellington Ic HX431 'O'　　　　　　**Tobruk**

| | | |
|---|---|---|
| F/Lt H. Grant | POW | Crash-landed after a mid-air collision with another |
| Sgt G. Whyte | POW | Wellington. Hull and Dauphin baled out; Hull too |
| P/O A.E. Hull | Killed | low for his parachute to open. He is |
| Flt/Sgt C.E. Dauphin | | commemorated on the El Alamein Memorial. |
| RCAF | POW | |
| Flt/Sgt A.W. Dunn | POW | |
| | Injured | |
| Flt/Sgt J. Ware, DFM | FOW | |
| | Injured | |

Wellington Ic DV663 'U'

| | | |
|---|---|---|
| Flt/Sgt L.P. Kerr RNZAF | Killed | Possibly collided with HX431. Lost without trace. |
| Flt/Sgt E.K. Hainey | Killed | All are commemorated on the El Alamein Memorial. |
| Sgt J.I. Thomson RNZAF | Killed | |
| Sgt F.R. Smith RAAF | Killed | |
| Sgt R.StC. Gowdie RAAF | Killed | |
| Sgt D. Wolstenholme | | |
| RCAF | Killed | |

## 9/10 August 1942

Wellington Ic HX560 'S'　　　　　　**Tobruk**

| | | |
|---|---|---|
| Flt/Sgt G.P.A. Yates RCAF | | An engine failed on the return journey and the |
| Sgt G.A. Westthorp | | crew baled out after reaching the allied lines at El |
| F/O F. Waterman | | Alamein. |
| Sgt J. Dickenson | | |
| Sgt R. Gardiner | | |
| Sgt J. Egan | | |

## 11/12 August 1942

Wellington Ic HX377 'A'　　　　　　**Tobruk.**

| | | |
|---|---|---|
| Sgt C.E. Hickman | POW | Engine failure. Crew baled out, and covered 90 |
| Sgt G.S. Ferrero RAAF | POW | miles in 7 days before capture. |
| Sgt P.C. Lloyd | POW | |
| Sgt G. Martin | POW | |
| Sgt L.R.A. Beasley | POW | |
| Sgt G.T. Holt | POW | |

## 16/17 August 1942

Wellington Ic HX425 'H'  **Tobruk**

| | | |
|---|---|---|
| Sgt J. Mason | POW | Engine failure, perhaps because of flak damage. |
| Sgt D. Syddall | POW | |
| Sgt L.W. H. Stevens | POW | |
| Sgt C.A. Boyer RNZAF | POW | |
| Sgt D.A. Carmichael RNZAF | POW | |
| Sgt D. White | POW | |

## 22/23 August 1942

Wellington Ic HX488 'Y'  **Mersa Matruh: flare dropping**

Sgt R. Ceha
Sgt G. Dawson
Sgt D. MacMichael
Sgt T. Vickers
Sgt F. Mason
Sgt K. Davidson

Loss of port propeller and failing starboard engine caused crew to bale out over allied territory.

## 2/3 September 1942

Wellington Ic X9938 'T'  **Alam Halfa Battle Area**

| | | |
|---|---|---|
| Sgt V. Baker | Injured | Blew up on landing because of a bomb hang-up. |
| P/O G.J. Nicholson | Killed | The dead are buried in Heliopolis War Cemetery. |
| Flt/Sgt R.D. Walker RAAF | Killed | |
| Sgt A.R. Duncanson RAAF | Killed | |
| Sgt R.J. Evans RAAF | Killed | |
| Sgt J. Roach | | |

## 25/26 September 1942

Wellington Ic HF846 'P'  **Tobruk**

| | | |
|---|---|---|
| Flt/Sgt G.F. Langham RNZAF | Killed | Perhaps the a/c which was seen to crash south west of L.G. 146. All are commemorated on the El |
| F/O D.A. Adams, m.i.d., RNZAF | Killed | Alamein Memorial. |
| Sgt J.M. Welsh RNZAF | Killed | |
| Sgt R.H. Cook RNZAF | Killed | |
| Sgt M.G. Smart RAAF | Killed | |
| Sgt W.G.J. Price | Killed | |

## 7/8 October 1942

Wellington Ic DV504 'G'  **Tobruk**

| | | |
|---|---|---|
| Flt/Sgt R.L. Spence RCAF | Evaded | Engine failure. Spence and Wood reached allied |
| Sgt K. Bowhill | POW | lines after 24 days in the desert. |
| Sgt C.C. Hill RCAF | POW | |
| Sgt J.K. Wood RAAF | Evaded | |
| Sgt E.A. Linforth | POW | |
| Sgt A.W. Butteriss | POW | |

**1/2 November 1942**

Wellington Ic BB516 'A'                **El Alamein Battle Area**
Sgt M. McKiggin                        Engine malfunction led to loss of height. Crew
Sgt W. Sercombe            Injured     baled out over allied territory.
Sgt G.M. Rea
Sgt R.A. Brown
Sgt G. Armstrong
Sgt A.D. Price

**10 November 1942**

Wellington Ic HX571 'F'                **Tobruk**
Sgt R.G. Workman           Killed      Crashed and caught fire immediately after take-off.
Flt/Sgt R.A. King          Killed      The dead are buried in Heliopolis War Cemetery.
Flt/Sgt L. Greenwood       Killed
Sgt C.S. McCormick         Killed
Sgt P.P. Armstrong         Killed
Sgt Quinn                  Injured

**10/11 November 1942**

Wellington Ic R1182 'D'                **Almas aerodrome**
Sgt W. Setterfield                     Forced by engine failure to ditch 15 miles off Gozo.
Sgt R.E.C. Rainey RNZAF                Crew rescued by fishermen.
Sgt W. Heffernan
Sgt G. Agnew
Sgt M. Churchman
Sgt W. Nicholson

**12/13 November 1942**

Wellington Ic DU489 'A'                **Motor Transport: Tobruk-Derna road**
P/O R.G. MacInnes                      A/c crash-landed in the desert.
Sgt J.F. Turner
P/O Cottell
Sgt A. Venner
Flt/Sgt A. Challand        Injured
Sgt A. Liston

**3/4 December 1942**

Wellington Ic HX395                    **Ragusa**
P/O V.M. Todd                          Blew up on landing at Luqa; bomb hang-up. Sgts
P/O N. Simmonds                        Aspell and Semley are buried in Capuccini Naval
Sgt E.A. Aspell            Killed      Cemetery, Malta.
Sgt A.W. Ward
Sgt R. Semley              Killed

## 7/8 December 1942
Wellington Ic HF834 'C'  **Bizerta Docks**

| | | |
|---|---|---|
| F/O A.D. Bell | Killed | Flt/Sgt Wigley is buried in the Catania War |
| Sgt A. Marshall | Killed | Cemetery; the others are commemorated on the |
| Sgt R. Gill | Killed | Malta Memorial. |
| Flt/Sgt H.J. Wigley RAAF | Killed | |
| Sgt S. Heywood | Killed | |
| Sgt L.L. McDonnell | POW | |

## 31 December 1942/1 January 1943
Wellington Ic HB955  **Sfax**

| | | |
|---|---|---|
| W/O D.L. Iremonger | Killed | Does not appear on the 40 Squadron ORB. |
| Sgt T.J. Pritchard | Killed | Apparently a 37 Squadron crew detached to Luqa, |
| Sgt E.H. Wright | Killed | and attached to 40 Squadron. All are |
| Sgt J. Bell | Killed | commemorated on the Malta Memorial. |
| Sgt A. Campbell | Killed | |
| Flt/Sgt S.Q. Schrump RCAF | Killed | |

## 2/3 January 1943
Wellington Ic HE107 'C'  **Sousse**

| | | |
|---|---|---|
| Sgt C. Richardson | | Flak damage caused engine failure. Crew baled out. |
| Sgt C.F. Last | Injured | |
| Sgt J.S. Dovey, DFM | | |
| Sgt R.A. Brown | Injured | |
| Sgt W.R. Burton RCAF | | |

## 9/10 January 1943
Wellington Ic HX446 'Q'  **Tripoli**

| | |
|---|---|
| F/O R.C. Earl RNZAF | Radio u/s and navigation difficulties meant a/c ran |
| Sgt J. Whale | out of fuel short of Malta and ditched. Crew |
| P/O J. Liversidge | rescued by HSL. |
| Sgt R.F. Cooper | |
| Sgt R.J.H. Milne | |
| Sgt R.D. Turner | |

## 29/30 January 1943
Wellington Ic HX494  **Palermo**

| | | |
|---|---|---|
| Sgt T. Patterson | Killed | Hit by flak during the bombing run and crashed in |
| Sgt C.S. Carroll | Killed | flames. On attachment to 70 Sq. at Magrun North. |
| P/O R.B. Carlson RCAF | Killed | All are commemorated on the El Alamein Memorial. |
| Sgt R. Stansfield | Killed | |
| Sgt R.B. Smith | Killed | |
| Sgt J.H.P. Evans | Killed | |

## 22/23 February 1943

| Wellington Ic DV569 'F' | | **Palermo** |
|---|---|---|
| WO1 J.D. Massey RCAF | Killed | Attached from 37 Sqn. All are commemorated on |
| F/O P.R. Ward | Killed | the El Alamein Memorial. |
| Sgt R. Scott | Killed | |
| Flt/Sgt J.H.G. Nash RAAF | Killed | |
| Flt/Sgt J.T. Lindsay | Killed | |

## 23/24 February 1943

Wellington Ic BB478 'C'        **Gabes**

F/O A.B. Smith RNZAF          Port engine failed off Djerba. The a/c was ditched

F/O E.A. Moir                successfully, but the crew was adrift in a dinghy for

Flt/Sgt W. Throup            82 hours before landing near Zuara, where help was

F/O K. Bingham              obtained from Arabs.

Sgt C.R. Harrison

Sgt M.J. Vail

## 3/4 March 1943

| Wellington Ic HX 601 'H' | | **Motor transport near Mareth** |
|---|---|---|
| F/Lt L. McLachlan RNZAF | Killed | Shot down by Hpt. Dr. Horst Petuschka of |
| Flt/Sgt J.T. McRae | Killed | II/NJG2. All are commemorated on the El Alamein |
| Sgt J.F. Arrowsmith | Killed | Memorial. |
| Flt/Sgt F. Hughes | Killed | |
| Sgt A.G. Sawyer | Killed | |
| Sgt K.D. Tookey | Killed | |

## 9/10 March 1943

| Wellington Ic AD651 'D' | | **Palermo** |
|---|---|---|
| Sgt J. Whale | Injured | A/c ran out of fuel and in trying to ditch crashed in |
| Sgt R. Rickard | Injured | a coastal palm grove 15 km from Homs. Sgt |
| Sgt P.G. Hartley | Injured | Sprattley is buried in Tripoli War Cemetery. |
| Sgt L.A. Turner | Injured | |
| Sgt L. Knight | Injured | |
| Sgt J.A. Sprattley | Killed | |

| Wellington Ic HX778 'R' | | |
|---|---|---|
| F/O K.F.D. Attwell | Injured | Crashed on return to base. No entry in ORB Form |
| . . . . . . | | 541 |
| P/O C.C. Goldsmith | | |
|   RAAF | Injured | |
| . . . . . . | | |
| . . . . . . | | |
| Sgt A.C. McTier | Injured | |

## 6/7 April 1943

Wellington Ic HZ 207 'J'

**Sfax**

| | | |
|---|---|---|
| Sgt R.A. Atterton | Killed | Sgt Atterton and F/O Laycock are buried in Sfax |
| P/O A. Ittkin RCAF | Killed | War Cemetery. The others are commemorated on |
| Sgt A. Kenyon | Killed | the El Alamein Memorial. |
| F/O P.H. Laycock | Killed | |
| Sgt R.J. O'Brien | Killed | |

## 11/12 April 1943

Wellington HE109 'E'

**St. Marie du Zit Airfield**

| | | |
|---|---|---|
| F/O H.E. Wilkinson | Killed | Hit by flak while illuminating the target and crashed |
| F/Lt A.J. Meldrum RAAF | Killed | in flames. All are buried in the Medjez-el-Bab War |
| Sgt L.P. Grace | Killed | Cemetery. |
| Sgt R. Milbourne | Killed | |
| Sgt A.R. Graves | Killed | |
| Sgt P.C.P. Kipling | Killed | |

## 15/16 April 1943

Wellington III HZ125 'P'

**St. Marie du Zit Airfield**

| | | |
|---|---|---|
| Flt/Sgt J.G. Hibbert | Killed | Shot down over the target by Fw. Lubenka of |
| Flt/Sgt J.T. Knox | Killed | II/NJG2. All are buried in the Enfidaville War |
| Sgt H.J. Wheeler | Killed | Cemetery. |
| Sgt C.B. Freeman | Killed | |
| Sgt B.C. Marling | Killed | |
| Sgt R.M. Jay | Killed | |

## 19 April 1943

Wellington III HZ146 'B'

**Soliman South Landing Ground**

| | | |
|---|---|---|
| W/O G.R. Webb RAAF | Killed | Perhaps lost to flak but claimed by Oblt. Stefen |
| Sgt M.F. McKeon | Killed | Machat of II/NJG2. Crashed in flames. The dead |
| Flt/Sgt J.W.F.S. Liley RAAF | POW | are commemorated on the El Alamein Memorial. |
| Sgt A.S. Quick | POW | |
| Sgt I.W. Sanderson | Killed | |
| Flt/Sgt L.N. Bain RAAF | Killed | |

Wellington III HZ248 'R'

| | | |
|---|---|---|
| Flt/Sgt A.St.C. Turner RAAF | Killed | Shot down by Oblt. Machat. All but Sgt Allwright |
| Flt/Sgt D.N. Dawson RAAF | Killed | (commemorated on the El Alamein Memorial) are buried in Enfidaville War Cemetery. |
| Flt/Sgt W.S. Sinclair RAAF | Killed | |
| Flt/Sgt R.B. McIlroy RAAF | Killed | |
| Sgt A.G. Allwright | Killed | |

## 4/5 May 1943

| Wellington III HF 743 'N' | | **Motor transport and troop concentrations** |
|---|---|---|
| Sgt W. Dench | Injured | Unable to locate base in bad weather, despite a |
| P/O H.E. Kessock-Philip | | square search and dropping flares. Crew finally baled |
| Sgt J. Richardson | | out. |
| Sgt R.J. Herbert | | |
| Sgt Kay | | |

## 6/7 May 1943

| Wellington III HZ243 | | **Roads; Tunis area** |
|---|---|---|
| Sgt J.R. Hough | Killed | Believed crashed over target area. All are buried in |
| P/O K. Madin | Killed | the Massicault War Cemetery. |
| Sgt P.F. Jackson | Killed | |
| Sgt C.V. Scadden | Killed | |
| Sgt D.W.E. Batch | Killed | |

## 10 June 1943

| Wellington III HF687 T' | | **Pantelleria** |
|---|---|---|
| W/O1 N. Kennedy RCAF | Killed | A/c crashed on take-off and was completely |
| Sgt I.A. Roy | Killed | destroyed. All the dead are buried in Enfidaville |
| Sgt S. Underwood | Killed | War Cemetery. |
| Flt/Sgt D.N. Hall | Killed | |
| Sgt R.A. Powell | Injured | |

## 5/6 July 1943

| Wellington X HE793 'Y' | | **Gerbini aerodrome** |
|---|---|---|
| Sgt W. Dench | Killed | A/c crashed N of the target area. All but W/O2 |
| P/O H.E. Kessock-Philip | Killed | Petz (who is buried in Agira Canadian War |
| Sgt J. Richardson | Killed | Cemetery) are buried in Catania War Cemetery. |
| Sgt R.J. Herbert | Killed | |
| W/O2 M.G. Petz RCAF | Killed | |

## 8/9 July 1943

| Wellington X HE144 'W' | | **Catania aerodrome** |
|---|---|---|
| F/O J.K. Piry | Killed | All are commemorated on the El Alamein Memorial. |
| Flt/Sgt G.A. Westthorp | Killed | |
| F/O R.R.W. Peters | Killed | |
| Sgt S. Knowles | Killed | |
| Sgt N. Waddington | Killed | |
| Flt/Sgt A.A. Mansell | Killed | |

| Wellington X HE707 'L' | | All are commemorated on the Malta Memorial. |
|---|---|---|
| Sgt S.H.N. Hart | Killed | |
| Flt/Sgt W.V. Williams RAAF | Killed | |
| Sgt J. Howartson | Killed | |
| Sgt G.S. Dryden | Killed | |
| Sgt H.H. Sharpe | Killed | |

## 5/6 August 1943

Wellington X HE796 'P' — **Messina Beaches**

| | |
|---|---|
| P/O D.C. Challis, DFM | Killed |
| Sgt R.K. Cox | Killed |
| Sgt J.G. Noblett | Killed |
| F/O M.S. D'Abadi | Killed |
| Sgt F.A. Hitchcock | Killed |

All are commemorated on the El Alamein Memorial.

Wellington X HE759 'A'

| | |
|---|---|
| Sgt W.L. Boundy | Killed |
| F/O R.W. Holdsworth | Killed |
| Sgt H.W.S. Ducklin | Killed |
| Sgt K. Lyne | Killed |
| Sgt G.L. Abrahams | Killed |

All are commemorated on the El Alamein Memorial.

## 11/12 August 1943

Wellington X HZ544 'Z' — **St. Agata Beaches**

| | |
|---|---|
| W/O H.S. Shepherd RNZAF | Killed |
| Flt/Sgt L.A. Cox | Killed |
| Sgt G.W. Payne | Killed |
| Sgt H. Cameron | Killed |
| Flt/Sgt A.R. Murray | Killed |

Shot down in flames over the target. All are commemorated on the El Alamein Memorial.

Wellington X HF525 'R'

| | |
|---|---|
| Flt/Sgt H. Bartlett, DFM | POW |
| P/O W. Lester, DFC | Killed |
| Sgt R. Curtis | POW |
| Sgt L.D. Atkins | POW |
| Sgt A.F. Ash | POW |

Shot down over the target area. After several days in the hands of Italian troops Atkins met advancing American troops, and returned to his unit. P/O Lester is commemorated on the El Alamein Memorial.

## 12/13 August 1943

Wellington X HZ570 'U' — **Messina beaches**

| | |
|---|---|
| Flt/Sgt W.R. Walters RAAF | Killed |
| Flt/Sgt W.O Gaze RAAF | Killed |
| Flt/Sgt J.P. Hall RAAF | Killed |
| Flt/Sgt D.H. Morgan RAAF | Killed |
| Sgt J.K. Kirk | Killed |

Shot down over the target area. All are buried in Syracuse War Cemetery.

## 15/16 August 1943

Wellington X HE646 'D' — **Scalea beaches**

| | |
|---|---|
| Sgt K. Bamford | Evaded |
| Sgt C.W.H. Heels | Killed |
| Sgt A.G. Payne | Evaded |
| Sgt P.O Pearson | Killed |
| Sgt W.M. Bladen | Killed |

Crashed in flames near San Giovanni, Calabria. The dead are buried in Naples War Cemetery.

### 16/17 August 1943

| | | |
|---|---|---|
| Wellington III HF688 'P' | | **Viterbo aerodrome** |
| Flt/Sgt C.S. Field | | A/c came under heavy AA fire. The rear gunner |
| Sgt B.C.L. Boyd | | found the rear hatch open, a torch on the floor and |
| Sgt N.J. Madigan RAAF | POW | Sgt Madigan and a parachute missing. |
| Flt/Sgt B.F. Sedgley RAAF | | |
| Sgt C.G. Taylor | | |

### 19/20 August 1943

| | | |
|---|---|---|
| Wellington III HF688 'P' | | **Beaches, Sapri-Paola** |
| Flt/Sgt C.S. Field | Killed | Believed crashed in flames near Scalea. All are |
| Sgt B.C.L Boyd | Killed | commemorated on the El Alamein Memorial. |
| Sgt R.S. Facey | Killed | |
| Flt/Sgt B.F. Sedgley RAAF | Killed | |
| Sgt C.G. Taylor | Killed | |

### 17/18 September 1943

| | | |
|---|---|---|
| Wellington X HF534 'D' | | **Cerveteri aerodrome** |
| WO1 B.M. Berven, DFM, | | Caught fire shortly after leaving the target area. All |
| RCAF | Killed | save WO2 Nicholls (buried in Bolsena War |
| WO2 P.E. Nicholls RCAF | Killed | Cemetery) are commemorated on the Malta |
| WO2 H.A. Pennell RCAF | Killed | Memorial. |
| Flt/Sgt J. Hawkyard | Killed | |
| Flt/Sgt W.G. Webster | Killed | |

### 1/2 October 1943

| | | |
|---|---|---|
| Wellington III HZ244 'G' | | **Formia: coastal road** |
| Sgt S. Costin | | Unable to locate base owing to dense cloud and |
| Sgt J.V. Griffiths | Injured | eventually crash-landed near Djeida. A/c severely |
| Sgt F. Roberts | | damaged. |
| Sgt J.H.J. Bruxby | | |
| Sgt W.E. Batty | | |

### 8/9 October 1943

| | | |
|---|---|---|
| Wellington X LN340 'R' | | **Isernia: choke point** |
| Flt/Sgt R. Rickard | | A/c unable to lower undercarriage on return to |
| F/O F. McCrudden | | base. One bomb was believed to have 'hung up', so |
| Flt/Sgt L.A. Turner | | a belly landing was ruled out. Crew baled out. |
| Flt/Sgt L. Knight | | |
| Sgt J. Bates | | |

### 30/31 October 1943

| | | |
|---|---|---|
| Wellington X HE269 'E' | | **Perugia: aerodrome** |
| Sgt S. Costin | | Bomb aimer hit by flak. A/c landed El Alouina. |
| Sgt J.V. Griffiths | | |
| Sgt F. Roberts | | |
| Sgt J.H.J. Bruxby | Wounded | |
| Sgt W.E. Batty | | |

## 24/25 November 1943

Wellington III DF734 'G'

**Turin, ballbearing factory**

| | | |
|---|---|---|
| Flt/Sgt N. Carter | Killed | Crashed into mountains near Genoa in severe |
| Flt/Sgt W.L. Carr RNZAF | Killed | weather. All are buried in Staglieno Cemetery, |
| Sgt F. Middleton | Killed | Genoa. |
| F/O K.J. Strong | Killed | |
| Flt/Sgt G.W. Crowe | Killed | |

Wellington X HZ552 'M'

| | | |
|---|---|---|
| Flt/Sgt F.H. Haegi | Killed | Crashed into mountains near Genoa. This crew is |
| F/O W.A. Eagles | Killed | also buried in Staglieno Cemetery, Genoa. |
| Flt/Sgt W.C. Andrews RAAF | Killed | |
| P/O J.C. Harthill | Killed | |
| Sgt R.S. Colvin | Killed | |

Wellington X HE487 'M'

| | | |
|---|---|---|
| | | Crew radio'd that it was baling out over Sardinia, |
| P/O T.J. Gosling, DFM | Killed | but came down in the sea. P/O Gosling and Flt/Sgt |
| P/O G. Bushell RAAF | Killed | Chalmers are buried in Cagliari (S. Michele) |
| Flt/Sgt G. Chalmers | Killed | Communal Cemetery; the others are commemorated |
| Flt/Sgt D.E.L. Crosse | Killed | on the Malta Memorial. |
| Flt/Sgt D.L. Cooper | Killed | |

## 7/8 January 1944

Wellington X HF586 'U'

**Reggio Emelia: aircraft factory**

| | | |
|---|---|---|
| F/ Sgt L.J. Redden RAAF | | W/Op was thrown from the a/c over Bologna |
| Sgt L. Gillespie | | when it dived steeply to avoid flak. |
| Flt/Sgt T.L. Fielder RAAF | POW | |
| Sgt W.R. Black | | |
| Sgt J. Whitlock | | |

## 10/11 January 1944

Wellington X HZ514 'G'

**Sofia**

| | |
|---|---|
| Flt/Sgt C. Allen | Tyre burst on take-off; a/c wrecked, but did not |
| Sgt I M. Matley | burn or explode. |
| Sgt A. Parr | |
| Flt/Sgt E. de Blaquiere RCAF | |
| Sgt A. Howes RCAF | |

Wellington X HE287 'W'

| | | |
|---|---|---|
| Flt/Sgt J. Coape-Smith RAAF | | On return could not locate base. Short of fuel, the |
| Flt/Sgt G. Cormie | | crew baled out. |
| Flt/Sgt R. Kilroy RAAF | Injured | |
| Flt/Sgt G.H. Dealtry | | |
| Flt/Sgt R. Bayliss RAAF | | |

**18/19 January 1944**

| Wellington X JA122 'K' | | **Fano-Ancona railway** |
|---|---|---|
| P/O L.T. Puddephat | Killed | Crashed among the hills near San Marco on the |
| Sgt R.H. Davies | Killed | return journey. All are buried in Bari War Cemetery. |
| Sgt G.W. McNab | Killed | |
| Flt/Sgt M.N. Jones | Killed | |
| Flt/Sgt T. Owens | Killed | |

**16/17 February 1944**

| Wellington X LN513 'T' | | **Porto San Stephano** |
|---|---|---|
| Flt/Sgt A.F. Mason RAAF | Killed | Crashed in the hills near Murhe Sarachelle. All are |
| Sgt J.C. Keighley | Killed | buried in Bari War Cemetery. |
| Flt/Sgt E.E. McGilvery | | |
|   RAAF | Killed | |
| Sgt E.S. Sayer | Killed | |
| Sgt A. Bayliss | Killed | |

**17/18 February 1944**

| Wellington X HE237 | | **Genzano – Velletri** |
|---|---|---|
| F/O K.W. Lyon RAAF | Killed | Crashed into a house immediately after take-off: |
| Flt/Sgt S.E.P. Pillinger | Killed | cause unknown. A soldier and several civilians were |
| Sgt K.R. Reader | Killed | also killed. Three bombs exploded. The dead are |
| Sgt D.H. Knight | Killed | buried in Bari War Cemetery. |
| Sgt F. Jones RAAF | Injured | |

**24/25 March 1944**

| Wellington X LN898 'R' | | **Sofia** |
|---|---|---|
| Lt F.F. Williamson SAAF | POW | |
| W/O R.R. Sanderson | POW | |
| Sgt A.E. Servis | POW | |
| Sgt R. Madi | POW | |
| Flt/Sgt F.M. McBain | POW | |

| Wellington X LN874 'H' | | |
|---|---|---|
| Sgt G.S Waddell | | Starboard engine cut over Manfredonia, on the |
| Flt/Sgt H. Davison | | Adriatic coast. A/c lost height, and when the port |
| P/O J.W. Campbell | | engine began cutting, a crash-landing was made. |
| Sgt T.C. Hardwick | Injured | |
| Sgt K. Withnall | | |

**12/13 April 1944**

| Wellington X LP177 'B' | **Ferencvaros Marshalling Yards, Budapest** |
|---|---|
| Sqn/Ldr C. Mervyn-Jones, DFC | Ditched in the Adriatic off Yugoslavia after flak |
| Flt/Sgt G.E. Arnott RCAF | damage caused fuel loss. |
| P/O. J. Hardy | |
| F/O C.F. Mohs RCAF | |
| P/O D.F. Tester, DFM | |

### 15/16 April 1944

| Wellington X LN562 'C' | | **Turnul Severin, Marshalling yards** |
| Sgt J.C.J. Bailey | Killed | Shot down by flak near Bor, Yugoslavia. All are |
| Sgt E.F. Deadman | Killed | buried in Belgrade War Cemetery. |
| Sgt K. Richardson | Killed | |
| Sgt H.H. Francis | Killed | |
| Sgt J.B. Lucas | Killed | |

### 17/18 April 1944

| Wellington X JA509 'K' | | **Plovdiv Marshalling Yards** |
| F/O E.P. Payne | Injured | A/c burst a tyre on take-off and crashed, catching |
| Flt/Sgt E. Edmonds | Injured | fire, and setting off two other a/c. Bomb load |
| Sgt G. Leach | Injured | exploded. F/O Emery died of burns, 21.4.44, and is |
| F/O J.E. Emery | Injured | buried in Bari War Cemetery. |
| Sgt A. Knight | | |

### 5/6 May 1944

| Wellington X LP191 'R' | | **Cimpina, Marshalling yards** |
| Flt/Sgt D.H. Royle | Killed | Crashed at Valea Lungha, 10km SW of the target. |
| Flt/Sgt J.A. Smith | Killed | All are buried in Bucharest War Cemetery. |
| W/O A. Brown | Killed | |
| Sgt G.W. Ward | Killed | |
| Sgt A.R. Wood | Killed | |

### 6/7 May 1944

| Wellington X LP128 'O' | | **Bucharest** |
| W/O J.D. Coape-Smith | | Attacked by a night fighter, which set the a/c on |
| RAAF | POW | fire and killed the rear gunner. LP128 crashed at |
| Flt/Sgt G. Cormie | POW | Castranova, 30km S of Craiova, Romania. Flt/Sgt |
| W/O R.D. Kilroy RAAF | POW | Sauerwald is buried in Bucharest War Cemetery. |
| | Wounded | |
| Flt/Sgt G.H. Dealtry | POW | |
| Flt/Sgt R.G. Sauerwald | | |
| RAAF | Killed | |

| Wellington X LN982 'Q' | | |
| Flt/Sgt K.C.J. Martin RAAF | POW | Engines damaged by flak and failed on route to |
| Flt/Sgt G.M. Groat | POW | target. The crew baled out and the a/c crashed at |
| Flt/Sgt E.G. Carey | POW | Balta Greaca |
| Flt/Sgt K.G. Chambers | POW | |
| Flt/Sgt R. Tyrell | POW | |

**7/8 May 1944**

Wellington X LN804 'T'

| | | **Filiasi bridge** |
|---|---|---|
| W/O T.R. Bradshaw | | A/c crippled by light flak on bombing run and |
|   RCAF | Evaded | crashed at Zagubica, Yugoslavia. P/O McKenna is |
| W/O N.L. Reid RCAF | Evaded | buried in Sofia War Cemetery. The survivors met |
| Flt/Sgt W. Taylor | Evaded | up with Yugoslav partisans and returned to Italy in |
| P/O I.B.H. McKenna | Killed | August 1944. |
| Sgt L.R. Somers | Evaded | |

Wellington X ME878 'X'

| | | **Bucharest** |
|---|---|---|
| F/Lt G.W. Williams, DFC | Killed | Hit by flak soon after bombing. The rear gunner |
| W/O L.F. Dutton RCAF | Killed | baled out at very low level. A/c crashed at |
| Flt/Sgt F.W.A. Head | Killed | Vartoapele, 11km S of Belciug, Romania. The |
| Sgt L.J. Carey | Killed | dead are buried in Bucharest War Cemetery. |
| F/O H.D. Calvert | POW | |

**9/10 May 1944**

Wellington X LP180 'K'

| | | **Port-les-Valences** |
|---|---|---|
| F/O J. Huggler, m.i.d. | Killed | In 10/10ths cloud crashed into hills surrounding the |
| F/O H.C. Lane | Killed | target. All are buried in Mazargues Cemetery |
| Flt/Sgt N. Green | Killed | Extension, Marseilles. |
| Sgt K.W. Jackson | Killed | |
| Flt/Sgt E.J.H. Howell | Killed | |

**11/12 May 1944**

Wellington X HE991 'V'

| | | **Porto Ferrajo, Elba** |
|---|---|---|
| P/O D.M. Cleeve | Killed | All are buried in Coriano Ridge War Cemetery. |
| 2/Lt P. van Staden SAAF | Killed | |
| Sgt A.S. Smith | Killed | |
| Sgt A.D.B. Poole | Killed | |
| Sgt R.A. Moore | Killed | |

**24/25 May 1944**

Wellington X LP127 'P'

| | | **Valmontone** |
|---|---|---|
| Sgt F.J. Broad | Killed | All are buried in Salerno War Cemetery. |
| Sgt F.H. Baker | Killed | |
| Sgt R.R.C. Bartram | Killed | |
| W/O1 P.A.J. Desico RCAF | Killed | |
| Sgt K.J. Nuttycombe | Killed | |

**2/3 June 1944**

Wellington X LP120 'N'

| | | **Giurgiu** |
|---|---|---|
| Flt/Sgt F.R. Hughes RAAF | Killed | Crashed 20km S of Pirot, Yugoslavia. All are |
| Flt/Sgt K. Shaw | POW | commemorated on the Malta Memorial. |
| Sgt W.E. Samler | Killed | |
| Flt/Sgt A Millar | Killed | |
| Sgt F.R. Sweeney RAAF | Killed | |

## 13/14 June 1944

Wellington X LP324 'A'

**Munich**

| | |
|---|---|
| P/O M. Denson RAAF | POW |
| Flt/Sgt A. Goodman-Jones RAAF | POW |
| Sgt P.S. Kirby | POW |
| Sgt A.W. Belverstone | POW |
| Sgt A.L. Sorzano | POW |
| Sgt R. Haughton | POW |

Coned over target and the aircraft became uncontrollable after flak damage. Sgt Belverstone was doing a 'second dicky' wireless operator op.

## 1/2 July 1944

Wellington X LP497 'A'

**Minelaying, Pancevo - Smederevo**

| | |
|---|---|
| P/O G.S. Waddell, DFC | Killed |
| Flt/Sgt H. Davison | Killed |
| Flt/Sgt T.C. Hardwick | Killed |
| F/O J.W. Campbell | Killed |
| Sgt K. Withnall | POW |

Shot down by light flak on mining run. Rear gunner blown clear in his turret. The dead are buried in Belgrade War Cemetery.

Wellington X LM744 'N'

| | |
|---|---|
| Sgt W. Booth | Evaded |
| Sgt W. Goodbrand | Evaded |
| Sgt M. Mason | Evaded |
| Sgt L.F. Wetherill | Evaded |
| Sgt A.R. de Schrynmakers | Evaded |

Crippled by flak during the mining run. Pilot gained sufficient height for the crew to bale out. Hidden by Chetnik partisans, they returned to Italy in August.

Wellington X ME960 'U'

| | |
|---|---|
| Sgt E.E.R. Paterson | |
| Sgt W.T. Quinlan | |
| Sgt W.D. Mackenzie | |
| Sgt G.V. Lea | |
| Sgt T. Horwood | Killed |

A/c damaged by intense cross fire from the river banks. Sgt Horwood is buried in Bari War Cemetery.

## 2/3 July 1944

Wellington X LP253 'R'

**Prahova Oil Refinery**

| | |
|---|---|
| Flt/Sgt R.D. Sutcliffe RCAF | POW |
| Sgt J.D. Yole | Killed |
| Sgt E.H. Turner | POW |
| Sgt J.E. Turnbull | Evaded |
| Sgt H. Beeson | Killed |

Aircraft crippled by night fighter attack in which the rear gunner was killed. Sgt Yole was shot as he descended, or on the ground. Turnbull was sheltered by Yugoslav partisans, and returned to Italy in August. Sgts Yole and Beeson are buried in Belgrade War Cemetery.

Wellington X MX990 'R'

| | |
|---|---|
| F/O L.F. Tichbourne RAAF | POW |
| Flt/Sgt L.J. Goodlet RNZAF | POW |
| F/O A. Poole | POW |
| F/O A.T. Duff RAAF | POW |
| F/O J.C. Murphy | Killed |

A/c crippled by a night fighter attack in which the rear gunner was killed. Crashed at Macesul, 45km S of Craiova, Romania. F/O Murphy is buried in Bucharest War Cemetery.

**6/7 July 1944**

| Wellington X LN759 'M' | | **Feuersbrunn aerodrome** |
|---|---|---|
| P/O R.T. Collins RAAF | Killed | All are buried in Klagenfurt War Cemetery. |
| Flt/Sgt R.C. Dalton RAAF | Killed | |
| Sgt D.W. Niccols | Killed | |
| W/O M.W. Marsh | Killed | |
| Sgt V. Charles | Killed | |

| Wellington X LP210 'D' | | |
|---|---|---|
| P/O E. Hall | Killed | All are buried in Klagenfurt War Cemetery. |
| Flt/Sgt G.A.C. Coldridge | Killed | |
| Sgt D.C. Brennan | Killed | |
| Sgt A.P. Tarr | Killed | |
| Sgt S. Clubb | Killed | |

**10/11 July 1944**

| Wellington X MF399 'D' | | **Milan Lambrate Marshalling Yards** |
|---|---|---|
| Sgt N. Walters | Killed | All are buried in Milan War Cemetery. |
| Sgt A.H. Mabey | Killed | |
| Sgt A. McKenzie | Killed | |
| Sgt A. Ross | Killed | |
| Sgt A.J. Ellworthy | Killed | |

**13/14 July 1944**

| Wellington X LN270 'O' | | **Milan Lambrate Marshalling Yards** |
|---|---|---|
| P/O C. Charalambous | Killed | All are buried in Padua War Cemetery. |
| 2/Lt K. Hoyer SAAF | Killed | |
| F/O E.C. Martin | Killed | |
| Flt/Sgt E.R. Shepherd | Killed | |
| Sgt A.J. Knight | Killed | |

**16/17 July 1944**

| Wellington X LF118 'P' | | **Smederevo Oil Refinery** |
|---|---|---|
| Sgt A.W. Radley | Killed | All are buried in Belgrade War Cemetery. |
| P/O K.R. Evans | Killed | |
| Sgt O. Thomas | Killed | |
| Sgt J. Magee | Killed | |
| Sgt J.E. Hughes | Killed | |

**21/22 July 1944**

| Wellington X LP301 'A' | | **Fanto Oil Refinery, Pardubice** |
|---|---|---|
| Sgt R.W.F. Bodley | Injured | Turned back with fuel problems. Crew baled out |
| Sgt S. Eustace | | over Italian coast. |
| Flt/Sgt A. Joyce | | |
| Sgt A.G. Butcher RAAF | | |
| Flt/Sgt E.C. Fitzgerald RAAF | | |

**17/18 August 1944**

| Wellington X HF476 'X' | | **Xenia Oil Refinery, Ploesti** |
|---|---|---|
| Sgt D.J. Francis | Killed | Lost without trace, but perhaps crashed near Lake |
| Sgt S.B. Goddard | Killed | Scutari. All are commemorated on the Malta |
| Sgt J.W. Davies | Killed | Memorial. |
| Sgt D.A. Beaven | Killed | |
| Sgt D.W.R. Moore | Killed | |

| Wellington X LP237 'N' | | |
|---|---|---|
| Sgt E.E.R. Paterson | Killed | Crashed at Contesti, 25km N of Pitesti, Romania. |
| Sgt W.T. Quinlan | Killed | All are buried in Bucharest War Cemetery. |
| Sgt W.D. Mackenzie | Killed | |
| Sgt G.V. Lea | Killed | |
| Flt/Sgt I. Campbell | Killed | |

| Wellington X ME476 'B' | | |
|---|---|---|
| Flt/Sgt I. Arrowsmith RAAF | | Returned early because of fuel shortage and cloud. |
| Sgt J. Rowlinson | | Bombs jettisoned live. The a/c caught fire (cause |
| Sgt N. Greenaway | | unknown) while landing at base, and burnt out. |
| Sgt G. Mounfield | | |
| Sgt B. Stone | | |

**21/22 August 1944**

| Wellington X LN652 'S' | | **Szony Oil Refinery, Komarom** |
|---|---|---|
| F/O J. Barnett | Killed | All are buried in Budapest War Cemetery. |
| Lt S.B. Haagner SAAF | Killed | |
| Sgt L.F. Bonnet | Killed | |
| Sgt R.F. Vicary | Killed | |
| W/O F.W. Griffiths | Killed | |

**6/7 September 1944**

| Wellington X LN753 'P' | | **Bologna Marshalling Yards** |
|---|---|---|
| F/O G.P. Roberts RAAF | Killed | All are buried in Bologna War Cemetery. |
| Sgt J.M. Dobson | Killed | |
| Sgt T. Morris | Killed | |
| P/O A.J. Quin | Killed | |
| Sgt V.S.J. Belt | Killed | |

**20/21 September 1944**

| Wellington X LN816 'Z' | | **Hegyeshalom Marshalling Yards** |
|---|---|---|
| Flt/Sgt C.C. Westwood | | Came down in Northern Yugoslavia, cause |
| RAAF | Evaded | unknown. Sheltered by Tito's YNA, and returned |
| Sgt W.T.G. Samuel | Evaded | to the squadron in November. |
| Sgt T. McKenna | Evaded | |
| Sgt Ashworth | Evaded | |
| Sgt R. Douglas | Evaded | |

## 4/5 October 1944

| Wellington X MF458 'A' | | **Minelaying, Danube** |
|---|---|---|
| P/O A.L. Mayers | Killed | Hit by flak on mining run and port wing set on |
| Flt/Sgt V. McCall | Killed | fire. A/c exploded as the pilot attempted to ditch. |
| W/O C.H. Gunby | Killed | W/O Gunby is buried in Prague War Cemetery; |
| Sgt H.W. Hesketh | Killed | the others are commemorated on the Malta |
| Sgt R.C.R. Johnson | Killed | Memorial. |

## 11/12 October 1944

| Wellington X LP464 'D' | | **Verona, Porto Nuovo Marshalling Yards** |
|---|---|---|
| W/O R.W.F. Bodley | Killed | All are commemorated on the Malta Memorial. |
| Flt/Sgt L.R. Johnston | | |
|   RAAF | Killed | |
| Sgt G. Coyle | Killed | |
| Sgt A.G. Butcher | Killed | |
| Flt/Sgt E.C. Fitzgerald | | |
|   RAAF | Killed | |

| Wellington X MF630 'S' | | |
|---|---|---|
| P/O F. Wood | Killed | All are commemorated on the Malta Memorial. |
| F/O M. Enright | Killed | |
| P/O D.A.R. Rutland | Killed | |
| Sgt E. Crooks | Killed | |
| Sgt F.J. Edwards | Killed | |

## 13/14 October 1944

| Wellington X LF556 'X' | | **Szekesfehervar Marshalling Yards** |
|---|---|---|
| Sgt G.W. Moore, m.i.d. | Killed | All are buried in the Budapest War Cemetery. |
| Sgt B.N. White | Killed | |
| Sgt D.C. Berrisford | Killed | |
| Sgt H.R. Williams | Killed | |
| Sgt W.J. Lawn | Killed | |

## 10/11 November 1944

| Wellington X LN511 'Q' | | **Partisan supply drop: Chiapovano area** |
|---|---|---|
| Flt/Sgt J.P. Baker | Killed | Crashed in the hills near San Severo shortly after |
| Sgt B.W. Weston | Killed | take-off. All are buried in Bari War Cemetery. |
| Sgt D.W. Ayers | Killed | |
| Sgt T.J. Walaron | Killed | |
| Sgt J.McP. Mackenzie | Killed | |

## 22/23 November 1944

| Wellington X LP732 'O' | | **Szombathely Marshalling Yards** |
|---|---|---|
| P/O A.J.M. Starr | Killed | All are buried in Budapest War Cemetery. |
| Sgt W.G. Colgrave | Killed | |
| Sgt F.S.R. Smith | Killed | |
| Sgt E.T. Prior | Killed | |
| Sgt O.A.M. Cook | Killed | |

## 4 February 1945

Wellington X LP559 'L'

| | | **Partisan Supply drop: 'Crayon' area,** |
|---|---|---|
| F/O C.F. Wellman | Killed | **Yugoslavia** |
| Sgt A. McLeod | Killed | Crashed at San Severo shortly after take-off in bad |
| Sgt J. Purdon | Killed | weather. The dead are buried in Bari War Cemetery. |
| F/O D.T. Blain | Killed | |
| Sgt E. Lambert | Injured | |

Wellington X ME993 'F'

| | | |
|---|---|---|
| F/O J.N. Hickey | Killed | Crashed at Aprechina shortly after take-off. All are |
| Sgt C.H. Jones | Killed | buried in Bari War Cemetery. |
| Sgt P.M. Holt | Killed | |
| Sgt K.V. Dennis | Killed | |
| Sgt A.C. Lloyd | Killed | |

Wellington X MF371 'X'

| | | |
|---|---|---|
| Flt/Sgt C. Sunderland | Killed | Crashed at San Severo on the return journey. The |
| Sgt R.C. Burton | Killed | dead are buried in Bari War Cemetery. |
| Sgt E. Mulpeter | Killed | |
| Sgt D. Stott | Killed | |
| Sgt R. Coles | Injured | |

## 3/4 April 1945

Liberator VI KL579 'H'

**Novska Marshalling Yards**

Sqn/Ldr R.D. Thirsk
Flt/Sgt J Feltham
Flt/Sgt R. Ellicott
Sgt J. Parkinson
Sgt F. Tinsley
Sgt P. Simpson
Sgt J. Flint
Flt/Sgt B. Blakeman
Sgt J. Litchfield

Stalled and crashed on final approach. Starboard undercarriage collapsed.

## 15/16 April 1945

Liberator VI KK347 'N'

**Villach North Marshalling Yards**

Flt/Sgt R. Millett
Flt/Sgt L. Hall
Sgt F. Law
Flt/Sgt S. Day
Flt/Sgt L. Ingram
Sgt J. Wray
Flt/Sgt A. Cornick
Sgt B. Carton

Control lost on landing, and a/c reared up and crashed, being completely wrecked.

## 16/17 April 1945
Liberator VI KL581 'U'                    **Casalecchio Bridge**

| | | |
|---|---|---|
| W/O V.W. Greensmith | Injured | Crashed on landing with bombs on board. W/O |
| Flt/Sgt L.A. Burns | Injured | Greensmith, who died of his injuries on 17 April, is |
| Flt/Sgt J.J. Elliott | Injured | buried in Bari War Cemetery. |
| Sgt T.H. Coope | Injured | |
| Flt/Sgt P.J. Harrison | Injured | |
| Sgt R.H. Lloyd-Abbott | Injured | |
| Sgt A. Penfold | Injured | |
| Sgt T. Walliker | | |

# Appendix B
# Non-operational flights resulting in injury or death

**7 June 1916**
DH 2 6014                           **Practice**
2/Lt G.H.E. Rippon          Killed   When the engine cut as a result of 'improper
                                     adjustment of petrol supply', the pilot tried to turn
                                     back to the aerodrome, but stalled. Crashed at
                                     Alverstoke. 2/Lt Rippon is buried at Bath.

**Between 15 & 21 June 1916**
Lt A.W. Morey              Injured  **Practice**

**Between 29 June & 5 July 1916**
Sgt A. Armstrong          Injured  **Practice**

**29 September 1916**
FE8                                  **Practice**
2/Lt G.F. Campbell        Injured

**1 November 1916**
FE8 6379                            **Air Test**
Capt G.D. Hill            Injured   Crashed shortly after take off.

**13 November 1916**
FE8 6418                            **Air Test**
Sgt F.E. Darvell          Injured   Crashed taking off.

**23 March 1917**
Nieuport 17/23 A6669                **Practice**
2/Lt W.H. Ryder           Injured   Swung on take-off, propeller hit the ground and
                                    machine overturned.

**10 April 1917**
Nieuport 17/23 B1505      Injured  **Practice**
2/Lt A.C. Dunlop                     Lost control of a/c in snowstorm. Came out of
                                     cloud at 500 ft. Severe concussion, head injuries and
                                     broken legs.

**9 May 1917**
Nieuport 17/23 B1634                    **Practice**
2/Lt A.O.F. Bigg-wither    Injured    Crashed.

**20 August 1917**
Nieuport 17/23 A6646                    **Practice**
Sgt L.A. Herbert           Injured    .Crashed.

**15 September 1917**
Nieuport 17/23 B1578                    **Air Test**
2/Lt A.C. Nutter           Injured    Spun, flattened out too late and crashed.

**21 September 1917**
Nieuport 24 B3601                       **Practice**
2/Lt H.M. Hutton           Injured    Crashed on landing.

**17 May 1918**
SE5a B189                               **Target practice**
Lt P.S. Kerr               Injured

**15 August 1918**
SE5a D6122                              **Esquerdes - Bruay**
Maj A.W. Keen              Injured    Returning from 70 Sqn did a stall turn low down
                                        and struck a bank. A/c burst into flames, and Maj
                                        Keen died of burns on 2.9.1918. He is buried in
                                        Terlincthum British Cemetery, Wimille.

**29 September 1918**
SE5a D3991                              **Ferry Flight**
Lt T.H. Turnbull           Injured    Returning to aerodrome after a forced landing.
                                        Machine overturned on take-off.

**30 October 1918**
SE5a F5528                              **Practice**
2/Lt E.H. Mulley           Killed     Attempted to pull out of a steep dive too sharply;
                                        port wings gave way and machine crashed. 2/Lt
                                        Mulley is buried in Douai British Cemetery.

**6 January 1919**
SE5a                                    **Practice**
2/Lt L.A. Brais            Injured    On take-off engine cut, machine stalled, struck a
                                        tree, and crashed into the chateau moat.

**26 September 1933**
Fairey Gordon I                         **Montrose - Abingdon**
F/O N.C.M. Styche          Killed     Attempted forced landing at Bamborough,
AC1 M.A.C. White           Killed     Northumberland, in heavy fog.

Fairey Gordon I
Sgt J.W.E. Christian | Killed | Crashed in sea off Hartlepool in heavy fog. Sgt
Cpl A.C. Lewis | Killed | Christian's body was washed ashore, but Lewis's was never found.

## 9 November 1935
Fairey Gordon I K2720 | | **Cardington - Abingdon**
Sgt W. Park | Killed | After breaking formation, No. 2 of the Hart section climbed and dived and turned 180° and flew into a Gordon of the section following.

Hawker Hart (Special) K4371
F/O A. Ross | Killed
LAC J. Waugh | Killed

## 6 June 1938
Airspeed Envoy 252 | | **Salisbury - Pretoria**
P/O R. Moseby | Killed | P/O Moseby was one of three members of the RAF boxing team killed when a South African Air Force Envoy [Capt Koch] crashed near Tuli, Rhodesia. The SAAF crew of two also died. P/O Moseby's brother, F/Lt W.G. Moseby, also a member of the Boxing Team, was flying in an accompanying aircraft.

## 2 September 1939
Fairey Battle I L4979 | | **Abingdon - Betheniville**
F/Lt W.G. Moseby | Injured | Engine failure: ditched in the Channel. Rescued by
Sgt A. Cody | | Newhaven - Dieppe ferry. F/Lt Moseby was
AC1 W. Furby | | concussed and admitted to hospital in England.

## 14 April 1940
Blenheim IV L9207 | | **Unauthorised flight**
LAC J.F.B. Lewis | Killed | Lewis took up an a/c he was guarding without authority. He crashed in the Thames Estuary and is commemorated on the Runnymede Memorial.

## 12 December 1940
Wellington Ic T2718 | | **Training flight**
Sqn/Ldr R.G.C. Arnold | | Swung on take-off, hit lighting cables on the airfield
P/O B.H. Tweedale | Injured | boundary and crashed.
. . . . . .
Sgt H. Smith | Injured
. . . . . .
. . . . . .

**18 March 1942**

| | | |
|---|---|---|
| Wellington Ic Z9104 | | **Fuel consumption test** |
| Flt/Sgt H.W. Garvin RCAF | Killed | A/c suddenly dived into the ground. Cause not |
| W/O F.E. Johnson | Killed | established, but possibly pilot illness. All are buried |
| Sgt J.C. Joss | Killed | in the Suez War Memorial Cemetery. |
| Sgt R.J.J. Robb | Killed | |

**22 November 1942**

| | | |
|---|---|---|
| Wellington Ic HX438 'R' | | **Bone – Luqa** |
| P/O J.L Dickenson | | Forced-landed at Bone after bombing Bizerta. Left |
| Flt/Sgt G.T. Dawson | Killed | for Malta after repairs, crashing shortly after take-off. |
| Sgt L. Hadley | | Flt/Sgt Dawson and Sgt Golby are buried in Bone |
| Sgt D.A.D. Golby | Killed | War Cemetery. |
| Sgt A.P. Jones | | |
| Sgt W. Jones | | |

**22 May 1943**

| | | |
|---|---|---|
| Wellington Ic HX606 'C' | | **Air test** |
| Flt/Sgt W.A. Stewart | Killed | Crashed from 300'. Cause unknown. Flt/Sgt Stewart |
| | | is buried in Tripoli War Cemetery. |

**27 August 1943**

| | | |
|---|---|---|
| Bristol Beaufighter | | **Trapani – Blida** |
| Flt/Sgt F.A. Noonan | | Flt/Sgt Noonan and crew landed at Trapani after an |
| RAAF | Killed | engine caught fire during a raid on Bagnoli |
| | | Marshalling Yards, 26/27 August. Noonan was |
| | | killed when the Beaufighter in which he was a |
| | | passenger was shot down by USAAF Spitfires. He is |
| | | commemorated on the Malta Memorial. |

**19 September 1945**

| | | |
|---|---|---|
| Lancaster VII NX 690 'A' | | **Trooping: UK – Egypt** |
| F/O D.R. Faber | Killed | Crashed shortly after take-off from Castel Benito en |
| Flt/Sgt P.H. Bond | Killed | route for Shallufa. All are buried in Tripoli War |
| W/O D.J.J. Frost | Killed | Cemetery. |
| Flt/Sgt A.A.G. Steele | Killed | |
| Flt/Sgt J.H.E. Ashfield | Killed | |
| Flt/Sgt W.E. Bailey | Killed | |
| Flt/Sgt L.J. Clarkin | Killed | |
| Passengers | | |
| 37 Sqn | | |
| W/O N.S. Beames | Killed | |
| F/Lt G.R. Coleshill | Killed | |
| Flt/Sgt R.H.J. Harris | Killed | |
| W/O D.J. Law | Killed | |
| Wg/Cdr E.L.F. Meynell, | | |
| MBE | Killed | |

Flt/Sgt C.J. Pearce            Killed
W/O R.S. Shepherd             Killed
70 Sqn
Flt/Sgt F.H. Butterworth       Killed
Flt/Sgt W.H. Davies            Killed
W/O F.W.J. Denyer             Killed
W/O B.F. Hillyer              Killed
F/Lt G.P. Jakins              Killed
Flt/Sgt T.G. Lawson            Killed
W/O G.T. Lee-Roberts          Killed
F/O M.F.G. Long               Killed
Flt/Sgt K.S. Morris            Killed
Flt/Sgt J.H. Piper             Killed

## 23 July 1954

Canberra B2 WJ720              **Operation Dividend**
F/Lt G.S. Wilkes              Killed  Diverted to Marham in bad weather and crashed on
P/O D. Nelson                 Killed  final approach.
Sgt G. White                  Killed

# Appendix C
# Deaths or injuries from other causes

**3 September 1934**

AC2 F.W. Holland     Injured    Holland was standing beside a Gordon, using arm and hand signals, when his right hand was amputated by the propeller.

**27 September 1938**

P/O W.W. Macfarlane     Died    Air embolism after a faultily administered innoculation.

**28 October 1940**

AC2 W.J. McDonald     Killed    Struck by a propeller. AC2 McDonald is buried in Grantown-on-Spey New Burial Ground, Cromdale, Morayshire.

**2 August 1941**

LAC F. Gilleard     Died    Natural causes, Alconbury. LAC Gilleard is buried in York Cemetery.

**23 August 1941**

LAC S. Ballance     Killed    Road accident outside Alconbury aerodrome. LAC Ballance is buried in Great Walsingham, Norfolk.

**24 November 1941**

| | | |
|---|---|---|
| P/O W.F. Ingles | Injured | When the bomb doors of Wellington Ic X9662 |
| AC1 T. McCann, BEM | Killed | were opened on return to Luqa an anti-personnel |
| LAC F. Matley | Injured | bomb dropped out. AC1 McCann and Sgt Shearsby |
| AC2 J. Power | Injured | are buried in Capuccini Naval Cemetery, Malta. |
| Sgt W. Shearsby | Killed | |
| Sgt J.C. Williams | Injured | |

**18 December 1941**

| | | |
|---|---|---|
| Sgt F.J. Sunley | Killed | Waiting at Luqa to board Wellington X9907 for |
| Sgt A.J. Brogan | Injured | take-off when it was bombed. Sgt Sunley is buried |
| Sgt J.A. Tipton | Injured | in Capuccini Naval Cemetery, Malta. |
| Sgt J.D. Martin | Injured | |
| Sgt D.T Taylor RCAF | Injured | |
| Sgt S. Shepherdson | Injured | |

**15 February 1942**

| | | |
|---|---|---|
| Sgt J.A. Webb | Killed | Sgt Webb died when the a/c he was running up at Luqa prior to take-off was bombed. He is buried in Capuccini Naval Cemetery, Malta. |

| | | |
|---|---|---|
| F/Lt J.S. Reeves | Injured | Attending the Regent Cinema, Valetta, when it was |
| P/O E.G. Watson, MM | Injured | bombed F/Lt Reeves and P/O Watson were rescued after several hours trapped in the rubble. |

**24 March 1942**

| | | |
|---|---|---|
| LAC L.H. Quinn | Died | Natural causes, Malta. LAC Quinn is buried in Capuccini Naval Cemetery, Malta. |

**8 May 1942**

| | | |
|---|---|---|
| LAC D.J. Clarke | Died | Natural causes, Malta. LAC Clarke is buried in Capuccini Naval Cemetery, Malta. |

**21 November 1942**

| | | |
|---|---|---|
| F/Lt B.L. Blackbourn | Died | Natural causes, Egypt. F/Lt Blackbourn is buried in Fayid War Cemetery. |

# Appendix D
# Helpers

(Note: I have chosen to refer to individuals by first names or initials, as they wrote to me. If any offence is thereby given, my apologies.)

I gratefully acknowledge the help of the following former members of 40 Squadron:

Doug Adamson; Bob Alldrick; Denis Allen; W.J. Ames; Ron Anderson; Bob Andrew; Doug Angus; Ken Annable; Bill Armstrong; George Arnott; Ian Arrowsmith; A.F. Ash; Jack Atkinson, J.D. 'Bunny' Austin.

Stanley Bacon; Eric Baddeley; Doug Bagnall; G.D. Bain; R.A. Bain; Curley Baker; Guy Baker; Len 'Shorty' Baker; Ray Ball; Bill Ball; John Barling; Denis Barnett; A.H. Barrington; Harry Bartlett; Keith Beattie; T.B. Beattie; Jack Bellock; Willie Beringer; Stuart Biggin; Peter Billyeald; Eddie Bircher; John Bishop; Ron Black; Jim Bodman; R.D. Bone; Rowley Bowering; Rom Bradshaw; J.R. Brandish; Stan Brew; Dick Broadbent; Alan Brodie; Joe Brogan; Bill Bromley; Jim Brooker; A.C. Brown; Eddie Brown; Russell Brown; Ted Bunnin; Bernard Burdsall; Bill Burton; Ron Bush; Harry Butler; Arthur Butteriss.

Douglas Calvert; B.H. Cameron; N.E. 'Conk' Canton; J. Carruthers; T.E. Carter; Jack Casper; Ron Ceha; Steve Challen; David Chalmers; George Chant; R.L. Chidlaw-Roberts; Vic Claney; Arthur 'Nobby' Clarke; Don Clarke; F.T. Clee; R. Clish; Fred Cocker; A. Cody; Keith Coleman; Eric Coombe; Ken Coombe; J.P. Cooper; Eric Coppins; Gordon Cormie; Jack Cornelius; Ted Corns; Bertram Cornwell; Harry Corrin; John Corser; J.R. Cox; Bill Craigen; Tony Craven; Bryan Crespin; Don Crossley; Bob Currie; Reg Curtis.

James Davidson; H. 'Taffy' Davies; Ivor Davies; G.E. Davis; George Dealtry; Reg Dolden; J.W. Doull; John Dovey; John Dunling; Ken Dunn; E. Dunnell.

Gerald Easton; Brian Edwards; Stan Elcock; Peter Elliott; Alyn Elvey; Bill Emmett; Cyril Enoch; Lawrence Ewels.

John Fairbairn; A.R. Fasham; Laurie Field; Tom Fielder; Pat Fincher; Frank Fitton; Bob Fleming; Don Flint; Terry Foreman; Blake Forrest; Fred Fox; Len Francis; Ernest Frost; John Funnell.

W.T.G. Gabriel; H.F. Galvin; C. Gill; David Gladstone; Harry Godfrey; Bill Goodbrand; John Goodlet; Charles Goodridge; Dennis Gouge; H.G. 'Dodd' Gray; David Green; Ted Green; Bill Greengrass; P.F. 'Shorty' Greenway; Alex Greer; Bill Griffiths; Dave Grindell.

F.A. Haden; Jack Hall, Jim Halligan; Fred Harburn; Maurice Harmes; James Harper; John Harrison; Art Harvey; John Harvey; Lorne Haunts; Ted Hawes; Jim Higgins; George Hill; Alec Hipperson; Jim Holland; John Holmes; Geoff Holt; Bert Horton; George Howard; Ron Hughes; Bill Huntley; Arthur Husk; G.F. Hutchinson.

Bob Jackson; Algy Jane; Peter Jenkins; Ken Jenner; Frank Jewell; Martin Johnson; William A. Johnson; C. Jones; George 'Jonah' Jones; J.H. Jones; Taff Jones; Strat Judd.

Gil King; Phil Kirby.

Eric Laithwaite; Jo 'Ollie' Lancaster; W.J. Lawson; Hugh Le Good; Peter Lewin; Gwilym Lewis; Ken Liles; Jack Liley; Vic Lilley; Clifford Lowe; Denis Ludman; Hugh Lynch-Blosse.

Angus MacAskill; M. McCullagh; Harry McDonald; Bob McDonald; Peter McGoldrick; Ronald MacInnes; Stuart Mackay; Angus McLean; Alastair McNab; Jack McWicker; V. Mais; Dick Maling; Tom Mapplebeck; Les Marlow; John Marr; Ted Marriott; Ed Martin; John Mason; Maurice Mason; Ian Matley; Dougie Melrose; Cameron Mervyn-Jones; Bob Mills; Geoffrey Mills; Cecil 'Eski' Mohs; Cyril Moore; Bill Moseby; Alan Mott; G.I. Muir; Bob Mullins.

Freddie Newall; J.T. Newsholme; Ken Newton; E.F. Nichols; Joe Noble; L.D. Noddings; Red Norbury; Peter Norton-Smith.

Gordon Ogden; Jack O'Hara; John Oram; Bill Oxley.

Geoffrey Paget; Colin Palmer; Stanley Palmer; Ted Palmer; Percy Panting; Donald Parker; H.J. Parry; George Parsons; Ted Paterson; Pat Pattinson; Eddie Pauley; Peter Payne; Roger Peacock; Cedric Pearce; John Perry; Roger Phillips; Haydn Poole; Allan 'Gillie' Potter; Fred Powell; Bill Power.

Andrew Raeside; Cec Rainey; Joe Raybould; Leo Redden; George Reddy; Ken Rees; Norman Reid; John Rettie; R.F. Richardson; J.M. Riddell; Dick Ridgway; Tony Rippengal; Jim Robbins; Stan Roberts; J. Robertson; Jack Robinson; Stewart Robinson; C.A. 'Smokey' Robson; Phil Rockingham;

Keith Rogers; Rhys Rogers; Fred Rooke; Peter Rowe; Charles Ruggles; Ken Ruskell.

Ted Sammons; Tom Sayers; Harry Scholar; Charles Scott; Tom Scullion; Tom Seel; Stuart Sigley; Eric Simpson; H. Smart; Hugh Smeddle; Alan Smith; Danny Smith; E. Alan Smith; John Smith; Bob Spence; R.L. 'Jock' Stark; Jim Steel; Frank Stevens; Jo Stevenson; Bob Stewner; Ron Street; Dick Sutcliffe; John Sykes.
　　Arthur Taylor; Eric Taylor; Denis Telfer; Vic Tennant; Reg 'Gordon' Thackeray; Ron Thirsk; Bill Thompson; Dick Tindell; Pat Tipping; John Tipton; Stan Todd; Henry Towler; Patrick Towsey; Peter Travers-Wakeford; Eric Turner; Ron Turner.

John Verrall.

Jack Wade; Bertie Wallace; Jim Wallace; Jim 'Ginger' Ware; Allan Weller; Jack 'Spindy' Wey; Cyril Wheeler; Henry Wheeler; Jack Whitlock; Herbert Whyte; George Williams; Douglas Wilson; Richard Wilson; Trevor Wilson; John Wood; T.J. Wood; George Wootton; John Wray; John Wright; A.D. Wyles.

E. Yandell; Patrick Yarrow; Guy Yates; Wilfrid Young.


I also acknowledge, with equal gratitude, the help of the following:

Gurth Addington; J.A. Agius; Sid Ainsworth; Tom Alston; R.A.N. Andrews; Arthur Arculus; Valerie Austin; Karen Atherton.

Pamela Barnett; John Barron; John Bishop; Theo Boiten; E. Bovett; Chaz Bowyer; Guy Britton; Robin Brooks; Jack Bruce.

Geoffrey Cardew; Geoffrey Carter; Allan Challis; David Chamberlain; Roy Chappell; Frank Cheeseman; Arthur Christmas; Danny Clements; Chris Cole; Peter Connon; F.G. Cook; Peter Cooksley; Frank Cooper; Peter Coppins; Dorothy Cox; Tom Cranmer; Mary Crouch; George Crump.

Jeffrey Day; H. Dennis; Anne de Winton; Norman Didwell; Philip Duckham; Charles Dutt.

Jack Eder; Anthony Edwards; Sam Elworthy; Reg Emsden; Bill Evans.

Margaret Fenwick; Phil Fougere; Norman Franks; George Furby.

Betty George; Jim George; Robert Ginn; Christina Goulter; Frank Graf; Connie Graham; Barry Gray; Peter Green.

John Hager; George Haines; James Halley; Colin Hanson; Paul Hare; Paul

Harris; Ken Harrison; Phyllis Heap; Chris Holmes; J.B. Hopley; Rochford Hughes.

Tom Jeffares; Michael Jeffery; Jeff Jefford; Mike Jermy.

George Kay; Catherine Kennedy; Ted Killen; Tom Killoran; Mary Kirwan.

Peter Landon; Ian Lawson; Stephen T. Lawson; Stuart Leslie; Frank Letchford; Peter Liddle; Lanayre D. Liggera.

Pat Macdonald; Jim MacDonald; Fred McMillan; Nev McNamara; Alex McQuarrie; David Major; Patrick Mallahan; Robert Martin; Monica Michell; Martin Middlebrook; Audrey Morris; Ken Molson; Ivy Morton.

Roy Naylor; Don Neate; Roy C. Nesbit; Veronica Nicol.

Tom Parker; Mollie Penwarn; Jim Pettigrew; Stella Pynton; Ron Powers; Chas Price.

Alex Revell; Ray Rimell; Heather Robinson; David Rockel; Trevor Richards; Alan Riches; Jessie Rowan; Max Ruane; Arnold Russell Vick.

Enrico Sallustio; Tom Scotland; Somnath Sapru; Karl S. Schneide; Diana Searby; Chris Shores; Bill Simpson; Gordon Smith; Stephen Smith; John Starr; Ray Sturtivant; Frank Sullivan; Michael Swann.

Paul Taylor; Stewart Taylor; Andy Thomas; John Thompson; G.B. Tonkin (Abingdon Town Council); Bob Trotter.

John Wallen; Leslei Ward; Harry Widdup; George H. Williams; S.F. Wise; Hugh Wynne.

Richard Yole; Roger Young.

# Index of people mentioned

Note: The appendices and illustrations are not indexed.

(Ranks, where given, are those attained on Squadron or, with others, at the time of reference.)